State Feminism and Political Representation

D0746456

How can women maximise their political influence? Does state feminism enhance the political representation of women? Should feminism be
established in state institutions to treat women's concerns? Written by
experts in the field, this book uses an innovative model of political
influence to construct answers to these and other questions in the
long-running debate over the political representation of women. The
book assesses how states respond to women's demands for political
representation in terms of both their inclusion as actors and the consideration of their interests in the decision-making process. Debates on
the issue vary from country to country, depending on institutional
structures, women's movements and other factors, and this book offers
the first comparative account of the subject. The authors analyse eleven
democracies in Europe and North America and present comprehensive
research from the 1960s to the present.

JONI LOVENDUSKI is Professor of Politics at Birkbeck College,
University of London. She is author of *Women and European Politics*
(1986) and *Feminising Politics* (2005) and editor of *Feminism and
Politics* (2000). She has co-authored and co-edited a number of other
books and has published numerous papers, articles and chapters on
gender and politics.

State Feminism and Political Representation

edited by

Joni Lovenduski

with

Claudie Baudino
Marila Guadagnini
Petra Meier and
Diane Sainsbury

CAMBRIDGE
UNIVERSITY PRESS

CAMBRIDGE UNIVERSITY PRESS
Cambridge, New York, Melbourne, Madrid, Cape Town,
Singapore, São Paulo, Delhi, Mexico City

Cambridge University Press
The Edinburgh Building, Cambridge CB2 8RU, UK

Published in the United States of America by Cambridge University Press, New York

www.cambridge.org
Information on this title: www.cambridge.org/9780521617642

© Cambridge University Press 2005

First published 2005

A catalogue record for this publication is available from the British Library

ISBN 978-0-521-85222-7 Hardback
ISBN 978-0-521-61764-2 Paperback

Contents

Figures

Tables

Notes on contributors

CLAUDIE BAUDINO received her Ph.D. in Political Science from Paris IX-Dauphine University in 2000. A member of the French RNGS (Research Network on Gender Politics and the State) team, she teaches courses on social science, and her research focuses on political and linguistic representation of women in France. Her publications include *Politique de la langue et différence sexuelle. La politisation du genre des noms de métier* (L'Harmattan, 2001), 'La cause des femmes à l'épreuve de son institutionnalisation', *Revue Politix*, 51, 2000, and 'Le genre gâché. La féminisation de l'action publique' (in collaboration with Amy G. Mazur), Revue Espace-Temps, 2001.

BRIGITTE GEISSEL received her Ph.D. in political science from the Technische Universität Berlin and she has been employed as Research Fellow at the Social Science Research Centre Berlin (WZB) since 2004. She is also Lecturer (*Lehrbeauftragte*) at the Technical University of Berlin and in the winter term of 2004/5 she was guest professor at the University of Münster. She has worked at several universities within Germany and the USA. Her research interest is the relation between citizen and democracy in developed democracies, especially participation and new forms of governance. She has published on civil and political participation, e.g. on women in parties and parliaments in Germany, on civil society and on participatory governance. Her recent publications include 'Dynamiken der politischen Partizipation. Politische Partizipation von Frauen und Männern', http://www.fu-berlin.de/gpo/geissel_penrose.htm, 2003 (with Virginia Penrose), and *Zivilgesellschaft und Sozialkapital*, with Ansgar Klein, Kristine Kern and Maria Berger (VS Verlag, 2004).

MARILA GUADAGNINI is Associate Professor of Political Science at the University of Turin. She is author of *Il sistema politico italiano. Temi per una discussione* (Il Segna libro, 1997) and *La stagione del disincanto? Cittadini, cittadine e politica alle soglie del 2000* (Il Segna libro, 2001), co-author of *Il soffitto di cristallo? Le donne nelle posizioni decisionali in*

Europa (Edizioni Fondazione Olivetti, 1999) and editor of *Da elettrici a elette. Riforme istituzionali e rappresentanza delle donne in Italia, in Europa e negli Stati Uniti* (Celid, 2003). She has published numerous chapters and articles on gender and politics, and wrote the chapters on Italy in *Comparative State Feminism*, edited by D. McBride Stetson and A. Mazur (Sage, 1995) and *State Feminism, Women's Movements and Job Training: Making Democracies Work in the Global Economy*, edited by A. Mazur (Routledge, 2001).

ANNE MARIA HOLLI is currently Researcher (Academy of Finland) at the Department of Political Science, University of Helsinki. Her major areas of research are in the fields of public equality policies, women in the media, and women and politics in general. Her most recent publications include *Discourse and Politics for Gender Equality in Late Twentieth Century Finland* (Helsinki University Press, 2003) and an edited volume (together with T. Saarikoski and E. Sana) on Finnish equality policies, *Tasa-arvopolitiikan haasteet* (WSOY, 2002). She is also a co-author of *Equal Democracies? Gender and Politics in the Nordic Countries*, edited by C. Bergqvist et al. (Scandinavian University Press, 1999), and wrote the chapters on Finland in *State Feminism, Women's Movements and Job Training: Making Democracies Work in the Global Economy*, edited by A. Mazur (Routledge, 2001) and *The Politics of Prostitution: Women's Movements, Democratic States and the Globalisation of Sex Commerce*, edited by Joyce Outshoorn (Cambridge University Press, 2004).

LYNN KAMENITSA is Associate Professor of Political Science and Women's Studies at Northern Illinois University. Her previous research has focused on abortion policy, local women's offices, the women's movement in united Germany, and women's and other social movements from the former East Germany. Her work has appeared in the journals *Comparative Politics*, *Women & Politics*, *Problems of Post-Communism*, *Mobilization*, and *German Politics & Society*.

JOHANNA KANTOLA obtained her Ph.D. from the University of Bristol and is currently a researcher at the Politics Department of the University of Helsinki, where she is also teaching feminisms and inter-national relations. She has published in *International Journal of Feminist Politics*, *European Journal of Women's Studies* and *European Political Science*, as well as in *The Politics of Prostitution: Women's Movements, Democratic States and the Globalisation of Sex Commerce*, edited by Joyce Outshoorn (Cambridge University Press, 2004). She is the co-editor of the Finnish women's studies journal, *Naistutkimus*.

REGINA KÖPL is Associate Professor of Political Science at the University of Vienna, Austria. She received her Ph.D. from the University of Vienna and has a postgraduate diploma from the Institute of Advanced Studies, Vienna. She is the author of articles and research reports on feminism and women's movement organisations in Austria, for example on the status of women for the Austrian government, Frauen bericht 1985 and 1995. She was the Austrian expert in the European Expert 'Women in Decision-Making' Network. She contributed the chapter on Austria in *Abortion Politics, Women's Movements and the Democratic State*, edited by Dorothy McBride Stetson (Oxford University Press, 2001). She has also published on subjectivity and gender and on media and politics, including an essay on subjectivity and political marketing in *Demokratie and Kritik*, edited by Helmut Kramer (Helmut Kramer, 2004).

JONI LOVENDUSKI is Professor of Politics at Birkbeck College. Her most recent book is *Feminizing Politics* (Polity Press, 2005) and her other work includes *Women and European Politics* (Harvester Whealsheaf, 1986), co-author of *Political Recruitment* (Cambridge University Press, 1995), *Contemporary Feminist Politics* (Oxford University Press, 1993) and *Politics and Society in Eastern Europe* (Macmillan, 1987). She edited *Feminism and Politics* (Dartmarth Press, 2000), and co-edited, *Women in Politics* (HarperCollins, 1996), *Different Roles, Different Voices* (HarperCollins, 1994), *Gender and Party Politics* (Sage, 1993), *The New Politics of Abortion* (Sage, 1986), *The Politics of the Second Electorate* (Routledge and Kegan Paul, 1981) and numerous papers, articles and essays on gender and politics. She was co-director of the British Candidate Study from 1988 to 1992 and the British Representation Study 2001. She was a founding convener of the Standing Group on Women and Politics of the European Consortium for Political Research and of the Women and Politics Group of the Political Studies Association of the UK.

PETRA MEIER is a research fellow at the Politics Department of the Vrije Universiteit, Brussels and the Radboud Universiteit, Nijmegan. Her major areas of research are feminist theories on representation, the conceptualisation of, logic behind and measures to promote social groups in decision-making and their interaction with electoral systems, feminist approaches to public policies, the conceptualisation and integration of feminist frames in public policies, the political opportunity structures of the Belgian women's movement and state feminism. She recently co-edited (with Bérengére Marques-Pereira) *Genre et science politique en Belgique et en Francophonie* (Academia-Bruylant 2005) and (with Karen Celis) *Vrouwen vertegenwoordigd, Wetstraat gekraakt? Representativiteit feministisch bekeken* (VUBpress, 2004). She has published in *Party Politics, European Political Science, Acta Politica, Res Publica, Tijdschrift voor Sociologie, Ethiek en Maatschappij* and in various edited volumes.

JANTINE OLDERSMA studied politics and communication at the University of Amsterdam. She is a fellow of the Joke Smit Insitiue, Research Centre for Women's Studies, and teaches at the Department of Public Administration, both at the University of Leiden in the Netherlands. She specialises in the study of women in political elites and in public policy for women. Her Ph.D. dissertation is on the representation of women in corporatist bodies in the Netherlands: 'De vrouw die vanzelf spreekt, gender en representatie in het Nederlandse adviesradenstelsel'. Her published articles and essays include 'Can a Woman be Just like a Man? The Representation of Women in the Corporatist Channel in the Netherlands', in *Participation, Citizenship and Gender*, edited by J. Bussemaker and R. Voet (Ashgate, 1998) and 'More Woman or More Feminists in Politics? Advocacy Coalitions and the Representation of Women in the Netherlands 1967–1992', in *Acta Politica, International Journal of Political Science* (2002). She co-edited a volume on the use of theories of power in women's studies, with K. Davis and M. H. Leijenaar, *The Gender of Power* (Sage, 1991), and has also published articles on civil society and social capital, mass culture and feminist detectives.

JANINE A. PARRY is Assistant Professor of Political Science and Director of the Arkansas Poll at the University of Arkansas, Fayetteville. She completed her BA at Western Washington University, magna cum laude, and her MA and Ph.D. at Washington State University. Her fields of teaching and research include gender, politics, and policy and state and local government, with an emphasis on Arkansas politics. Her work has appeared in *Social Science Quarterly, Policy Studies Journal, Arkansas Historical Quarterly, National Women's Studies Association Journal, Review of Public Personnel Administration, Pacific Northwest Quarterly, Current Municipal Problems, Transportation Quarterly* and various edited volumes.

DIANE SAINSBURY is Lars Hierta Professor of Political Science at Stockholm University. She is author of *Gender, Equality and Welfare States* (Cambridge University Press, 1996) and editor of *Gendering Welfare States* (Sage, 1994) and *Gender and Welfare State Regimes*

(Oxford University Press, 1999). Her recent publications include 'Rights without Seats: the Puzzle of Women's Legislative Recruitment in Australia', in *Elections: Full, Free and Fair*, edited by Marian Sawer (Federation Press, 2001), 'Gender and the Making of Welfare States: Norway and Sweden', in *Social Politics* (2001), 'US Women's Suffrage through a Multicultural Lens: Intersecting Struggles of Recognition', in *Recognition Struggles and Social Movements*, edited by Barbara Hobson (Cambridge University Press, 2003) and 'Women's Political Representation in Sweden: Discursive Politics and Institutional Presence', in *Scandinavian Political Studies* (2004).

CELIA VALIENTE is in the Department of Political Science and Sociology of the Universidad Carlos III de Madrid (Spain). Her major area of research is gender equality policy and the women's movement in Spain from a comparative perspective. She has published articles and chapters including 'Central State Child Care Policies in Postauthoritarian Spain', in *Gender & Society* (2003), 'State Feminism and Central State Debates on Prostitution in Post-Authoritarian Spain', in *The Politics of Prostitution: Women's Movements, Democratic States and the Globalisation of Sex Commerce*, edited by Joyce Outshoorn (Cambridge University Press, 2004), 'Pushing for Equality Reforms: the European Union and Gender Discourse in Post-Authoritarian Spain', in *Gendering Europeanisation*, edited by Ulrike Liebert (Peter Lang, 2003) and 'The Feminist Movement and the Reconfigured State in Spain (1970s–2000)', in *Women's Movements Facing the Reconfigured State*, edited by Lee Ann Banaszak, Karen Beckwith and Dieter Rucht (Cambridge University Press, 2003).

Preface

This book is the result of almost ten years of collaboration by its authors. Although at first glance it appears to be an edited collection, it is in fact co-written on the basis of a collaboratively designed research project. The contributors are all members of the Research Network on Gender Politics and the State. In the project as a whole some forty scholars from the USA, Canada and Europe have met over a period of ten years, sustaining a cross-national, longitudinal research project on gender and public policy. Since 1995 this network has met to design, conduct and write up research on state feminism in advanced industrial democracies. As chapter 1 describes, we decided to assess the impact of state feminism on women's representation by examining the part played by women's policy agencies in key policy debates since their establishment. In this volume we assess the impact of those agencies on the issue of political representation itself to offer a systematically comparative account of how and to what effect women's movements have engaged the important issue of women's political representation.

This volume is jointly edited by a team of five. Each member of the team took responsibility for some country chapters and for assessing and analysing parts of the model. Each supplied feedback to authors, prepared text that was incorporated into the concluding chapters and supplied feedback on drafts of the concluding analysis. The final manuscript was prepared by Joni Lovenduski who was responsible for drafting the introduction and conclusions and preparing the manuscript for publication.

We accumulated many debts along the way. Our project depended upon finding time, places and resources to meet, to solve problems and to share research. A number of individuals and organisations have assisted us. The American Political Science Association annual conference organisers welcomed us to convene workshops around the annual meetings. Many early findings were presented at the European Consortium for Political Research Joint Sessions of Workshops. The American National Science Foundation International Programmes Grant (#9411142) funded the first meeting in Leiden in 1995. CREDEP of the University of Paris hosted our meeting in 1998. The European Science Foundation funded a meeting at Chilworth in Southampton in 1999. Professor Ed Page made funds available from the ESRC Future Governance Programme for a meeting on this volume at Belfast in 2000. He also commented extensively on draft versions of the introduction and conclusions, as did Amy Mazur, Dorothy Stetson and Alan Ware. Both the American National Science Foundation and the European Science Foundation supported the group with further grants. The ESF and the NSF supported the RNGS Network meetings at which the chapters in this book were reviewed and discussed in Turin in 2002 and Leiden in 2003. The final manuscript benefited from Rainbow Murray's help with proofreading and data checking. We are all grateful for the support, skill and patience of an editor, John Haslam, and copy-editor, Carol Fellingham Webb, at Cambridge University Press who guided us through the production of this volume.

Our project would not have been possible without electronic communication. It owes much to the support we have been given. Most of all it has depended on the continuing commitment, good will, intellectual liveliness and curiosity of its members and the sheer will power of its conveners, Amy Mazur and Dorothy Stetson.

Abbreviations

QWPA	quasi-women's policy agency
RNGS	Research Network on Gender Politics and the State
WMA	women's movement actor
WPA	women's policy agency

Austria

FPÖ	Austrian Freedom Party
ÖVP	Austrian People's Party
SPÖ	Social Democratic Party

Finland

SKDL	Finnish People's Democratic League
SNDL	Finnish Women's Democratic League

France

RPR	*Rassemblement pour la république*

Germany

ASF	*Arbeitsgemeinschaft Sozialdemokratischer Frauen*
BMFJ	Ministry for Women and Youth
CDU	Christian Democratic Union
CSU	Christian Social Union
FDP	Free Democratic Party
PDS	Party of Democratic Socialism
SPD	Social Democratic Party

Italy

AN	National Alliance Party (*Alleanza Nazionale*)
CC	Central Committee (*Camitato centrale*)
CNELD	National Commission for Women's Emancipation and Liberation (*Commissione nazionale per l'emancipazione e la liberazione delle donne*)
CNPPO	National Commission for Equality and Equal Opportunities between Men and Women (*Commissione nazionale per la parità e le pari opportunità tra uomini e donne*)
COREL	Committee for Electoral Reforms (*Comitato per le riforme elettorali*)
DS	Democrats of the Left (*Democratici di sinistra*)
MSI	Italian Social Movement (*Movimento sociale italiano*)
PCI	Communist Party of Italy (*Partito Comunista italiano*)
PDS	Democratic Party of the Left (*Partito democratico della sinistra*)
RC	Communist Refoundation (*Rifondazione Comunista*)

The Netherlands

CPN	*Communistische Partij Nederland*
DCE	*Directie Coördinatie Emancipatiebeleid*
ER	Emancipation Council
MVM	*Man-Vrouw-Maatschappij* (Man-Woman-Society)
NVR	National Women's Council
PSP	Pacifist Socialist Party
PvdA	Social Democratic Party
SGP	*Staatkundig Gereformeerde Partij*
TECENA	*Tijdelijke Expertise Commissie voor Emancipatie in het nieuwe Adviestelsel*

Spain

CC	Constitutional Court (*Tribunal Constitucional*)
ETA	*Euskadi Ta Askatasuna*
IU	United Left (*Izquierda Unida*)
PP	People's Party (*Partido Popular*)
PSOE	Spanish Socialist Workers' Party (*Partido Socialista Obrero Español*)
WI	Women's Institute (*Instituto de la Mujer*)

Sweden

SSKF	Social Democratic Women's Federation
VPK	Left Party-Communist

UK

EOC	Equal Opportunities Commission
MSF	Manufacturing Science and Finance
NEC	National Executive Committee
WNC	Women's National Commission

USA

CCWI	Congressional Caucus for Women's Issues
ERA	Equal Rights Amendment
GCSW	Governor's Commission on the Status of Women
LWV	League of Women Voters
NOW	National Organisation for Women
NVRA	National Voter Registration Act

1   Introduction: state feminism and the political representation of women

Joni Lovenduski

The representation of women in a political system is a good test of its claims to democracy. The claims that women make for representation are claims for their citizenship and at the heart of their engagement with politics. Political representation is therefore a fundamental feminist concern, although its importance has not always been acknowledged. The women's liberation movements that began in the 1970s were, in many countries, ambivalent about formal political representation. However, by the end of the twentieth century women's movements were active to secure equality of representation throughout the world. From the moment that women's movements were making demands on the state the issue of their political representation was in play. Whilst suffrage campaigns were explicit movements for political participation and representation, campaigns over rights to education, to paid work, to equal pay, to personal dignity and security, to sexual autonomy were also in part about the inclusion of women's interests in policy-making. Later movements for representation in legislatures and assemblies were movements for presence that challenged political arrangements and sought to insert women's interests into policy-making by ensuring they were amongst the policy-makers.

The connection between agenda status for women's interests and the claim for equal political representation continues. Since the nineteenth century women's movement activists have demanded state action on a range of issues that includes anti-discrimination policies, anti-violence policies, reproductive rights, childcare and political equality. In the late twentieth century governments responded, some more slowly than others, by developing a set of agencies to take responsibility for such demands. These women's policy agencies (WPAs) vary in scope, size, resources, stability and location. They appeared at different times in different countries but are now part of the political landscape. Their existence is, at least in symbolic terms, an acknowledgement of women's demands for representation.

Assessing women's political representation

How should women's representation be assessed? What factors, in a world of rapid and massive change, might enable us to assess the impact of women's movement claims for representation? Have democracies become more representative in the sense that they have incorporated women in ways which ensure that their interests are advocated and considered? What mechanisms exist to facilitate gender-balanced policies and how effective are those mechanisms? How, if at all, do women's movements participate in processes of decision-making? Have states responded to demands to incorporate women as political actors? Anne Phillips (1995) points out that post-industrial democracies are deficient because they fail to represent women's interests and needs adequately. They neither include women in positions of power nor routinely incorporate gender perspectives in the policy process. Her observations are supported by feminist analysts in Europe and North America who show that the absence of women in positions of power may explain the extent to which public policies in many post-industrial democracies are gender-biased and therefore discriminate against women (Hernes 1987; Lewis 1993; Sainsbury 1994; Lovenduski and Norris 1993; Meehan and Sevenhuijsen 1991; Haavio-Mannila et al. 1985; Lovenduski 1986; Bergqvist et al. 1999; Abrar et al. 1999). For these analysts, the democratic deficit may be addressed by ensuring that an appreciation of gender differences informs government policy.

Women's political representation as a subject for comparison

Research on state institutions shows considerable variation in the presence of women in elected office, even amongst otherwise similar countries. In the democracies considered in this volume the proportion of women legislators in 2003 ranged from 12.3 per cent in France to 45 per cent in Sweden (Appendix 1). These differences invite comparative analysis to determine the circumstances under which women achieve higher or lower shares of political office. In addition, comparative research shows that there is generally a pattern of decreasing numbers of women as decision-making hierarchies are ascended. There are exceptions: in Sweden there have been no differences since the 1970s and in the 1980s more women were elected to parliament than to local councils. Other exceptions are the Netherlands, Finland and Norway. Finally, this research shows that there is a functional division of labour between women and men representatives whereby women are more likely to specialise in 'soft' and less prestigious policy areas such as health, cultural affairs, education and social welfare while men dominate the traditionally more prestigious areas of economic management, foreign affairs and home affairs. Paradoxically the 'soft' policy areas in which women are more likely to be found constitute the major part of state activity and absorb the bulk of government budgets. The patterns raise the important question of what if any influence women representatives have and where and how they are able to exercise it. They also raise questions about the nature of political representation.

What is political representation?

Political representation has many definitions and takes many forms. A standard and widely cited definition by Hannah Pitkin (1967) identifies four types of political representation: *authorised*, where a representative is legally empowered to act for another; *descriptive*, where the representative stands for a group by virtue of sharing similar characteristics such as race, gender, ethnicity or residence; *symbolic*, where a leader stands for national ideas; and *substantive*, where the representative seeks to advance a group's policy preferences and interests. In this volume we are interested in women's access to political institutions and the effects of that access on policy. Accordingly, we investigate the descriptive and substantive representation of women as concepts that enable us to compare the extent to which policy processes in democratic regimes are inclusive of women.

Political representation underpins the legitimacy of democratic states. Ideas about political representation shape institutional arrangements and definitions of citizenship. The requirements of political representation are matters for negotiation, and subject to change. Therefore debates on political representation are part of the process by which democracies evolve. Such debates include concerns about the nature of political institutions, the processes of decision-making and the quality of policy implementation. Frequently they are constitutional debates directly aimed at institutional reorganisation. In representation debates definitions of citizenship are invoked and decisions are made about who is and is not a citizen, and who may and may not be a representative. Debates about the implementation of representation policy highlight the inclusion and exclusion of social groups and individuals. In short, claims for representation are part of the process of claiming membership of a polity; hence the debates they generate illuminate the way political actors understand democracy.

Women's policy agencies and state feminism

Since the last quarter of the twentieth century there has been a proliferation of (state) agencies established to promote women's status and rights, often called women's policy agencies. WPAs are sometimes termed *state feminist*. State feminism is a contested term. To some it is an oxymoron. It has been variously defined as the activities of feminists or femocrats in government and administration (Hernes 1987; Sawer 1990), institutionalised feminism in public agencies (Eisenstein 1990; Outshoorn 1994), and the capacity of the state to contribute to the fulfilment of a feminist agenda (Sawer 1990; Stetson 1987). In this book we define state feminism as the advocacy of women's movement demands inside the state. The establishment of WPAs changed the setting in which the women's movement and other feminists could advance their aims, as they offered, in principle, the possibility to influence the agenda and to further feminist goals through public policies *from inside the state apparatus*. WPAs could increase women's access to the state by furthering women's participation in political decision-making, and by inserting feminist goals into public policy. Thus WPAs may enhance the political representation of women. WPAs vary considerably in their capacity, resources and effectiveness, raising questions about the circumstances under which they are most likely to enhance women's political representation. To understand them we need to consider in detail the part they play in processes of incorporating women's interests (substantive representation) into policy-making, a requirement that is particularly important when the decisions are about political representation itself.

Accordingly, the part played by women's policy agencies in securing women's political representation is the subject of this book. We can expect WPAs to provide the strongest evidence of the impact of women on the political agenda because they ostensibly build women into the policy process. The comparison of WPAs' activities in different countries over time makes possible an assessment of their effects on women's political representation in both its procedural and substantive senses. The research that is described in chapters 2 to 12 addresses the roles of women's policy agencies in eleven post-industrial democracies. The research question is: how, and under what circumstances, have WPAs furthered the impact of women's movements on arrangements for political representation?

In addressing this question the book raises issues about the nature of political representation in different countries. Do the variations in arrangements for political representation suggest different ways of think-ing about democratic representation? Do those differences impact on women's representation? How do conventions about representation affect the capacity and mandate of women's policy agencies? Are women's policy agencies able to represent feminist movements? What happens to women's movement agendas when activists collaborate with the state? These are issues that studies of women's movements have attempted to address (Hernes 1987; Franzway et al. 1989; Watson 1990; Sawer 1990; Eisenstein 1990, 1996; Outshoorn 1994, 1998).

Such questions invite consideration of method, of how to assess impacts in policy-making. Feminist political scientists have developed a common method for assessing such impacts in the collaborative project on which this book is based. In the Research Network on Gender Politics and the State (RNGS) scholars met to formulate such a methodology from the early 1990s. The resulting framework was developed by a net-work of scholars who participated in an extended series of international meetings. The starting point was the volume edited by Amy Mazur and Dorothy Stetson, *Comparative State Feminism*, published in 1995. The collection generated a series of debates about what explains the success or otherwise of state policy machinery. The debates addressed fundamental questions about the comparative method, case selection, policy analysis and the nature of democracy. Contributors to the original volume were soon joined by others in a collaborative effort that makes it difficult to separate the contributions of any one individual (though Mazur and Stetson have been central to the project's leadership). One of the outcomes of the co-operation is the model on which this book is based. The model, which draws on current approaches to the study of politics to combine the intellectual concerns of feminist and democratic theory, is embedded in theories of political representation, the study of social movements and of public policy. In order to explain the model and hence the approach of this book, it is necessary first to develop the ideas presented so far in more detail.

Women and policy-making

Making women more central to government concerns is partly about electing and appointing more women to public office, that is, descriptive representation. It is also about incorporating women's concerns into the policy process, that is, substantive representation. Whilst increasing women's descriptive representation may lead to the inclusion of women's concerns, it is only one of the several ways of enhancing women's repre-sentation. Hence, in this study, while we *take note* of women's representa-tion in terms of how many women are in public office, we *focus* on the question of whether women are included in day-to-day processes of decision-making. To do this we have elected to study patterns of debates about policy decisions over time. So, instead of concentrating on the state and its institutions as a whole, we are looking at particular decisions and the policy debates that lead up to them. We identify core activities in the process of policy-making that we classify according to the inclusion of women and women's concerns. We address the question of the roles of WPAs in debates to determine whether agencies are active or whether they are symbolic bystanders. We ask whether WPAs participate in debates, advocate women's movement goals and contribute to successful outcomes for women. To capture agency variations, for each debate we gather information on the activities of agencies and on their characteristics.

Our case studies are drawn from eleven countries: Austria, Belgium, Finland, France, Germany, Italy, the Netherlands, Spain, Sweden, the UK and the USA. The countries included in this volume are all post-industrial democracies. They represent about half of the twenty-three countries that fall into this category of systems. They have relatively similar and large levels of national wealth and, with the exception of Spain, have had relatively stable democratic political systems since 1949. All the countries have had stable democratic systems since the 1970s. Within this category they differ by type of democratic regime, a variation that is reflected in the selection of countries that we consider. For each debate we identify the women's movement's goals and characteristics. The debate outcome is assessed as a success or failure for the movement, enabling us to classify women's movement impacts. From the literature on social movement impact we developed a set of variables that might explain women's movement success or failure.

Gender and framing

We start by considering the way in which policy debates are or become gendered, an exercise that requires working definitions of the terms gender, gendering and framing. *Gender* is a concept that has acquired several different meanings (Harding 1986). As originally adapted for social science, it provided a way to distinguish between biological sexual differences and the cultural and social meanings attached to those differences (Nelson 1989). In this study, we define gender as the meaning or ideas people attach to biological and demographic differences between men and women. Gender is not a synonym for sex, which is also a contested term. Most simply, sex is a biological category that separates men and women, while gender is the set of social meanings attached to the categories 'male' and 'female'. Another way of conceptualising gender is to think of it as a scale of attributes ranging from masculinity to femininity. Women are more likely than men to possess feminine attributes but such attributes do not belong exclusively to women. Gender also expresses the effects of relationships between and among women and men. These relationships are manifested in differences of political power, social roles, images and expectations resulting in recognised characteristics of masculinity and femininity that differ over time and across cultures. Thus gender is not only a set of attributes, it is also a process, *gendering*, that should be thought of as a changing contextualised social, psychological and political pheno- menon that affects the way groups of women and men define and express their interests. *Gendering* therefore refers to the way in which debates are framed in terms of gender. It is the process whereby phenomena, such as identities, observations, entities and processes, acquire symbols based on ideas about men and women. *Framing*, in this context, refers to the order, logic and structure in which an idea is enclosed. Framing may be more or less contrived and deliberate, but it always affects how we understand phenomena, ideas or events. A strong version of its meaning is found in the slang term 'frame up' which is the false establishment of blame through a particular description of events. The frames that are used to express an idea or event play an important part in the meaning that is conveyed. For example, to paraphrase Carol Bacchi (1999, p. 5) women's political under-representation may be described by equality advocates as a problem of discrimination but by traditionalists as a matter of women's choices. Framing occurs in policy debates as competing actors offer competing issue definitions and policy goals. The way a policy is framed or a problem is defined favours some interests over others: 'the definition of the alternatives is the supreme instrument of power; the antagonists can rarely agree on what the issues are because power is involved in the definitions' (Schattschneider 1975: 66). The dominant frame of a policy debate has implications for decisions because it establishes the nature of the problem to be solved. Thus gendered debates are those policy debates framed in terms of ideas about how the problem and proposed solutions will affect women in comparison with men.

Gender is therefore an important component of the way in which issues are framed in policy debates. Policy-making can be construed as a set of arguments among policy actors about what problems deserve attention, how those problems are defined and what the solutions are (John 1998; Mazur 2002). In this conflict of ideas only a few issues are taken up for action. The problem for women's advocates therefore is twofold: first, they must gain attention for their issues and the ideas they promote, and second, they must ensure that the problem is defined in terms that are compatible with movement goals. The public definition of a problem is amongst other things a frame that affects how an issue is considered and treated.

Paradoxically gender issues are often framed in gender-blind terms. Historically the gendering of debates about political representation has been 'invisible', built on the unspoken assumption that the political actor (the voter, the citizen) is male. Feminist theorists have unmasked this convention (Pateman 1988; Lister 1997) pointing out not only that women are citizens, voters and activists, but also that women in traditional gender roles have made possible the functioning and dominance of the male political actor. Historically, when issues of political representation were discussed, traditional gendering went unnoticed until the suffrage movements claimed votes for women.

Gendering policy debates therefore consists of inserting ideas about women and men into the discussion. This does not necessarily mean the debates become feminist, or that their participants support women's movement goals. Rather, this is a form of process change that, by making gender differences explicit, provides the basis for a second form of process change: increased participation by groups of women in the policy-making process. One women's movement strategy therefore is to insert its frame into the debate in order to affect policy content and outcome. The purpose is to frame debates in terms that will highlight the status of women in order to bring about its improvement. Once successful the movement then acts to maintain their frames so that the debate is conducted in feminist terms.

Consideration of the gendering of policy debates illuminates how policy debates are influenced by the women's movement. Do WPAs insert ideas of gender into the definition of policy problems? And if they do, are the ideas congruent with those of the women's movement? Adapting a line of reasoning established by Schattschneider and others (Przeworski 1991; Schneider and Ingram 1993; Cobb and Elder 1983; Jenson 1988; Schattschneider 1975), we propose that WPAs may facilitate the goals of the women's movement within the state, not only by advocating its agenda, but also by *changing the terms of debate*. In other words, the WPAs may attempt to reframe the debate to accommodate the problem definitions made by women's movement actors.

Analysing debates: the model and the cases

To summarise so far, our comparative approach to the study of the impact of women's movements on debates about political representation contains a number of elements or variables. For each we expect to find variation across countries, over time and across debates within countries. Our model is the product of a cross-national research project in which authors developed the design collectively, and then individually, as experts, made assessments of a selected country. The efforts of WPAs are examined in each country to determine how they behave in relation to women's movement attempts to affect state action. Each author has selected, described and classified three debates on political representation, making

Policy debates will vary by

activities and characteristics of the women's policy agencies

and

women's movement impact; policy content and participation

explained by variations in

characteristics of women's movements

and/or

the policy environment

Figure 1.1 The elements of the research problem

an assessment of the impact of the women's movement on the decision and the role of the WPAs in achieving that decision.

From the literature on social movement impact we developed a set of variables that might explain women's movement success or failure. To do this we drew on resource mobilisation theory, which highlights the characteristics of women's movements, and on political opportunity structure theory, which addresses the policy environment in which the movement operates. Accordingly each author has also gathered information about the characteristics of the women's movements and the policy environment at the time of each of three selected debates.

In all of the countries discussed in this volume, debates on political representation have led to explicit policies to increase the political representation of women. In most cases, however, the policies did not fully incorporate women's movement goals. The meeting of women's movement goals is only one of the criteria that we use to assess the policy impact of the women's movements. We also consider whether movements affected policy processes to make them more inclusive of movement concerns and to provide for the inclusion of women. Finally we consider the extent to which policy frames have become gendered, the relationships between frames and movement perspectives, and the extent to which processes include women and women's movements.

The elements of the research problem are shown in figure 1.1.

A theory of state feminism

The state feminist framework presented here incorporates the variables we have discussed so far into a theory in which the units of analysis

Women's movement impact

Dependent variable

Activities and characteristics of women's policy agencies

Intervening variables

Characteristics of women's movements

Independent variable cluster

The policy environment

Independent variable cluster

Figure 1.2 The RNGS framework

are political representation policy debates. We use the language of variables to give precision to our model, which is structured on relationships between dependent, independent and intervening variables. To construct the theory it is necessary, first, to establish the extent of variation in the success of women's movements in achieving substantive and descriptive representation in the state at the end of these debates. Thus the *dependent* variable, what we are trying to explain, is women's movement impact. The next step is to examine patterns of activities of women's policy agencies in changing the policy-making process on behalf of women's movements. At this stage the women's policy agency characteristics are *independent* variables that explain differences in movement impact. The third and most important step in our theory building is to assess the state feminist explanation in terms of alternative explanations for movement success in political representation policy debates. When the association between these variables, women's policy agency activities and movement impacts are examined, women's policy agency activities become an *intervening* variable. These associations are depicted in figure 1.2.

The model is built on a set of classifications. Categories from democratic representation and social movement impact theories are synthesised into typologies to measure the intervening and dependent variables: women's policy agency activities and women's movement impact. At the same time, these typologies analytically separate the variations in agency activities from the state's policy and procedural responses to permit examination of the effects of one on the other. They also separate substantive representation from descriptive representation.

The classifications illuminate our three-part research question:
Dependent variable
– What is the impact of women's movements on state policy? This question
implies an analysis and classification of the success of the women's movement in framing public policies according to a feminist understanding of
the policy problem under consideration.
Intervening variables
– What is the extent to which the WPAs further this impact? This question
implies an analysis and classification of WPAs' activities to effect changes
in the policy-making process in order to make the policy outcome correspond to women's movement goals and to establish the WPAs'
characteristics.
Independent variables
– Which characteristics of the women's movement and which features of
the policy environment provide a favourable setting for women's movement impact on state policy? How do variations in WPA activities and in
the women's movement relate to both the women's movement characteristics and features of the policy environment?

The research question translates into the five hypotheses set out in Box 1.

Box 1: RNGS hypotheses

H.1 Women's movement activists in democratic states have tended to
     be successful in increasing both substantive representation
     as demonstrated by policy content, and procedural/descriptive
     representation as demonstrated by women's participation.

H.2 Women's movement activists in democratic states have tended to
     be more successful where women's policy agencies have acted as
     insiders in the policy-making process, that is, have gendered policy
     debates in ways that coincide with women's movement goals.

H.3 Women's policy agencies with institutional capacity as defined by
     type, proximity, administrative capacity and mandate have been
     more effective than agencies with fewer resources and less capacity in
     providing linkages between women's movements and policy-makers.

H.4 Variations in women's movement representatives' characteristics
     and/or policy environments explain variations in both women's
     policy agency effectiveness and movement activists' success in
     increasing women's representation.

H.5 Women's policy offices have tended to provide necessary and
     effective linkages between women's movement activism and
     substantive and procedural responses by democratic states.

H.5A If women's policy offices are necessary and effective linkages between movement activism and state substantive and procedural responses, then variations in movement resources and policy environments will have no independent relation to state responses.

H.5B If women's policy offices are not necessary and effective linkages between movement activism and state substantive and procedural responses, then variations in women's movement resources and policy environments will be directly related to variations in state responses, regardless of women's policy office activities.

Applying the RNGS framework to debates on political representation

Each of the cases presented in chapters 2 to 12 follows the format used in the studies edited by Mazur (2001), Stetson (2001) and Outshoorn (2004). First WPAs in the political system are identified and the institutions that make the most important decisions about political representation are described. Next the major policy debates on political representation that took place during the lifetime of the WPAs are identified. Debates must have taken place in a public arena such as legislature, bureaucracy or political parties; they must have ended in a decision or other output, for example a law or official report. Once the universe of policy debates is established, researchers then select three debates for analysis that reflected the decisional system, the life cycle of the WPAs and the salience of the debates.

A feature of the case selection in this volume is that we are analysing debates about political representation itself in order to determine whether political representation arrangements ensure women's inclusion. In other words we are looking at the heart of the representative process. To do this effectively we have adapted the debate selection requirements of the RNGS model. In order to determine whether WPAs raise the issue of women's representation in wider debates about political representation authors were asked to include, where possible, at least one debate that was not explicitly about *women's* political representation. Eleven such debates in seven countries are included.

Each selected debate was traced to determine how it reached the public agenda, what frame dominated at the time and whether the debate was gendered. Researchers then assessed whether or not new gender meanings were introduced into the debate and who inserted such new meanings. To determine the extent to which a debate was framed in terms of gender, researchers examined the explicit statements of policy actors and noted

Table 1.1 *Political representation debates by country*

AUSTRIA	
AU_1	Access to the cabinet, 1975–9
AU_2	Civil service reform, 1981–93
AU_3	Public party subsidies, 1994–9
BELGIUM	
BE_1	Quotas for electoral lists, 1980–94
BE_2	Quotas for advisory committees, 1990–7
BE_3	Quotas for federal government, 1991–9
FINLAND	
FI_1	Independent electoral associations to nominate candidates, 1972–5
FI_2	Quotas for party executive in the Finnish People's Democratic League (SKDL), 1986–7 *Party debate*
FI_3	Quotas in the Equality Act of 1995, 1991–5
FRANCE	
FR_1	Change in voting system for local elections, 1982
FR_2	Change in voting system for parliamentary elections, 1985
FR_3	The parity reform, 1999–2000
GERMANY	
GR_1	Quota rules in the Social Democratic Party (SPD), 1977–88
GR_2	Second Federal Equal Rights Law, 1989–94
GR_3	Reform of Nationality Law, 1998–9
ITALY	
IT_1	Creation of the Democratic Party of the Left (PDS), 1989–91
IT_2	Reform of electoral law for the lower chamber of parliament, 1991–5
IT_3	Constitutional amendment to promote equal opportunities for access to political office, 1997–2003
NETHERLANDS	
NL_1	Reform of Social Democratic Party (PvdA), 1966–77
NL_2	Equality Policy Plan, 1981–5
NL_3	Corporatism, 1989–97
SPAIN	
SP_1	Women's quota of 25% in the Socialist Party (PSOE), 1987–8
SP_2	Women's quota of 40% in the PSOE, 1992–7
SP_3	Mandatory quotas for all parties, 1998–2003
SWEDEN	
SW_1	Greater democracy and more women in politics, 1967–72
SW_2	Quotas for appointed positions, 1985–7
SW_3	The establishment of a women's party, 1991–4
UNITED KINGDOM	
UK_1	Reform of public bodies, 1979–81
UK_2	Candidate selection in the Labour Party, 1993
UK_3	Parliamentary working hours, 2001–2
UNITED STATES	
USA_1	Equal rights amendment ratification in Arkansas, 1972–7
USA_2	Term limits in Michigan, 1991–2
USA_3	National Voter Registration Act, 1988–93

		Policy and movement goals coincide	
		Yes	No
Women involved in policy process	Yes	Dual response	Co-optation
	No	Pre-emption	No response

Figure 1.3 Women's movement impact/state response

how they described the policy problem, the solutions they suggested and whether they mentioned women or groups of women. Attention was paid to the various ways women were portrayed in the debates, especially to the images that were invoked of women and men and the significances of gender differences in the debate. Researchers described the end point of each debate. This could be a law, or report, or other kind of decision. In the course of debate tracing, close attention was given to the part played by the WPAs and women's movement and the characteristics of the movement; agency and policy environment were classified according to the schemes sketched out below. To maximise comparability, common variable descriptors were developed for each set of characteristics. These are described in Appendix 2.

Movement impact

The impact of the women's movement on the outcome was assessed using Gamson's (1975) two dimensions of substantive responses and procedural acceptance. The impact of the movement was then classified in terms of a fourfold typology. When the state accepts individual women, groups and/or constituencies into the process and changes policy to coincide with feminist goals, it is a case of *dual response*. When the state accepts women and women's groups into the process but does not give policy satisfaction, it is classified as *co-optation*. *Pre-emption* occurs when the state gives policy satisfaction but does not allow women, as individuals, groups or constituencies, into the process. Finally, when the state neither responds to movement demands nor allows women or women's groups into the process, there is *no response*.

WPA and QWPA characteristics and activities

The WPAs and their activities and possible interventions are examined for each debate. For these debates about political representation we also use the concept of quasi-women's policy agencies (QWPAs). These are WPAs that are not formally established by the state but operate at state level to improve women's status and policy influence. All but one of the QWPAs discussed in the following chapters are located in political parties.

		WPA advocates movement goals	
		Yes	No
WPA genders frame of policy debate	Yes	Insider	Non-feminist
	No	Marginal	Symbolic

Figure 1.4 Typology of women's policy agency activities

Each agency is described in terms of a number of characteristics: scope, type, proximity, administrative capacity, individual leadership, and policy mandate and orientation. These dimensions have the potential to allow the agency to enhance movement ideas, promote demands and facilitate movement actors in the policy process. *Scope* refers to the policy mission of the agency; some have a cross-sectional approach and others are single-issue agencies. *Type* refers to the form the agency takes; there are a large variety of structures such as commissions, departments, advisory councils and ministries. *Proximity* refers to its location within the executive and the closeness to the major locus of power there. *Administrative capacity* refers to budgets, staff and period of mandate, which can be temporary or unlimited. The professional and political background of the *leadership* can also determine the activities of the agency on the issue. Some agency heads are feminist and have close ties to the movement. Finally, *policy mandate* and *orientation* determine priorities of the agency and how the political representation issue fits these.

The debate is then classified according to agency activities within a fourfold typology based on two variables: (1) whether or not the agency is an advocate of women's movement goals in the policy process on the issue; (2) whether or not the agency was effective in changing the frame of the debate to these terms. When the agency incorporates the goals of the movement and is successful in gendering, i.e. inserts the gendered policy definitions into the dominant frame of the debate, it is classified as *insider*. If the agency asserts movement goals, but is not successful in gendering the policy debate, it is classified as *marginal*. When the agency is not an advocate for movement goals but genders or degenders the debate in some other ways, it is classified as *non-feminist*. Finally, when the agency neither advocates movement goals nor genders the policy debate, it is classified as *symbolic*.

Women's movement characteristics

Women's movement actors (WMAs) are examined to discover characteristics that are considered to be important for mobilisation in policy debates. Characteristics such as stage of development, closeness to the political left, priority of the political representation issue on the movement agenda, cohesion of the movement on the issue, and the strength of a possible counter-movement were used to assess this first independent variable. Four stages of development, a combined measure of size, support and mobilisation (Rosenfeld and Ward 1996), are employed: emerging/ re-emerging, growth, consolidation and decline/abeyance. Closeness to the political left refers to movement ideology and organisational closeness to the parties and trade unions of the left. Cohesion is present when movement groups active on the issue agree on the frame of the debate and the policy proposal. Issue priority refers to the expert's assessment of the priority of the political representation issue to overall movement concerns.

Policy environment

Policy environment characteristics are divided into three variables. First, the policy sub-system in which the debate takes place is examined on its degree of open- or closed-ness. When its organisation is amorphous, with no formal rules or conventions, allows the broad participation of varying interest groups and individuals, and has no fixed power balance or chain of command, it is classified as open. It is classified as moderately open/ closed when it shows some degree of organisation but opportunities are affected by shifting balances of power. It is classified as closed when it is bounded by regular procedures and rules, the limited participation of interest groups and free agents, and typically one major actor in control of the policy space and area. Second, the dominant policy discourse is compared with that of the women's movement. This frame can match that of the women's movement, be partly compatible or incompatible. Third, the party or coalition in power is classified according to ideological position on the left–right spectrum of the country concerned. In many countries party QWPAs established to promote women in the party are not only more important actors in debates on political representation than WPAs, but they also have similar characteristics and mandates to state WPAs. The role of QWPAs is explored in the conclusions.

The RNGS model and democratic representation

How can feminists maximise their political influence? Do WPAs enhance the political representation of women? Should feminism[1] be established

---

[1] Feminism is defined as an ideology that seeks to further the interests of women within a gender hierarchy and to undermine that hierarchy. The authors are well aware of controversies over the definitions of feminism and over what constitutes a feminist outcome. Thus we do not offer a universal definition of feminism. Instead we accept the prevailing definition or definitions in each country at the time of the debate. We return to this issue in chapter 13.

in state institutions to treat women's concerns? Do state equality agencies diminish women's movements? What can women's advocates expect from the expansion of the agencies, ministries, departments that have proliferated in governments since the 1970s? We demonstrate in this volume that it is possible to treat these questions systematically, using a genuinely comparative framework.

The model described above enables us to assess how states respond to feminist demands for political representation. Descriptive representation is considered in terms of the inclusion of women as political actors and substantive representation in terms of the consideration of their interests in decision-making processes. The remainder of this book consists of case studies of debates in eleven countries followed by a comparative concluding chapter. Chapters 2 to 12 are country studies, presented in alphabetical order. Chapter 13 offers a conclusion, in which we return to the questions raised here by combining the findings for each debate in a comparative analysis based on the hypotheses generated by the model.

References

Abrar, Stefania, Joni Lovenduski and Helen Margetts 2000, 'Feminist Ideas and Domestic Violence Policy Change', *Political Studies* 48: 239–62

Bacchi, Carol Lee 1999, *Women, Policy and Politics: the Construction of Policy Problems*, London: Sage

Bergqvist, Christina Annette Borchorst, Ann-Dorte Christansen, Viveca Ramstedt-Silén, Nina C. Raum and Auður Stynkarsdottin (eds.) 1999, *Equal Democracies: Gender and Politics in the Nordic Countries*, Oslo: Scandinavian University Press

Cobb, Roger and Charles D. Elder 1983, *Participation in American Politics: the Dynamics of Agenda-Setting*, Baltimore: The Johns Hopkins University Press

Eisenstein, Hester 1990, 'Femocrats, Official Feminism and the Uses of Power', in S. Watson (ed.) *Playing the State: Australian Feminist Interventions*, London: Verso, pp. 87–103

1996, *Inside Agitators: Australian Femocrats and the State*, Philadelphia: Temple University Press

Franzway, S., D. Court and R. W. Connell 1989, *Staking a Claim: Feminism, Bureaucracy and the State*, Sydney: Allen & Unwin

Gamson, William A. 1975, *The Strategy of Social Protest*, Homewood, IL: The Dorsey Press

Haavio-Mannila, E., D. Dahlerup, M. Eduards, E. Gudmundsdóttir, B. Halsaa, H. M. Hernes, E. Hänninen-Salmelin, B. Sigmundsdóttir, S. Sinkkonen and T. Skard 1985, *Unfinished Democracy: Women in Nordic Politics*, New York: Pergamon

Harding, Sandra 1986, *The Science Question in Feminism*, Ithaca: Cornell University Press

Hernes, Helga 1987, *Welfare State and Woman Power*, Oslo: Norwegian University Press

Jenson, Jane 1988, 'Changing Discourse, Changing Agendas: Political Rights and Reproductive Policies in France', in M. F. Katzenstein and C. M. Mueller (eds.) *The Women's Movements of the United States and Europe: Consciousness, Political Opportunity and Public Policy*, Philadelphia: Temple University Press, pp. 64–88

John, Peter 1998, *Analysing Public Policy*, London: Pinter

Lewis, Jane (ed.) 1993, *Women and Social Policies in Europe*, Aldershot: Edward Elgar

Lister, Ruth 1997, *Citizenship: Feminist Perspectives*, London and Basingstoke: Macmillan

Lovenduski, Joni 1986, *Women and European Politics: Contemporary Feminism and Public Policy*, London: Wheatsheaf

Lovenduski, Joni and Pippa Norris (eds.) 1993, *Gender and Party Politics*, London: Sage

Mazur, Amy (ed.) 2001, *State Feminism, Women's Movements, and Job Training: Making Democracies Work in the Global Economy*, New York and London: Routledge

  2002, *Theorizing Feminist Policy*, London: Oxford University Press

Meehan, Elizabeth and Selma Sevenhuijsen (eds.) 1991, *Equality Politics and Gender*, London: Sage

Nelson, Barbara J. 1989, 'Women and Knowledge in Political Science: Texts, Histories and Epistemologies', *Women & Politics* 9: 1–25

Outshoorn, Joyce 1994, 'Between Movement and Government: "Femocrats" in the Netherlands', in H. Kriesi (ed.) *Yearbook of Swiss Political Science*, Berne, Stuttgart and Vienna: Paul Haupt Verlag, pp. 141–65

  1998 '"Furthering the Cause": Femocrat Strategies in National Government', in Jet Bussemalier and Rian Voet (eds.) *Gender, Participation and Citizenship in the Netherlands*, Aldershot: Ashgate, pp. 108–22

  (ed.) 2004, *Prostitution, Women's Movements and Democratic Politics*, Cambridge: Cambridge University Press

Pateman, C. 1988, *The Sexual Contract*, Stanford, CA: Stanford University Press

Phillips, Anne 1995, *The Politics of Presence*, Oxford: Clarendon Press

Pitkin, Hanna Fenichel 1967, *The Concept of Representation*, Berkeley: University of California Press

Przeworski, Adam 1991, *Democracy and the Market: Political and Economic Reforms in Eastern Europe and Latin America*, Cambridge: Cambridge University Press

Rosenfeld, Rachel A. and Kathryn B. Ward 1996, 'Evolution of the Contemporary US Women's Movement', *Research in Social Movements, Conflict and Change*, 19: 1–73

Sainsbury, Diane (ed.) 1994, *Gendering Welfare States*, London: Sage

Sawer, Marian 1990, *Sisters in Suits: Women and Public Policy in Australia*, Sydney: Allen & Unwin

Schattschneider, E. E. 1975, *The Semisovereign People: a Realist's View of Democracy in America*, Hinsdale, IL: The Dryden Press

Schneider, Anne and Helen Ingram 1993, 'Social Construction of Target Populations: Implications for Politics and Policy', *American Political Science Review* 87: 334–47

Stetson, Dorothy 1987, *Women's Rights in France*, Westport, CT: Greenwood Press (ed.) 2001, *Abortion Politics, Women's Movements and the Democratic State: a Comparative Study of State Feminism*, Oxford: Oxford University Press

Stetson, Dorothy McBride and Amy Mazur (eds.) 1995, *Comparative State Feminism*, Thousand Oaks: Sage

Watson, Sophie (ed.) 1990, *Playing the State: Australian Feminist Interventions*, London: Verso

2   Gendering political representation: debates and controversies in Austria

Regina Köpl

Introduction

Historically, political representation in Austria was defined in terms of inclusion and exclusion. Exclusion corresponded with ethno-linguistic cleavages but was also based on class and gender. Class restrictions on men's voting were removed in 1907, and women were granted the right to vote and stand for election in 1918. Suffrage was now universal and equal, and elections free and secret. From 1918 to 1934 female MPs, especially from the highly organised and centralised women's working class movement, which was part of the Social Democratic Party, represented women as an interest group in decision-making bodies at federal and local levels. In 1934 the Christian Social Party abandoned its commitment to parliamentary democracy, and the parties of the left were outlawed. Between 1938 and 1945 Austria was part of the German Third Reich.

After the Second World War the party system was re-established. In the decades following the war political representation was primarily understood in terms of economic interest representation, and women's representation in parliament hovered around 6 per cent. It was not until the emergence and growth of the second wave of the women's movement that the political representation of women became an issue. In the late 1970s the movement called for a higher percentage of female MPs by linking descriptive representation to questions of substantive representation, and women's parliamentary representation began to increase up to 10 per cent. By 2003 the proportion of women MPs was 31.7 per cent.

Universe of debates

Modern Austria is a 'consociational' type of democracy characterised by a 'party state' and corporatism. Parties structure all elections, and all office holders in representative institutions are party nominees and, mostly, also party members and functionaries. The cabinet is chosen from the party or coalition of parties holding a majority in the Lower House of parliament

(National Council). The parties represented in parliament are highly disciplined, and MPs vote along party lines. Accordingly, the party or the coalition of parties in government commands a majority of votes in parliament, and it is able to pass and implement its policies (Pelinka 1998).

There is a complex network of formal and informal relations among the large interest associations and between them and the government/state bureaucracy. Negotiations with the social partner organisations, the Wage Earner's Associations on the one hand and the Employers' Association on the other, are often part of the pre-parliamentary stage of the legislative process (Talos 1996). Political decision-making is synchronised not only by structural links but also by personal links. Leaders of interest associations are usually MPs or even members of the cabinet.

The most important debates on political representation focused on women's representation, citizenship rights of immigrants, the principle of equality in the constitution, and changes in the electoral system. In 1971 parliament passed a new electoral law to reduce the number of electoral districts and increase the number of seats in the National Council. The measure gave smaller or new parties a better chance of winning seats. Although in 1979 the Social Democratic Party (SPÖ) owed its victory in the national elections to the support by women, barriers to the representation of women remained. Women's organisations and women's groups inside and outside the SPÖ demanded increases in the number of women in parliament and government. Responding to women's demands, Chancellor Kreisky asked the 1979 party conference to increase his cabinet in order to accommodate the appointment of four women as under-secretaries of state, two of them in charge of the promotion of women's policy concerns. In the early 1980s an action programme was agreed to promote qualified women for high-level civil service positions. This programme provides evidence of the symbolic nature of support by male office holders for women's demands. The outcome of the debate was the 1992 Law on the Equal Treatment of Men and Women in the Civil Service. In the same year, electoral law was changed again. Once more the main focus was on the division of electoral districts. Additionally, the personal element within the voting process was strengthened. Voters were still required to vote a straight party ticket but could now cast one preference vote. However, in the following elections only a small number of candidates received enough preference votes to win seats. In 1995 and 1996 Green Party women MPs brought in private member's bills that would connect state subsidies and public party finance to the promotion of women in politics. Both measures were rejected by the governing parties and thus settled. In Austria a minimum standard of basic rights was incorporated in the Federal Constitutional

Law. Only a very general principle covered equality between men and women. On the basis of the gender-related principles of the Amsterdam Treaty of 1997, Austrian feminists mobilised in support of a constitutional amendment on equality between men and women that included provision for affirmative action to decrease gender inequality. However, the new amendment was formalised only as a state goal (*Staatsziel*) and not as a basic or constitutional right. Universal suffrage is connected to Austrian citizenship. In the late 1990s, in Austria as in other European countries, rising immigration prompted questions about the hegemonic concept of citizenship and led to demands for voting rights for foreign residents. In 2002 the Council of the City of Vienna decided to allow foreign residents to vote at city level. However, in June 2004 a supreme Constitutional Court ruling argued that this reform was unconstitutional.

Debate selection

The first debate selected concerns women's access to cabinet positions and the chancellor's decision in 1979 to expand his cabinet by appointing four women as under-secretaries of state. The second debate focuses on the 1993 Law on Equal Treatment of Men and Women in the Civil Service. The third debate deals with public party subsidies as an instrument to increase women's representation. These debates represent the life cycle of the representation issue, from the first to the most recent major debate. They also represent different facets of political representation. The three debates additionally meet the criterion of decisional system importance – given that the debates resulted in decisions made in the internal party arena, in pre-parliamentary negotiations in the cabinet and with social partner organisations, and in parliament.

Debate 1: Women's access to the cabinet, 1975–1979

How the debate came to the public agenda

The first debate on the political representation of women was sparked by disappointment. During the first half of the 1970s, more and more women regarded the Social Democratic Party (SPÖ) as a party that supported women's interests, and women became an increasing part of the party's electorate. In the 1979 national election women of the left, linked to autonomous women's groups, undertook a great deal of campaigning for the SPÖ and its leader, Bruno Kreisky. In election addresses, Kreisky promised that the SPÖ would champion women's struggle for emancipation. At the polls, the SPÖ not only retained their majority but also gained seats. However, only one female candidate on the party's list profited from the gain in seats. In the cabinet there were only two female ministers and one female under-secretary of state. Matters became worse when only a few months after the electoral triumph, Chancellor Kreisky announced a cabinet reshuffle, dismissing the Minister of Health, a woman. At this point, women's movement activists demanded that the chancellor and the Party's elite set an example and choose a woman in the cabinet. Initially Kreisky wanted to expand the cabinet by recruiting two female under-secretaries of state. The resulting interplay between different power brokers, interest groups and traditional wings of the SPÖ saw this number doubled.

Dominant frame of debate

When the issue came onto the political agenda, it was framed in terms of injustice. Beyond lip-service on the promotion of women, Social Democratic men refused to share electoral success. Although women participated in the party organisation at all levels and in election campaigns through support networks and action committees, there was little increase in their representation on candidate lists or in cabinet appointments. It was men who controlled access to power.

The dominant frame of the debate changed after the chancellor's decision to increase the proportion of women in his cabinet. Women's activists outside and inside the SPÖ were satisfied, but the opposition parties, the media and also some Social Democratic Party officials complained that the enlargement of the cabinet occurred at the taxpayers' expense. Opponents carefully avoided questioning women's political representation, and none of the new under-secretaries of state was attacked personally in public. However, opponents agreed that there was no need to enlarge the cabinet.

Gendering the debate

Proponents and opponents pointed out that women in political office had different perspectives from those of their male colleagues and that they made a substantive difference in public policy. Women were more active and involved than men in issues that flow from their different life experiences. In particular, women's position in the workplace, influenced by their experiences as mothers, affected their views on policy. There was a divergence of attitudes between women and men on social issues including the role of women, social welfare and environmental protection. More feminist proponents argued that without women's input, issues such as battered women, child abuse and rape would have taken longer to reach the political agenda.

After the cabinet reshuffle, debate gendering concerned the role under-secretaries of state played in government. According to the Austrian constitution, under-secretaries of state are under the direct control of federal ministers. With respect to their policy mandate, secretaries of state participate in the Council of Ministers, where the chancellor, vice-chancellor and ministers have a vote, but the under-secretaries of state do not. Their roles are rather ambivalent as they are both cabinet members and highest rank bureaucrats. The opposition parties soon focused on this fact by comparing under-secretaries of state to housewives: both were 'little helpers' (*Gehilfen*). Opponents – both feminists and male critics – argued that by appointing four women as under-secretaries of state Chancellor Kreisky had reaffirmed women's traditional role.

Policy outcome

Kreisky was well known for his sensitivity to hot issues. Political representation of women was a hot issue in most western countries at the time. Two of the four new under-secretaries of state were explicitly responsible for women's issues, one for women's affairs in general and one for working women. Kreisky presented this proposal to the Social Democratic Party executive, which accepted it. As a result, 26.1 per cent of the members of the new cabinet were female, which far exceeded women's representation in other decision-making bodies. Chancellor Kreisky was correct in presenting his proposal as a 'venture with multi-plier effects'. It also created a change in atmosphere and male party officials could not publicly deny or reject women's demands without great difficulty.

One further outcome was the integration of women's interests into the policy-making process for the first time at the cabinet level through the establishment of two women's policy agencies. The under-secretary of state for the affairs of working women was abolished in 1983, when the SPÖ lost its majority in parliament and was forced to form a coali-tion government with the Austrian Freedom Party (FPÖ). The under-secretary of state for women's affairs in general took over the mandate of the abolished unit, and the agency was granted the status of a ministry in 1992. The Minister of Women's Affairs existed until February 2000 when the coalition government of the Austrian People's Party (ÖVP) and the Austrian Freedom Party decided to reduce the number of cabinet members.

Women's movement impact

Women participated in the debate, both as individuals and as group members. The SPÖ women's organisation successfully lobbied and found opportunities to intervene. They also participated in the decision-making process because the head of the women's organisation was an *ex officio* member of the party's highest decision-making bodies. Of course a male-dominated party executive made the final decision. Women also participated in the parliamentary debate discussing the cabinet reshuffle, which was highly reported in the media. Thus, women's movement impact in this debate is a dual response, satisfying goals of the women's movement.

Women's movement characteristics

The 1970s have been described as the decade of Austria's socio-economic modernisation. The Social Democrats had promised a major reform programme covering all parts of society. Two main reforms had a direct impact on women's lives. The abortion reform, giving women control over their reproductive capacities (Köpl 2001), and the replacement of patriarchal paragraphs in the marriage code and family law by gender-neutral ones based on a partnership, enhanced women's personhood and autonomy. Against this backdrop the women's movement experienced a surge in growth. Feminist consciousness expanded and women organised events and activities or set up their own groups at the local level. Gaining access to the political arena had become one of the major goals of the women's movement close to the left. Most of its leading members were also members of the SPÖ. Only small groups distrusted traditional politics and formed the autonomous (non-politically affiliated) wing of the women's movement. Most movement actors agreed on the demand to increase the number of women in political office as well as the necessity to establish a women's policy agency at national level. There was no counter-mobilisation at the time of the debate.

Women's policy agency activities

There was no state women's policy agency during the first debate. The establishment of two such agencies at national level was an outcome of the debate. There was, however, a quasi-WPA, the SPÖ women's organisation (*Bundesfrauenorganisation der SPÖ*). This organisation is directly represented at party conferences as well as in party decision-making bodies. Its brief was to organise the Social Democratic women's movement at local, state and national level. In the decision under question it was near the power centre. The *Bundesfrauenorganisation der SPÖ* not only advocated but also pushed and organised for more appointments. It had only a small independent budget and marginal administrative resources. The women's organisation was entitled to make policy recommendations and to forward proposals to the party's annual conference. Historically, its major policy orientations were directed to social and welfare policies.

At the time of the debate the chairwoman, who was elected by the women's organisation, was a moderate feminist. She supported most demands of the new women's movement but was not a second-wave feminist herself. She and the women's organisation played an insider role by gendering the policy debate through emphasising women's under-representation in politics, accusing the party elite of being unwilling to promote women's concerns, and advocating the establishment of women's policy agencies. The head of the SPÖ women's organisation advocated demanding the increase of women's political representation in the party's highest decision-making bodies as well as in parliament. At the time of the debate she was Minister of Science and she was believed to be one of the few persons Chancellor Kreisky feared.

Policy environment

Between 1971 and 1983 the Social Democrats had held an absolute majority in the legislature and Chancellor Kreisky headed a single-party government. The policy sub-system was very closed because government formation has always been the domain of party politics. Decisions on cabinet members are formally made in the party executive bodies. Very strong chancellors, like Bruno Kreisky, have successfully managed to make the party's approval of their personal decisions a pure formality (Müller 1996: 32). The matching issue frame at the beginning of the debate was expressed in similar terms to those of the feminist movement.

Debate 2: Equal treatment of men and women in the civil service, 1981–1993

How the debate came to the public agenda

The 1979 Equal Treatment Law established obligatory adherence to the principle of equal treatment of men and women in terms of employment, especially regarding equal pay. This law covered only the private sector since wage statistics underscored that gender-related income differentials were much larger in the private sector than in public administration where there are set salary scales. For federal employees, the under-secretary of state responsible for women's affairs introduced an action programme for the promotion of women in the civil service in 1981. The core of the programme comprised three main goals: to increase the pool of female applicants through special training programmes, to increase women's access to professional degrees needed for entry into decision-making administrative bodies, and to establish women's networks within the bureaucracy. Authorised only by a decision of the Council of Ministers, this programme had little effect. In 1988, an evaluation report showed some progress in increasing the pool of applicants and in net-working. However, the number of women in decision-making positions had not increased in real terms. Because female officers reported that they encountered frequent resistance, the experts' report also recommended 'legalising' the action programme by introducing an Equal Treatment Law for the public service (Kreisky and Walther 1990).

Courts have not traditionally played an important role in Austrian pol-itics. However, in December 1990 the Constitutional Court handed down a major decision. According to Austrian pension law, women could retire at sixty and men at sixty five. This was to compensate for prior disadvantages related to women's familial duties. The Constitutional Court decided to remove this paragraph from the pension law because they deemed it incompatible with the general principle of equality laid down in the Austrian constitution. Therefore the government was obliged to reform the pension law. The Minister of Women's Affairs used the court's decision as an opportunity to force government to introduce measures to reduce the inequality of men and women in economic and social life.

The Minister of Women's Affairs proposed a comprehensive package of measures related to welfare policies and social issues. Central to this pack-age, known as the 'equal treatment package' (*Gleichbehandlungspaket*), was a proposal to reform the Equal Treatment Law for the private sector and introduce a similar law for the civil service. By combining all these different policy proposals the minister wanted to push them through as a single piece of legislation. Only when the whole package was negotiated and passed, she stated, was she willing to agree to reform the pension law. Otherwise she intended to make use of her veto in the Council of Ministers to prevent the pension law reform.

Dominant frame of debate

All major actors agreed that there was a need to 'feminise' bureaucracy to make it more representative. Also there was no dissent on the introduction of measures to overcome gender-related job segregation. The new law was meant to provide the legislative basis for descriptive and substantive feminisation of public administration. However, there was dissent over the policy instruments proposed by the WPA and its allies to remove discriminatory practices as well as to reach the future goal of de facto equality between men and women in the civil service.

Gendering the debate

Women's movement representatives exposed existing gendered procedures that worked against women. They asked for objective criteria and more transparency regarding qualifications and promotion procedures in public administration. Thereby they directly challenged male-dominated practices deeply embedded in the bureaucracy. Appointments to administrative bodies were traditionally confined to old boys' networks and determined by patronage politics in political parties. Unsurprisingly, some high-ranking civil servants countered that recruitment or promotion decisions are always somewhat arbitrary. They complained that objective criteria and measurements would erode the role of experience and empathy in guiding the recruitment process. Proponents defended their demand, arguing that only by this measure would (male) superiors provide detailed information on job qualifications. Gender-specific qualifications – e.g. men's experiences in the military vs. women's experiences as mothers – would be described explicitly in terms of their relevance to the job.

One major goal of the Minister of Women's Affairs was to shift the burden of proof in cases of unlawful discrimination. First, shifting the burden of proof to the employers would raise their awareness of discrimination. Second, it would help to eliminate recruitment practices that discriminate indirectly by having a differential impact. Third, a woman who experiences discrimination is disadvantaged if she must assemble evidence of a prima facie case. Critics of this proposal feared that the number of complaints and litigation would snowball. In arguing against the proposal, spokespersons of the ÖVP and the Austrian Business League pointed out that only big business has the money to pay top attorneys. Some legal scholars joined the critics, defending the assumption of innocence as a basic principle guiding the rule of law.

Convinced that removing discriminatory barriers alone would not achieve de facto equality, advocates of affirmative action measures favoured preferential treatment to overcome the effects of past discrimination, and argued that a change in attitudes and mentalities would take time. Opponents (MPs of the FPÖ) took the position that preferential treatment of women would result in reverse discrimination.

Prominent members of the civil servants' trade union opposed some of the women's movement's demands. The trade union's leader rejected both the demand to nominate equal treatment officers at department level and the demand to establish an Equal Treatment Commission to advance women's interests. He saw no need to establish new bodies and contact persons separate from the existing works councils.

Debate gendering was feminist in the sense that movement actors focused on de facto equality as the main goal. They also raised taboo issues, such as sexual harassment.

Policy outcome

In Austrian-style consociational democracy, important decisions are made prior to parliamentary deliberations. In addition to negotiations with the social partners, the Minister of Women's Affairs had to clear controversial issues with the other cabinet ministers. Special agreements, such as an extended time span to fulfil the 40 per cent women's quota, were negotiated with the Minister of Internal Affairs and the Minister of Defence. The most controversial issue was shifting the burden of proof to the employer. As a compromise, the negotiating partners agreed on a soft version of this demand. The employer – the federal ministries and agencies – would not have to prove non-discrimination of women in cases of conflict; rather they needed only to explain in detail that they did not discriminate against women, if requested to do so.

The policy outcome was the 1993 Equal Treatment Law for Men and Women in the Civil Service (*Bundesgleichbehandlunggesetz*). The law expressly prohibited both direct and indirect discrimination. Discrimination was defined as any form of non-objective prejudicial treatment. The law required positive action in favour of women, which has been translated into detailed provisions for the preferential treatment of women in hiring, promotion and training. The ministers must adopt individual plans for the advancement of women within their units and submit detailed reports to parliament. To monitor equal treatment and the various provisions relating to the plans for the advancement of women, an Equal Treatment Commission as well as equal treatment officers and working groups at the department level were established.

Women's movement impact

The women's movement's impact was a dual response. Prominent female MPs and spokespersons from the women's organisations of the political parties as well as the trade unions promoted the equal treatment package – not only within their organisations but also in the media. In pre-parliamentary negotiations, social partnership organisations from the labour sector nominated women to represent their interests in the negotiating committee. In parliament, women MPs dominated the final reading of the draft. Forming a cross-party network, women successfully framed the debate. Most of the women's movement goals found their way into the final policy formulation.

Women's policy agency activities

The Ministry of Women's Affairs initiated the policy proposal. Its staff, together with feminist legal experts, drafted the proposal. The policy mandate of the WPA was a cross-sectional one, co-ordinating all policies related to women's issues at a federal level. Clearly, the policy mandate covered the issue under study. The minister, Johanna Dohnal, like all cabinet appointees, was politically appointed. She was also the chair-woman of the SPÖ women's organisation, and in this capacity was a member of the party executive. Using her veto, she was able to prevent the passage of drafts proposed by other ministers and was thus at the centre of power. However, the WPA's administrative capacity was not great. Three separate divisions supported the minister, and every year there were struggles to increase a modest budget.

The head of the WPA was a second-wave feminist who supported autonomous feminist groups. Her major policy goals were to increase the representation of women in political and administrative bodies and place controversial issues, such as domestic violence against women including marital rape, on the public agenda. By networking and interceding, she sought to increase her influence (Dohnal 1992). The role of the WPA in the policy process is therefore insider.

Women's movement characteristics

The major women's organisations were those of the SPÖ and the ÖVP. The women's organisation of the Austrian Trade Union Federation also played an important role in the debate. There was only a small autonomous women's movement, mostly dealing with single issues and projects such as rape crisis centres, critiques of patriarchy, and lesbian and gay rights. As a whole, the women's movement was in a stage of consolidation. At that time the SPÖ women's organisation was the most powerful. Because of the corporatist structure of Austrian politics it was interconnected with women organised within the trade unions. For instance, the chairwoman of the women's organisation of the Austrian Trade Union Federation represented her organisation as an MP of the SPÖ. Of course these women's organisations only hold limited power within the party and trade union hierarchy and in general have to tailor their ideas to fit the party line.

The advancement of equal treatment policies was an issue uniting most movements' organisations and activists. At the beginning of the debate, female politicians from the major parties as well as Green Party MPs and trade union representatives formed a cross-party women's coalition to promote the WPA's proposal. However, during pre-parliamentary negotiations the women's phalanx collapsed. Brought back into line by their mother organisations, ÖVP women's representatives as well as female civil servant trade unionists did not support the WPA's efforts to push through the more radical demand of shifting the burden of proof. Otherwise, the women's movement can be characterised as cohesive. The women's movement was feminist insofar as most women's movement actors and organisations portrayed affirmative action and quota regulations as necessary measures to overcome women's under-representation. No counter-movement mobilised to prevent the passage of the new law. However, there were strong lobbies – e.g. employers' associations, some civil servant trade unionists as well as some ministers and high-ranking civil servants – who tried hard to dilute women's demands.

Policy environment

The policy sub-system was closed. Women's movement actors had direct access to policy formulation as representatives of women's party organisations, as functionaries in social partnership organisations, as cabinet members or as civil servants involved in drafting the ministerial proposal. During the evaluation procedure, when all groups involved are asked to formulate their consent, criticism or rejection of the draft, criticisms came from the Austrian Business League and some ÖVP ministers, as well as the civil servants' trade union, which is ÖVP-dominated. The most controversial issues were negotiated at the pre-parliamentary stage by several round tables in which the Minister of Women's Affairs, the Minister of Social Affairs (male), top representatives of the Austrian Trade Union Federation's women's organisation, a female representative of the Chamber of Labour, and the General Secretary of the Austrian Business League (male) took part. The policy frame matched the dominant frame. Especially at the beginning of the debate, it was expressed in terms that corresponded to women's movement goals. Male allies also supported women's demands in general. However, on the more controversial feminist issues such as shifting the burden of proof or introducing detailed affirmative action, support eroded.

At the time of the debate, Chancellor Vranitzky led a coalition government dominated by the SPÖ. Since the SPÖ and ÖVP possessed an
absolute majority in parliament, the government was able to control
decision-making. Therefore, the policy environment was characterised
by moderate left-wing control.

Debate 3: Public party subsidies, 1994–1999

How the debate came to the public agenda

The most important source of income for political parties in Austria is
public party subsidies. Donations have traditionally played a relatively
small role, and membership fees are of less importance as a result of the
decline in party membership. Direct and indirect forms of public party
financing – campaign subsidies, funding of parliamentary caucuses and
subsidies to the parties' political education activities – constituted nearly
half of the parties' budgets in the mid-1990s (Sickinger 1997).

In the 1990s the federal deficit dominated public discussion.
International recession, which reached Austria in the early 1990s, and
the costs of joining the EU in 1995 deepened the federal deficit. The need
to consolidate public finance was widely recognised. After the 1994
parliamentary elections the SPÖ/ÖVP coalition government proposed
an austerity programme, cutting back expenditures, e.g. welfare payments. At the same time, the governing parties opted to increase public
party subsidies. Initially the debate centred on the necessity of austerity
measures to consolidate the federal budget, on the one hand, and the
coalition parties' demands to increase public party financing, on the
other. An increase of state subsidies to political parties did not seem
appropriate during a period of budgetary restraint. Protesting against
the political establishment, the populist chairman of the FPÖ, Jörg
Haider, successfully integrated increasing public party financing into his
strategy of fighting corruption, mismanagement and waste in public
spending.

In the 1994 federal election the proportion of female MPs fell for the
first time since the 1970s. The two major parties, the SPÖ and the ÖVP,
lost seats and sent fewer women to parliament. Women's representation
in the legislature declined from its peak of 25.14 per cent in March 1994
to 21.85 per cent in 1995. Women also remain vastly under-represented
in elective office at a regional and local level (Bundesministeruim für
Frauenangelegenheiten/Bundeskanzleramt 1995). Faced with the failure
of the party elites to support women as candidates and office holders, the
chairwoman of the Green parliamentary caucus announced at a

conference on women and politics in 1994 that she would introduce a private member's bill to make 15 per cent of public subsidies contingent upon the number of female representatives being proportional to their presence in the population, which is more than 50 per cent. At that time nearly 60 per cent of the MPs of the Green Alternative (GAL) were female. She also announced that public party finances should also fund concrete action plans and training programmes to promote women. Shortly after the first reading of the bill, the cabinet resigned and new elections took place in 1996. After the election the Greens launched a new parliamentary initiative on this subject.

Dominant frame of debate

All actors involved in the debate, mainly female representatives of the political parties, believed that representation of both men and women was a basic criterion of democracy. All agreed that increasing the number of women in politics was essential. Their main concern was how to do this. Were strong measures such as quota rules appropriate and – most important – was it the task of the legislature to intervene by linking quota regulations and party finances? In 1996, the inherently gendered structure of politics was explicitly questioned. Old boys' networks and high incumbency rates coupled with no term limits for legislative offices were only a few of the factors contributing to lower percentages of women in politics. At the end of the debate, the main emphasis was on legislative intervention.

Proponents of the bill, mainly members of the Green Party, justified their demand by arguing that political leaders had failed to increase the number of women in elected offices. Although there was no formal/legal discrimination and party officials declared their support for women, the increase in the number of female representatives was only very gradual. Quota rules, they argued, while not desirable, were an auxiliary engine towards equality. Linking quotas for women to public party subsidies at a federal level could provide an example for regional and local legislative bodies and social partnership organisations.

Only two parties in the Austrian parliament, the Green Alternative and the SPÖ, have introduced gender quotas into their party statutes. In 1986 the GAL established a quota system committed to a strict 50 per cent representation of women by the principle of gender alternation. In 1985, the SPÖ first introduced a 25 per cent quota for women on candidate lists and for appointed offices. In 1993, the party decided to increase the quota to 40 per cent and make it mandatory. The ÖVP is verbally committed to a 30 per cent quota for women but there are no regulations in its statutes.

The FPÖ rejects gender quotas, arguing that they are discriminatory towards women because they imply that women are less capable than men. The female founder and head of the *Liberales Forum* (LIF), a group of MPs that split away from the FPÖ in 1993, described quota rules as a contradiction of the principle of self-regulation (Bundesministerium für Frauenangelegenheiten/Bundeskanzleramt 1995: 593).

Not surprisingly, female speakers from the Liberals and the FPÖ rejected the term 'incentive'. They described linking quota regulations to public party subsidies as a coercive measure. Public subsidies should not determine the composition of political parties or the extent to which they represent social interests. In the debate during the final reading, female SPÖ and ÖVP representatives declared that parties' interest in votes (of the female electorate) should govern recruitment practices rather than legislative intervention.

Gendering the debate

Both proponents and opponents focused on barriers to women's representation. The chairwoman of the ÖVP women's organisation, as well as some female SPÖ speakers, considered women's disadvantaged political position to be an outcome of the division of housework and constraints posed by women's domestic duties. Preconceptions of proper female behaviour hindered women from pursuing public office, especially in the more Catholic, rural parts of Austria; and socialisation effects led to less confidence about becoming a candidate.

Opponents claimed that a targeted transfer of party subsidies was not in women's interests. Compulsory intervention would not only undermine the principles of the market economy and self-regulation, it would also be misused. Party elites would promote token women rather than qualified ones. Women would thus be reduced to a financial product. FPÖ party officials were not alone in stressing the qualification argument; they were joined by a senior SPÖ MP. Contrary to those women put in an elected office by quotas, he stated, successful female politicians must be highly qualified and politically committed. The chairwoman of the ÖVP women's organisation also argued that gender should not matter in politics. Personal commitment was a much better criterion for promotion.

Proponents responded by pointing to 'hidden quota rules' that have traditionally regulated access to political office. Besides regional representation, the impact of economic interest group representation (mainly employers and unions) moderates the extent to which women can gain representation. In the two major parties, the SPÖ and the ÖVP, a certain number of seats have been traditionally reserved for prominent members of the social partnership organisations.[1]

The importance of women in politics now extended beyond influencing policy. Women were seen as agents of change, who not only bring different experiences and perspectives to their jobs but will also change legislative style. Female opponents, who would not label themselves as feminists, agreed that women in office operate differently from their male peers. Women, it was said, tended to favour co-operation rather than confrontation, were less aggressive and approached the world more contextually. Dealing with gendered stereotypes such as women's tendency towards harmony, the chair of the conservative ÖVP women's organisation noted that women displayed a style of consensus rather than one of command and control. Feminist proponents of the proposal stressed arguments based on critical mass theory to give weight to their demand for quota regulations. When women's representation reached parity with men's, they would transform the way in which legislators do business. Changing the norms and rules of legislative life would alter the gendered nature of the political institutions.

Policy outcome

During the first reading of the Greens' bill in 1996, prominent female speakers from all parties agreed that women's participation was important to democracy and that political parties must promote women's entry into politics. Speakers of the SPÖ and the ÖVP, but also the SPÖ Minister of Women's Affairs, explicitly welcomed the Greens' initiative. Only Liberals and MPs of the FPÖ opposed the bill. After the first reading, the bill was assigned to the parliamentary committee on equality. In June 1999 the equality committee, dominated by the governing parties, the SPÖ and the ÖVP, advised parliament to reject the bill. In the final debate, female speakers of the SPÖ, ÖVP, FPÖ and LIF argued against the proposal. The bill was rejected – all female MPs voted along party lines. There has been no further effort to introduce quota rules by legislation or to link public party subsidies with the advancement of women in politics.

---

[1] Internal party rules make the inclusion of women's organisation representatives on every list mandatory. But the number of seats reserved for women's organisation officials is limited. Therefore, increasing the number of female MPs in the national parliament depends on opening up conventional means of access to elected offices.

Women's movement impact

After the introduction of the bill, women's movement actors were integrated into the decision-making process. All parties found it important to have women play visible roles in the process. Women were thus party spokespersons on the issue throughout the debate. Some female speakers of the SPÖ and the ÖVP were representatives of their parties' women's organisation. Two female participants were chairwomen of their party's parliamentary caucuses – the GAL and LIF. The Green Party has always had strong connections with social movements, including the more radical autonomous branch of the women's movement. Since the head of the GAL proposed the bill, feminist women's movement interests gained direct access to the policy sub-system. Women were also accepted as experts in committee hearings. In short, women were involved in the policy process, but feminist goals of the women's movement were not achieved. Accordingly, this debate was a case of co-optation.

Women's policy agency activities

The Minister for Women's Affairs would have been able to play a role in the policy process by virtue of the ministry's cross-sectional policy mandate. As a minister, she also had a veto right in the cabinet and was formally close to the centre of power, but she was dependent on the party that appointed her. During the third debate the minister was moderately feminist and appointed by the SPÖ. She did not initiate debates on controversial issues such as domestic violence or parity in housework as had some of her predecessors. Attempting to avoid conflict, the minister refused to take a position on public party subsidies as an instrument to promote women in politics. On this issue, the WPA did not support feminist goals, e.g. by forwarding a ministerial proposal to the Council of Ministers. The role of the WPA can thus be classified as symbolic.

Women's movement characteristics

In the 1990s the women's movement was consolidated but fragmented. Women had successfully entered the bureaucracy; the number of women's projects with regular state support had increased. Femocrats were working on the regional and local levels to implement women's programmes and set up women's offices. Most feminist women's movement actors were allied with the left-wing political parties, the SPÖ and GAL, and they viewed quota regulation as a means to achieve the feminist goal of equal representation. Female representatives of the ÖVP, the chairwoman of the LIF and the spokeswoman of the FPÖ did not consider themselves feminists and opposed legislative intervention on gender relations. In other words, linking public party subsidies and women's political representation did not unite the women's movement. Furthermore, many movement actors gave priority to social issues. Faced with cutbacks in the public sector and welfare payments, which were detrimental to women's economic situation, feminist women's groups and actors tried to force parliament to deal with women's demands by organising a women's popular initiative (*Frauenvolksbegehren*) in 1997. Increasing women's political representation through mandatory quotas was a priority only for some activists. During the third debate no overt counter-movement against women's issues emerged but the climate changed and anti-feminist attitudes slowly re-emerged.

Policy environment

The policy sub-system in the third debate was closed. The site of the debate was parliament and the main actors were political parties. Only high-ranking party officials took a position in public discussion and legislative deliberations. Non-institutionalised participants were present as experts at committee hearings, workshops or in the media. With a majority in parliament, the coalition parties (SPÖ and ÖVP) were successful in voting down the opposition's parliamentary initiative. However, having lost seats in all federal elections since 1979, and confronted with the success of the FPÖ in the 1990s, the SPÖ had to cater to its coalition partner. At the time of the third debate, left-wing control was further weakened. In that all actors agreed that increasing the proportion of women was a step towards democracy, the policy frame that initially shaped the debate met the goals of the women's movement. However, strong, mandatory measures were not party executives' main interest. Neither male allies nor non-feminist decision-makers supported the proposals to introduce quota regulations and action programmes for women through the vehicle of public party subsidies.

Conclusion

Comparing the three debates on political representation discussed in this chapter we find changing patterns of movement impact and state response. In the first debate (representation of women at the cabinet level) and in the second debate (Law on the Equal Treatment of Men and Women in the Civil Service), the women's movement succeeded in getting its demands on to the political agenda and keeping them there. In both cases the state enacted policies that reflected the movement's goals. On the issue of public party subsidies and the promotion of women in politics (the third debate), however, 'the state' refused to act on women's claims even though – as in the first and second debates – women's movement representatives were involved in decision-making and Social Democrats had a major say. How can these findings be accounted for?

Analysing the first and second debates we find movement actors networking to achieve their demands. In both cases the issue was of top priority to the major branches of the women's movement. During the first debate autonomous feminist groups and individuals joined with women organised within the SPÖ women's organisation, which promoted the plea for more women in politics. In enlisting the support of the chancellor and the party's elite – the SPÖ had an absolute majority in 1979 – the SPÖ women's organisation, led by a long-established and very prominent party official, played the role of a quasi-WPA. However, there was no state women's policy agency at the time of this debate. In the case of the second debate the heads of the political parties' women's organisations, supported by spokespersons of the Trade Union Federation's women's organisation, forged a cross-party alliance to force government to deal with the 'equal treatment package'. In the early 1990s the Social Democrats had lost absolute control but still dominated in cabinet and parliament. Neither in the first nor the second debate was there any counter-movement in existence that mobilised to defeat women's proposals. Of course, individual men and also some women opposed movement goals, in particular feminist ones. Nevertheless, most political actors portrayed women's demands in terms of justice and democracy. Thus, the cultural environment was more encouraging for movement activists to make claims. In the second debate on Equal Treatment in the Civil Service, the policy was initiated and shaped by the WPA. Seasoned by many years of experience in politics, the head of the agency played a key role in networking and pushing the proposal through pre-parliamentary negotiations. She did not hesitate to threaten to use her veto in the cabinet. The Minister of Women's Affairs, who was also in contact with autonomous movement activists, operated as a veritable insider. As the chairwoman of the Social Democratic party's women's organisation she was also a member of the Party's executive bodies at a federal level. Accordingly, the second debate not only testifies to the fact that state feminism exists but also indicates how it works. In the third debate women also played a visible role in persuading party leaders tacitly to recognise the importance of including women in the public discussion. Backed by their parliamentary caucus, female MPs of the Green Party introduced the bill on linking public party financing to the increase of the number of female candidates and MPs. Nevertheless, the Green Party was in opposition. As a result of the power structure in Austrian politics, opposition proposals are only adopted when supported by the majority. In contrast to the second debate, no women's cross-party network or alliance was in existence to force their party elites to deal with the proposal. During the late 1990s the proposal was a priority only for some individual women and women's groups, but it was not on the agenda of the major women's organisations, which focused on welfare policies and social issues instead. The Minister of Women's Affairs, a newcomer in cabinet, neither advocated nor rejected the bill in public. Nor did she make use of her position as chairwoman of the SPÖ women's organisation to start a debate on the subject within her party. Compared with her predecessors she was not supported by feminist groups outside the party and she was not in close contact with the women's spokespersons of the other parties.

Still dominating cabinet and parliament, the SPÖ, which had held power for almost thirty years, had lost much of its attraction. Unlike in the 1970s, when the SPÖ was at its peak, younger well-trained urban people, academics and intellectuals shifted their votes to the LIF or the Greens. Blue-collar workers, who historically sympathised with the SPÖ, became increasingly attracted by Jörg Haider, the populist leader of the FPÖ, who by successfully playing upon people's emotions was able to define the dominant discourse.

Summing up, the Austrian debates provide evidence that the success of movement actors in achieving state responses, in line with movement goals, depends on the following key factors:

- The role taken by the WPA's leader. Is she willing to go against the party that appointed her in advocating movement demands? Is networking within as well as outside the political parties one of her main goals? Do (male) allies holding power positions support her?
- A strong left that is not only in power but also willing to frame issues in a way that is not always popular.
- A women's movement that treats the issue as a high priority, is unified in its demands and connected to institutionalised women's bodies operating within political institutions, such as political parties, social partnership organisations, parliament and the cabinet.

References

Bundeskanzleramt (ed.) 1995, *Frauenbericht 1995. Bericht über die Situation der Frauen in Österreich*, Vienna: Bundesministerium für Frauenangelegenheiten

Dohnal, Johanna 1992, 'Die Überwindung des Patriarchats. Grenzen und Möglichkeiten staatlicher Frauenpolitik', *Zukunft* 4: 5–7

Köpl, Regina 2001, 'State Feminism and Policy Debates on Abortion in Austria', in Dorothy McBride Stetson (ed.) *Abortion Politics, Women's Movements and the Democratic State: a Comparative Study of State Feminism*, Oxford: Oxford University Press, pp. 17–38

Kreisky, Eva and Ingrid Walther 1990, *Quantitative und Qualitative Evaluierung des 'Förderungsprogrammes für Frauen im Bundesdienst' für den Zeitraum 1981/ 1988*, Vienna: Forschungsbericht im Auftrag des Bundeskanzleramts

Müller, Wolfgang C. 1996, 'Political Institutions', in Volkmar Lauber (ed.) *Contemporary Austrian Politics*, Boulder: Westview Press, pp. 23–58

Pelinka, Anton 1998, *Austria: Out of the Shadow of the Past*, Boulder: Westview Press

Sickinger, Hubert 1997, *Politikfinanzierung in Österreich. Ein Handbuch*, Vienna: Thaur.

Talos, Emmerich 1986, 'Corporatism – the Austrian Model', in Volkmar Lauber (ed.) *Contemporary Austrian Politics*, Boulder: Westview Press, pp. 103–24

3 The Belgian paradox: inclusion and exclusion of gender issues

Petra Meier

Introduction

The Belgian understanding of representation is intimately related to the conception of citizenship, which itself is connected to the specific history of the Belgian state. In 1830 Belgium became a unitary constitutional monarchy, but Belgian society has never been homogeneous. Its political and institutional landscape is characterised by a segmented pluralism, reflecting basic social cleavages. Religious and economic divisions played a predominant role until the 1960s when the cleavage between the Flemish and the Francophone language groups gained priority. Although both the economic and religious cleavages led to descriptive representation, it was above all the increasingly salient linguistic cleavage that led to a redefinition of the institutions of political representation. The federalisation of the Belgian political system, a process that started in the 1960s, led to an institutionalisation of the prevailing interpretation of citizenship (on the Belgian political system see Deschouwer 2002, 2004).

Belgian citizenship is believed to be embedded in its social groups. Like the Netherlands, Belgium is a consociational society that integrates social groups into processes of decision-making. Such recognition supports provision for descriptive representation according to which the membership of public bodies and elected assemblies should mirror the society by containing the salient groups, although not necessarily in proportional terms. Whereas segmentation of political and civil society is decreasing, the balanced representation of key social groups continues to be seen as an essential legitimising feature of the political system (Paye 1997). There is, furthermore, a consensus that it is legitimate to institutionalise the presence of specific social groups (Meier 2000). There is no reluctance to enshrine structural measures in party statutes, legislation or the constitution to ensure the presence of particular social groups in bodies of representation.

Compared with other European countries female suffrage came late. From 1919 widows, women active in the resistance and single mothers of soldiers who died during the First World War were awarded the right to vote, but only until they (re)married. In 1921 women gained the right to vote in local elections. Universal female suffrage began in 1948. From 1921 onwards women were entitled to run for elections. Until the middle of the 1970s elected women were an exception; at the beginning of the 1990s they comprised about 10 per cent of the representatives. Only in the 1990s did the percentage of female representatives begin to rise. In the federal Lower and Upper Houses about 35 per cent of MPs are women. In the regional assemblies the percentage varies from 45 per cent (Brussels Capital Region) to 18 per cent (Walloon Region). On average, about 30 per cent of representatives at the local and provincial level are women.

Selection of debates

The Belgian political system is a paradigmatic case of the allocation of presence in decision-making institutions on (mainly) linguistic, ideological and philosophical grounds. Thirty-five years of constitutional reform turned the Belgian state into a federal system reflecting debates on the fair representation of the linguistic groups. Reserved seats were introduced for the linguistic groups in the European parliament, in the federal Upper House and in the council of Brussels Capital Region. Similar arrangements were made for the federal government and for the government of the Brussels Capital Region. The representation of linguistic groups is also required in the composition of public administration, advisory committees and public boards. Debates about the institutionalisation of gender quotas in politics began at the beginning of the 1980s. The need for more women in politics and especially in government was an issue in 1973 when the two female secretaries of state did not survive a reshuffle of the Leburton government. From then onwards the women's movement, and later also the women's policy agency, tried to mobilise both public opinion and decision-makers on the issue of increasing the presence of women in politics. From the beginning of the 1980s, gender quotas for the composition of electoral lists, of advisory committees and of the federal government were debated at regular intervals. In addition debates on positive action took place, mainly regarding the public sector and the political parties.

The most recent such debate concerned the constitutionalisation of parity democracy. Since the first half of the 1990s feminist intellectuals have defended the principle of parity democracy, defined as the explicit recognition of the equality of both sexes. To enshrine the principle of parity democracy in the constitution would oblige the government to act to achieve equality between the sexes (Vogel-Polsky 1996, 1997). Both equality and difference arguments were invoked to justify parity democracy. The argument is that there are as many women as men and this proportion should be reflected everywhere in society. The Belgian advocates of parity democracy emphasise that the concept fits well with the Belgian conception of a citizenship with many faces, and their concern is to ensure gender is recognised as one of those faces. A less salient debate in the second half of the 1990s concerned the voting and participation of foreign citizens and was partly influenced and crosscut by the EU agenda on these matters. The issue of representation also arises in economic and labour market decision-making. Whilst not all of the examples refer to political representation in the strict sense of the term, between them they show how the Belgian political and institutional landscape is full of procedures distributing positions on descriptive grounds.

Thus Belgian debates on representation involve several institutions. The main institutions of political representation are the federal Lower and Upper Houses of parliament as well as the federal government. In practice the most important institutions are the governing parties. Decision-making is strongly dominated by the political agenda of the parties and the elements of most policies are set out in coalition-formation agreements.

This chapter examines three debates about gender quotas in three different institutions. Debate selection was constrained by the late establishment of the women's policy agency and the nature of debates on representation that have dominated the agenda since it was established. Neither the debates on the representation of the linguistic groups nor those on multiculturalism meet RNGS selection criteria. While several claims by linguistic groups were settled in the 1990s, those debates had their roots in the 1960s and were well advanced by the time the women's policy agency was established. The debates on multicultural society have not yet reached their end point. Moreover, as we will see, studying other debates than those on gender issues would make it impossible to understand the way in which the organisational logic of the Belgian political system influences the potential scope and activity of the women's policy agency.

Debate 1: Quota for electoral lists, 1980–1994

How the debate came to the public agenda

The question of the political representation of women first made it to the political agenda in January 1980. Paula D'Hondt, a Flemish Christian Democrat senator, introduced a bill stipulating that no more than 75 per cent of the candidates on local lists should be of the same sex. The issue was described in terms of the desirability of political equivalence.

Advocates sought a society in which both sexes would have the same political rights and duties (Senaat Gedr. Stuk. 1979–80: 370/1). The Council of State rejected the bill on the grounds that a gender quota would violate the principles of equality and of non-discrimination.

Ten years later, in March 1991, Trees Merckx, also a Flemish Christian Democrat MP, introduced a new bill. She advocated only a maximum of 80 per cent of candidates of the same sex, but wanted it to be applied to all except local and European elections. She also suggested that at least one winnable seat on electoral lists be designated for the under-represented sex (Kamer Gedr. Stuk. 1990–1: 1538/1, 1539/1). The Belgian electoral system is a proportional list system. And although the closed character of lists has declined, voting behaviour still tends to reinforce the list order. Hence, only winnable seats are interesting, which explains Merckx's focus on eligible list positions. The bill, along with many others, fell when elections were called a few months later. From then on the government took the lead on electoral gender quotas.

The first government of Jean-Luc Dehaene declared its intention to stimulate an improved participation of women in political decision-making in 1991. The (Flemish male Social Democrat) Minister of Internal Affairs, Louis Tobback, supported by the (Flemish female Christian Democrat) Minister of Equal Opportunities, Miet Smet, pro-posed to impose gender quotas on electoral lists through legislation. The bill they submitted to the Council of Ministers stipulated that electoral lists may contain a maximum of two-thirds of candidates of the same sex. This principle would apply to the list as such and to the top – and most winnable – list positions (De Win 1994). Parties that did not respect these stipulations would face sanctions, losing, amongst other things, part of their state subsidy and financial advantages (Leye 1992). The Council of State did not condemn the idea of a gender quota but argued that the sanctions were disproportionate (Kamer Gedr. Stuk. 1993–4: 1316/1). Following disagreement within the Council of Ministers, a working group was set up, consisting of the chairmen of the parties in the government coalition. This group seriously reduced the scope of the bill. It wanted the act to be a temporary measure and applicable only to local and provincial elections. It dropped the stipula-tions on the distribution of fe/male candidates over the lists. And it offered only one sanction: parties that did not find enough candidates of the under-represented sex had to present incomplete lists (Carton 1995). The Council of Ministers accepted the new formulation of the sanction and retained the idea that the quota should be applied to all elections, but only from 1999 onwards. With these alterations the government submitted the bill to parliament.

Dominant frame of debate

It took nearly two years to prepare the bill, an indication of difficulties in securing a majority within the government willing to submit a bill stipulating gender quotas on electoral lists to parliament. Although all actors involved thought the under-representation of women in politics to be problematic (Marques-Pereira 1998), opinions on what should be done diverged. There are no accounts of discussions within the government, but the parliamentary debates reflect these divergences. Not all of the advocates of gender quotas thought that quotas were ideal. Rather, many took a pragmatic view of quotas, as the most efficient and reliable solution, reasoning that without structural measures nothing would change. Their case was that quotas were the only means to overcome the subtle mechanisms of discrimination women encounter when trying to find their way in a man's world (Kamer Hand. 29/3/1994; Senaat Hand. 6/5/1994). A few female MPs explicitly mentioned men's desire to preserve their dominant power position, and cited the weakening of the initial draft of the bill as an example (Senaat Hand. 6/5/1994). Advocates of gender quotas were mainly found among MPs of the governing majority. But the Greens, an opposition party, also defended quotas. Later on, however, they would vote against the bill, employing the argument that it did not go far enough.

The opponents of quotas, mainly MPs from the Liberal and far right opposition parties, claimed they preferred sensitising and training measures for women, or even a neutralisation of the list order[1] because a quota would diminish the status of women so elected. They saw the problem in terms of both a lack of concern by the electorate, and a lack of aspiration to political office by women. They argued that women lacked interest in politics by comparison with men, probably because of the demanding rules of the political game. Women's putative lack of interest was sometimes overtly invoked, but it was mainly disguised by an argument often put forward by the Liberals, that there were no barriers to women (Kamer Hand. 29/3/1994). In addition, the opponents of quotas explicitly rejected the idea that men would not be willing to share power.

Gendering the debate

Although both advocates and opponents gendered the debate, they did so in different ways. While everybody claimed to consider women and men

[1] A neutralisation of the list order implies that the number of preferential votes for an individual candidate determines his/her chances of being elected whereas the position on the list plays no role.

to be equal, the opponents of quotas thought women and men had different interests and needs and that as a result, women might not be interested in politics. The advocates of quotas did not reject the idea of gendered interests, but did not think that it explained the different positions of men and women in politics. A woman's choice not to be interested in politics was not an individual one; it was structural. Making this case, quota advocates referred to an argument invoked by their opponents, namely the rules of the political game. However, advocates approached the rules argument differently. They argued that politics is a male world that is difficult for women to enter, precisely because they are not male. This is so because male politicians accept a gendered profile both of the ideal representative and of the political world as a whole. The very dominance of male power serves to maintain an androcentric norm. Advocates and opponents situated the problem of women's underrepresentation at different levels, and hence preferred different solutions.

Policy outcome

Despite the parliamentary debates and various amendments to stipulate the positions of both sexes on the lists, the parties of the majority adopted the bill in May 1994 without changing its content.[2] From 1999 onwards no electoral lists should contain more than two-thirds of candidates of the same sex. Between 1996 and 1999 electoral lists had to respect a maximum of three-quarters of candidates of the same sex on their lists. The same temporary quota was applied to the 1994 local and provincial elections. The most women-friendly parties criticised the lack of ambition of both the act and the governing coalition (Kamer Hand. 29/3/1994). For the Greens this was a reason to reject the act, although their rejection of the bill might also have been inspired by the fact that they were in the opposition. But on the whole, the voting behaviour of parties in the opposition corresponded with their perception of quotas. The Belgian Liberals and the far right are generally opposed to any form of gender quota.

Women's movement characteristics and impact

The most conspicuous feature of the Belgian women's movement is its fragmented nature as it reflects the traditional cleavages that characterise Belgian politics. It is further divided into an integrated and an

---

[2] Wet van 24/5/1994 ter bevordering van een evenwichtige verdeling van mannen en vrouwen op de kandidatenlijsten voor de verkiezingen. BS 1/7/1994.

autonomous wing. Whereas the first is part of the 'pillars' structuring Belgian civil society, the second consciously dissociates itself from traditional power institutions (Hooghe 1994). The autonomous women's movement is to a large extent co-ordinated by the Flemish and the Francophone Women's Council respectively. Within the Flemish sector another important umbrella is the Women's Consultation Committee (*Vrouwen Overleg Komité*) (VOK 1997). Although the autonomous women's movement was partly set up as a reaction to the highly sectarian character of Belgian society, most women's movement branches are close to parties that espouse social equality. Many women's organisations had their origin in the second feminist wave of the 1970s, though some date from the beginning of the 1900s. While the integrated women's movement has steadily grown since the 1970s and was partly consolidating during the 1990s, the autonomous movement has weakened since its heyday between 1979 and 1984.

On the whole, the women's movement advocated an equal or balanced participation of both sexes in decision-making. The evolution of its claims has been similar over time for both parts of the movement. The demand for representation escalated from *at least some* via *more* to an *equal share of* women. Between 1980 and the 1990s actors from both the autonomous and the integrated women's movements claimed a *greater*, and from the middle of the 1980s an *equal* presence of women in politics. One of the best-known claims was made in March 1988, when the presidents of the political women's organisations, at the invitation of the State Secretary of Social Emancipation, proclaimed the charter of women in politics, requesting an equal representation of women in (the top positions of) electoral lists (Staatssecretaris voor Maatschappelijke Emancipatie 1988). However, although the autonomous women's movement's claim is generally more progressive (Van Mechelen 1996), the issue is of greater priority to the integrated women's movement. Arguably equal political representation is of moderate priority to the autonomous women's movement although it gained in weight in the 1990s. For the integrated women's movement, the issue had greater priority, not least because of its direct involvement in politics. On the whole, the women's movement characteristics did not change substantially between the first and the other two debates. Finally, the Belgian women's movement does not face an organised counter-movement with respect to the issue of democratic representation.

The integrated women's movement in the governing coalition welcomed the bill as a step towards parity. The view of the Minister of Equal Opportunities – 'better this act than no act at all' (*De Morgen* 1993) – was typical of their position. The Green women's political organisations, as well as the autonomous women's movement, rejected the act, regarding it as a step backwards. They feared that the male majority could hide behind an act that offered no feminist outcome at all (*Het Volk* 1993).

Thus the policy was one of co-optation. The policy content did not coincide with the women's movement goals even though women were involved in the policy-making process. Indeed the integrated women's movement was involved both through MPs and through the Minister of Equal Opportunities. However, although they participated in the policy-making process, the women's movement had no direct say in the decision-taking process. It was the group of the ruling coalition's party chairs who mainly determined the content of the legislation. This group contained no women, all party chairs being men.

Women's policy agency activities

What is generally considered to be the first real Belgian women's policy agency was set up in the wake of the 1985 Nairobi UN world conference on women. However, as far as the women's movement and the political women's organisations were concerned, there had been a Minister of Equal Opportunities since the 1980s. When Miet Smet, a former president of the Flemish Christian Democrats' political women's organisation, became State Secretary of Environmental Affairs in 1985, she negotiated an Equal Opportunities portfolio. At this point the state secretary of Social Emancipation was established. A year later the government also established an Emancipation Council (Hondeghem and Nelen 2000). When compared with earlier consultative committees the council can be seen as an early version of a women's policy agency. The sphere of action and the potential of the State Secretary and of the Emancipation Council had substantially increased. The scope of issues covered everything related to social emancipation. The State Secretary focused not only on violence against women but also on women's economic and political position. It is therefore not surprising to find that the women's policy agency itself helped to bring the debate to the political agenda in the final stage. However, a state secretary is the lowest level of the governmental hierarchy and subordinate to a minister, in this case the Minister of Public Health and Environment (as is the Emancipation Council; in this respect it did not differ from former advisory bodies on women's issues). When Miet Smet became Minister of Labour and Employment in 1991 she retained the Equal Opportunities portfolio. Since then the portfolio has been officially termed Equal Opportunities and is linked to the Minister of Labour and Employment, where a Unit of Equal Opportunities has operated since 1992. Hence, we can see that the government took up the quota act at the same time as a Minister of Equal Opportunities was established. However, there is no direct link between these two facts, as will become clear below. In 1993 the Council of Equal Opportunities for Men and Women replaced the Emancipation Council and the older Committee on Women's Employment. It can advise on its own initiative, but its advice is (still) not binding (Raad van Gelijke Kansen voor Mannen en Vrouwen 1997). In summary, over time the federal Belgian women's policy machinery rose in the government hierarchy, in autonomy and in scope. In terms of resources such as budget and personnel, however, it has always been marginal compared with those awarded to other ministers and state secretaries.

When the 1994 bill finally made it through the political process, the women's policy machinery was an important actor, represented by the Minister of Equal Opportunities herself. She was not the official initiator of the act but she strongly defended the bill introduced by her colleague responsible for electoral matters. She did so within the Council of Ministers, within the parliamentary assemblies, vis-à-vis the press and last but not least within her party, one of the coalition partners most opposed to the bill. The women's policy agency gendered the debates. Like the other advocates of quotas it did so by recognising and criticising the underlying gendered power relations that characterise politics and society as a whole. Although the final act was much weaker than that initially suggested by the Minister of Internal Affairs and backed by the women's policy agency, we can say that the women's policy agency promoted feminist goals and acted as an 'insider'. But it had no alternative other than to accept the act.

Policy environment

The Belgian political system is a typical example of a consensus democracy, ruled by a political elite subscribing to a fragile consensus. This implies a rather rigid allocation of resources. The political system is closed to outsiders and new actors in the field (Hooghe 1998). Many issues are dealt with by a small but select club of insiders, most of the time directly linked to and often mandated by the governing parties. This is well illustrated by the impact that the chairmen of the governing parties had on the bill. This logic underlying the policy environment has an important impact on the women's policy agencies' potential scope for activity.

On the whole, the characteristics of the policy environment did not change substantially between the various debates. Throughout this debate Christian Democrats were in power, forming a coalition first with the Liberals (until 1988) and then with the Social Democrats. Throughout the second and third debates, the Christian Democrats continued to form coalitions with the Social Democrats.

Debate 2: Quota for advisory committees, 1990–1997

How the debate came to the public agenda

In contrast to the previous case, no individual MPs submitted a bill to regulate the composition of federal advisory committees. In March 1990 the State Secretary of Social Emancipation, Miet Smet, submitted a bill requiring that for each mandate in a federal advisory committee, all nominating bodies would present a male and a female candidate (Kamer Gedr. Stuk. 1989–90: 1129/1). She argued that the under-representation of women in advisory committees did not coincide with the principle of equality between the sexes (Kamer Gedr. Stuk. 1989–90: 1129/2). The Council of State received the bill favourably. But it pointed out the weakness of this type of quota, emphasising that since there was no obligation to appoint the women nominated, the bill did not automatically interfere with the actual composition of advisory committees (Kamer Gedr. Stuk. 1989–90: 1129/1).

The Lower House debated the bill in June 1990 and the Upper House did so a month later. Compared with the previous case, there was little discussion, a fact reflected in the limited duration of the debate, in the small number of interventions and in the lack of amendments. However, not everybody agreed on the mechanism suggested by the state secretary. The far right were against any such mechanism, while the Greens wanted to apply a quota to the composition of the advisory committees as such. They further argued that the act would remain ineffective as long as it did not stipulate sanctions for non-compliance (Senaat Hand. 13/7/1990). Nonetheless, the bill was passed in July 1990.[3]

Six years later the issue reappeared on the political agenda. It was again Miet Smet who presented a bill, but by now she was Minister of Equal Opportunities. The new bill provided for a maximum of two-thirds of members of the same sex on federal advisory committees. This bill also provided for sanctions. Mandates would remain vacant and advice would lack binding force where the quota was not respected. The reason for a new bill was that the previous act had no impact. The number of women

---

[3] Wet van 20/7/1990 ter bevordering van de evenwichtige aanwezigheid van mannen en vrouwen in organen met adviserende bevoegdheid. BS 9/10/1990.

had not risen on advisory committees. And even the nomination of female candidates was not taken seriously in all cases. Male candidates were deliberately nominated with less-qualified women. The advice of the Council of State contained only technical remarks. It included both the principle of applying a quota to the composition of advisory committees and provision for strong sanctions (Kamer Gedr. Stuk. 1996–7: 860/1). The Lower House debated the bill in May 1997, and the Upper House did the same two months later.

Dominant frame of debate

Once again, advocates conceived quotas as a tool necessary to put into practice what theory and law promised. But the opinions diverged over what made quotas necessary. At the beginning of the 1990s the state secretary referred to inequality in the functioning of democratic institutions. In a normally functioning system more women would be members of advisory committees. Specific measures were necessary to overcome the gender bias of the system. The underlying assumption, therefore, was that the presumed equality of the sexes should translate itself in a numerical equality at the level of fe/male participation in decision-making. But the causes of the problem were not analysed. By 1997 quotas were considered to be necessary because six years of practice had shown that the 1990 'soft approach' of stimulating the nomination of female candidates had not been successful. The Minister of Equal Opportunities herself explicitly stated that men hindered women from reaching the top. She cited the notorious example of an organisation that nominated a male director and a cleaning lady as candidates for the same function (Kamer Hand. 15/5/1997). Hence, what was considered to be the cause of the problem and the justification of quotas was explicitly named. The discourse was no longer on theoretical principles and in this respect it was more open and radical. Advocates of quotas also justified their claim by referring to the panoply of quotas characterising the Belgian political system. To them sex was a defining social characteristic equivalent to the other social characteristics that underlay traditional cleavages (Senaat Gedr. Stuk. 1989–90: 989/2; Kamer Hand. 15/5/1997).

The opponents of quotas wondered why gender should constitute a basis for representation when many other social characteristics, for example, age, carried no such entitlement to particular attention. They further argued that being nominated as a member of an advisory committee is an issue of capacity and not of sex. Finally, they wondered whether women face discrimination on sexual grounds, or whether they encounter problems of combining professional and family life. This last argument can actually be read as a version of the claim that women were not really interested in political decision-making, an argument also encountered in the first debate. During the 1997 debates, Alexandra Colen, a female Flemish far right MP, argued that many women might want to lead a life away from a career. She stated that the entire bill was based on the prejudices that men are not willing to share power with women and that women absolutely want to obtain power (Kamer Hand. 15/5/1997). She argued that the real issue was to determine the extent to which these prejudices are correct. Like in the previous case such ideas were marginal.

Overall, the debates were more technical and less intense than those about electoral quotas. Arguably the path was smoothed for the 1997 debates both by the fact that the new bill provided for what had been the major request some years before and also because the 1994 debates on electoral lists had established the acceptability of gender quotas. However, the lack of intensity of the debate is more likely a result of the fact that those concerned were not present. Within the advisory committees themselves there was considerable opposition to any form of legally imposed quota.

Gendering the debate

To a large extent the debate followed the same pattern of gendering as did the first debate. While the opponents of quotas gendered the issue of political interest, their advocates gendered the power relations underlying society. However, the advocates of quotas did so most explicitly in 1997 and more extensively than in the debates on electoral lists, a consequence perhaps of the bad experience with the 1990 act.

Policy outcome

The bill adopted in July 1997[4] was an update of the 1990 bill. All federal advisory committees had to consist of at least one-third of members of the under-represented sex. In the case of non-compliance seats would remain vacant and advice would not be binding.

---

[4] Wet van 17/7/1997 tot wijziging van de wet van 20/7/1990 ter bevordering van de evenwichtige aanwezigheid van mannen en vrouwen in organen met adviserende bevoegdheid. BS 31/7/1997.

Women's movement impact

Advisory committees, uniting specialists and/or interest groups, are an important element of the Belgian political system and can considerably influence politics at the highest level. Given their repeated demands for more women in politics, it is not surprising that the women's movement criticised the dominant male composition of advisory committees. For example, the charter of women in politics also included a demand for an equal representation of both sexes on advisory committees. Despite the claims by the women's movement, most of its members took a different position as an MP. Although the women's movement demanded such quotas, many female MPs, including those belonging to the women's movement, defended a more moderate point of view, even though women dominated these discussions. The intervention of Miet Smet during the 1990 debates explains this difference in attitude. She declared that she herself would not have objected to a gender quota applied to the actual composition of advisory committees. But she had adapted her position to that favoured by the government, which rejected any form of quota on the advisory committees and chose what it called a 'softer' method (Senaat Hand. 13/7/1990). The Lower House's Advisory Committee for Social Emancipation, made up entirely of female MPs, also subscribed to this softer approach, arguing that it might be more effective than a quota that defined the composition of advisory committees. The opinion of the women's movement was actually best reflected by the Greens who argued both for a quota to be applied to the composition of advisory committees and for sanctions to enforce implementation.

A similar discrepancy was apparent during the 1997 debates. While the women's movement demanded an *equal* participation of women at all levels of decision-making from the 1990s onwards, the 1997 act imposed only a one-third quota (Coordinatie van politieke vrouwengroepen voor paritaire democratie 1994; Raad van Gelijke Kansen voor Mannen en Vrouwen 1997; *De Morgen* 1994). Thus although the 1990 bill had imposed the nomination of an equal number of candidates of both sexes, the proportion was reduced when the measure was made compulsory. The Advisory Committee on Social Emancipation of the Lower House was asked for advice but formulated no criticism. And the Advisory Committee on Equal Opportunities of the Upper House, established in 1995, did not intervene in the debates although it included many members of the integrated women's movement. Thus although the women's movement had a voice in the parliamentary debate, female MPs who belonged to the women's movement took a moderate stance in the parliamentary debates. The women's movement impact was 'co-optation'.

Women's policy agency activities

In this case the women's policy agency was more active than in the previous one because the State Secretary of Social Emancipation and later Minister of Equal Opportunities not only defended the bills and gendered the debates in a feminist way, she also brought the issue to the official agenda. Nevertheless the women's policy agency should be considered as non-feminist because it did not advocate the women's movement's equality goals. In defence of the women's policy agency we should emphasise that the attitude of the integrated women's movement itself was ambiguous, because it had not used the numerous opportunities available to criticise the bill from a women's movement perspective. The lack of criticism reflected the party loyalties of the integrated movement, a sensibility that had previously prevented the state secretary from claiming a quota for the composition of advisory committees.

Debate 3: Quotas for the federal government, 1991–1999

How the debate came to the public agenda

The issue first appeared on the political agenda of the Lower House in March 1991, as an amendment to the revision of article 86 of the constitution. Trees Merckx, who had introduced a bill on electoral quotas in 1991, proposed that at least one minister and one state secretary of the federal government be of the under-represented sex. The underlying idea was a perceived need for measures to increase the participation of women in decision-making because their actual number is not only low but also stagnating. The first woman in the federal government held office between 1965 and 1966. In the period from 1980 to 1981 and from 1985 onwards there were about two to four female ministers, slightly more than 10 per cent of the ministers. But their number did not rise. The bill was aimed at actively promoting the reduction of the gap between formal and substantive equality (Kamer Gedr. Stuk. 1990–1: 10/86–1464/2). Initially, the revision of article 86 was meant to limit the size of the federal government. Legal and technical discussions reduced the revision to a resolution that a minimum representation of each sex in the federal government was to be promoted (Kamer Gedr. Stuk. 1989–90: 961/3). Such a resolution does not have the same legal status as an article of the constitution. While a resolution can be interpreted as advice to the federal government, Trees Merckx's initial idea was to impose a minimal presence of each sex in the federal government through the constitution. The Lower House adopted the resolution in May 1991.

Two legislatures later, in 1996, the issue made it to the political agenda again, this time in the Upper House. Flemish Christian Democrat Sabine de Bethune submitted a proposal to declare articles 99 and 104 (formerly 86) of the constitution open for revision. This time the demand was for equal representation of both sexes. The underlying argument was that of parity democracy, and comparisons were made with the federal government's policies of linguistic parity (Senaat Gedr. Stuk. 1996–7: 1–657/1). The Advisory Committee on Equal Opportunities of the Upper House adopted the proposal (Senaat Gedr. Stuk. 1998–9: 1–584/2) and sent it to the Committee on Institutional Affairs of the Upper House where it was ignored. It was not considered during the subsequent debates and was rejected when votes were taken (Senaat Gedr. Stuk. 1998–9: 1–1374/2). The issue received much the same treatment during the debates in the Upper House's plenary in April 1999, which was the end point of the proposal to declare articles 99 and 104 open for revision (Senaat Hand. 30/4/1999).

Dominant frame of debate

Touching on the composition of the federal government and embedding it in the constitution is a delicate matter. As in the two previous debates, the issue at stake was the under-representation of women and the need to increase their presence. During the 1991 debate this claim was not successfully justified. Eight years later the advocates of an equal representation of both sexes in the federal government argued in terms of parity democracy and of a new political culture. Contrary to the two previous cases, no explicit reference was made to the causes of women's under-representation. The argumentation was an abstract theoretical plea for a constitutionally embedded quota. Actually, the most comprehensive justification for increased participation of women in political decision-making appeared towards the end of the decade and not at its beginning when it might have helped better to justify the claim. Throughout the decade a theoretical discourse on the issue of equal representation evolved. By the end of the decade it was known and used by the advocates of gender parity in the federal government. Arguably this debate was more of a discourse because there was no explicit discussion of the issue. In the Advisory Committee on Equal Opportunities of the Upper House, the principle of parity as well as quotas meant to translate parity into practice was accepted. Their discussion was of a strategic nature: although the original request was for parity, some members preferred to claim a balanced presence of both sexes, arguing that a 60:40 repartition of ministerial and state secretary posts might be more acceptable (Senaat Gedr. Stuk. 1998–9: 1–584/2).

Although certain female MPs are convinced advocates of parity democracy, including a strict equal participation of both sexes in all institutions of political decision-making, they tend to claim less far-reaching measures. The underlying idea is that the majority might more easily accept a weaker measure. Thereafter, in the rest of the parliamentary process there was no debate; instead the proposal was simply ignored. The Advisory Committee on Equal Opportunities debates were probably framed in such a favourable way because only advocates of the issue were present. Most of its members are in favour of an improved promotion of gender equality. Also different from the previous two debates is the fact that all female MPs present in the Advisory Committee on Equal Opportunities were in favour of the measures discussed, regardless of whether their party was a member of the majority or of the opposition. This does not necessarily imply that female MPs of the opposition became more feminist. Rather, it could be argued that they spoke in their name and not on behalf of the party.

Gendering the debate

It is therefore not surprising that the issue was gendered in a way different from that of the two previous cases. What had been implicit in the first two debates now became explicit. The focus was no longer directly on gendered power relations. There was a consensus that equal gender power relations were a problem. But the advocates of parity democracy went a step further and tried to provide an explanation for these imbalances, thereby highlighting the gendered nature of the basic concepts underpinning contemporary state institutions.

Policy outcome

The final outcome was the decision within the Upper House's plenary not to declare articles 99 and 104 open for revision. This decision was not defended, arguably because the majority of (male) MPs did not even think it necessary to explain this decision. While the gender quotas for electoral lists and advisory committees of the first and second debates had become an issue associated with a notion of 'political correctness', the same could not be said for sex parity in the federal government. Hence, it was not an issue worth considering.

Women's movement impact

Higher, and later equal, participation of both sexes in the federal government was just as much on the agenda of the women's movement as in the two previous debates. For decades the women's movement demanded more female ministers and on numerous occasions from the 1980s onwards they pointed out the low female presence in government and demanded correction. After the middle of the 1990s the entire women's movement without exception demanded parity democracy (VOK 11/11/1997; *De Standaard* 1996). The integrated women's movement also pushed its parties to appoint more female ministers. This goes especially for the political women's organisations of the Flemish Christian Democrats (*De Standaard* 1995a, 1998) and Social Democrats (Socialistische Vrouwen 1991), the two dominant Flemish coalition partners in the time span of this debate.

In contrast to the previous cases, women were the only participants in the debate. Female MPs with an explicit link to the Flemish Christian Democrat political women's organisation submitted both proposals and the integrated women's movement generally participated in the debate. And the other actors of the integrated women's movement were well represented in the Advisory Committee on Equal Opportunities of the Upper House. The autonomous women's movement was not officially represented in the debates but the demand perfectly reflected its claim. On the whole, therefore, not just women but women with a link to the women's movement were the only participants in the debate. The women's movement was the motor behind the debate but it did not achieve its feminist goal. The reason for this is that although it had a stake in the policy-making process, the women's movement had only a limited presence in the decision-taking process. Even though the point was adopted in the Advisory Committee on Equal Opportunities of the Upper House, the governing parties did not take it up in the plenary for the reasons already mentioned. Hence, again the women's movement's impact was 'co-optation'.

Women's policy agency activities

The women's policy agency was the big absentee in the debate. It neither came up with an initiative, nor (with the exception of one member of the ministerial cabinet participating in the debates held within the Advisory Committee on Equal Opportunities of the Upper House) did it intervene in the issue. Theoretically there was nothing to prevent the women's policy agency from intervening. This point is well illustrated by the fact that in 2001 Laurette Onkelinx, a Francophone Social Democrat who had taken over the portfolio of Equal Opportunities from Miet Smet in 1999, brought the issue to the agenda and pushed for an act requiring a minimal presence of members of each sex in the executive. However, during the 1990s the women's policy agency influence was 'symbolic'.

Conclusion

The three debates map an evolution in the thinking on the under-representation of women in decision-making, escalating from the request for at least *one* woman, via the need for *more* women, towards the conviction that men and women should *equally share all functions of political decision-making*. There is also an evolution in the way in which the political establishment reacted to the claims. In the first instance the feminist claim was ignored. When ignoring it was no longer possible, the claim was minimised. When minimising was no longer politically acceptable, rhetorical correction was offered. When rhetoric was shown to be hollow, a real measure was taken. But the measures did not necessarily correspond to feminist claims; hence the issues reappeared on the agenda. We described this pattern for the case of the advisory committees, but it can also be found in the case of a quota applied to electoral lists. In 2002 the government coalition that emerged from the 1999 elections passed a series of laws to require future electoral lists to comprise an equal share of fe/male candidates, including the two top positions.

Linked to the evolution of attitudes towards feminist claims, we can also see that the identity of the actor putting the issue on the agenda indicates the extent to which it is accepted. Except in the case of the advisory committees, MPs put the issue on the agenda first but these attempts were rejected or minimised. However, when the State Secretary or Minister for Equal Opportunities puts the issue on the agenda it is a formal measure. This pattern obtained both in the case of electoral lists and for the composition of the federal government. As we saw in 2001 the federal coalition voted for an initiative by Laurette Onkelinx to make executives include at least one member of each sex, whereas earlier attempts of individual MPs did not succeed. And once the government had agreed on the modalities of a gender quota for electoral lists at the beginning of the 1990s and submitted a bill to parliament, it was accepted by the legislature. The point is that by the time the State Secretary or Minister for Equal Opportunities defends an issue, it has the necessary support within the coalition to be accepted by parliament. For instance, in the case of the electoral lists several male MPs of the majority openly admitted that they voted for the bill only because it emanated from the majority. But this also means that the women's policy agency can defend an issue only once it has the necessary support within the coalition. Miet Smet is arguably more of a feminist than Laurette Onkelinx. But when the last debate first appeared on the agenda Miet Smet would not have found enough support within the government to impose a gender quota in the federal government.

All these patterns explain why the influence of the women's policy agency was respectively labelled as insider, non-feminist and symbolic. Our assessment expresses neither a change of attitude of the women's policy agency nor a decrease of its power. The apparently less impressive influence over time of the women's policy agency actually reflects the stage of acceptance of the issue debated and the functioning of the Belgian political system. Thus the characteristics of the women's movement are less influential than the policy environment in securing the desired state response and women's policy agency activities. Both the women's policy agency and the women's movement function within a particular policy environment, which to a large extent determines their scope of action. What is politically acceptable or not is prescribed by the governing parties. The State Secretary or Minister for Equal Opportunities, other members of the women's policy agency and feminist MPs are in the first instance members of their political parties. This leads to a gap between what they want from a feminist perspective and what they could defend as coalition partners. In both the first and the second debate we saw the extent to which the women's policy agency was unable to achieve what it thought would be a valid solution.

Submission to the general rules of the political game is required from both the women's policy agency and the integrated women's movement. During the debates the political women's groups had an important forum to express their claims in both the Lower and the Upper Houses. But when it came to voting on an issue, the female MPs mainly followed their parties. Party positions were inspired more by majority versus opposition conventions than by gender relations. Attempts to go against the dominant party line, as in the case of the revision of the constitution, proved impossible. In such cases women were simply outvoted. The problem of submission to the parochialism of the party elites is part of the reason for the existence of an autonomous women's movement. They are not bound by party opinion. They thus have more room to advance far-reaching claims but at the expense of limited or no formal impact. It seems that the Belgian policy system to a large extent determined the outcome of the debates. In this respect the Belgian case presents a paradox. On the one hand the specific character of Belgian society facilitates a representation of women as a social group. Yet other facets of this character limit the scope and effectiveness of the activity available to the women's policy agency and to the women's movement.

References

Carton, Ann 1995, Paritaire democratie: een definitieve stap vooruit, *Jaarboek van de vrouw*: 71–89

Coordinatie van politieke vrouwengroepen voor paritaire democratie 1994, *Persmap*, Brussels: Coordinatie van politieke vrouwengroepen voor paritaire democratie, 25 May

De Morgen 1993, 'Smet over vrouwen op kieslijsten: liever deze wet dan geen wet', 14 October

1994, 'Voortaan minstens één derde vrouwen op kieslijsten', 7 May

Deschouwer, Kris 2002, 'Falling apart together. The changing nature of Belgian consociationalism, 1961–2000', *Acta Politica*, 37: 68–85

forthcoming 2004, 'Belgium: Federalism and the Art of Constitutional Compromise', in A. Tarr and J. Kincaid (eds.) *Constitutional Origins, Structure, and Change in Federal Democracies*, Ottawa: Forum of Federations

De Standaard 1995a, 'Een derde van ministers vrouwelijk', 27 April

1995b, 'Gelijke vertegenwoordiging taak voor de volgende regering', 3 May

1998, 'CVP-vrouwen willen helft of niets', 11 September

De Win, Linda 1994, *De afwezige vrouw*, Leuven: Kritak

Het Volk 1993, 'Beter geen wet dan een slechte wet', 23–24 October

Hondeghem, Annie and Sarah Nelen 2000, 'Een beleid op weg. Situering van het Gelijke-Kansenbeleid in België', *Tijdschrift voor Genderstudies* 3: 36–48

Hooghe, Marc 1994, 'De organisatiestructuur van de Vlaamse vrouwenbeweging', *Sociologische Gids* 41: 144–61

1998, 'Selectieve uitsluiting in het Belgisch politiek systeem', *Res Publica* 40: 3–21

Kamer van Volksvertegenwoordigers, gedrukte stukken: GZ 1989–90: 961/3, 1129/1–2; GZ 1990–1: 1538/1, 1539/1, 10/86–1464/2–3; BZ 1991–2: 432/1–3; GZ 1993–4: 1316/1–6; GZ 1996–7: 860/1–4

Kamer van Volksvertegenwoordigers, parlementaire handelingen: 7/6/1990, 8/6/1990, 08/5/1991, 29/3/1994, 31/3/1994, 15/5/1997

Leye, Els 1992 'Vrouwen in de politieke besluitvorming', *Jaarboek van de vrouw*: 67–77

Marques-Pereira, Bérengère 1998, *La citoyenneté politique des femmes*, Brussels: Crisp

Meier, Petra 2000, 'From Theory to Practice and Back Again: Gender Quota and the Politics of Presence in Belgium', in Michael Saward (ed.) *Innovations in Democratic Theory*, London: Routledge, pp. 106–16

Paye, Olivier 1997, 'Féminiser le politique: recitoyennisation ou tribalisation?', *Sextant* 7: 139–61

Raad van de Gelijke Kansen voor Mannen en Vrouwen 1997, *Activiteitenverslag 9.93–10.97*, Brussels: Ministerie voor Arbeid en Tewerkstelling

Senaat, gedrukte stukken: GZ 1979–80: 370/1; GZ 1989–90: 989/1–2; GZ 1993–4: 1053/1–5; GZ 1996–7: 1–633/1–2, 1–657/1–3; GZ 1998–9: 1–584/2, 1–1096/1–4, 1374/2

Senaat, parlementaire handelingen: 13/7/1990, 6/5/1994, 10/7/1997, 28/4/1999, 30/4/1999, 28/4/1999, 30/4/1999

Socialistische Vrouwen 1991, *Persmap*, Brussels: Socialistische Vrouwen, 7 March

Staatssecretaris voor Maatschappelijke Emancipatie 1988, *Persmap*, Brussels: Staatssecretaris voor Maatschappelijke Emancipatie, 22 March

Van Mechelen, Renée 1996, *De meerderheid. Een minderheid. De vrouwenbeweging in Vlaanderen: feiten, herinneringen en bedenkingen omtrent de tweede golf*, Leuven: Van Halewyck

Vogel-Polsky, Eliane 1996, 'Les actions positives, les quotas au crible du droit de l'égalité', in Kathrin Arioli (ed.) *Quoten und Gleichstellung von Frau und Mann*, Basle: Helbing & Lichtenhahn, pp. 109–37

1997, 'Démocratie, femmes et citoyenneté européenne', *Sextant* 7: 17–39

VOK 1997, *25 vrouwendagen in beelden en woorden*, Brussels: VOK

1997, *Persmap*, Brussels: VOK, 11 November

Anne Maria Holli and Johanna Kantola

Introduction

In Finland women gained the right to vote by 1906, and women's parliamentary representation has increased steadily since (Karvonen and Selle 1995: 5; Raaum 1999), rising from 9.5 per cent in 1907 to 30 per cent in 1983 and 37.5 per cent in 2003. In contrast, women's representation at the local level and in the corporatist structures of Finnish society has remained lower (Raaum 1999; Haavio-Mannila et al. 1985).

The high proportion of women in parliamentary politics has been explained by socio-economic factors (women's high education level and their full-time participation in the labour market), the existence of relatively strong and independent women's political organisations and, last but not least, the structural characteristics of the Finnish political system (Bergqvist et al. 1999; Karvonen and Selle 1995; Dahlerup 1989; Haavio-Mannila et al. 1985). Finland is a parliamentary democracy with a unicameral parliament and a multi-party system. The electoral system is based on proportional representation and multi-member constituencies. The open list system and mandatory preferential voting also make it possible for the electorate to express their gender preferences at the polls. Traditionally, women have voted for female candidates and men have voted for male candidates.[1]

In this chapter, we will analyse the substantive impact of women's movements and the role of state feminism on debates concerning political representation. The results suggest a link between women's descriptive

---

[1] International political research has so far failed sufficiently to take notice of this tendency, which has been important in increasing women's political representation, although Elina Haavio-Mannila (1979) initially drew attention to this phenomenon (see also Pesonen 1991, 1995; Pesonen et al. 1993: 74).

and substantive representation in issues that explicitly concern strengthening women's presence in decision-making arenas. The analysis shows how in such cases, a token female presence translated into critical acts and a critical mass turned into women's successful co-operation across party lines (cf. Dahlerup 1988).

Although internationally rare, in Finland cross-party alliances between women became more prominent during the 1990s on issues that were regarded as 'women's common interests', for example, day-care arrangements (Aalto 2003), prostitution (Holli 2004), gender equality policies and women's representation. Several factors have contributed to the emergence of such co-operative mechanisms; for instance, the strong presence of women in parliamentary politics, the relatively strong women's party sections and the greater independence of parliamentary representatives vis-à-vis the party.

Political representation

In the Finnish context, political representation can be understood on two different levels which, however, are deeply intertwined. First, there is formal democratic representation in both directly (municipal, national and the European Union) and indirectly (regional councils, inter-municipal joint companies) elected bodies and politically appointed posts. The electoral laws, party laws and citizenship laws have shaped formal representation in Finland. Three crucial debates have concerned limiting the power of parties, restraining presidential powers and extending citizenship rights to non-natives. Gender has hardly featured in these debates.

Second, there are the corporatist structures of Finnish democracy. In Finland, the descriptive and substantive representation of interest groups is guaranteed through institutionalised co-operation with the state (Nousiainen 1998: 106). The stages of Finnish policy deliberations typically include an initial committee proposal, a remittal process, and expert and interest group statements. The descriptive representation of minority groups (the Roma and the Sami people, immigrants) is moreover secured through the establishment of special advisory representative bodies. Two recurrent themes in the corporatist arena have been criticisms of trade union power and male dominance.

Selection of debates

The legalistic nature of Finnish political culture is demonstrated by the strict legislative control of both formal democratic representation and party activity. The electoral and party laws were set in place at the end of the 1960s, and thus before the era of Finnish state feminism (from 1972 onwards). Only minor amendments have been made since then, although in 1998, a single act was created to combine the four separate electoral laws. The laws regulate the procedures of candidate selection, party democracy and party funding. Therefore, the cabinet, the parliament and the Ministry of Justice are the most central decision-making arenas. Parties are prominent actors but, as a result of legislative regulation, their influence is restrained (Sundberg 1995, 1997).

For the first debate, a change in the electoral law in 1975 was chosen. The 1969 electoral law gave the parties a monopoly over candidate nominations for elections. This received huge criticism. In 1975, the law was changed to allow again the nomination of candidates by independent electoral associations. The change in the law thus restricted the power of the parties, which, at the time, was at its peak.

As the second debate, a decision that shaped the internal decision-making process of a party is analysed. In 1987, the Finnish People's Democratic League (SKDL), as the first established party in Finland, decided to adopt gender quotas for internal decision-making bodies. The SKDL followed in the footsteps of the Green League, which had made the same decision earlier when it was still a grass-roots movement. The decision of the Greens set a precedent on internal quotas, followed by the SKDL, the Social Democratic Party (SDP) (1996), the Christian Democrats (1997) and the Swedish People's Party (2001).

In contrast to formal representation and the functioning of political parties, the corporatist channel is much less regulated. It has been the focus of state feminism and women's movements since the 1970s, fuelled by a growing realisation of the disparity between women's high level of representation in parliament and their low share in policy preparation processes. In the third debate, the 1995 Equality Act prepared by the Ministry of Social Affairs and Health is examined. The final law included a minimum of 40 per cent of both sexes in all publicly nominated bodies. As a result of this single decision, the proportion of women in newly appointed public bodies almost doubled.

The selection of debates thus includes one debate from each decade of the existence of the women's policy machinery in Finland. The sample also represents some of the most salient debates on political representation, as well as two central decision-making systems on the issue, the party arena and the parliament. The two selected parliamentary laws were also prepared administratively by different policy subsystems, the Ministry of Justice and the Ministry of Social Affairs and Health.

Debate 1: Change in the electoral law, 1972–1975

How the debate came to the public agenda

In 1969, a new electoral law was enacted in Finland. One of the most important changes was that the law granted parties a monopoly over nominating candidates in parliamentary elections (Tarasti 1998: 41). Previously (since 1955), the electoral law had provided for independent electoral associations, which registered at times of elections and had the right to put forward one candidate each (Nousiainen 1998: 158). In 1966, an electoral law commission suggested that the right to nominate candidates in parliamentary elections should be given to parties alone, which would strengthen their position in relation to elections.[2]

The new law was resented from the beginning by the people and by many MPs. The debate fully emerged in 1972 when the first parliamentary elections were held according to the new 1969 electoral law. The Supreme Administrative Court had to settle a number of disputes resulting from the elections and it wrote a letter to the Ministry of Justice criticising the 1969 electoral law as problematic from the point of view of democracy in the country. The government was obliged to change the law. The initial government position was hostile towards granting independent electoral associations the right to nominate candidates. However, in 1974 the Constitutional Law Committee took the opposite view, and in the end the government gave in and drafted a new proposal that recognised the right of independent electoral associations to nominate candidates (Gov. prop. 178/1974).

In its new proposal, the government accepted independent electoral associations but did not want to allow alliances among them, either with one another or with other parties. However, the Parliamentary Standing Constitutional Law Committee changed the government's proposal so that the independent electoral associations were allowed to make an electoral alliance with other independent electoral associations, though not with parties.

Dominant frame of debate

The debate was framed in terms of democracy. Supporters of the change in the law understood independent electoral associations to be a source of democracy. Most citizens did not belong to any parties and, the argument went, if these citizens could not participate fully in parliamentary

---

[2] Independent electoral associations were allowed in municipal elections.

elections, it was bad democracy. If participating in the elections required establishing a new party in order to nominate alternative candidates, the threshold for participation would be too high.

The debate took place at a time when Urho Kekkonen had been the president of Finland for almost twenty years. This period was generally perceived as undemocratic. J. Juhani Kortesalmi (Rural Party) argued: 'The Finnish people and electorate have been turned into servants, over-powerful parties have replaced the Finnish people and electorate. The basic rights of citizens have been moved to the few registered parties, and at the same time it has been made very difficult to establish new competing parties' (Parliamentary documents 1975: 774).

In parliament the governing parties, the SDP and the Centre Party, backed up by the Liberals, supported the government's proposal. The radical left-wing parties and the populist Rural Party thought that the government did not go far enough in enhancing democracy. They argued that independent electoral associations should be allowed to form electoral alliances with parties, not just among themselves.

For the government, the issue was one of unity and disunity. The ministers saw independent electoral associations as a force that could divide the unity of Finnish party politics. Before the government changed its proposal, Matti Louekoski (Minister of Justice, SDP) argued: 'To allow for electoral alliances between the independent electoral associations in practice signals the strengthening of the forces of disunity both between the parties and within the parties' (Parliamentary documents 1975: 759).

Gendering the debate

In 1974 there were forty-three female MPs in the Finnish parliament (21.5 per cent). What is remarkable in this debate is the absence of women's voices. Only one woman, Terttu Tuominen (Finnish People's Democratic League, SKDL), spoke briefly in the parliament on the issue. Male MPs from the Rural and Communist parties led the debate. In her speech, Tuominen focused on democracy and stressed the right of every citizen to participate in elections, but did not try explicitly to gender the debate (Parliamentary documents 1975: 900).

The electoral law was perceived as a gender-neutral issue. It was part of high politics, like security issues, and was not thought to have anything to do with gender. Some parliamentarians, however, resorted to sexist language to emphasise the importance of the issue: 'Establishing a party should not, of course, be as easy as establishing some kind of sewing society because parties are bodies which fundamentally influence society and political decision-making' (Olavi Borg, Liberals, Parliamentary documents 1974: 897).

Policy outcome

As a result of the debate, the government had to change its proposal and to accept both independent electoral associations and alliances between them. However, the government did not agree to electoral alliances between independent electoral associations and political parties. In the 1979 elections, an independent electoral association put only one candidate forward. However, in 1983, when the Green movement was gathering momentum, some fifty candidates were nominated by independent electoral associations (Nousiainen 1998: 159), which prefigures their later significance. In the 1999 parliamentary elections, sixty-eight candidates came from outside the party system (3.4 per cent), fifty of them being men and sixteen women. Of these, one male candidate was elected to parliament.

Women's movement impact

There were no women's movement goals in this debate. No women's movement activists participated in the debate, and no one tried to gender it. Therefore, there was no response from the state.

Women's policy agency characteristics

The Council for Equality between Women and Men was established in 1972 and its role was to prepare and propose reforms for gender equality. The agency was a cross-sectional, national, permanent government advisory body with a secretariat and a small budget. Institutionally, the secretariat was placed in the planning section of the Prime Minister's Office and, therefore, it was near to the top in the governmental hierarchy. However, its administrative capacity was limited by its small budget (Holli 2001). The council consisted of twelve members and a chairperson, all of whom were political nominations. During the highly politicised era of 1972–5, partisan fights characterised the work of the council. During this debate, Meeri Kalavainen (SDP MP, chairperson of SDP women's section) headed the council. The secretary general was Leila Räsänen, a member of the Finnish People's Democratic League. She had been a prominent feminist activist in the 1960s women's movement and also, earlier, a secretary of the Committee on the Status of Women (Holli 2001: 198). During this period, the right-wing council representatives often accused the secretariat of serving left-wing interests only (Holli 1991: 74).

Changes in the electoral law were not excluded from the council's policy mandate and the council was concerned with issues concerning women's political status. However, the electoral laws, and proportional representation in particular, were considered to work for women and were not mentioned in the council's statements. A clear priority at the time was the fight for funding for the women's sections of the parties. In addition, on a more general level, the council had adopted the policies and ideas of the women's movement, Association 9, and it believed that general societal reforms, such as education, social policies and labour market policies, would automatically increase women's political representation to equal men's (Council for Equality between Men and Women 1973; Holli 1988, 1991). Therefore, the women's policy agency played a symbolic role in this debate. There were no movement goals and the policy agency did not gender the debate.

Women's movement characteristics

The women's movement was going through a period of growth when the debate took place. Second-wave feminism gave rise to new consciousness-raising groups which, however, had little public visibility or impact (Jallinoja 1983). The older women's sections in political parties remained the central players in the arena. Some of them were inside, while others were in conflict with the left. The change in the electoral law was not a priority for any part of the women's movement and there was no counter-movement. The women's movement was therefore also unified in its agreement that this was a 'non-issue' from a gender perspective.

Policy environment

The policy sub-system was moderately closed during the debate. Political parties and lawyers were the main actors. Nevertheless, there was a public debate on the topic and all the political parties participated. In parliament, 46 per cent of the MPs came from left-wing socialist parties and 54 per cent from non-socialist parties. The government was an SDP-Centre Party coalition government. The political parties, the women's policy agency and the women's movements shared the view that women's low political representation resulted from inequalities in education and the labour market, not from the electoral system as such. The electoral law was not a gender issue for anyone in this debate.

Debate 2: Gender quotas in SKDL, 1986–1987

How the debate came to the public agenda

The Finnish People's Democratic League (SKDL) was the first established party in Finland to debate and to introduce gender quotas for its decision-making bodies in 1987. At the beginning of the 1980s, the SKDL was the fourth biggest party in Finland and women comprised 32 per cent of its members (Tuominen 1984). The SKDL was a radically left-wing hierarchical party, with clear traces of a communist legacy (Sundberg 1997: 111). In its report to the party congress in 1988, the SKDL described itself as a male-dominated party of the working population (Finnish People's Democratic League 1988). Nevertheless, general equality goals formed a central part of the party ideology and the SKDL was one of the first parties in Finland to include new feminist ideas into its party programme in the early 1970s (Nupponen 1968: 51–2; Jallinoja 1983: 178–81; Holli 1988: 140–1). The party also had a separately organised women's section, the Finnish Women's Democratic League (SNDL).[3]

The introduction of quota regulations in the SKDL coincided with the introduction of the Finnish Equality Act (1986). Both the party and its women's section had strongly supported the act. The aim of the Equality Act was to prohibit discrimination on the basis of sex. The new law also promoted proactive measures to improve the position of women in society. In the parliamentary debate, the SKDL advocated a wider definition of discrimination that would have included the private sphere of the family (Saarikoski 2001: 37).

The SKDL's commitment to the Equality Act generated pressures for the party to achieve gender equality in its own male-dominated party structures. However, the idea for quotas did not come from the party's women's section.[4] Instead, the general secretary of the party, Reijo Käkelä, asked Sinikka Mustakallio, who was working in the party administration at the time, to formulate a statement which would appeal to female voters and enhance the party's image among women in the 1987 elections (interview with Mustakallio 2002).

Mustakallio was active in a feminist group Näytit ('Tokens') that was set up in 1986 as part of the SKDL's self-governance project, whose aim, in turn, was to enhance political participation in society in general. In its

---

[3] For a brief history see Katainen (1994).

[4] For example, there are no references to quotas in the women's section's publication *Pippuri* during the years 1986–8. Instead, *Pippuri* wrote about the Equality Act and its significance to women's labour market participation (see for example *Pippuri* 4, 1986).

meetings, the feminist group discussed in particular how patriarchal structures discriminated against women in the party. The women were disappointed with the SKDL as a gender equality movement and Mustakallio felt that there was 'conscious resistance' against appointing women to top positions. With the support of the feminist group, and particularly Ulla-Leena Alppi, MP and another party activist, Mustakallio wrote a statement that argued for the introduction of gender quotas into the party (interview with Mustakallio 2002). The introduction of quotas was heatedly debated in the party executive, and initially, in December 1986, there was strong resistance to the idea. However, in January 1987, the executive recommended a quota rule for the decision-making bodies of the party.

Dominant frame of debate

The debate was framed in terms of different conceptions of equality. There were differences in emphasis between the women who brought forward the idea of quotas, and the party's official line. For the women active in Näytit, the quotas would challenge the patriarchal structures of the party. Equal representation of women and men in the party was a basic principle as such for these women (interview with Mustakallio 2002). Quotas were regarded as the only effective way to transform the male domination in the party and in politics.

For the party leadership, the ultimate goal was not gender equality but economic equality. Economic inequalities were seen to require political solutions: 'The core question is to change the division of labour which confines women to traditional women's jobs and consigns them to a marginal role in decision-making' (*Kansan Uutiset* 16 January 1987). While the feminist activists emphasised the patriarchal structures of society, the official party line also blamed people's attitudes: 'The use of such quotas is necessary in order to change people's attitudes and to build a new, equal society' (*Kansan Uutiset* 15 January 1987).

The statements of the women's section, the SNDL, were in tune with the party's official line. Outi Ojala, MP and the chairperson of the women's section, argued: 'True equality is not achieved in society without economic equality, and this we don't yet have' (*Kansan Uutiset* 17 January 1987). Ojala also stated: 'Quotas for women are not a solution forever, but a tool with which you can endorse aspirations for gender equality, for example, solutions to the low pay problem' (*Kansan Uutiset* 8 February 1987). For Ojala, quotas were thus a means to other ends rather than an end in themselves. In these statements, the persistence of the gender pay gap was regarded as one of the most important gender inequality issues and it was hoped that an increase in women's political representation would result in positive changes in tackling the problem. Characteristically, the women's section's publication, *Pippuri*, stated that the foremost aim of the women's section was to use the Equality Act to demand a six-hour working day and a solution to women's low pay (*Pippuri* 3, 1985).

A further difference in framing the debate was evident in discussions about the nature of the quota. For feminist activists, the decision about quotas was binding (interview with Mustakallio 2002; see also Alppi 1988). For the party leadership, in contrast, the quota principle was just a recommendation. Esko Helle, MP and the leader of the party, stated that it was clear that it could not be one hundred per cent implemented (*Kansan Uutiset* 17 January 1987). The party leadership saw quotas as a temporary measure required for a certain transition period.

Gendering the debate

The debate focused explicitly on gender and the party women were active in bringing forward ideas about gender. The feminist activists, the women's section and the party leadership all portrayed women as active workers: 'Women are not a temporary labour reserve in the labour market; rather their work is a necessary prerequisite for the functioning of our society' (*Kansan Uutiset* 15 January 1987). Furthermore, all participants in the debate emphasised the problem of having a segregated labour market where women's jobs were less well paid and less valued than men's jobs. Implicitly the introduction of quotas was also a challenge to labour market inequality.

In the debate, both sides emphasised the difference between women and from men. In its statement, the SKDL executive argued: 'Women are the best experts on women's position. Currently, it is possible to find expert women for all positions. However, women are continuously discriminated against in the selection procedures' (*Kansan Uutiset* 15 January 1987). Were women to participate in decision-making, they would 'change the political culture' (*Kansan Uutiset* 17 January 1987). The arguments reflect a shift in the Finnish equality discourse from aspiring to equality according to the male norm, to a position stressing women's positive difference from men (Holli 1991).

However, elderly men in the party placed part of the blame on women themselves. The party newspaper, *Kansan Uutiset* (17 January 1987), portrayed women as passive and argued that the quota law would end up 'kicking women to participate', reflecting the idea that passive women had to be forced by quotas to participate. Feminist activists resented such arguments, believing as they did that the patriarchal structures of the party and its masculine rules of conduct prevented women from full participation (interview with Mustakallio 2002). Only when more women were allowed to participate in politics would such barriers come down.

The women were not united in their assessment of the quotas. For example, in her column in *Kansan Uutiset*, Tuula-Liina Varis accused women who had argued for quotas of elitism, and expressed deep scepticism about the significance of quotas to 'ordinary women' (interview with Mustakallio 2002). When Salme Kandolin was appointed as the party's general secretary in spring 1987, she immediately denied that quotas had helped her. This disappointed the activists who had fought for the quota rule (interview with Mustakallio 2002; see also Alppi 1988).

Policy outcome

The party executive adopted the internal party quota of at least 40 per cent of both sexes in all decision-making structures in January 1987. The positive impact of the quota rule was immediately seen at the party congress that convened in May 1988, where a new executive was elected (Finnish People's Democratic League 1988). Of the 163 representatives at the congress 41 per cent were women. The new ten-member party executive included five women, and three of the deputies were men and two women. This was a clear improvement over the previous executive. Since then, the SKDL has had a gender balance in its party executive unlike most parties in Finland (Veikkola 1998: 24).

Women's movement impact

Feminists participated actively in the debate and achieved their goals; hence they achieved a dual response from the party.

Women's policy agency activities

As in the previous debate, the Council for Equality between Women and Men was the relevant women's policy agency in this debate. It had become a part of the Social Affairs and Health Ministry in the autumn of 1986 and its resources remained small. The chairwoman of the council was Eeva Kuuskoski-Vikatmaa (Centre Party MP, Social Affairs and Health Minister) and Eeva-Liisa Tuominen, an active feminist, was the secretary general. The council was composed of seven members from the centre-right parties and six from the left.

The council demanded fairness and a gender balance in democratic decision-making and focused especially on public commissions and corporatist structures. Party quotas were excluded from its mandate, as the council could not intervene in the internal decision-making procedures of parties. As a consequence, the role of the council was symbolic in this debate. The council had strongly advocated the Equality Act, which the feminist activists in the SKDL were able to use to their benefit. However, the goals of the council were not the same as the goals of the feminist activists and, therefore, it had only a mediating role in this debate.

The party had no internal machinery for women or gender equality that would have been relevant to the debate. It had a women's section, the SNDL, which did not, however, have the status of a quasi-women's policy agency.

Women's movement characteristics

The women's movement was in a continued period of growth when this debate took place. Women's studies were expanding in academia and women's political organisations on the left started drawing on the ideas generated by women's studies (Katainen 1994: 376–8). The relevant sections of the women's movement, Näytit and the SNDL, were inside the left. The priority of the issue was high for the feminist group Näytit and moderate for the SNDL, the women's section of the party. These two sections of the women's movement within the party disagreed over the significance and necessity of quotas, but nevertheless appeared moderately unified on the issue towards the party executive. There was also resistance to quotas within SKDL and the strength of the countermovement was therefore moderate.

Policy environment

The policy sub-system was closed, as the decision for quotas was made within the SKDL's party executive. As noted above, the party itself was male-dominated and hierarchical. However, the party was facing a number of external and internal challenges. At the end of the 1980s, transformations in the Soviet Union questioned the legitimacy of radical left-wing parties in Finland. In the previous elections, in 1983, the SKDL lost eight seats in the parliament (from 35 to 27 of 200 seats) and had changed from being a member of the coalition government to being an opposition party. Furthermore, Democratic Alternative, a communist faction that had broken away from the party's ranks, challenged the party in the 1987 elections (Nousiainen 1998: 39). The SKDL also had to compete with a newcomer in Finnish politics, the Green League, which was appealing to some of SKDL's voters with radical equality politics. The SKDL was therefore confronted by internal and external crises that created pressures for structural change and spaces for women's demands for quotas (cf. Perrigo 1995). Both the executive and the feminist activists wanted increased female participation in the party and both framed their demands in the language of equality, although in a slightly different manner. The frame fit between the feminist activists and the party executive was therefore compatible.

Debate 3: Gender quotas in the Equality Act, 1991–1995

How the debate came to the public agenda

The Equality Act of 1987 included a loosely formulated paragraph on the gendered composition of public bodies. Government commissions, advisory boards and similar bodies, including municipal boards, should include both women and men, unless there were special reasons to the contrary. The implementation proved difficult, however, especially because municipal authorities insisted on interpreting the law in a minimal way. Even after the law was slightly modified in 1988, the Equality Ombudsman, Paavo Nikula, repeatedly had to remind authorities that 'women' and 'men' were written in plural terms in the law (Ministry of Social Affairs and Health 1989: 19–20). Moreover, efforts to implement the law were seriously undermined by a 1990 decision by the Supreme Administrative Court that did not consider the presence of only one woman or man in a public body to be in breach of the Equality Act.

The idea of specifying numerical quotas (a minimum 40 per cent of each sex) in the law in order to ensure its implementation was presented by two state inquiry commissions in 1991–2 (Committee report 1991, 1992). However, the suggestion met with great criticism from most ministries and employers' organisations.

The final government proposal was a compromise solution that excluded numerical quotas in favour of a looser formulation concerning 'a balanced representation' of both sexes. Two female ministers of the centre-right government[5] formally dissented from the decision. Furthermore, the Minister for Gender Equality Affairs, Elisabeth Rehn (Swedish People's Party), who was responsible for the preparation of the law, personally supported specified numerical quotas but did not want

---

[5] Minister of Justice, Anneli Jäätteenmäki (Centre Party) and Minister of Environmental Affairs, Sirpa Pietikäinen (National Coalition Party).

the conflicts to cause the bill to be withdrawn or delayed. She told this to parliament in May 1994, urging it to change the law (Parliamentary documents 1994: 1326–8, 1359–60). Two private member's bills (Law initiatives 34/1994 and 35/1994) for the inclusion of numerical quotas were prepared by the Network of Women MPs in parliament as alternatives to the government's proposal. Mobilisation by women MPs was also successful within parliament: the Parliamentary Standing Committee for Labour Market Affairs decided to recommend specified numerical quotas in its statement to the plenary.

Dominant frame of debate

The debate was framed in terms of gender equality, which was supported unanimously throughout the debates regardless of one's opinion on gender quotas. The problem was defined as women's lack of opportunities to participate in policy-formulation processes and the subsequent gender imbalance in public bodies. It was thought that women's descriptive under-representation had also led to an under-representation of women's substantive interests in policy-making. Nor was there enough utilisation of women's resources and expertise in the service of society either (see Gov. prop. 90/1994).

However, there was a conflict about the causes and solutions of inequalities. For the right-wing parties and the employers' associations, the causes were to be found at the level of attitudes and the solution was to change them through enlightenment and education. Numerical quotas would not solve the real problem. Additionally, quotas were seen as an inflexible method that would lead to more inequality between individuals. Quotas of men and women would disregard the individual expertise and merits that were required of persons recruited to political posts.

For the left-wing and the majority of female MPs, the causes of gender inequalities were also considered to exist at the structural level, in gender discrimination and the exclusive selection practices exercised by the closed, male networks in society. Quotas would be an effective method to counteract discrimination and to achieve change, as the Norwegian example had illustrated. Moreover, many female MPs expressed their extreme disappointment with the manner in which the Equality Act 1987 had been side-stepped in practice.

Gendering the debate

The debate was framed in a gendered manner from the very beginning. In parliament, conflicts over the acceptability of gender quotas were closely intertwined with different gendered interpretations of the concept of 'political competence' (see Raevaara and Saarikoski 2002; Saarikoski 2001; Raevaara 1999, 2001, 2003). Basically, there were three different approaches to women's political competence in the debate.

The first standpoint, favoured by some male and female MPs from the right-wing parties, took the idea of political competence for granted. The absence of women in various decision-making bodies was regarded as proof of women's political incompetence or political passivity. 'The issue is about your, the female gender's sense of worth and a lack of it ... There are more of you as voters than there are men. Nevertheless you have to resort to legislative powers in the form of quotas in order to get your gender equality' (Sulo Aittoniemi, Centre Party, Parliamentary documents 1995: 6835).

The other two positions both conceived women as politically competent but held opposing views on quotas and political competence.

Some young female right-wing MPs were the proponents of the second standpoint. They heatedly opposed quotas, which they regarded as an insult to competent women: '(T)oday's women are more and more educated and knowledgeable and they want to succeed on their own merits, not as so-called obligatory quota-women. At least I would not like to see my education, achievements and the regard I receive because of my work to be spilled in vain because of deprecatory quota-thinking of that kind' (Kirsi Piha, National Coalition Party, Parliamentary documents 1995: 1385).

However, the majority of female MPs from both the left-wing and right-wing parties supported the third standpoint. They stressed that Finnish women were already more educated than men. Women were politically competent but nevertheless, because of discrimination or outdated attitudes, they did not get their due in public policy-making. Therefore quotas were necessary, at least as a temporary measure. The female MPs also utilised a persuasive rhetoric by repeatedly pointing out that gender quotas would help men, too, especially in the future when men would be in a minority among the high-educated women in all areas of public life.

In this discourse, women and men were constructed as inherently different. Demands for women's increased representation were justified by the need to include women's different experiences and interests in public policy-making. Often women were portrayed as 'experts on everyday life', which can be regarded as an attempt to broaden the concept of political competence. In contrast, rarely did the debate blame men for current inequalities, or question the level of men's political competence (Raevaara and Saarikoski 2002).

Policy outcome

From 1991 to 1995, there was a world record of 39 per cent of female MPs in the Finnish parliament. The majority of them, across party lines, supported numerical quotas of men and women and joined forces with the opposition left-wing party men to form a parliamentary majority on the issue. As a consequence, the government's proposal, supported by right-wing male MPs and some National Coalition Party and Centre Party women, lost the vote in the parliament.

Since 1995, the Equality Act has included a paragraph that decrees that all indirectly elected public bodies (government inquiry commissions, other similar bodies, municipal executive boards and other municipal boards) must be composed of at least 40 per cent of both women and men. There were also attempts to include similar numerical quotas in the regulations concerning the decision-making bodies of state-owned companies, but the initiative did not gain enough support. Instead, they are to have 'a balanced representation of both sexes'.

As a result of the quota decision, in the late 1990s the proportion of women in newly appointed public commissions increased from 30 per cent to 48 per cent (Vähäsaari 1995; Kaasinen 1996); in municipal executive boards from 25 per cent to 45 per cent; and in municipal preparatory boards from 35 per cent to 47 per cent (Pikkala 1999: 478).

Women's movement impact

Women's movement actors (including the Network of Women MPs in Parliament), government ministers and individual female MPs were central to the debate and they also achieved their goal. Therefore, the state made a dual response to movement demands.

Women's policy agency activities

From 1987 onwards, the Council for Equality shared responsibility over equality policy with the Equality Ombudsman, a cross-sectional, judicial, formally independent official charged with supervising the Equality Act. Both institutions were located under the Ministry of Social Affairs and Health. They both played active, albeit mutually complementary and even conflicting, roles in the policy debate.

In the initial stages, it was the ombudsman who played an insider role. As the expert on the scope and implications of equality legislation, the ombudsman and his staff were central actors in the policy preparation within the ministry and other policy deliberations. Ombudsman Paavo

Nikula (1987–91), a strong male supporter of feminist demands, headed one of the commissions proposing the quota, participated in all the others and also, after his resignation, supported gender quotas as a Green Party MP in parliament.

During 1991–4, the ombudsman was Tuulikki Petäjäniemi, a former National Coalition Party MP with close ties to organised management. In contrast to her predecessor, Petäjäniemi actively resented numerical quotas of women and men, arguing that they would jeopardise respect for the Equality Act (Committee report 1992: Appendix; Constitutional Law Committee 1994: Appendix). Although the ombudsman continued to gender the debate during this period, the standpoints deviated from those of the women's movement and can thus be classified as non-feminist in terms of the model.

The Council for Equality had worked actively since 1974 to promote equal representation of both sexes in public bodies (Holli 1991: 78). In the early 1990s, however, the division of work between the women's policy agencies had transferred the issue to the Equality Ombudsman. The council continued to participate in the policy deliberations by providing expert statements. However, because of its partisan composition, the council was divided on the issue of whether numerical quotas were a solution to the problem of women's under-representation. In late 1992, however, the council started to take a more active role in the debate and it issued a protest against the exclusion of women's organisations in the 1992 hearings (Council for Equality between Men and Women 1992a, 1992b, 1992c). The complaint led to additional hearings and a stronger presence of women's movement actors in the policy debate.

In the final stages, the council started to support numerical quotas more strongly (Committee for Labour Market Affairs 1994: Appendix) and also to play the insider role now abandoned by the ombudsman. During 1992–5, the chair of the council was Tuula Kuittinen, MP (Centre Party). For example, Kuittinen and another council member, Anneli Taina, MP (National Coalition Party), as members of the Parliamentary Standing Committee for Labour Market Affairs, were active in mobilising political support for the numerical gender quota in parliament. In the 1990s, the secretariat of the council, with diminishing administrative capacity and a more non-partisan profile than before, was headed by the same two feminist women (Eeva-Liisa Tuominen, Leila Räsänen) as before.

Women's movement characteristics

In the 1990s, women's movements entered into a stage of consolidation, where women's networks became a more common form of organising. In political terms, the most important ones were NYTKIS (*Naiset Yhteistyössä – Kvinno-organisationernal Samarbete*, the Coalition for Joint Action of Finnish Women's Organisations, from 1988) and the Network of Women MPs in Parliament (from 1991). Both worked for gender equality and women's rights from within established structures and across party lines. All parts of the women's movement agreed on the high priority of redressing women's political under-representation. However, there was initially some disagreement about the methods, as some (left-wing, Centre and Swedish party women, and feminists) supported the Norwegian model (explicit legislative quotas) and some (especially right-wing women) opted for the Swedish model instead (no quotas, but a strong political commitment for gender balance) (Ministry of Social Affairs and Health 1992a, 1992b, 1993). During the policy process, unity among women increased significantly as many right-wing women adopted the left-wing standpoint. The counter-movement was extremely strong, consisting of the government, most ministries, right-wing parties, organised management and the majority of male MPs.

Policy environment

The policy sub-system headed by the Ministry of Social Affairs and Health was moderately closed. Gender equality affairs had been delegated to the Minister of Defence, Elisabeth Rehn (Swedish People's Party), and later, her successor Jan-Erik Enestam (from the same party). In the 1991 elections, the socialist parties had faced defeat with only 33.5 per cent of MPs. The Social Democrats were in opposition for the first time in twenty-five years, and the right-wing and centre parties formed a coalition government led by Prime Minister Esko Aho (Centre Party).

All the policy actors shared the view that the issue concerned gender equality and political competence, but female MPs and other movement representatives, however, redefined women's political competence. Consequently, the frame fit was compatible.

Conclusion

In this chapter on Finland, the impact of women's movements in three debates on political representation from the 1970s to the 1990s has been analysed.

On the one hand, the results show a significant policy success (dual response in the second and third debates) by women's movements in debates that explicitly link to women's political representation. On the other hand, the structures of formal representation in the country are commonly regarded as gender-neutral or relatively favourable to women's representation. As a consequence, system-level reforms tend to remain non-gendered in the context of an open-list PR-system, multi-member constituencies, legislative regulation of party activity and a strong presence of women in electoral politics. In the absence of gendering attempts by women's movements, the policy outcome in the only case in our selection (the first debate) that concerned a reform of the electoral system was a 'no response' by the state.

Women's movement characteristics are decisive to movement impact, whereas policy environment characteristics do not appear to play a role. Movement success was achieved in both a closed and a moderately closed policy sub-system; in a closed left-wing party environment; and in the parliamentary arena with the right-wing parties in government. By contrast, the two women's policy successes occurred in a context of women's movement mobilisation. The issue at hand was considered to be a high movement priority, various sections of the movement were relatively unified on the issue, and the left-wing parts of the movement participated in the debate. In the sole policy failure (the first debate), there was no mobilisation by women's movements.

The results appear to concur with earlier findings (Holli 2002, 2003) that argue that there is a tendency for Finnish women's movements to achieve policy success, if they manage to mobilise to a sufficient degree on an issue. Various parts of the movement co-operate on pragmatic political issues by way of 'strategic alliances' (Halsaa 1992). From a comparative perspective, it is remarkable that cross-party alliances are formed by women on gender issues. For instance, in the third debate, the majority of right-wing female MPs joined forces with the opposition left-wing MPs, against their government proposal and their party line.

The results also show that even if the role of the women's policy agencies is not necessary in securing a successful policy outcome, they can nevertheless efficiently promote movement goals. In the third debate both existing women's policy agencies played central roles in preparing the legislation and in giving statements. However, none of the women's policy agencies was active in the other two debates.

Interestingly, some women's policy agency characteristics, such as the policy mandate and leadership characteristics, seem to have affected agency activities in the two successful debates. In the second debate, the issue was excluded from the women's policy agency mandate, which prevented the agency from entering the closed party arena. In the later stages of the third debate, the two existing women's policy agencies were at odds on the issue of quotas. The Council for Equality played an insider role and the ombudsman a non-feminist role in the debate. The difference may be explained by the specific leadership characteristics of the latter.

In conclusion, the analysis illustrates that Finnish women's movements tend to mobilise successfully when women's political presence is at stake. However, there seems to be a blind spot in regard to more general system-level reforms, which are typically considered 'gender-neutral'. For example, a recent proposal to reform the electoral system (2001) did not invoke any gendered analysis. It remains to be seen whether Finnish women's mobilisation for political presence could be considered a reactive strategy, made necessary by their tendency to 'think positively' in the first place and a subsequent disappointment at the exclusion of gendered interests.

References

A Government and party documents

Committee for Labour Market Affairs 1994, Pöytäkirja eduskunnan työasiainvaliokunnan kokouksesta 11.10.1994, no. 44/1994 vp, Liite B 6 §: Eeva-Liisa Tuomisen muistio, Helsinki: Eduskunta

Committee report 1991, Naiset ja miehet valtionhallinnossa. Suunnittelu, valmistelu ja tulosohjaus, Komiteanmietintö 1991:47, Helsinki: Valtion painatuskeskus

1992, Tasa-arvolain uudistamistoimikunnan mietintö, Komiteanmietintö 1992: 35, Helsinki: Valtion painatuskeskus

Constitutional Law Committee 1994, Pöytäkirja eduskunnan perustuslakivaliokunnan kokouksesta 9.11.1994, no. 90/1994 vp, Liite B 3 §: Tasa-arvovaltuutettu Tuulikki Petäjäniemen lausunto eduskunnan perustuslakivaliokunnalle (tasa-arvovaltuutetun diaarionumero 36/31/94), Helsinki: Eduskunta

Council for Equality between Men and Women 1973, Lausunto sosiaali- ja terveysministeriölle koskien YK:n pääsihteerin kyselyä hallituksen ehdotuksista kansainvälisen naisten vuoden 1975 ohjelmaksi, Diaarionumero 32/51/73, Helsinki: Tasa-arvoasiain neuvottelukunta

1992a, Kannanotto 3.12.1992, Helsinki: Tasa-arvoasiain neuvottelukunta (also available in Ministry of Social Affairs and Health 1992b)

1992b, Kirjelmä tasa-arvoministeri Elisabeth Rehnille. 3.12.1992, Helsinki: Tasa-arvoasiain neuvottelukunta (also available in Ministry of Social Affairs and Health 1992b)

1992c, Lausunto tasa-arvolain uudistamistoimikunnan mietinnöstä, Hyväksytty 4.12.1992, Helsinki: Tasa-arvoasiain neuvottelukunta (also available in Ministry of Social Affairs and Health 1992b)

Finnish People's Democratic League 1988, Vasemmisto Liikkeellä, SKDL 15. Liittokokous 20–22.5.1988, Turku, Helsinki: Kansan arkisto

Gov. prop. 178/1974, Hallituksen esitys laiksi vaalilain muuttamisesta, Helsinki: Eduskunta

90/1994, Hallituksen esitys Eduskunnalle laiksi naisten ja miesten välisestä tasa-arvosta annetun lain muuttamisesta, Helsinki: Eduskunta
Law initiative 34/1994, Lakialoite 34/1994 vp: Varpasuo ym.: Ehdotus laiksi naisten ja miesten välisestä tasa-arvosta annetun lain 4 §:n muuttamisesta, Helsinki: Eduskunta
35/1994, Lakialoite 35/1994 vp: A. Ojala ym.: Ehdotus laiksi naisten ja miesten välisestä tasa-arvosta annetun lain muuttamisesta, Helsinki: Eduskunta
Ministry of Social Affairs and Health 1989, Vuosikertomukset 1988. Kertomus tasa-arvovaltuutetun toimialalta. Tasa-arvoasiain neuvottelukunnan toimintakertomus, Tasa-arvojulkaisuja, sarja B: Tiedotteita 1/1989, Helsinki: Valtion painatuskeskus
1992a, Valtion tasa-arvotoimikunnan mietinnöstä (KM 1991: 47) annetut lausunnot, Diaarionumero 5/059/92, Helsinki: Sosiaali- ja terveysministeriö
1992b, Tasa-arvolain uudistamistoimikunnan mietinnöstä (KM 1992: 35) annetut lausunnot, Diaarionumero 35/059/92, Helsinki: Sosiaali- ja terveysministeriö
1993, Tasa-arvolakityöryhmän ehdotuksesta (Työryhmämuistio 1993: 14) annetut lausunnot, Diaarionumero 22/059/93, Helsinki: Sosiaali- ja terveysministeriö
Parliamentary documents 1974–5, 1994–5, Helsinki: Eduskunta. (From 1994 Diet onward, all parliamentary documents except committee minutiae are also available at http://www.eduskunta.fi)

B General

Aalto, Terhi 2003, 'Kuka vie? Naiset, politiikka ja päivähoitolainsäädäntö. Tapaukset päivähoidon subjektiivinen oikeus 1994 ja kotihoidon tuen leikkaus 1995', unpublished Master's thesis, Helsinki: Helsingin yliopisto
Alppi, Ulla-Leena 1988, *Kosketuskohtia*, Helsinki: Kirjayhtymä
Bergqvist, Christina, Annette Borchorst, Ann-Dorte Christiansen, Viveca Ramstedt-Silén, Nina C. Raum and Auŏor Stynkarsdottin (eds.) 1999, *Equal Democracies: Gender and Politics in the Nordic Countries*, Oslo: Scandinavian University Press
Dahlerup, Drude 1988, 'From a Small to a Large Minority: Women in Scandinavian Politics', *Scandinavian Political Studies* 11: 275–98
1989, *Odotuksen aika on ohi. Naispolitiikan käsikirja*, Kööpenhamina: Pohjoismaiden ministerineuvosto
Haavio-Mannila, Elina 1979, 'How Women Become Political Actors: Female Candidates in Finnish Elections', *Scandinavian Political Studies* 2: 351–71
Haavio-Mannila, Elina, Drude Dahlerup, Maud Eduards, Esther Gudmundsdóttir, Beatrice Halsaa, Helga Maria Hernes, Eva Hänninen-Salmelin, Bergthora Sigmundsdóttir, Sirkka Sinkkonen and Torild Skard 1985, *Unfinished Democracy: Women in Nordic Politics*, Oxford: Pergamon Press
Halsaa, Beatrice 1992, *Policies and Strategies on Women in Norway: The Role of Women's Organisations, Political Parties and the Government*, Skriftserien no. 74, Lillehammer: Oppland Distriktshøgskole

Holli, Anne Maria 1988, ' "Tätä vääryyttä vastaan ei taistella kukkasin?" *Yhdistys 9:n politiikan ja politiikka käsityksen suhteen merkityksestä* tasa-arvopolitiikan syntyhistoriassa', unpublished, Master's thesis, Helsinki: Helsingin yliopisto.
  1991, 'Miehisestä tasa-arvosta kohti naisten käsitteellistä tilaa. Tasa-arvoasiain neuvottelukunnan tasa-arvopoliittinen diskurssi vv. 1972–86', unpublished licentiate thesis, Helsinki: Helsingin yliopisto
  2001, 'A Shifting Policy Environment Divides the Impact of State Feminism in Finland', in Amy Mazur (ed.) *State Feminism, Women's Movements and Job Training: Making Democracies Work in the Global Economy*, New York and London: Routledge, pp. 183–212
  2002, 'Suomalainen tasa-arvopolitiikka vertailevan tutkimuksen valossa', in Anne Maria Holli, Terhi Saarikoski and Elina Sana (eds.) *Tasa-arvopolitiikan haasteet*, Helsinki: WSOY and Tasa-arvoasiain neuvottelukunta, pp. 128–45
  2003, *Discourse and Politics for Gender Equality in Late Twentieth Century Finland*, Acta Politica 23, Helsinki: Helsinki University Press
  2004, 'Towards a New Prohibitionism? State Feminism, Women's Movements and Prostitution Policies in Finland', in Joyce Outshoorn (ed.) *The Politics of Prostitution: Women's Movements, Democratic States and the Globalisation of Sex Commerce*, Cambridge: Cambridge University Press, pp. 103–22
Jallinoja, Riitta 1983, *Suomalaisen naisasialiikkeen taistelukaudet. Naisasialiike naisten elämäntilanteen muutoksen ja yhteiskunnallis-aatteellisen murroksen heijastajana*, Helsinki: WSOY
Kaasinen, Päivi 1996, Naisten osuus valtion komiteoissa ja työryhmissä sekä valtion virastojen ja laitosten, liikelaitosten ja valtionyhtiöiden johto- ja hallintoelimissä 1995–1996, Tasa-arvon työraportteja 3/1996, Helsinki: Sosiaali- ja terveysministeriö.
Karvonen, Lauri and Per Selle 1995, 'Introduction: Scandinavia: a Case Apart', in Lauri Karvonen and Per Selle (eds.) *Women in Nordic Politics: Closing the Gap*, Aldershot: Dartmouth, pp. 3–23
Katainen, Elina 1994, *Akkain aherrusta aatteen hyväksi*, Tampere: Tammer-Paino
Nousiainen, Jaakko 1998, *Suomen poliittinen järjestelmä*, tenth edition, Juva: WSOY
Nupponen, Terttu 1968, 'Puolueohjelmat ja sukupuoliroolit', in Katarina Eskola (ed.) *Miesten maailman nurjat lait*, Helsinki: Tammi, pp. 45–61
Perrigo, Sarah 1995, 'Gender Struggles in the British Labour Party from 1979 to 1995', *Party Politics* 1: 407–17
Pesonen, Pertti 1991, 'Puolueen ja edustajaehdokkaan painottuminen äänestyspäätöksissä', *Politiikka* 2: 98–105
  1995, 'The Voter's Choice of Candidate', in Sami Borg and Risto Sänkiaho (eds.) *The Finnish Voter*, Tampere: The Finnish Political Science Association, pp. 114–28
Pesonen, Pertti, Risto Sänkiaho and Sami Borg 1993, *Vaalikansan äänivalta. Tutkimus eduskuntavaaleista ja valitsijakunnasta Suomen poliittisessa järjestelmässä*, Juva: WSOY
Pikkala, Sari 1999, 'Sukupuolikiintiöt kunnallishallinnossa', *Kunnallistieteellinen aikakauskirja* 4: 473–83

Raaum, Nina C. 1999, 'Women in Parliamentary Politics: Historical Lines of Development', in Christina Bergqvist et al. (eds.) *Equal Democracies: Gender and Politics in the Nordic Countries*, Oslo: Scandinavian University Press, pp. 27–47

Raevaara, Eeva 1999, 'Keskustelu sukupuolten tasa-arvosta Suomen ja Ranskan politiikassa', *Historiallisen Yhdistyksen julkaisusarjat, Historiallisia Papereita*, Helsinki: Historiallinen yhdistys (http://www.helsinki.fi/hum/hist/yhd/julk/tasaarvo/raevaara.html)

 2001, 'Naiset ja miehet liikkeessä. Toimijuus ranskalaisessa ja suomalaisessa tasa-arvopuheessa', Paperi politiikan tutkimuksen päivillä 10-1212001 Helsinki-Tukholma, työryhmä Esityksiä ja/vai edustuksia? Sukupuolen representaation politiikkaa.

 2003, 'Talking about Equality, Acting for Change: Conceptualisations of Gender Equality in Parliamentary Debates in Finland and France', paper presented at the second Conference of the European Consortium for Political Research, Panel 2–2: Translating Political Equality into Practice, Marburg, 18–21 September 2003

Raevaara, Eeva and Terhi Saarikoski 2002, 'Mikä nainen, mikä mies? Tasa-arvo ja toimijat eduskunnan kiintiökeskustelussa', in Anne Maria Holli, Terhi Saarikoski and Elina Sana (eds.) *Tasa-arvopolitiikan haasteet*, Helsinki: WSOY and Tasa-arvoasiain neuvottelukunta, pp. 264–86

Saarikoski, Terhi 2001, 'Naiset tasa-arvon ongelmana ja asiantuntijoina: Puolueiden tasa-arvodiskurssit vuosien 1986 ja 1995 tasa-arvolakeja koskeneissa eduskuntakeskusteluissa', unpublished Master's thesis, Helsinki: Helsingin yliopisto.

Sundberg, Jan 1995, 'Women in Scandinavian Party Organisations', in Lauri Karvonen and Per Selle (eds.) *Women in Nordic Politics: Closing the Gap*, Aldershot: Dartmouth, pp. 83–111

 1997, 'Compulsory Party Democracy: Finland as a Deviant Case in Scandinavia', *Party Politics* 3: 97–117

Tarasti, Lauri 1998, *Suomen vaalilainsäädäntö*, fourth edition, Helsinki: Edita

Tuominen, Eeva-Liisa 1984, Naisten osuus puolueiden, työmarkkinajärjestöjen ja osuustoimintajärjestöjen jäsenistössä ja päättävissä elimissä vuoden 1982 lopussa, Tasa-arvoasiain neuvottelukunnan monisteita 3/1983, Helsinki: Tasa-arvoasiain neuvottelukunta.

Vähäsaari, Maarit 1995, Naisten osuus valtion komiteoissa ja työryhmissä 1991–1995, Tasa-arvon työraportteja 3/1995, Helsinki: Sosiaali- ja terveysministeriö

Veikkola, Eeva-Sisko (ed.) 1998, Naiset ja miehet yhteiskunnallisessa päätöksenteossa, *Katsauksia* 8, Helsinki: Tilastokeskus

Newspapers and magazines cited include: *Kansan Uutiset* and *Pippuri*

5 Gendering the republican system: debates on women's political representation in France

Claudie Baudino

Introduction

The Fifth Republic constitution was adopted in 1958 during the French–Algerian war, in a period of violent political crisis. De Gaulle's text, which was framed to prevent governmental instability, is therefore grounded in the fear of division. In different ways, and despite numerous revisions, the political system favours efficiency at the expense of pluralism. From its inception, the regime was the target of sharp criticisms. Despite the direct election of the president, introduced in 1962, opponents of the regime pointed out its lack of democracy. Claims for democratisation have led to numerous debates on political representation; some paved the way for the debate on women's quotas. Few of them ended up in reforms.

Decisions about political representation are made at the centre. The powerful executive, consisting of both a president and a prime minister, plays a significant part in the decision-making process. Some policies take place through legislation, others require a special process of constitutional revision. The voting system falls within the competence of the legislature. Legislation is made by collaboration between the government and the two chambers of the legislature. The government controls the agenda through a system of party government. French deputies (Lower House) and senators (Upper House) may amend bills, 90 per cent of which are initiated by the executive. A Constitutional Council, the *Conseil constitutionnel*, may declare a law to be unconstitutional, thus making later revisions a constitutional matter. Constitutional revision must be initiated by the executive and may be decided either by referendum or by the joint vote of both chambers of the legislature. Lack of pluralism is the main weakness of the Fifth Republic. Criticism accelerated at the end of the twentieth century, partly in response to dissatisfaction with periods of cohabitation in which the prime minister and the president represented different parties. Renewed demands for a Sixth Republic were further strengthened by the entry of the far right *Front national* leader, Jean Marie Le Pen, into the second round of the presidential elections, thus excluding the candidate of the left, Lionel

Jospin, from the final round of votes and paving the way for right-wing control of both the presidency and the legislature.

The main results and surprises of the elections that took place in spring 2002 may be summed up in three points. First, the far right-wing candidate Jean-Marie Le Pen, leader of the *Front national*, won access to the second round of the presidential election, preventing Lionel Jospin, the socialist candidate, from playing the part of the expected challenger of Jacques Chirac. Second, the right-wing parties won both the presidential and the legislative elections, thus gaining an overall control of the political assemblies. Third, the low percentage of women elected to the chamber of deputies, 12.3 per cent (up from 10 per cent in the previous assembly), revealed how limited were the effects of the so-called parity reform at the national level. Any account of the wealth of debates on political representation after 1980 must keep in mind this moment of political crisis and its constitutional implications.

Selection of debates

For the past two decades, debates on political representation have been numerous and diverse. They have concerned each dimension of the issue: the representatives, the electorate and the election. However, only the debates on the representatives and the rules of the game ended up with formal decisions.

The three selected debates concern the change of electoral system for local council elections (1982), the change of electoral system for the parliamentary elections (1985) and the parity reform (1999–2000). In the first and the second debates, the rules of the game were at stake; in the third, it was the characteristics of the representatives. All three debates took place at the national level. Change to the electoral system was mainly discussed in the two chambers of the parliament while the parity debate, as a constitutional matter, was more widespread. It included a lively and diverse social movement and the highest levels of the state. Whilst the introduction of the proportional system was a short-lived reform, debates on the electoral system were of great significance during the 1980s. The Socialists accepted the constitution when they came to power in 1981, but change to the electoral systems was a way of challenging one of the pillars of the constitution without altering it. However, the proportional system was later said to be responsible for the resurgence of the *Front national*. The parity reform also challenged the sexual neutrality of the Republic. It gave rise to a huge number of articles and debates in the media. From the beginning of the 1990s to 2000, parity was the subject of a controversial debate of exceptional salience.

The first women's policy agency (WPA) in charge of furthering equality between the two sexes was established in the mid-1970s – it was the state secretary in charge of women's issues (*Secrétariat d'état à la condition féminine*) with Françoise Giroud at its head. But the high-ranking and well-funded Ministry of Women's Rights (*Ministère des droits de la femme*), led by Yvette Roudy, was not created until 1981. The three selected debates cover the full time span of French WPAs.

Debate 1: The change of the voting system for the local council elections, 1982

How the debate came to the public agenda

The introduction of a proportional electoral system (PR) was one of 110 proposals in the platform of the Socialist candidate, François Mitterrand, in the 1981 presidential and legislative elections. Local councils were due to be renewed in 1983. Hence the manifesto promise was quickly put to the test.

Dominant frame of debate

Mitterrand's proposal was listed in the manifesto section called 'The Respected Democracy'. It read: 'The proportional system will be instituted for the elections at the National Assembly, at the Regional assemblies, and at the town councils for towns of less than 9,000 inhabitants. There will be 30 per cent of women on every list' (Jenson and Sineau 1995, p. 353). The PR proposal challenged the very basis of the Fifth Republic. PR supporters framed their arguments for reform in terms of justice and faithfulness to the people's will. PR was presented as a means to express citizens' diversity.

Positive action to increase the number of women elected was not a new idea. In 1979, under a right-wing government, the Ministry of Women's Issues headed by Monique Pelletier sponsored a bill to introduce a women's quota at the local level. Opponents claimed that a women's quota would be unconstitutional, while its supporters argued the opposite (Vedel 1979). In the event, the measure was never put on the legislative agenda. The 1982 pledge of a women's quota in their platform was, for the Socialists, a way to show that they would do what the right wing failed to do, hence demonstrating their alliance to feminism. However, although the manifesto promised both a proportional system and a women's quota, the governmental bill offered only a change in the electoral system. Somehow the government forgot the gendered dimension of the electoral promise.

Gendering the debate

According to Jane Jenson and Mariette Sineau, presidential feminism peaked on 8 March 1982 (Jenson and Sineau 1995: 195). Government failure to include the women's quota in its bill showed the limitations of its commitment. Nevertheless, the public debate was explicitly gendered.

During the legislative debate, an amendment was put in by an independent deputy in alliance with the Socialist Party, Gisèle Halimi. Founder of *Choisir la cause des femmes* in 1971, Halimi had a long track record of feminist advocacy. Her amendment was well received by most of the left-wing deputies, who reacted as if the initiative of their feminist colleague put right an unfortunate oversight. In fact, Halimi was almost the only champion of a women's quota in the assembly. Her proposal, designed to gain maximum support, was not very ambitious. Following the advice of jurist Georges Vedel, she supported a rather neutral drawing up of the provision in which quotas were put forward as the best way to improve women's political representation, but their political significance was played down. Halimi tried to convince deputies that the amendment could be within the constitution. In gender-neutral language, the amendment referred to persons of the same sex. Halimi's amendment did not request the symbolic 50 per cent quota. More modestly, she supported the idea of a quota set at 30 per cent (Halimi 1982; *Débats parlementaires* 1982). Similarly another left-wing deputy, Odile Sicard, spoke in favour of the amendment, arguing that what was at stake was not the political representation of women but their taking part in the political game. In other words a quota would not overthrow the system, but would merely adjust its working.

Policy outcome

Passed quasi-unanimously, the amendment proposed that party candidate lists contain no more than 75 per cent of people of the same sex. A footnote would be useful to explain how the quota went from a mininium of 30 per cent women to a maximum of 75 per cent of the same sex. The few supporters of quotas did not really question the place of sexual difference in the political system. The real outcome of the process was the rejection of the quota by the *Conseil constitutionnel* on 18 November 1982, a decision that 'constitutionalised' the issue with significant impact on the policy sub-system ('Décision n° 82–146 du 18 novembre 1982'). The judges held that it was impossible to divide candidates into categories without seriously undermining the dogma of universal citizenship, interpreted to mean that citizens form a unitary and homogenous body. Their argument was grounded on article 6 of the *Déclaration des droits de l'Homme et du Citoyen* which says that 'all citizens being equal (in the eyes of the law), they are also eligible for all dignities, positions and public jobs according to their abilities and without any distinction other than their personal qualities and talents'. Written more than two centuries previously, in order to abolish privileges at a time when women were not citizens, the text was interpreted literally to enable judges to overturn the amendment. In a very republican mood and with a manifest lack of rigour, they asserted that the sex of the citizens should not be considered politically relevant. The decision made it impossible for successive women's ministries and departments to support any form of affirmative action.

Women's movement impact

The decision of the *Conseil* did not give rise to much protest, which is probably what the politicians expected. During the debate, many deputies foresaw the unconstitutionality of the provision. On behalf of the government, the Home Secretary suggested that it should be written down in a separate article so that its possible rejection wouldn't stop the rest of the text from being implemented (*Débats parlementaires* 1982). The unanimous vote of the lower chamber may have been made in the expectation that the measure would be overturned. In her standard work on this issue, Danièle Loschak describes the vote as 'collective hypocrisy' (Loschak 1983: 131).

Feminists did not play a great part in the political debate. Despite its diversity, the second wave of feminism was, in France, a movement more focused on the assertion of difference than on the quest for equality. Willing to challenge society from its margins, this movement was built on the rejection of reformism. Most activists had a high regard for political institutions and wanted to change the rules of the political game from the outside. In the 1980s, therefore, the institution of a women's quota did not coincide with women's movement goals.

By contrast, the reformist feminist and politician Halimi felt strongly about the issue of women's political representation. But she couldn't generate significant support for quotas. She was isolated in the feminist movement because of her political commitment and in the Socialist Party because of her feminist stand. Although quotas were on the legislative agenda, no key figure stood up for them and no real public debate took place on the issue.

Apart from Halimi, few feminists or women politicians paid much attention to the issue or took part in the debate. Women were not involved in the policy process. Halimi's 30 per cent quota was amended by the legislature to 25 per cent. Presented by the Socialist deputy Alain Richard and supported by the Socialist group at the National Assembly, its text exemplified the pre-emption of the feminist claims. The absence of assembly debate and movement engagement meant that only the *Conseil constitutionnel* explicitly gendered the debate. While the decision was to remove the category of sex from the law, the argument of the court referred to the place of men and women (citizens) in the political system.

Women's policy agency activities

At the beginning of the 1980s, the Ministry of Women's Rights was relatively powerful and well resourced. But it played only a symbolic part in the debate. Although Yvette Roudy was both a key figure of the left and a reformist feminist, unlike Halimi, she was an insider in the party and a member of the government. So, having advocated quotas during the presidential campaign, she realised that the window for feminist policy was closing. As interest in women's issues faded in the government, her ministry made equal opportunity at work its top priority. The ministry kept silent about the amendment. Hence WPA activities matched neither the reformist goals nor the new movement goals.

Ministry coolness towards a women's quota was partly the result of the political context at that time, and partly a reflection of the general frame of women's policy in the 1980s (Baudino 2000). Instead of claiming gender difference and asking for positive action, Roudy intended to improve women's status by providing equality of rights between the two sexes. In the aftermath of the quotas failure, she wrote an article published in *Le Monde* (Roudy 1982b). This text was the sole contribution she made to the debate. It used the *Conseil constitutionnel* decision as an opportunity to reassert the need for her ministry. In effect she accepted the decision of the court. The ban on the quota should have made the public aware of the problem. Hence political parties would be motivated to select more women. Roudy still believed that political will could close the gender gap in representation, and considered quotas to be acceptable only as a last resort. In this debate Roudy showed her preference for 'gender neutral' equality policies. As it neither advocated quotas nor gendered the debate, the ministry's activities were symbolic.

The debate had a significant impact on the policy sub-system. After 1982, the WPAs could no longer sponsor a bill on women's political representation. Thus the analysis of the second debates on the voting system is an opportunity to compare the WPA's actions in two different legal contexts and to assess the impact of the social movement on women's policy goals.

Women's movement characteristics

The first debate on the voting system was gendered not by the WPA but by the *Conseil constitutionnel*, which opened the debate but then immediately closed it again. The debate was a wasted opportunity. Activists did not succeed in putting forward an alternative frame for the issue. They missed the debate because they had little interest in the running of the institutions. French feminism was, in the 1980s, entering a stage of abeyance. Although the activists of women's movements did not agree with the Socialists on what a feminist policy should be, they were closer to the left than to the right. The election of François Mitterrand raised many hopes, but left most of them pending. The debate exemplifies the consequences for feminist activists of avoiding the public arena.

Policy environment

The main variable that explains the poor outcome of the policy process is the political culture. In the republican system, citizens are defined as a united and homogeneous body. Thus, the recognition of the sexed nature of candidates and therefore of citizens would have undermined this dogma. During the legislative debate, deputies showed that they feared the consequences of such a provision. They feared a law that might entail a system in which they would have to grant quotas to other groups of citizens as well. Above all, they feared a text that could jeopardise one of the main pillars of the system. They signalled their views by separating the amendment from the main PR reform, enabling quotas to be treated separately.

Debate 2: The change of electoral system for parliamentary elections, 1985

How the debate came to the public agenda

In 1985 the Socialists tried to complete their democratisation project by introducing PR at national level. But according to the right, this bill was part of a petty political strategy. The removal of the winner-takes-all system was seen by opponents as a way of minimising the expected losses of the Socialists in the National Assembly. The electoral timetable was a major pressure for the reform.

Dominant frame of debate

During the legislative debate, right-wing deputies defended the Gaullist legacy. They strongly opposed the reform. They argued that majority rule had ensured stable governments in the Fifth Republic, but PR would cause government instability as it had done in the Fourth Republic. Moreover, the reform aimed to prevent the incoming elected government from governing. The Socialists claimed their reform would strengthen the part played by all the parties in the political game. In the name of minorities, the left supported a reform that promised to improve their representation. At that time women were defined with 'other minorities'. Hence the reform argument prioritised the representation of different political ideologies.

Gendering the debate

The government and all the supporters of the bill claimed women were among the citizens who could benefit from the reform. Roudy supported the 1985 change as a substitute for a women's quota. No specific measure was included to improve women's representation, but the interest of women in the reform was invoked, hence the debate was explicitly gendered.

Policy outcome

The bill was passed in 1985 and the proportional system was first implemented in March 1986. While the change of the electoral system probably limited the success of the right, it did not prevent the first 'cohabitation' (of a prime minister and president from different political tendencies) nor did it provide a better representation for women. The proportion of women in the National Assembly remained around 5 per cent.[1]

Women's movement impact

In 1985, most feminist activists still regarded political institutions with contempt. Female politicians who had feminist sympathies demonstrated

---

[1] In June 1981, among the 491 deputies, there were 26 women. They represented 5.3 per cent of those elected. In March 1986, among the 577 deputies – in changing the electoral system, the reform also increased the number of deputies – there were 34 women, that is to say only 5.9 per cent. The new right-wing majority restored a permanent majoritarian electoral system for general elections on 22 October 1986.

their support for positive actions. Halimi exemplified this trend. In the Socialist Party, the group of women who advocated feminist goals had pressed for a women's quota in the party leadership some years previously. They adopted a clear stand against a policy that considered women as 'the immigrants from within' (Roudy 1982a: 207). They objected to a policy that grouped women's interests with those of minorities. In classifying women as a minority, the bill did not match the expressed feminist description of the problem.

The interest of women in the reform was mentioned but not questioned. Roudy was the only woman involved in the policy process. Later, in August 1985, a short debate followed the drawing up of the lists of candidates for the next election. In an article published in *Le Monde*, three members of the government, Edwige Avice, Édith Cresson and Yvette Roudy, complained about the low number of women on the Socialist lists (*Le Monde* 25 August 1985). Answering them in the same newspaper, Hélène Goldet, a Socialist activist, claimed that caring about sex on the political scene was stupid (Goldet 1985). By contrast, without openly giving her support to the ministers, Christiane Papon, a member of the RPR (*Rassemblement pour la République*, a Gaullist party) and also the president of a women's association *Femme-Avenir*, asked for more women on the lists and talked about quotas as a solution (Papon 1985). The short exchange of views demonstrated that the low number of women in the assemblies was not unanimously considered to be a problem. Although the exchange took place after the bill was passed, it reveals the lack of consensus and may help to explain why women did not get involved in the policy process. The silence of women during the debate ensured that the state did not respond to the women's movement.

Women's policy agency activities

The Minister of Women's Rights gave her support to PR. Roudy supported the bill but she did not really enter the debate. Activists, however, were either indifferent to the political representation issue or supporters of quotas, so the post-debate stand that Roudy took could not be considered to be supportive of (divided) feminist goals. In approving the bill in the name of women, she underlined the gendered consequences of the reform. Her contribution could have been the starting point of a real feminist approach to public debates. Instead she chose to avoid a gendered way of solving problems. Moreover she presented her point of view in a newspaper rather than in a political arena (Roudy 1985). In her article, she reasserted that the failure of the 1982 women's quota had been a missed opportunity.

She argued that the 'missed law' made the political leaderships aware of the problem. Her argument was that a gender-neutral approach to the issue could be relevant. This symbolic activity of the minister was more about supporting a government that was said to be on the road to ruin rather than being aimed at the improvement of women's political representation. In other words, Yvette Roudy entered the debate as a member of the government, not as a supporter of women.

Women's movement characteristics and policy environment

The absence of feminist concerns from the policy process can be linked to the decline of both the left and the women's movement. In the mid-1980s, disappointment with the record of the Socialist government became widespread, paving the way for the first period of cohabitation. In this difficult context the activists were less demanding and the movement continued to wane.

The 1986 election was a setback for women. By this time, Roudy understood her mistake. Talking about women on the Socialist candidates' slates, she asserted: 'We have been treated like doormats' (Frappat 1985). The experience marked a turning point as those who trusted in a gender-neutral approach began to regard the involvement of women in the policy process as crucial.

Debate 3: The parity reform, 1999–2000

How the debate came to the public agenda

At the end of the 1980s, several international institutions such as the UN, the Council of Europe, the European Commission and the OECD drew attention to the over-representation of men in political arenas. The idea of parity, defined as the equal representation of men and women in the assemblies, emerged from their deliberations. 'Parity' (*parité*) was a French word that corresponded with French political culture and values. As a result, it was more resonant in argument than English terms such as gender mainstreaming, a term not readily translatable into French. And while the notion of parity won a certain popularity, the term 'quotas' was rejected by the French public. As the implementation of quotas is obviously the main means to achieving parity, this observation may appear paradoxical. The explanation for this apparent contradiction lies in the different possible meanings of the word. While keeping difference in play in its implication that human nature is two-sided (made of men and women), the term parity also suggests equality between the sexes. Thus the idea of parity advances sexual differences as a basis for claiming equality. This combination of difference and equality allowed a wide range of women activists – feminist and non-feminist – as well as politicians to support the reform. The ambiguity of the word was an asset in the first part of the reform process. The term itself is politically significant. In a way, it worked as a Trojan horse for quotas.

Parity not only convinced but also revived the French feminist movement. Associations such as *Parité, Parité 2000* or *Elles aussi* were to further the reform process. In the 1990s, feminist groups and women's associations gathered together in two main networks – *Femmes pour la Parité* and *Demain la Parité* – to support the idea of parity. As French feminism has always been highly divided, it is important to underline that all of these activists supported the same goal. The development of a great, lively and united movement in favour of parity was the first factor that brought the reform into the public debate. The second was the strategy of the movement. The activists made good use of opportunities to raise the issue: they entered each debate on democratisation and above all in each electoral campaign to obtain promises from the political leaders. During the 1990s parity gave rise to political debate on three occasions.

In 1995, the disappointing results of the 1993 parliamentary elections and the Beijing International Conference on Women highlighted the need for reform. Presidential candidates were questioned on the issue. By then the gender gap in the assemblies was broadly considered to be a public problem. On 7 April, each candidate appeared before *Le Conseil national des femmes* to explain what he or she intended to do to improve women's political representation. Jacques Chirac, who promised only the implementation of incentives to nominate more women, was elected. The dissolution of the National Assembly in 1997 was an opportunity for both the Socialists and the parity activists. The Socialist Party campaigned as a progressive force and supported parity. Nearly 30 per cent of the Socialist candidates were women and the party leader, Lionel Jospin, promised a constitutional reform. But, once installed, the new government delayed reform. Agreements between right-wing candidates and far right-wing candidates during the 1998 local elections generated another debate on democracy. With most political leaders calling for a renewal of democracy, the parity activists were able to remind them that the improvement of democracy was also at stake in the parity reform. Accordingly, in December 1998, the bill to amend the constitution to allow parity was presented to the Assembly. In each of the three cases a wider debate on political representation permitted parity advocates to raise the issue of increasing women's presence.

Dominant frame of debate

The parity reform was introduced as a means of improving democracy. One of the first events that contributed to promote the idea of parity was a seminar organised by the Council of Europe in 1989. The seminar was reported by Élisabeth Sledziewski, and the report is considered a founding text on the issue of parity (Sledziewski 1992). In her report, Sledziewski discussed the need to ponder upon the modern doctrine of democracy. A democratic doctrine that ignored the existence of two sexes was not only unable to prevent discrimination, it was also 'unfinished'. Equality between men and women was as important as universal suffrage and the separation of powers. Sledziewski's framing of the issue was very effective in the way that parity was expressed as a means to *complete* the system. Although not all supporters of the reform developed such an argument, most claimed parity would improve democracy by restoring the balance of power between the two sexes.

Opponents of the reform invoked the republican system. Parity, they argued, was dangerous because it jeopardised the indifference to differences of French Universalism. Both sides concentrated on the expected effects of parity on the political system. Although the need to improve women's representation was unanimously acknowledged, there was major disagreement over the means. As the debate polarised, parity was considered by its advocates as a way to complete the regime and by its opponents as a way to destroy its foundations.

Gendering the debate

The starting point of the parity movement was a statement of failure: the equality of rights between the two sexes was unable to close the gender gap in political representation. In the process of gendering the political representation debates of the 1990s, the part played by women, including feminist activists and women involved in political life, was crucial. The supporters of parity referred to sex difference as if it were the primary human difference and, consequently, they introduced the reform as if this were obvious. If humanity is twofold – made of men and women – power must also be shared equally between the two sexes. Their argument made the formation of the assemblies appear unfair and, in so doing, paved the way for the reform. While activists called for positive action in the assemblies, their main goal, broadly defined, was to introduce an explicitly gendered approach to each public problem. For its supporters the parity debate was not only gendered, it was also a way to question the gendering of all public debates.

Despite the serious divisions between the supporters of parity and their opponents, the debate was framed in very general terms. For example, they did not really discuss the scale of differences in society, nor did they enter into a discussion of benefits or consequences in the debate. The generality of the debate concealed disagreements among supporters of the reform. It helped parity to advance on the agenda without really convincing public opinion.

Policy outcome

On 8 July 1999 two amendments to the constitution were adopted and, on 6 June 2000, a law implementing the principle of equal access of women and men to political mandates and functions was passed. The first amendment to the constitution read: 'The law promotes the equal access of women and men to political mandates and functions' and the second that: 'Political parties contribute to the implementation of this principle' ('Loi constitutionnelle n° 99–569 du 8 juillet 1999'). The provisions are the outcome of a compromise. Initially the proposal consisted only of the first amendment containing the word 'guarantee' instead of the word 'promote'. Under pressure from the Senate, the National Assembly changed the wording of the original amendment and also added the second. This compromise weakened the reform. The law and political parties are both responsible for its implementation.

The law establishes obligations and financial incentives ('Loi n° 2000–496 du 6 juin 2000'). The actual legal obligations for presenting women as candidates are established only for elections held under systems of PR in France: European, regional and municipal. The law requires political parties to present lists that alternate male and female candidates. If they do not comply, they are not allowed to register their list. However, at national level the election of the National Assembly and the president occur under plurality rules where, of course, no lists are presented. The device to ensure parity at national elections is financial incentives. Parties that fail to present equal proportions of female and male candidates lose part of their funding. They are not prevented from presenting their candidates. Financial incentives are less restrictive than legal obligations. Thus, the rules of the electoral game have narrowed the scope of the reform. Moreover, as all the provisions deal with candidates and not with the elected representatives, the law does not ensure parity in actual electoral results. To summarise, the more important an election, the less constraining are the provisions.

Women's movement impact

Activists played an important part in the policy process. However, as the supporters of parity had to cope with a strong opposition, the reform only partly achieved movement goals. Of the numerous militant actions during the decade, some had a greater impact than others. In 1992, three well-known activists, Françoise Gaspard, Claude Servan-Schreiber and Anne Le Gall, researcher, journalist and femocrat respectively, published a book entitled *Au pouvoir citoyennes! Liberté, Égalité, Parité*. The book brought the idea of parity to public opinion. The creation of the network of associations, *Femmes pour la Parité*, organised a round-table on the issue at the National Assembly, on 8 March 1993. Several months later, this network was behind the publication of the first petition for parity in *Le Monde*. The 'Manifesto of the 577 for a Parity Democracy' (*Le Monde* 1993) was signed by 289 women and 288 men – 577 is the number of deputies in the National Assembly. The women included politicians from each side. Roselyne Bachelot and Françoise Giroud were from the right; Huguette Bouchardeau and Yvette Roudy were from the left. There were also researchers such as Françoise Héritier and Michelle Perrot and activists such as Antoinette Fouque or Françoise Gaspard. In the shadow of parliamentary elections, another manifesto for parity made the front page of a news magazine in June 1996 (Barzach et al. 1996). In this text, ten women, from both the left and the right, advocated parity. In the mid-1990s, parity gave rise to many comments. A huge number of articles were published. For supporters, the articles of Sylviane Agacinski, a philosopher who was also Lionel Jospin's wife, led the debate (1996, 1999). Parity gave her the opportunity to come into the limelight and her articles showed the determination of the left to push the reform onto the agenda. On the opponents' side, the intellectual Élisabeth Badinter became the champion of the republican legacy (1999). Women led the debate.

In October 1995, the new right-wing government established the *Observatoire de la Parité entre les femmes et les hommes* ('Décret n° 95–1114 du 18 octobre 1995'). This agency was commissioned to question the gender gaps in all spheres of power and to suggest ways to reduce them. Although the *Observatoire* was only a consulting body it played a great part in shaping the reform. The *Observatoire* became an arena for the supporters of parity. It was led by Roselyne Bachelot, a right-wing woman who signed the first manifesto for parity, and Gisèle Halimi. Halimi was in charge of running the committee for parity in politics and wrote the report on the issue.[2] The consultation process involved the collection of data as well as seeking the views of experts. The experts included a number of feminist activists and supporters of quotas. Hence, while a wide range of political and ideological opinion was canvassed, the arguments of feminist activists were officially taken into account. In each category of experts, the *Observatoire* included at least one supporter of parity. Four jurists of the six consulted were in favour of a constitutional reform; one of them, Olivier Duhamel, had taken a clear public stand for parity. If Alain Finkielkraut voiced the argument of Élisabeth Badinter, other intellectuals and researchers such as Geneviève Fraisse, Michelle Perrot or Françoise Gaspard who supported the idea of parity were consulted. In addition to the representatives of the main political parties, three politicians, Michèle Barzach, Édith Cresson and Simone Veil, who had signed petitions in favour of parity, were also heard. In the category of 'women's associations', six groups were represented: *Choisir-la-Cause-des-femmes, Club parité 2000, Demain la parité, Parité, Parité-infos* and the *Union des femmes françaises*. All agreed the necessity to revise the constitution. Halimi's final report was pluralist in the sense that it considered a range of different ways to achieve parity, from mere incentives to legal constraints. Framed by lawyers and activists, in effect it was a plea for constitutional reform (Halimi 1999). The Minister of Justice, Élisabeth Guigou, presented the government bill to the National Assembly on 15 December 1998. Her speech paid tribute to all the women, from Olympe de Gouges to Yvette Roudy, who had played a part in the struggle for equal rights. She thanked activists, politicians and famous names, including Françoise Gaspard, Antoinette Fouque, Roselyne Bachelot, Gisèle Halimi, Simone Veil and Yvette Roudy. Thus the way she introduced the constitutional reform affirmed the involvement of women in the process (Journal officiel 1998).

The government bill encountered strong opposition in parliament. Under the pressure of senators, the first amendment was redrawn and the second amendment was also adopted. These changes limited the effectiveness and coverage of parity reform. In the Senate, opposition took the form of a coalition of key figures of the left – Robert Badinter was the most famous[3] – and the conservative right-wing majority. Against

---

[2] Originally, the *Observatoire* was divided into several committees. But it concentrated its efforts on the political arena.

[3] Constitutional lawyer, human rights activist, Robert Badinter has been a key figure of the Socialist Party. Minister of Justice under the first Socialist government in 1981, he initiated the abolition of the death penalty and remains famous for his involvement with the cause. He is the husband of Élisabeth Badinter.

them were the numerous associations and groups of activists who sought constitutional reform.

Activists lost control of the political process. The results of the recent elections are evidence that parity is yet to be achieved. Predictably women did better in municipal than in parliamentary elections. Equally predictably, municipal results were also disappointing. In the first municipal elections, legal obligations for parity only applied to elections held in towns with more than 3,500 inhabitants. As 34,000 of all the 36,000 French towns have populations less than 3,500, 94 per cent are excluded from the new parity stipulations: approximately 20 million of 56 million people in France, and a third of all city council representatives. In the 2001 municipal elections, political parties, public attention and the media focused on larger cities like Paris, Lyons or Marseilles not mentioning that smaller municipalities were not subject to parity requirements. The legal provisions of the parity reforms do not apply to the placement of women at the top of the list or in cabinet appointments. The 2001 municipal election results show near-parity between men and women council members.[4] However, women have not gained access to positions of power, either as mayors or as members of mayoral cabinets. Thus, the male-dominated party hierarchies have not been changed. Mayors gain office as a result of their positions at the top of electoral lists, and hence of the chain of command within their party, and mayoral cabinets follow from list positions. The elections made it clear that there is no shortage of women in politics; however, for the most part, the women who were recruited for the municipal elections were newcomers with little political experience. Indeed, many observers claim that predominantly male party leadership has purposefully avoided selecting experienced women politicians or women politicians with feminist records. In other words, candidate nominations of women were made to avoid challenging the real balance of power between men and women within the parties. Another important observation to be made about the impact of the parity reforms is that they apply only to the number of candidates, not the number of elected representatives. The logic of the law was to establish an obligation with regard to the input side of elections but not the actual outcome.

In the parliamentary elections, the percentage of women in the National Assembly did not rise substantially. Political parties preferred to lose a part of their public financing rather than field sufficient numbers

---

[4] In towns with fewer than 3,500 inhabitants, women represent 30.05 per cent of municipal councillors. In towns with more than 3,500 inhabitants, they represent 47.5 per cent of municipal councillors. When all the municipalities are considered together, women represent 33 per cent of councillors and 10.9 per cent of the mayors.

of women candidates.[5] Thus the reform did not restore the balance of power between the sexes in the assemblies, nor did it change political practices. Women became involved in the political process but quickly lost control over it. The debate on parity is a case of co-optation.

Women's policy agency activities

The creation of the *Observatoire de la Parité* may be considered as a first step towards the reform. During the 1990s, several agencies were, simultaneously or successively, in charge of women's rights. However, they were unable to act and were limited to expressions of the idea that women's representation had to be improved. They did not take a clear stand on the reform. In the speech she gave for the setting up of the *Observatoire*, Colette Codaccioni, the conservative minister in charge of women's rights, underlined the limited effects of the law (1995). She argued that only the evolution of political practices could bring about change. She appeared very doubtful about quotas. But, because two supporters of the parity reform were to take control of the new agency, her point of view did not carry much weight in the debate.

The *Observatoire* was a platform for the movement argument. Although Halimi's report gave a fair account of the different stands taken on the issue, its conclusion clearly took the part of the activists. Following the standard strategy of the parity activists, she first brought up the gender gap in the assemblies, framing her statement in terms of danger for the institutions. She then showed that the goodwill of the political leaderships could not achieve equality of political representation. She discussed how the leaders of the main political parties complained about the poor number of women in the assemblies but admitted that they did nothing to reduce the gender gap. The report paved the way for the defence of a constitutional reform. In December 1996, the first report was handed in to the prime minister. Although the right-wing government was slow to follow up this report, a debate was organised in March 1997 at the National Assembly. On that occasion Alain Juppé, the prime minister, claimed that women had to be initiated into political practices, and he

---

[5] The financial incentives introduced by the 2000 law are linked to the public financing of political parties. The public grant is made of two parts. The amount of the first part depends on the number of votes obtained at the first round of the parliamentary election. And, since 2000, if the gap between the number of candidates of each sex is above 2 per cent, this first part of the grant will be reduced by half the percentage of the gap. For example, if among all the candidates of a party, there are 60 per cent of men and 40 per cent of women, the grant will be reduced by $(60 - 40) \div 2 = 10$ per cent. The second part of the grant is proportional to the number of candidates elected at the National Assembly.

suggested the implementation of temporary incentives at the local and European levels. In the usual way of holding women responsible for their own exclusion, he meant that women had to make up for lost time, not that the political system should be questioned. The government feedback was disappointing. But the *Observatoire* report succeeded both in pushing the issue onto the parliamentary agenda and in gendering the legislative debate.

After the June 1997 elections, the *Observatoire*'s powers were extended. Instead of merely studying gender gaps, it was now able to assess the gendered consequences of bills and to put recommendations forward. Thus, the government gave the *Observatoire* the means to gender the debate.

At the same time, a new WPA was created. The *Délégation interministérielle aux droits des femmes* was given a cross-governmental mission: to co-ordinate and to boost the gender policy of the different ministries. Geneviève Fraisse was appointed as its head. Several months later she made a critical assessment of government policy in *Le Monde* (Fraisse 1998). Using clear examples, she showed that public problems were gendered and she called for gendered solutions. For instance, she underlined that most single-parent families were single-mother families; in the same way, she reminded people that women's unemployment rate was higher than men's. In each case, she called for the implementation of gender-sensitive policies.

The personalities in charge of the WPAs were strongly pro-parity; they had or took the means to take part in the debates, and they did gender these debates. Against resistance from the political institutions, both the *Observatoire* and the *Délégation* played a part in the policy process. From 1995, it was obvious that WPAs were insiders in the policy process.

Women's movement characteristics

The movement for parity reform renewed French feminism. At a time when fewer women said they were feminists, parity mobilised a range of activists. Moreover, because the idea of a reform was argued in terms of human nature and because the proposal also came from international institutions, parity gave a progressive image to feminist claims, once said to be old-fashioned. Some feminist and women's associations reworded their demands in parity terms. The involvement of feminist activists in the parity movement was a turning point in their relationship with political institutions. They managed not only to bind the presidential candidates to publicly made promises, they also worked in close collaboration with politicians. Activists began to behave in a reformist manner that contrasted with the past. They were united in support of the same goal: a constitutional reform. In the first part of the process, both their unity and their diversity were assets that helped to put the reform on the agenda. But, in the second part of the policy process, they were divided and did not design a real strategy; hence they lost control over the process.

Policy environment

It took a co-operative left-wing government to put the constitutional reform on the legislative agenda and to give the *Observatoire* the means of taking a real part in the process. The political swing to the left in 1997 was a key factor for the reform. But the limited implementation of the laws confirmed that the culture had not really changed. With no legal obligations applying to parliamentary elections, the gender gap in the National Assembly remains the same. At national level, the parity reform did not really improve French democracy. The republican system still needs to be effectively challenged (Baudino and Mazur 2001).

Conclusion

For the past twenty years, WPAs have been numerous and diverse. Some of them were short lived, such as the *Délégation interministérielle aux droits des femmes* or several *secrétariats d'État* (junior minister's offices). Others have seemed to outlive the swings of political majority, such as the *Observatoire*. Above all, despite the disappointing results of the parity reform, their activities have come to be more and more in line with movement objectives. Two factors can be put forward to explain why the institutions and the activists have come closer. First, parity was a turning point in the objectives of feminists. Where once they avoided the political arena, now activists called for the improvement of women's political participation. Political representation has become a priority. Second, the spread of the gender mainstreaming approach in Europe slowly pushed the institutions to take gender differences into account. The discourse of parity was an important factor in this process. Since the late 1990s, the naming and the missions of WPAs have been reframed in parity terms. Created in 2000, the *Comité de pilotage pour l'égal accès des femmes et des hommes aux emplois supérieurs des fonctions publiques* has to promote parity at the highest level of the civil service. In their first report, its members suggested the implementation of positive action in the recruitment of civil servants. In the new right-wing government formed in June 2002, Nicole Ameline is in charge of parity and equal opportunity at work; her post is titled the *ministre déléguée à la parité et à l'égalité professionnelle* (Junior Minister for Parity and Professional Equality).

While early WPAs could not play a major part in the reform processes dealing with political representation, the parity debate enabled them to gender their missions and may perhaps in the near future enable them to gender policy.

References

Agacinski-Jospin, Sylviane 1996, 'Citoyennes, encore un effort . . . ', *Le Monde*, 18 June

Agacinski, Sylviane 1999, 'Contre l'effacement des sexes', *Le Monde*, 6 February

Badinter, Élisabeth 1999, 'La parité est une régression', *L'Événement*, 4 February

Barzach, Michèle, Frédérique Bredin, Édith Cresson, Hélène Gisserot, Catherine Lalumière, Véronique Neiertz, Monique Pelletier, Yvette Roudy, Catherine Tasca, and Simone Veil 1996, 'Le manifeste des dix pour la parité', *L'Express*, 6 June

Baudino, Claudie 2000, 'La cause des femmes à l'épreuve de son institutionnalisation', *Revue Politix* 51: 81–112

Baudino, Claudie and Amy G. Mazur 2001, 'Le genre gâché. La féminisation de l'action publique', in *'Repérages du politique' Revue Espace-Temps. Les Cahiers*, 76/77: 68–80

Codaccioni, Colette 1995, 'Discours prononcé par Madame Colette Codaccioni, Ministre de la solidarité entre les générations lors de l'installation de l'Observatoire de la Parité', *Jeudi* 19 October: 6

Débats parlementaires 1982, Compte rendu intégral, séance du 27 juillet 1982, *Journal officiel* du 28 juillet 1982, p. 4899

'Décision n° 82–146 du 18 novembre 1982', *Journal officiel, Lois et décrets* 269, 19 November 1982, pp. 3475–6

'Décret n° 95–1114 du 18 octobre 1995 portant création d'un Observatoire de la parité entre les femmes et les hommes', *Journal officiel, Lois et décrets* 244, 19 October 1995, p. 15,249

Fraisse, Geneviève (Propos recueillis par Michèle Aulagnon) 1998, 'Une femme en colère', *Le Monde*, 7–8 June

Frappat, Bruno 1985, 'Marge', *Le Monde*, 11 July

Gaspard, Françoise, Claude Servan-Schreiber, and Anne Le Gall 1992, *Au pouvoir citoyennes! Liberté, Egalité, Parité*, Paris: Seuil

Goldet, Hélène 1985, 'Une ânerie', *Le Monde*, 25–26 August

Halimi, Gisèle 1982, 'Des municipales pour les hommes?', *Le Monde*, 27 July 1999, *La parité dans la vie politique*, preface by Lionel Jospin, *Pais:* La Documentation française

Jenson, Jane and Mariette Sineau 1995, 'Mitterrand et les Françaises. Un rendez-vous manqué', *Presses de la Fondation Nationale des Sciences Politiques*

Journal officiel 1998, Assemblée nationale, compte rendu intégral des séances du mardi 15 décembre, n°118 AN, p. 10,495

'Loi n° 2000–496 du 6 juin 2000 tendant à favoriser l'égal accès des femmes et des hommes aux mandats électoraux et fonctions électives', *Journal officiel de la République française*, 7 June 2000, pp. 8560–2

'Loi constitutionnelle n° 99–569 du 8 juillet 1999 relative à l'égalité entre les femmes et les hommes', *Journal officiel de la République française*, 9 July 1999, p. 10,175

Loschak, Danièle 1983, 'Les hommes politiques, les "sages" (?) . . . et les femmes (à propos de la décision du Conseil constitutionnel du 18 novembre 1982)', *Droit social* (February): 131–7

Martin, Jacqueline (ed.) 1998, *La Parité, enjeux et mise en oeuvre*, Toulouse: PUM

Le Monde 1993, 'Manifeste des 577 pour une démocratie paritaire', À l'initiative du Réseau Femmes pour la Parité, *Le Monde*, 10 November

Montebourg, Arnaud 2000, *La machine à trahir. Rapport sur le délabrement de nos institutions*, Paris: Denoël

Mossuz-Lavau, Janine 1998, *Femmes/hommes pour la parité*, La bibliothèque du citoyen Paris: Presses de la Fondation Nationale des Sciences Politiques

Papon, Christiane 1985, 'Mais où sont-elles donc?', *Le Monde*, 25–26 August.

Roudy, Yvette 1982a, *La femme en marge*, preface by François Mitterrand, La rose au poing Paris: Flammarion

  1982b, 'La "part qui revient à chacun"', *Le Monde*, 24 November

  1985, 'La proportionnelle: une chance pour les femmes. La fin d'un anachronisme', *Le Monde*, 16 April

Sledziewski, Élisabeth 1992, 'Les idéaux démocratiques et les droits des femmes', *La Démocratie paritaire – Quarante années d'activité du Conseil de l'Europe*, Actes du séminaire, Strasbourg, 6–7 November 1989, Strasbarg: Les éditions du Conseil de l'Europe, pp. 17–27

Vedel, Georges 1979, 'Les 20 per cent de femmes et la Constitution', *Le Monde*, 3 February

6   WPAs and political representation in Germany

Lynn Kamenitsa and Brigitte Geissel

Introduction

Since its 1949 founding, the political system of the Federal Republic of Germany (FRG) has rested firmly on the principle of representative democracy. The framers of the German constitution, fearing supposed anti-democratic popular tendencies, designed moderating institutions between the people and the exercise of power. Political parties became the most important of these. Political scientists have characterised the FRG as a 'party-state' in which parties make all of the most important political decisions. The German constitution, the Basic Law, explicitly assigns them the role of 'forming the political will of the people' (Conradt 1993: 84–85). Parties control access to the legislatures at all levels, in terms of both candidate selection and group access to the policy-making process. Strict party discipline, especially at the federal level, assures party dominance.

Germany has a neo-corporatist system in which interests are organised and articulated in a structured fashion. Interest groups must have state recognition to obtain formal representation in the policy process (Dalton 1993: 237, 271). Interest representation has traditionally been channelled through four major interest alignments (mainly business and labour, less crucially agriculture and churches), each with direct access to the parties and government bureaucracies. Groups outside of these four categories have had difficulty gaining access to policy channels (see Conradt 1993: 109).

Women's political representation in Germany has traditionally lagged behind some other western European countries, but began to catch up in the 1990s. Today women are represented at a rate above the European Union average. At the federal level, women comprised fewer than 10 per cent of elected legislators in the early 1980s, but this number climbed to 20 per cent in 1990, 30.9 per cent in 1998 and 33 per cent in 2002 (Penrose and Geissel 2001: 98). Women's representation in federal-level executive offices has increased as well. Before 1987 no more than two women served as ministers in a given cabinet. Three to five women served in each subsequent cabinet and in 2003 five of twelve ministers were women. Women have also made great strides in elective office at the state level, though these vary significantly by region. The percentage of women in state parliaments grew from about 10 per cent in 1984 to roughly 30 per cent by 2000 (Hoecker 1998; Penrose and Geissel 2001: 198). The lowest rates of women's representation (less than 22 per cent) were found in the two most southern and politically conservative states (Bavaria and Baden-Württemberg), while the highest (more than 35 per cent) were concentrated in the north-western states, along with Saarland and Berlin. In other states, including all of the eastern states, women held roughly 30 per cent of the seats (see Penrose and Geissel 2001: 198–200). On the local level the percentage of women in the local representative bodies climbed from 13 per cent in the early 1980s to 25 per cent in the middle of the 1990s, with substantial differences between the parties. The conservative parties, the Christian Democratic Union (CDU) and the Free Democratic Party (FDP), had the lowest percentages of women at 19.6 per cent and 18.4 per cent respectively; the Greens at 40.6 per cent and the Party of Democratic Socialism (PDS) at 39.4 per cent had the highest (Penrose and Geissel 2001: 197). There are also differences in the presence of women on the political parties' governing boards (*Bundesparteivorstand*). Women hold at least 50 per cent of the board seats in the parties of the left, including the Social Democratic Party (SPD), the Greens and the PDS, and between 24 per cent and 33 per cent in the conservative parties, the CDU, the FDP and the Christian Social Union (CSU) (Penrose and Geissel 2001: 194).[1] Altogether, women have made substantial progress in gaining representation in the political arena since the 1980s, but significant differences between the parties, regions and states (*Länder*) remain.

Selection of debates

Policy-making institutions

Major decisions about political representation are made at the federal level. The lower house of parliament, the *Bundestag*, passes legislation under the guidance of the federal government. The upper house, the *Bundesrat*, must also approve certain laws. Parties play a central role in the process by determining the legislative agenda and content in advance

---

[1] The CSU is the Bavarian affiliate of the CDU. At the federal level, they function as a single party, though they occasionally differ in their stance on specific policy measures.

of parliamentary action. Some policy about political representation is made at the state (*Land*) or local level. If the constitutionality of policy is challenged, the courts, particularly the Federal Constitutional Court, may play a role.

Universe of policy debates

In the quarter century since the establishment of the first women's policy agencies (WPAs), political representation debates have clustered around particular issues. Many key debates have taken place within the political parties, reflecting their importance in this policy area. The emergence of the Green Party in the 1970s helped spawn party debates about internal democracy and group representation within party organs and on electoral lists. The most important of these included debates about gender quotas in the Greens in 1986, the SPD in 1988, the PDS in 1990, and in the CDU in 1994–5. In the FDP quota rules were never discussed seriously.

Debates about representation in civil and public service positions began with a series of state-level equality laws in the 1980s that included provisions for quotas or affirmative action. The subsequent national debate resulted in new equal rights legislation and a modification of the constitution in 1994.

The events of 1989 and German unification ushered in a decade of discussion about political representation in the Federal Republic. The experience of East German opposition groups with a Round Table,[2] the possibility of a new constitution, and the incorporation of new voters and states all put pressures on the political system. Key debates concerned direct democracy (resulting in more rights to referenda and initiatives in several *Länder*), direct election of executives (resulting in the direct election of mayors in several *Länder*), and opening the neo-corporatist party-dominated system to effect broader representation of interests and civil society. A parallel SPD debate in the early 1990s resulted in a policy allowing party members, rather than party elites, to select the candidate for chancellor.

The election of Chancellor Gerhard Schröder's government in 1998 generated still more political representation debates. The SPD, having been out of power for nearly two decades, and the Alliance90/Greens,

---

[2] The Round Table was set up in the German Democratic Republic in late 1989 as communist control was waning. Delegates from fledgling opposition groups and the church met with representatives of the established political system to determine the direction of future political development, set election dates, etc.

combining the western Green Party and the remnants of the 1989 eastern movements, formed a coalition committed to opening the German political system. The government's efforts to reform the neo-corporatist system in favour of a more inclusive representation of interests spawned new legislative proposals and new debates about political representation in Germany.

Selection of debates

In this chapter, we examine three debates that have taken place since the formation of the German WPAs in the late 1970s. The first is the SPD's 1980s debate about a quota system for electoral lists. It provides an example of party-level decision-making in the German party state. It further represents two decades' worth of debates about who can stand for election, a central political representation issue in any democracy. The second debate, which deals with the federal equality law passed in 1994, is an example of a legislative policy debate at the federal level that illustrates the importance of political parties and the federal bureaucracies in policy-making. The third debate concerns the citizenship and, in turn, voting rights of foreign residents in Germany. This legislation, passed in 1999, was an important component of the Schröder administration's new emphasis on broadening German democracy. Two of the political representation debates deal explicitly with gender, though they are not necessarily gendered debates, while the third is not explicitly about gender.

Debate 1: Quota rules in the Social Democratic Party of Germany, 1977–1988

How the debate came to the public agenda

While some governments have imposed quota rules for political representation (e.g. Belgium), in Germany some political *parties* have decided to adopt quota rules.[3] Until the 1970s quota rules were hardly discussed in Germany. Debates about the need to increase women's political representation came to prominence with the rise of the Green Party, the emergence of the new women's movement, and the public mood on

---

[3] Inner-party quota rules mean that approximately equal numbers of men and women are represented on the party lists. The so-called zipper system, common in the FRG, alternates men's and women's names on the list. Thus, regardless of how many seats the party wins, half will go to women.

equality of the sexes. Since its inception in 1980, the Green Party has had a fifty-fifty rule where half of all candidates on electoral lists are female. Quota rules were fixed in their party statute in 1986. The Social Democrats adopted a 40 per cent quota rule in 1988. The PDS introduced a 50 per cent quota rule at its founding in 1990. The CDU and the FDP initially rejected any quota regulations, though the CDU eventually introduced a soft quota (*Quoren*) in the mid-1990s. The debate within the SPD will be discussed.

The support of women, equality between the sexes and women's representation has always been a part of the SPD's programme, but the reality looked somewhat different. For example, women comprised only 5.4 per cent of the SPD parliamentary caucus (*Fraktion*) in the *Bundestag* in 1972. Women within the SPD, especially the party's women's commission, the *Arbeitsgemeinschaft Sozialdemokratischer Frauen* (ASF),[4] had demanded a better representation of women for decades. Yet the majority of the ASF rejected quota rules until the mid-1980s (Weis 1995) and favoured other ways of increasing women's representation. Even at an ASF federal conference (*Bundeskonferenz*) in 1977 most members endorsed the view that quota rules were not necessary, because 'good politicians', be they men or women, would make their way up through the party machinery by performing well. The conference did, however, issue a statement with several non-binding demands and proposed correctives regarding the equality of the sexes. As it turned out these efforts to increase women's representation were hardly successful. The ASF eventually endorsed a quota rule in 1985 and pressed the topic on the SPD agenda. Other political realities also affected the agenda setting. The SPD had been losing votes throughout the 1980s. The trend was particularly evident in *Bundestag* elections, where the party lost large numbers of seats in both 1983 and 1987. In contrast, the Green Party, having successfully implemented a quota rule, continued to gain votes in this period.

Dominant frame of debate

The dominant frame used by actors on all sides concerned 'equality' and 'quality'. The German SPD is traditionally a party concerned with *equality* – at least in the party programme. Thus the feminist discourse on gender equality was perfectly compatible with the programmatic

---

[4] The ASF can be considered a quasi-WPA because it is a policy-making body in a party. It has the capacity to impact party policy-making directly and government policy-making through its party influence. Typically, several female members of parliament or government are actively involved in the ASF.

discourse on equality between human beings and the conviction that no group in society should be excluded from political representation. When the ASF initiated the discourse on quota rules, several 'male allies' began to support the idea.

Other debate participants referred to *quality* – its enhancement or preservation – as a central goal of their desired policy. They expressed either fear that 'quota rules hinder quality' or hope that 'quota rules improve quality'. Opponents declared that quota rules would only lead to a lack of quality in politics because they would undermine performance as the criterion for advancement. If gender were a criterion, people would be chosen who do not possess the necessary skills and abilities to be a politician and the quality of politics would deteriorate. Proponents argued that female politicians would enhance the quality of policy-making and political outcomes. These arguments were compatible with the dominant discourse within the SPD. As a party with its main tradition in the working-class movement, the argument that 'good politics' and 'good governance' require the representation of all groups within society, including women, was fully compatible with social democratic beliefs. In sum, while the debate shifted significantly over time, the dominant frame of 'equality' and 'quality' remained intact.

Gendering the debate

During the 1980s the debate on quota rules within the SPD became gendered in two ways. First, actors discussed whether having more women in office would make a difference to politics ('quality'). Inge Wettig Danielmeier, the ASF chair, and Hans Jochen Vogel, chair of the Equal Rights Commission of the SPD, argued in their speech at the 1988 SPD meeting that female politicians 'will change our party. They will also change politics (*die Politik*) ... and these changes are a tremendous opportunity' (*Sozialdemokratischer Informationsdienst* 1988). One argument was premised on an assumption that women and men have different interests, attitudes and experience. Quota proponents stressed that women live in different realms from men and that it is mostly women who have to combine family work and employment. They argued, in turn, that women – more often than their male colleagues – put topics related to the lives of women on the political agenda, thus leading to more equal policy outcomes (see Meyer 1997; Geissel 1999: 194).

Second, the debate increasingly focused on quota rules as a means of supporting women in the party and in politics ('equality'). Proponents argued that women should have the same possibilities and political opportunities as men, because they had experienced discrimination for such a long time.[5]

These arguments, put forth largely by the ASF, became central ones in the SPD quota debate of the 1980s. This gendering was clearly feminist in so far as it emphasised women's participation, importance, contributions and equality.

Opponents of quota rules resisted this gendering. They predicted that every special interest group might demand its own quota rules and thus contribute to the deterioration of politics. Opponents did not focus on gender in their official statements. Rather they put their concerns about recruiting mechanisms leading to quality and 'good politics' at the centre of their arguments.

To sum up, proponents gendered the debate by discussing quota rules in the context of 'under-representation of women', framing it with the idea of 'enhancing the quality of politics'. The framing of the opponents did not focus on gender, but rather on quality. It was, however, the gendered arguments of the proponents that ultimately won over a majority of the SPD policy-makers.

Policy outcome

The SPD passed the ASF proposal on quota rules in 1988 at the SPD conference (*Parteitag*) with an overwhelming majority (87 per cent) of conference delegates voting for it. These quota rules applied to all positions and mandates elected from lists. By 1993, 40 per cent of all internal SPD positions were to be held by women. By 1998, the same percentage of public SPD mandates were to be held by women. Thus, although quota rules were not implemented perfectly, one of the targets of the ASF was achieved.

Quota rules were certainly an important contributing factor to the subsequent increase in women's representation in legislatures at all levels of government and within the SPD. Whereas in the early 1980s 15 per cent of the local SPD politicians (members of the representative bodies) were female, that figure had increased to 29 per cent by the middle of the 1990s (Penrose and Geissel 2001: 197). In state parliaments the proportion of women in SPD delegations reached an average of roughly 35 per cent in 2000, with substantial differences between the states. The highest percentage was in Schleswig-Holstein at nearly 50 per cent and the lowest in Baden-Württemberg at 16.7 per cent (Penrose and Geissel 2001: 198).

---

[5] One strategic argument claimed that quota rules would attract women to join and vote for the SPD.

On the board of the SPD (*Bundesvorstand*) more than 50 per cent of members were women by the turn of the century. In the *Bundestag* women comprised 9.8 per cent of all members and 10.4 per cent of SPD members in the mid-1980s. By the early 1990s, those numbers had risen to 20.5 per cent and 27.2 per cent respectively. In the *Bundestag* elected in 2002, women comprised 32.8 per cent of all members and 37.8 per cent of SPD members.

Women's movement impact

The policy adopted coincided with the women's movement goals as articulated by the ASF. Women from that organisation were prominent and central players in the policy process. In all phases of the decision-making – from the agenda setting to the implementation – they were actively pushing the process. They took part in party meetings and conferences, as delegates of the ASF or as normal party members, and forced the party to act on the issue. The movement's impact can therefore be classified as dual response.

Women's policy agency activities

During the last few years of this debate, the federal WPA, the Ministry for Health, Family, Women and Youth, was a large, national ministry that was cross-sectional in scope. Although the minister was a political appointment from the conservative CDU during this period, she was moderately feminist on many issues. The SPD quota rule issue was clearly outside the mandate of the WPA. Given the fact that the federal WPA was not controlled by the SPD during this internal SPD debate, it is not surprising that the WPA made no effort to gender this debate, nor did it advocate feminist goals in the process. Nevertheless the ministry did not work against the efforts of the ASF feminists. The agency's activities thus fall into the symbolic category of the RNGS model.

The ASF functioned as a quasi-WPA in this debate in so far as it was a women's organisation that influenced party policy-making. By advocating women's movement goals and successfully gendering the debate, it played an insider role in this debate.

Women's movement characteristics

During the debate period, the West German women's movement was in a stage of growth, but was fragmented. The core of the West German movement, which originated in the 1970s abortion rights movement, consisted largely of autonomous groups focused on local women's projects and eschewed participation in 'men's' institutions (Ferree 1987). By the late 1970s, a separate group of women, referred to here as mainstream feminists, rejected the autonomous feminists' strategy and instead tried to influence public policy by working within political parties, trade unions, traditional women's organisations and state bureaucracies (Rosenberg 1996). These two movement branches had ideological and organisational disagreements with each other, with feminists from the Green Party, and with eastern German feminists after 1989.[6] Thus 'the' movement could not speak with a single voice on any issue.

The ASF women typified the mainstream branch of the women's movement. The ASF, having formed during the movement's heyday in the early 1970s, is the most important and relevant part of the women's movement for this debate. As an organisation within the SPD, it was clearly very close to the political left. Indeed, during this period the ASF had become a strong section with a large amount of influence on the SPD sub-system.

The fragmented nature of the movement makes it difficult to determine the priority of the issue. In the 1980s feminists still debated whether women and especially feminists should participate in 'male' political institutions. The autonomous part of the women's movement was not directly involved in internal party debates on quota rules. The mainstream feminists, who were interested in women's representation within parties, supported the idea. Thus, the issue was a high priority for the segment of the movement discussed here and of low priority for the autonomous part of the movement.

The counter-movement in the SPD was strong at the beginning, but it changed during the debate. It became less active in arguing against quota rules and finally became weaker than the feminist movement.

Policy environment

The SPD itself is the relevant policy sub-system for this debate. The policy environment in the SPD can be described as moderately closed. The SPD has a long history of supporting equal rights. In turn, the party programme maintains that the decision-making process is accessible to a

---

[6] On the 1970s and 1980s see Altbach (1984); Kolinsky (1988); Maier and Oubaid (1987: 38–40); Brox-Brochot (1984). On the emergence of the eastern movement and east–west tensions see Kamenitsa (1993, 1997); Kenawi (1995); Rosenberg (1996); Chamberlayne (1995); Ferree (1995b); Kiechle (1991).

wide range of party members, not only to a few. Therefore, the women's section and sections of other 'minorities' within the party can at least claim to take part in the decision process. In reality, though, the elite of the SPD had been purely male for decades. The official commitment to openness and equality, however, enabled female party members to criticise the discrepancy and argue for more female representation.

During the early years of this debate, an SPD and FDP coalition governed the FRG. After 1982 the SPD was the opposition to a CDU and FDP coalition. So, for the key years of this policy debate, a party of the right controlled both the executive and legislative branches.

Debate 2: Second Federal Equal Rights Law, 1989–1994

How the debate came to the public agenda

Since the 1970s, several German *Länder* debated equality laws dealing with women's political representation, primarily through affirmative action in civil and public service jobs.[7] In the early 1990s the debate reached the federal level, resulting in the 1994 Second Federal Equal Rights Law and a modification of the Basic Law. The federal women's ministry spearheaded this policy process, which resulted in a national public debate about women's political representation.

This policy debate has its origins in several places. The collapse of communism in the German Democratic Republic (GDR, East Germany) and German unification raised the issue of constitutional reform, because the Basic Law provided for its own revision in the event of unification. The unification treaty focused attention on gender and women by stipulating the need for additional measures to ensure gender equality in the new Germany (*Vertrag* 1990). In May 1990, the *Bundestag* requested a study of the status of women on public governing bodies that played a role in federal decision-making (i.e. governmental and quasi-governmental commissions or advisory boards). The resulting 1991 report revealed that women held only 7.2 per cent of positions on such bodies. Finally, unification itself raised questions about women's status in Germany. Compared with women in the FRG, women in the GDR were employed at much higher rates, had more formal legal rights vis-à-vis men, enjoyed more state affirmative action programmes in education and the workplace, and received many social welfare benefits designed to help them combine employment and family duties. Unification threatened to

---

[7] For an overview of equality policy issues in Germany, see Nassmacher (1993) and Berghahn (1993).

remove many of these rights and benefits, including the right to legal abortion. All of these issues helped place gender equality on the political agenda in the early 1990s.

Dominant frame of debate

All parties in this debate agreed on the basic problems: women held few positions in the public sector and fewer positions of authority in the public and private sectors, they lacked support for combining employment and family, and the constitutional promise of equality of rights was not a reality. There was less agreement about who was to blame for this situation. Most parties did not assign blame explicitly. Advocates of a larger state role implied that the state had not done enough to make equal rights a reality. Opponents of an expanded state role implied, vaguely, that individuals were responsible for discriminating or making personal choices that led to their advantaged or disadvantaged status.

Disagreements about proposed solutions centred around two issues. The first was whether a statement about the state's obligation to effect equal rights belonged in the constitution. Supporters argued that only inclusion in the constitution would indicate the seriousness of gender equality, demonstrate the state's responsibility for it, and protect the commitment from reversal by future governments. Supporters included the SPD, the PDS, Alliance90/Greens, women in the CDU and FDP, and many extra-governmental organisations including the trade unions. Opponents, including many in the liberal FDP, believed that proclamations about state policy goals did not belong in the constitution at all. They advocated writing and enforcing gender-neutral laws to effect equality and discourage discrimination. Many in the leadership and *Bundestag* caucus of the CDU/CSU simply argued that a constitutional statement was unnecessary given existing equality laws.

The second area of disagreement concerned the so-called compensation clause. This referred to measures designed to remedy – or compensate women for – past and existing discrimination. These ranged from vague affirmative action goals to the inclusion of gender preferences in hiring and appointments. The latter, usually labeled 'quota rules', were a hot topic in the debate. Compensation clause supporters wanted constitutional protection for compensatory gender preference laws, so they could not be construed as discrimination against men and thus violations of the Basic Law's prohibition against sex-based discrimination (Section 3, Article 3).[8]

---

[8] They were particularly concerned about several state equality laws that were being challenged in court.

The CDU/CSU opposed a compensation clause, although many CDU women and the party women's organisation supported some version of it. All other parties except the FDP supported some version of a compensation clause.

Gendering the debate

All parties engaged in gendering this policy debate. The major debate participants shared two assumptions. First, that widespread discrimination against women in Germany existed and was related to inequality between women and men. The more feminist actors, including party women and women's groups, women's movement groups and the trade unions, further looked at the underlying causes of systemic discrimination (e.g. traditional gender roles, the division of household labour).

A second common assumption was that the unification treaty's call for improving conditions for the combination of career and family was, de facto, a women's issue. Most debate participants, even those from conservative parties, discussed women's traditional roles in family life, especially time taken off from employment to raise children, as a source of women's disadvantaged position in society. Only the Women's Minister, Angela Merkel (CDU), gendered the career and family issue as one concerning women *and* men.

The main divergence of gendering concerned the solutions to women's disadvantaged status. Supporters of gender preferences and/or a compensation clause gendered the debate as being exclusively about women's disadvantages and discrimination against them. Opponents of 'quotas' and a compensation clause gendered the debate in a different way, arguing that such measures were gender discrimination against men.

Policy outcome

This debate resulted in two policy outcomes related to women's political representation. First, a modification of the Basic Law (Section 2, Article 3) declared that women and men deserve equality of rights and that the state is committed to promoting equal rights and working towards removing disadvantages. Second, the new Equal Rights Law of 1994, and, more specifically, its Article 11, dealt with representatives on governing bodies in Germany that play a role in federal decision-making. This article requires organisations nominating candidates for positions on such bodies to name a qualified man and a qualified woman for each position until parity is reached. If a qualified representative of each sex is not named, the rationale must be justified in writing.

Women's movement impact

This policy did not coincide with feminist goals. It did meet one basic goal, namely getting the constitution amended to specify some state obligation to realise gender equality, but the final language was weaker and more vague than that advocated by various feminist participants. More importantly, the changes excluded another basic feminist goal: a compensation clause. Many feminists, especially in the opposition parties and trade unions, were also critical of the Equal Rights Law for its narrow coverage (mainly of women in civil service jobs) and lack of meaningful sanctions for non-compliance with new rules, like the double-naming in Article 11 (see Jansen 1994; 'Neues Gesetz' 1994).

Women were active participants in this policy process and received significant media attention. These included parties' spokespersons on women and politics, individual politicians, and leaders of parties' women's organisations. Participation was not limited to feminists, but also included women from the conservative parties. The CDU/CSU women's parliamentary caucus and the Women's Minister advocated a compensation clause even in the face of opposition by the CDU/CSU leadership (*Frankfurter Allgemeine Zeitung* 17 March 1993). The CDU women's organisation was an important impetus for the equality law and constitutional changes throughout the process. The issue even spawned a broad, intra-party women's coalition in early 1993, when the constitutional changes confronted a parliamentary obstacle (*Frankfurter Rundschau* 4 March 1993). Coalition members spanned the spectrum from the CDU to Alliance90/Greens, including women from parties, unions, academia, media, civil rights groups and women's organisations. They lobbied publicly in favour of the constitutional expansion. Several members, including *Bundestag* president Rita Süssmuth (CDU), used it as a forum to call for a compensation clause as well.

In sum, women were very much involved and accepted as important legitimate actors in the debate. The policy content did not, however, coincide with movement goals. According to the RNGS model, the policy outcome was co-optation.

Women's policy agency activities

In the 1970s, the federal WPA originated within the Ministry for Health, Family and Youth (*Jahresbericht* 1979). 'Women' was added to the ministry's title when Süssmuth (CDU), a 'very visible spokesperson on women's policy issues', was appointed to head it in 1986 (see Ferree 1995a: 99). After a cabinet reorganisation split the ministry in

1991, the Ministry for Women and Youth (BMFJ) became a middle-level ministry in terms of administrative capacity. Its portfolio is cross-sectional, dealing with women's affairs broadly conceived. The issues of gender equality, women's employment, sexual harassment, and the combination of career and family placed this debate squarely within the mandate of the BMFJ.

The minister is a political appointment. Most staff, however, are civil servants, including many femocrats. They have some influence in shaping ministry proposals and positions, despite being bound to carry out the minister's directives. The minister during this debate, Angela Merkel, was a young, East German protégée of Chancellor Kohl, chosen largely to give the government an eastern and female face during the controversial post-unification abortion debates. She was able to act as a feminist minister in the equality debate, in part, because the government was so focused on the abortion debate, where she had little political room to advocate for women (Kamenitsa 2001).

The ministry under Merkel clearly worked to gender the debate. In speeches, press releases, newspaper articles, interviews and drafts of legislation, Merkel repeatedly emphasised discrimination against women and women's under-representation in decision-making positions; criticised the state for failing to realise the constitutional promise of gender equality; advocated measures to help women and men combine careers and family; and argued for more state recognition of women's economic contributions through household labor (see BMFJ 1993; Merkel 1993; *Frankfurter Rundschau* 15 January 1993). Media coverage and legislative transcripts reveal Merkel's influence in shaping this debate. Although not all of her gendering and policy preferences were successful, she played a central role in framing this debate in the media, in her party and in the government.

Although feminists criticised Merkel and her drafts of legislation, she did advocate movement goals throughout the process, most fundamentally an expansion of the constitutional equality clause. She initially advocated a compensation clause, but backed away when that proposal threatened to stop all CDU/CSU discussion of equality law reforms (*Frankfurter Allgemeine Zeitung* 17 March 1993). The government and CDU/CSU likewise rejected other state measures she advocated to improve women's status (see *Frankfurter Rundschau* 15 January 1993). Partisan political realities prohibited her from advocating any quota rules and from presenting stronger versions of feminists' goals in draft legislation.

In sum, Merkel's BMFJ advocated movement goals and gendered the policy debate. This makes the WPA an insider in this debate.

Women's movement characteristics

The German women's movement in the 1990s is best characterised as fragmented and in decline. The movement was close to the traditional political left during this debate. Although many mainstream feminists were active in the SPD, the movement as such had long been suspicious of ties to such male-dominated institutions. Individual feminists played important roles in the Green Party, the far-left PDS and Alliance90. Yet none of these groups was central to German politics during this debate and movement relationships with each were fraught with tension.

Movement fragmentation again makes it difficult to assess prioritisation. Throughout much of the 1980s, the autonomous women's movement seemed 'strangely indifferent' towards equality politics in general (Jansen 1995). Mainstream feminists, however, emphasised the utility of equality and anti-discrimination laws. Some eastern feminists, particularly those on Berlin's Women's Political Round Table, championed the inclusion of women's and gender issues in the constitutional reform process (see Arbeitskreis Verfassung 1992). Indeed, during the final months of this debate, feminists from various parties and some independent organisations showed an unusual degree of cohesion around this particular issue, even organising joint demonstrations in support of a constitutional change. For most feminists, however, the priority in the early 1990s was new abortion legislation. As a result, the equality debate was only a moderate movement priority at this time.

Potentially strong counter-movement forces were only moderately strong in this policy debate. Associations of employers and entrepreneurs opposed the proposed legislative and constitutional changes, arguing that these would decrease competitiveness, be expensive and limit growth opportunities (see *Frankfurter Rundschau* 11 March 1994, 15 January 1993). In Germany's neo-corporatist political structure, such groups have direct access to elected officials and even have their own, recognised representatives in the legislature. In this case, they influenced the position of the pro-business FDP, but did little more to shape this debate.

Policy environment

During the equality debate, the political right formed the government and controlled the *Bundestag*. The CDU/CSU led the governing coalition with the FDP as the junior partner. While both of these parties experienced internal conflict over the key issues in this debate, the leaderships of both blocked efforts by women in their respective parties to introduce a strongly worded constitutional statement or a compensation clause. The

SPD, which supported a stronger version of the amendment with a compensation clause, controlled a majority in the *Bundesrat* for most of this period, giving it the ability to block or slow government legislation. A Joint Parliamentary Committee on Constitutional Reform made the most important decisions pertaining to the constitutional changes.

The policy sub-system surrounding this issue is a moderately closed one, dominated by political parties and their parliamentary groups. Governmental ministries' substantial input comes in drafting government legislation and providing expertise to working groups and committees. Grass-roots groups' input is limited by the neo-corporatist system that favours established interests (see Conradt 1993; Dalton 1993).

Debate 3: Reform of German nationality law, 1998–1999

How the debate came to the public agenda

Several million migrants have entered the FRG since the end of the Second World War. Initially refugees of German descent fled communist-controlled countries after the war. Later millions of 'guest workers', largely from Turkey and southern Europe, came as 'temporary' residents to ease employment shortages. Because German nationality and citizenship law was based on *jus sanguinus* (law of the blood) rather than *jus soli* (law of the soil), the former were entitled to citizenship, even if neither they nor their parents had ever lived in Germany. The latter group and their children (often born and raised in Germany) were essentially denied German citizenship (see Klusmeyer 2000; Hailbronner 2000; Richter 1998–9). Despite this history of migration, the CDU-led governments of the 1980s and 1990s insisted that Germany was 'not a nation of immigrants', even though the foreign population of the FRG comprised 9 per cent of the country's total population (Klusmeyer 2000).

Several developments in the 1990s placed immigration and citizenship law on the German political agenda. First, German unification made FRG citizens of more than 17 million East Germans. Second, more than 2 million ethnic Germans migrated into Germany as communism collapsed throughout the continent (Rinaldi 1999; Richter 1998–9). The automatic citizenship granted to both of these groups increased dissatisfaction among the guest worker population and their German-born children who were denied citizenship rights – and, in turn, political representation – unless they participated in a long, onerous, costly naturalisation process and renounced citizenship in any foreign state. Third, Germany's once-liberal asylum laws attracted 1.6 million asylum seekers from 1987 to 1994

(Rinaldi 1999; Hailbronner 2000). These migrants, many fleeing war in the former Yugoslavia, became scapegoats for the post-unification economic hardships and unemployment. Fourth, in the late 1980s a few *Länder* and municipalities had passed legislation enfranchising permanent foreign residents in local elections. The Federal Constitutional Court's 1990 decision to overturn these laws made it clear that non-citizens did not enjoy equal political representation rights with citizens.

In the early 1990s, the CDU-led government responded to pressures with two stop-gap measures: minor liberalisation of the naturalisation laws and severe curtailment of the asylum policy. The 1998 federal election campaign returned the issue of reforming German citizenship laws to the political agenda. The FDP supported conditional naturalisation for children born in Germany, but received no support from its senior coalition partner (*Economist* 4 July 1998). The SPD and Alliance90/Greens included reform of nationality laws and an expansion of foreigners' citizenship rights in their campaign platforms. For candidate Schröder, this was an effort to make political representation in Germany more inclusive and to enlist future electoral support from foreign voters whom his party helped enfranchise.

Dominant frame of debate

The debate began with several overlapping meta-frames with all parties discussing questions about German national identity, who is a German, whether the country is an 'immigrant nation', and the post-war context of the *jus sanguinus* citizenship law (see Klusmeyer 2000). Parties vied to shape the dominant frame, with the SPD focusing on the widening gap between permanent residents and citizens[9] and CDU focusing on the question of dual citizenship (see Cahn 2000). The CDU won the contest and framing increasingly focused on dual citizenship rather than on more fundamental questions about German immigration and membership in the state.[10] This dominant frame was evident on magazine covers, in newspaper articles and interviews, and even as a subject heading in the parliamentary archive on this debate.

In turn, broad proposals for reforming immigration and nationality law were narrowed down to specific reforms of naturalisation requirements and the issues of dual citizenship for German-born children of foreign residents.

---

[9] Ministry of the Interior press release from 16 March 1999, quoted in Klusmeyer (2000: 10).
[10] Klusmeyer (2000) notes that the CDU used this frame to divide the public on the issue of reform of the nationality laws.

Gendering the debate

The debate about naturalisation and citizenship rights, including voting rights, remained ungendered, despite the fact that roughly half of all affected foreign residents were women. Earlier efforts by women's movement organisations, the SPD and the Greens to gender part of the immigrants' rights debate had focused very specifically on one paragraph of the immigration law, which relates to women obtaining or retaining permanent resident status in cases of divorce or domestic abuse. Yet efforts to gender the 1998–9 debate were almost non-existent. For instance, a spring 1998 special issue of the Alliance90/Green newspaper focusing on foreigners' rights made no gender-specific arguments about voting rights, despite grammar that made the inclusion of women explicit. In another 1998 example, the SPD women's organisation put out a special issue of its publication *Women's Issues: Information from the SPD* focused on women's politics in the SPD's campaign platform, but made no mention of foreign women or their enfranchisement.

A rare exception was a single 1999 issue of the periodical publication of the German Women's Council, a formerly conservative women's group that has been more influenced by women from the SPD in recent years. In response to the SPD draft legislation, the council devoted part of an issue of its magazine *Information for the Woman* to issues of foreign women in Germany and abroad. The editor notes that the German Women's Council had never previously considered any resolution concerning the issues of dual citizenship and naturalisation (Lieber 1999). One article in the publication argues that the nationality reform debate is a 'women's issue' and, thus, constitutes an effort to gender the debate, but the effort was late in the process and ineffective in shaping the debate.

Policy outcome

This debate resulted in new legislation, ratified in May 1999, that gives children born to non-Germans in the FRG dual citizenship until age 23, at which point they must choose one or the other citizenship (Cahn 2000).

Women's movement impact

Women were not high-profile participants in this debate. Women's movement representatives played no visible role in the process. Indeed, the movement had no clear-cut stance on the issue. Feminists did not oppose the government's efforts to reform the naturalisation process and thus voting rights, but neither did they work for such reform. In a search of women's movement archive materials, feminist periodicals and the publications of women's organisations, the norm was the complete omission of the voting rights issue in numerous articles, published interviews and speeches by advocates of the rights of female foreigners. There were only a few, isolated exceptions. As early as 1980, one Turkish women's group in Berlin called for the extension of voting rights to foreign women as a central criterion for their integration into German society (*Neue* 1980). In several cases, feminist groups joined dozens of other groups in organising demonstrations for foreign residents' rights, including, among others, the right to vote. The above-mentioned periodical by the German Women's Council was the only visible effort made by a women's group to participate in this debate. The authors were supportive of easing the naturalisation process, but were critical of the government's draft law for not going far enough and for not explicitly including women and their gender-specific issues in the new law. The policy outcome thus fell short of the demands of the few women's groups who expressed interest in the debate and was irrelevant to most women's movement groups. According to the RNGS model, the policy outcome in this case was no response.

Women's policy agency activities

During this debate the federal women's ministry remained a cross-sectional, middle-level ministry led by a minister with a political appointment. With the election of a SPD-Green government, a more feminist minister was appointed. This issue, however, was not within or adjacent to the mandate of the ministry despite the fact that many of the people affected by the legal reform were women. Instead, the mandate for this issue rested squarely with the Ministry of the Interior.

Our research revealed no comments about or engagement in this debate by the women's ministry. We found no evidence of efforts to gender this debate, nor any advocacy of women's movement goals. Thus, the women's policy agency's role was symbolic in this policy debate.

Women's movement characteristics

As noted above, the German women's movement in the 1990s was divided and in decline. It was close to the traditional political left during this debate. Mainstream feminists active in the SPD could, theoretically, have had influence and did address another immigration issue. As noted above, several women's movement groups and activists did focus on other immigration issues, specifically the rights of abused and divorced foreign women, but not on citizenship and voting rights. Thus, this debate was a low priority for the women's movement at this time. Because the women's movement was not engaged in the voting rights debate, there was no counter-movement to oppose it.

Policy environment

During the electoral campaign that marks the beginning of this debate, the conservative CDU controlled both the executive and the lower house of parliament. During the period when the legislation was debated and passed, however, the political left controlled the executive and both houses of parliament.

The new SPD government did make efforts to open up the policy process, but the realities of German parliamentary procedure left the policy sub-system around this issue moderately closed. The political parties and their parliamentary groups continued to dominate the sub-system. Inter-party negotiations about legislative content, the actual drafting of legislation and the determination of which outside groups could participate in the process were all controlled by the parties and the government of the day.

Conclusion

The cases discussed here represent very different outcomes in terms of state response/movement impact and WPA activities. Policy outcome did not coincide with movement goals in the second debate, which ended in co-optation, or the third debate, which ended with no response. Only in the first debate, which took place within a political party, was there dual response to movement efforts. The role of the WPA was symbolic in the SPD-quota and citizenship debates (first and third debates) and that of an insider in the equality law debate (second debate), although movement goals were not achieved in the latter.

The characteristics of the WPA did not vary much across the three debates and the variation generally did not correspond to differences in WPA activities or state response. The one partial exception is the closeness to mandate. The WPA was most active in the one debate (the second) where the issue was close to its mandate in terms of structure and substance. In the other two debates, the WPA was either structurally excluded (the first) or the substance was never framed as a 'women's issue' (the third). However, the one quasi-WPA included in this study, the ASF in the SPD-quota debate (the first debate), played a central role in achieving women's movement goals.

The explanatory value of the independent variable clusters is mixed. Movement characteristics do not appear to explain agency activities very well. The same symbolic response resulted from differences in stage, closeness to left, counter-movement strength and issue priority in the first and third debates, while different responses resulted from similarities in stage and closeness to left in the second and third debates. The only variable that may help explain agency activities in these three debates is cohesion. It was only in the second debate, where movement actors undertook some cohesive action on the policy, that the WPA achieved insider status.

The relationships between movement characteristics and movement impact/state response are similarly mixed. Neither similarities in stage and closeness to left (second and third debates) nor in counter-movement strength and cohesion (first and second debates) seem to have explanatory value. On the other hand issue priority seems to correlate with movement impact in all three debates, while stage, issue priority and closeness to the left all seem to be important factors in accounting for the dual response movement impact in the first debate. One movement impact not captured by the RNGS model, but evident in these cases, is the extent to which previous movement activities create expectations that women should be involved in the policy process when the topic has an obvious focus on women, as in the first and second debates.

The political environment variables do not appear to explain variation in agency activity or movement impact. We find that the WPA was most involved in working for feminist goals in the second debate and the movement impact was greatest in the first, both of which took place when the right was in power. The least WPA involvement and movement impact was in the third debate when the left led Germany. The lack of variation in sub-system cannot explain variation in other variables.

Other aspects of the policy environment that are not directly addressed in the RNGS model seem to be more important in explaining variation in these debates. The role of political parties in German democracy clearly affected the WPA activities in all three debates. Because the first debate took place within the SPD apparatus, the CDU-controlled women's Ministry could not effectively influence the debate. The WPA was thus not a player in securing the positive response to the movement. In the second debate, however, the CDU Women's Minister was able to act in a feminist manner that challenged her party's predisposition concerning equality laws. The prominence of the simultaneous abortion debate on the CDU's agenda actually created more space for the WPA to support feminist goals in the equality debate. Finally, the parties played a role in minimising WPA involvement in the third debate by defining the issue in a way that excluded that office. Without a mandate or any coherent women's movement pressure on the issue, the WPA was unable to foster women's participation or movement goals, despite the leadership of parties amenable to feminist ideas and activism.

References

Altbach, Edith Hoshino 1984, 'The New German Women's Movement', in Edith Hoshino Altbach, Jeanette Clausen, Dagmar Schultz and Naomi Stephan (eds.) *German Feminism: Readings in Politics and Literature*, Albany: State University of New York Press, pp. 3–26

Altbach, Edith Hoshino, Jeanette Clausen, Dagmar Schultz and Naomi Stephan (eds.) 1984, *German Feminism: Readings in Politics and Literature*, Albany: State University of New York Press

Arbeitskreis Verfassung des Frauenpolitischen Runden Tisches Berlin 1992, *Macht – Verfassung – Demokratie*, Berlin: Arbeitskreis Verfassung des Frauenpolitischen Runden Tisches Berlin (self-published booklet)

Berghahn, Sabine 1993, 'Frauen, Recht und langer Atem – Bilanz nach über 40 Jahren Gleichstellungsgebot in Deutschland', in Gisela Helwig and Hildegard Maria Nickel (eds.) *Frauen in Deutschland 1945–1992*, Berlin: Bundeszentrale für politische Bildung, pp. 71–138

BMFJ (Bundesministerium für Frauen und Jugend) 1993, *Informationsdienst Juni–Juli 1993*, Bonn: Bundesministerium für Frauen und Jugend (self-published collection of speeches, statements and press releases)

Brox-Brochot, Delphine 1984, 'Manifesto of the "Green" Women', in Edith Hoshino Altbach, Jeanette Clausen, Dagmar Schultz and Naomi Stephan, (eds.) *German Feminism: Readings in Politics and Literature*, Albany: State University of New York Press, pp. 315–17; trans. by Pamela Selwyn, originally published as 'Manifest der "Grünen" Frauen', *Courage* 5 (February, 1980): 13–17

Cahn, Claude 2000, 'Who is a German?' *SAIS Review* 20: 117–24

Chamberlayne, Prue 1995, 'Gender and the Private Sphere: a Touchstone of Misunderstanding between Eastern and Western Germany', *Social Politics* 2: 25–36

Conradt, David P. 1993, *The German Polity*, fifth edition, New York: Longman

Dalton, Russell J. 1993, *Politics in Germany*, second edition, New York: HarperCollins

Economist 1998, 'Who Should be German, Then?' 348 (4 July): 45

Ferree, Myra Marx 1987, 'Equality and Autonomy: Feminist Politics in the United States and West Germany', in Mary Fainsod Katzenstein and Carol McClurg Mueller (eds.) *The Women's Movements of the United States and Western Europe*, Philadelphia: Temple University Press, pp. 172–95

1995a, 'Making Equality: the Women's Affairs Offices in the Federal Republic of Germany', in Dorothy McBride Stetson and Amy G. Mazur (eds.) *Comparative State Feminism*, Thousand Oaks, CA: Sage, pp. 95–113

1995b, 'Patriarchies and Feminisms: the Two Women's Movements of Post-Unification Germany', *Social Politics* 2: 11–24

Geissel, Brigitte 1999, *Politikerinnen: Politisierung und Partizipation auf kommunaler Ebene*, Opladen: Leske und Budrich

Hailbronner, Kay 2000, 'Fifty Years of the Basic Law – Migration, Citizenship, and Asylum', *SMU Law Review* 53: 519–42

Hoecker, Beate (ed.) 1998, *Handbuch politische Partizipation von Frauen in Europa*, Opladen: Leske und Budrich

Jahresbericht der Bundesregierung 1979, Bonn: Presse- und Informationsamt der Bundesregierung

Jansen, Mechthild 1994, 'Gleiches Recht ist unverbindlich', *Die Tageszeitung* 3 May

1995, 'Wo die Quote erfüllt ist, beginnt demokratische Geschlechterpolitik', *Die Tageszeitung* 25 July

Kamenitsa, Lynn 1993, 'Social Movement Marginalization in the Democratic Transition: the Case of the East German Women's Movement', Ph.D. dissertation, Indiana University

1997, 'East German Feminists in the New German Democracy: Opportunities, Obstacles and Adaptation', *Women & Politics* 17: 41–68

2001, 'Abortion Debates in Germany', in Dorothy McBride Stetson (ed.) *Abortion Politics, Women's Movements, and the Democratic State: a Comparative Study of State Feminism*, Oxford: Oxford University Press, pp. 111–34

Kenawi, Samirah 1995, *Frauengruppen in der DDR der 80er Jahre*, Berlin: Grauzone

Kiechle, Brigitte 1991, *Selbstbestimmung statt Fremdbestimmung: zur aktuellen Auseinandersetzung um den §218*, Frankfurt am Main: isp-Verlag

Klusmeyer, Douglas 2000, 'Four Dimensions of Membership in Germany', *SAIS Review* 20: 1–21

Kolinsky, Eva 1988, 'The West German Greens – a Women's Party?' *Parliamentary Affairs* 41: 129–48

Lieber, Dorotea 1999, 'Liebe Leserin, lieber Leser', *Informationen für die Frau* 48 (March): 3

Maier, Marion and Monika Oubaid 1987, *Mütter – die besseren Frauen*, Braunschweig: Gerd J. Holtzmeyer

Merkel, Angela 1993, 'Von Frauenministerin zu Frauenministerin', *Frankfurter Rundschau* (26 February)

Meyer, Birgit 1992, 'Die "unpolitische" Frau, Politische Partizipation von Frauen oder: Haben Frauen ein anderes Verständnis von Politik', *Aus Politik und Zeitgeschichte* 25–26: 3–18

1997, *Frauen im Männerbund. Politikerinnen in Führungspositionen von der Nachkriegszeit bis heute*, New York: Campus Verlag

Nassmacher, Hiltrud 1993, 'Von der Gleichberechtigung zur Gleichstellung', in Aiga Stapf (ed.) *Frau und Mann zwischen Tradition und Emanzipation*, Stuttgart: Kohlhammer, pp. 167–80

Neue 1980, 'Wahlrecht Basis Für Integration', 25 September

'Neues Gesetz soll Bewusstseinswandel bewirken' 1994, *Sozialmagazin* 11: 10

Penrose, Virginia and Brigitte Geissel 2001, '"The Long Run": Partizipation und Engagement unter geschlechtsspezifischen Zusammenhängen', in Ulrike

Gentner (ed.) *Geschlechtergerechte Visionen. Politik in der Bildungs- und Jugendarbeit*, Königstein/Taunus: Ulrike Helmer Verlag, pp. 161–257

Richter, Anthony 1998–9, '"Blood and Soil": What It Means to be German', *World Policy Journal* 15: 91–8

Rinaldi, Alfred 1999, 'No Turks, Please, We're German', *New Statesman* 128: 23–4

Rosenberg, Dorothy 1996, 'Distant Relations: Class, "Race," and National Origin in the German Women's Movement', *Women's Studies International Forum* 19: 145–54

Sozialdemokratischer Informationsdienst 1988, 28: 10

Vertrag zwischen der Bundesrepublik Deutschland und der Deutschen Demokratischen Republik – Einigungsvertrag (Zweiter Staatsvertrag) 6 September 1990 [second unification treaty]

Weis, Petra 1995, 'Hürdenlauf an die Macht? Politische Partizipation von Frauen in der SPD und die Quote', in Eva Maleck-Lewy and Virginia Penrose (eds.) *Gefährtinnen der Macht. Politische Partizipation von Frauen im vereinigten Deutschland – eine Zwischenbilanz*, Berlin: Edition Sigma, pp. 65–82

Newspapers cited include: *Frankfurter Rundschau, Frankfurter Allgemeine Zeitung, Die Tageszeitung* (Berlin)

7 Gendering the debate on political representation in Italy: a difficult challenge

Marila Guadagnini

Introduction

In Italy, the concept of democracy has long been thought of as a means to represent social and political divisions. The need to guarantee access to decision-making arenas for the greatest number of social demands explains why, after the Second World War, a proportional-type electoral system with no minimum threshold was adopted. The results were a multi-party system and coalition governments (Verzichelli and Cotta 2003). Until the 1990s there was no alternation of government coalitions, but merely changes in coalition partners of the dominant Christian Democrats. After the late 1970s widespread discontent about the unstable and inefficient government coalitions increased and a debate about constitutional reforms developed.

By the early 1990s, discontent had become crisis. The legitimacy of the political elite collapsed leading to a widespread call for its replacement. Party identities dissolved and organisations disintegrated, making way for the rapid emergence of new political forces. The crisis accelerated the adoption of new institutional rules. Although there were many contributing factors (Cotta and Isernia 1996; Ginsborg 1996; Pasquino 2002), the determining event was the *Mani pulite* (Clean Hands) investigation launched by the judiciary in 1992. *Mani pulite* brought to light a widespread pattern of corruption involving the highest levels of the Italian political elite. It led to the dismantling of the party system. It focused on the government parties and, in particular, on their leaders. Between 1992 and 1994 the collapse of the party system involved an internal reorganisation whereby the original parties were replaced and new political forces created (Morlino 1996; Bardi 2002). None of the governing parties in power between 1945 and 1992 stood for election in 1994 with the same logo and same name. The crisis opened a public debate on the role of the political parties. Their capacity as organisations able to represent citizens was questioned. The need to adopt new rules of the political game was debated. Between 1993 and 2003, a series of reforms was adopted, including changes in the local and national electoral systems, reform of local government and devolution of policy-making powers from the state to local governments. Other proposals, including the reform of the upper chamber (the Senate) and of direct election of the head of state (or also of the chancellor), were put on the agenda but were not approved by 2004 (Ceccanti and Vassallo 2004).

One might think that the adoption of new rules of the game and the delegitimation and collapse of the party system would have created receptiveness to women's requests for representation. The parties were hostile to women's representation, as shown by the fact that the percentage of elected women has always been one of the lowest in Europe.[1] In the 1980s, advocates of women's political representation had begun a long struggle for equality. They achieved success in the early 1990s when, thanks to a quota system in the new electoral laws, a record number of women were elected at both national and local level. This, however, was a short-term success. The quota system was abolished in September 1995. Since then the number of women elected has steadily diminished, and by 2003 it was one of the lowest in Europe.

In the second half of the 1990s, several attempts were made to mobilise support for women's representation and to raise awareness in public opinion. Two regulations were passed to allow affirmative actions to increase women's presence in elective bodies: the adoption of a clause into the laws on federalism of 2001 establishing that regional laws should promote equal access of women and men to elective offices[2] and the amendment to article 51 of the constitution passed in 2003.

Institutions that make representation policy

Major decisions about political representation must be approved at national level by both houses of the legislature. Italian citizens may initiate referenda by collection of 500,000 signatures to remove or keep an adopted law, or they may vote in referenda to approve a constitutional law enforced by the National Assembly. The Constitutional Court can

---

[1] The percentage of women in the Lower House (Chamber of Deputies) was 5.6 per cent in 1953, 2.8 per cent in 1968, 8.4 per cent in 1976, 12.8 per cent in 1987 and 8.1 per cent in 1992 (Guadagnini 1993).

[2] It deals with the following laws: the amendment for the statutes of the autonomous regions (Constitutional Law 31 January 2001, n. 2) giving the law-maker the power to adopt measures suitable for promoting equal access to elective posts for both men and women, and the amendment to Titolo V of the constitution – Part II (Constitutional Law 18 October 2001, n. 3) (replacing article 117 of the constitution) 1st para., seventh new line. This amendment provides that 'regional laws remove any obstacles preventing equality of women and men in social, cultural and economical life and promote equal access to elective posts for both men and women'.

overturn legislation. Legislative initiative belongs to the government, to each member of the legislature, and to the citizens who may submit bills for legislative approval if they obtain the signatures of a certain number of voters (at least 50,000). Since the constitutional reform adopted in 1999 (Const. Law 1/1999), some policies on representation at local level (electoral system, form of government) may be decided at regional level (Fusaro 2000).

Parties play a crucial role in the process, as they determine the contents of the political agenda prior to policy-making action, they select the candidates for the election, and adopt decisions about the rules and procedures that establish who is to become a representative in the decision-making bodies. When the party system collapsed, new parties were created and the electoral system changed. In the process, parties were forced to adapt their candidate selection strategies. Even so, their crucial role in the selection of candidates remained unchallenged.

Selection of debates

From the 1980s and 1990s, the most important debates about political representation were of three types. First, there were debates on electoral system change. Second, constitutional debates considered the architecture of the political system. Examples included the introduction of federalism, the reform of the Senate and change from the existing parliamentary system to a presidential or semi-presidential form of government. Finally, the capacity and suitability of political parties as organisations for the representation of citizens' demands and interests was debated.

From the end of the 1980s to the end of the 1990s debates focused mainly on political parties and on institutional reforms. Accordingly the first selected debate is the creation of the *Partito democratico della sinistra* (PDS, Democratic Party of the Left) from the break up of the Communist Party (PCI). The PCI was the first party to undergo a process of transformation, before the *Mani pulite* investigation. The PDS is now the second largest party in Italy. The second debate is the reform of the system to elect the Chamber of Deputies. Among the debates about electoral system change,[3] this one most involved public opinion, as it was preceded by a referendum. Both these debates resulted in an end point decision in a major institution, gave rise to a lively debate and received broad media

---

[3] Besides the voting system for the Chamber of Deputies and the Senate, the voting systems for the election of municipal, provincial and regional councils were also reformed by introducing the direct election of the mayor, of the chairperson of the province (*provincia*) and the chairperson of the region (*regione*).

coverage. In both cases, the decision adopted marked the beginning of a new debate. The PDS, since renamed DS (*Democratici di sinistra*, Democrats of the Left) in the late 1990s, experienced an internal debate on the selection of candidate and party leadership as well as on procedures to promote greater participation and representation of the different groups and interests that continues into 2005. The debate on the opportunity to change the electoral system to the Chamber of Deputies was similarly protracted. Neither debate was gendered per se. Hence they are particularly suitable for an assessment of how the women's movement has been able to affect mainstream debate. By contrast, the third debate was directly about women's representation. The amendment to article 51 of the constitution, approved in February 2003, introduced the principle that the law should promote equal opportunities in access to political posts and public offices. This debate also illuminates wider debates on women's political representation.

Debate 1: The creation of the Democratic Party of the Left, 1989–1991

How the debate came to the public agenda

The renovation of the PCI was on the public agenda all through the 1980s, particularly after the death of its charismatic leader, Enrico Berlinguer, in 1984. During those years, the party experienced repeated electoral defeats (1979, 1983, 1987), as well as loss of membership. It was confined to political opposition and had no chances of participation in national government. The Socialist Party (PSI) led by Bettino Craxi fiercely opposed an alliance with the PCI. The PSI was in government in a coalition made up of centre parties. Until Achille Occhetto was appointed its party secretary (1988), the PCI internal organisation rested on the principle of 'democratic centralism', a characteristic of the Marxist-Leninist party. The distinctive features of the organisation were a strong centralisation of the decision-making process, the subjection of deliberative to executive organs, control from above and prohibition of any dissident group or faction.

The fall of the Berlin Wall and the collapse of the eastern communist regimes accelerated the process of reform. In 1989 Occhetto presented a proposal to be discussed at the next party congress. The proposal was to create a new reformist party. The new party would differ greatly from the Marxist-Leninist working-class party of previous years. It would accept the logic of the free market economy and would be a reformist party, similar to the social democratic parties of other European countries.

At the 1991 party congress at Rimini the Occhetto proposal was accepted by a majority of delegates (64.1 per cent) and a new party was formed with a new name and a new symbol. The dissident minority formed a second party, the Communist Refoundation (RC), which claimed to be the true heir of the old PCI, a claim that it signalled by maintaining the old party symbol (Bertolino 2004). The transformation process was characterised by a lively debate that involved PCI members, party officials and leaders, and received broad media coverage.

Dominant frame of debate

Between 1989 and 1991 debate turned to whether or not to abandon ideological and organisational tradition along with the name and symbol of the PCI. The question divided the party and the debate led to the formation of two new political forces. The PDS debate focused on the ideological redefinition of the party (the creation of a social democratic party based on European examples) and on the reform of internal organisation to bring about democratisation of the decision-making process, a streamlining of the bureaucratic apparatus and a turnover of the political elite (Baccetti 1997; Ignazi 1992). Matters concerning political representation included the procedures for the election of decision-making bodies, the selection of candidates and the promotion of members' participation in decision-making.

A central issue was 'who' the party should represent and how representation should be guaranteed in a bottom-up rather than top-down decision-making process. The new party embraced as its fundamental values freedom, equality and equal opportunities. Therefore, women's demands for representation were compatible with a programmatic approach aimed at democratising the party and ensuring representation of the greatest number of social groups.

Gendering the debate

Women were very active in the tumultuous phase leading to the creation of the PDS. At the Rimini conference the majority of women delegates voted for the creation of the new party, thus gaining the support of the party's secretary Occhetto and many other leaders of the new party. During the debate, women demanded both descriptive and substantive representation. The demands were a continuation of old business, of claims made and won in the old PCI. By 1986 PCI women had already obtained a minimum threshold (25 per cent) for women's representation in the party's executive board and in party delegations. In 1989 the percentage was raised to 33 per cent (Guadagnini 1993). In 1986, the women's section of the PCI, chaired by Livia Turco, drafted and published a document, the Women's Charter (*Carta delle donne*). The charter provided an overview of the way the request for women's representation was framed and the kind of strategies to be adopted. The point of departure was that the 'power of women can only come from women themselves'. Only women can represent women since sexual difference must be considered as one of the elements upon which society is founded. By publishing and disseminating the charter, the PCI activists launched a wide-ranging debate drawing in women from autonomous feminist groups, cultural centres, trade unions, associations, the universities and the labour market, trying to create a network of mobilisation and support outside the party. At the end of the 1980s, the women's movement in the PCI was very lively. It was becoming consolidated. There were by then a number of women (about 30 per cent) in party decision-making bodies.

In the debate, women activists, officials and MPs wanted the new PDS not only to include quotas for the presence of women in the party's decision-making bodies and on candidate lists, but also to express the point of view of women in the party programme. Crucial actors who gendered the debate included some prominent women in the party, in particular Livia Turco (who became a minister in the centre-left governments of the 1990s) and members of women's sections. Support also came from a number of party leaders and officials who were convinced that acceptance of women's demands would help consolidate a new image of the party in contrast with the old PCI, both in terms of its political elite and in its ideological content and programmes. Many thought that reform would help increase the appeal of the party to women voters (who, in Italy, had always tended to vote for centre parties, especially for the Christian Democratic Party).

Policy outcome

The demands for women's representation were accepted in the new party. This can be seen in three features of the regulations adopted in 1991. First, the PDS defined itself as 'a party of women and men' that proposed to create 'a society made to the measure of both sexes' and achieving full 'equal opportunities between women and men'. Second, it established quotas for the representation of women in all of the party's decision-making bodies, delegations at congresses, and in candidate lists on which neither of the sexes could constitute less than 40 per cent. Finally, the new PDS provided for the establishment of women's committees and sections within the party.

Despite the success achieved in terms of formal rules, the objectives established by the regulations in 1991, although included in later regulations adopted by the party in the following years, were not achieved by 2003 when women still did not constitute 40 per cent of all decision-making bodies. Women elected to the Lower Chamber in 2001 were only 24.3 per cent of the DS deputies. Those women's bodies that have been set up (there is now a *Coordinamento delle donne DS*, the Co-ordination Organisation for Women) still complain that they have not obtained satisfactory influence in party policy-making.

Women's movement impact

According to the RNGS model, because women were involved in the decision-making process and the party accepted women's goals, the response of the PDS to women's demands for representation can be classified as a dual response.

Women's policy agency activities

At the time of the debate, the PCI contained a quasi-WPA, the National Commission for Women's Emancipation and Liberation (CNELD, *Commissione nazionale per l'emancipazione e la liberazione delle donne*), which in 1989 included all women members of the party's Central Committee (CC) as well as others appointed by the CC. The commission was a body for discussion and debate about the recognition of sexual difference. Its task was to make decisions about proposals submitted by the CC, about the convening and the agenda of the CC, and to propose criteria for the inclusion of women in the candidate lists for local elections and for the national and European parliaments. There was also a Communist Women's National Conference (*Conferenza nazionale delle donne comuniste*) that had the task of drafting the guidelines for policies and initiatives.

When PCI secretary Occhetto advanced the proposal of transforming the party, the CNELD was divided on the issue. The vast majority of its members were in favour of the proposal while a minority disagreed. Nevertheless, the CNELD was united and cohesive in requesting women's descriptive and substantive representation. According to the RNGS model, the role played by the CNELD can be classified as insider.

Outside the party, there were two WPAs at the national government level: the National Committee for the Implementation of the Principles of Equal Treatment and Opportunity between Workers of Both Sexes (*Comitato nazionale per l'attuazione dei principi di parità di trattamento e uguaglianza di opportunità tra lavoratori e lavoratrici*), created in 1983 and attached to the Ministry of Labour and Social Security,[4] and the National Commission for Equality and Equal Opportunities between Men and Women (*Commissione nazionale per la parità e le pari opportunità tra uomini e donne*, CNPPO), attached to the Prime Minister's Office.

CNPPO consisted of representatives of the political parties, the social partners and women's associations. It provided guidance and consultation on the activities to be carried out to achieve equality between the sexes and equal opportunities for men and women. It had little funding, a modest staff and a purely advisory mandate for all issues not concerning employment.

The National Committee and the CNPPO had no mandate to intervene in a debate within a party.

Women's movement characteristics

During the period of the debate, the women's movement was re-emerging, but it was fragmented, divided into two broad segments of integrated and autonomous feminism. Heir to the 1970s, autonomous feminists were active in local women's projects and important cultural centres. The majority of them embraced the 'feminism of difference'. Difference feminist groups were opposed to participation in male institutions. They opposed quotas, which they thought were a way of emphasising the weakness of women. For this part of the movement, the issue of women's political representation was a low priority. By the late 1970s, a separate part of the movement, referred to here as the integrated women's movement, opposed the autonomous feminists' strategy and, on the contrary, tried to influence public policy by working within the political parties, trade unions, women's organisations and associations, and state bureaucracies. For integrated feminists, women's political representation was a high priority issue in the 1980s.

The lack of cohesion on the subject of political representation that resulted from the ideological and organisational disagreements between the components of the movement helped weaken its capacity to put forward an effective demand. The weakness was recognised by feminist activists in the PCI who attempted to create a bridge between these two sides. They tried to combine the idea of sexual difference and a radical renewal of politics with the demand for more posts within the institutions. Great emphasis was given to the need for a dual presence – in both the

---

[4] Consisting of representatives of trade unions and employers, women's associations and movements, it was a consultative organisation for matters concerning employment.

feminist movement and the institutions – in order to renovate politics. In fact, the operation was not a success since it neither convinced the autonomous groups nor fully involved integrated feminists, who simply demanded greater women's representation in the name of equality. Fragmentation not withstanding, the movement in this period was close to the left.

Policy environment

In this debate, the PDS itself was the relevant policy sub-system. The new party's regulations stated that the decision-making process should be open to a wide range of party members. The official commitment of the new PDS to openness and to equality enabled feminists, at least on paper, to achieve their goals. The policy environment in the PDS can be described as moderately open. During the debate (1989–91), the PDS was in opposition, and the governments of those years were formed by a coalition of five parties – *pentapartito* (Christian Democratic Party, Socialist Party, Social Democratic Party, Republican Party and the Liberals).

Debate 2: The change of the voting system for the members of the lower chamber – quotas in the electoral law, 1991–1995

How the debate came to the public agenda

Changes in the voting system for the election of local and national assemblies were on the agenda since the end of the 1970s (Fusaro 1995). In the 1980s, a parliamentary Joint Commission for Reforms (*Commissione bicamerale per le riforme*) was set up to address the issue. As a result of disagreements between political parties, no decision was adopted on the type of electoral system to be chosen. Since it proved impossible to change the existing electoral system through the parliament, a Committee for Electoral Reforms (*Comitato per le riforme elettorali*, COREL) was created in 1990 to get the reform adopted by means of a referendum. The committee consisted of some leading members of the PDS, of the Christian Democratic, Republican and Liberal parties and was presided by Mario Segni, a Christian Democratic MP. It was supported by a number of associations. The first referendum, held in 1991, did not address the change of the existing proportional system for the Chamber of Deputies, but it approved the reduction of the number of preference votes permitted from three or four to one.

The 1992 upheavals accelerated the reform process. In March 1993 the National Assembly approved a new electoral system for the election of mayors, municipal councillors, the presidents of provincial governments and provincial councillors. In April 1993, a second referendum concerning electoral laws was held. This referendum proposed the elimination of a short clause in the existing electoral law for the Senate. The elimination of the clause would have made it possible to transform the electoral system for the Senate into a primarily majority system. Its success would have shown that voters were in favour of a majority system.[5] Considerable participation in the referendum and the high number of votes in favour of the reform compelled the parties not only to implement the Senate reform according to the will of the voters, but also to change the voting system for the lower chamber.

Dominant frame of debate

Mainstream debate justified change in the electoral system to reduce the number of parties and to guarantee stability of government. Advocates of the adoption of a majoritarian system claimed that it would produce alternating party coalitions in government and direct responsibility of representatives to their electors. It would give the electorate the possibility to choose candidates on the basis of their personality, qualifications and qualities. Thus the reform would weaken the domination of the party 'barons' and the party organisations. The discussion concerned the type of electoral system to be approved and in particular the choice between the adoption of an English-style uninominal, majority system and a variation of the French two-round ballot system. The law that was approved provided that 75 per cent of seats would be assigned using the majority system and 25 per cent using a proportional system (Law no. 277, 4 August 1993) (D'Alimonte and Chiaramonte 1995; Parker 1996).[6]

---

[5] The size of the consensus was considerable. Not only was turnout high (77.1 per cent), but votes in favour of change were 82.7 per cent (with minimal differences between men and women). By the time of the referendum, the crisis of the political system was deepening and the old party system was being dismantled and decapitated. Faced with this deep crisis, what the electorate wanted was mainly to get out of it. The question posed by the referendum was perceived not so much as concerning a choice between two different electoral laws but as a positive or negative judgement on the need for change in view of the inefficiency of the political system.

[6] The path of the law towards approval was a difficult one. Discussion began in April 1993 and came to an end in August 1993. The debate first took place within the Committee on Constitutional Affairs (*Commissione affari costituzionali*) of the chamber (1 April 1993–13 July), then in the chamber (14–30 June), and then moved to the Committee on Constitutional Affairs of the Senate (7–12 July) before being discussed by the Senate

Gendering the debate

Aware that the adoption of a majority system would penalise women's representation, some women MPs demanded the introduction of quotas in the new voting system. A quota system had already been adopted in the previous electoral law approved in March 1993 for the election of the local councillors.[7] Among the strong advocates of the introduction of quotas were two well-known representatives of the largest parties: Tina Anselmi of the Christian Democratic Party, then president of the Equal Opportunities Commission at the Prime Minister's Office, and Livia Turco, a prominent PDS MP. The proposal to adopt quotas in the electoral system for the Chamber of Deputies was first submitted to the Parliamentary Committee on Constitutional Affairs (*Commissione affari costituzionali*) by a number of female MPs of the centre-left parties (mainly of PDS and RC). In the National Assembly debate on the text drafted by the committee, the quota proposal gave rise to a lively debate that divided the right-wing parties (MSI, the extreme right-wing party, heir to the fascist party, and *Lega Nord*, as well as the Republicans and the Liberals) from those of the centre-left (Dossier no. 128/II, pp. 838–46). Right-wing women MPs who took part in the debate included Irene Pivetti (*Lega Nord*), who was to become the president of the Chamber after the 1994 elections, and Alessandra Mussolini (MSI), while those in favour included important leaders such as Massimo D'Alema (later to become secretary of the PDS).

MSI female MPs openly stood by the official position of their party.[8] Other members of parliament opposed quotas, including Ombretta Fumagalli Carulli of the Christian Democrat Party, who voted in favour of the preliminary question on unconstitutionality presented by the MSI. The right wing and the Liberal Party called the quota system a 'panda' law as if it were a campaign to safeguard an endangered species. This slogan, widely quoted in the media, helped create popular opposition to quotas.

(13–15 July): the law returned for the second hearing in the chamber (23–28 July), before being examined by the Committee on Constitutional Affairs of the Senate, and obtaining final approval by the Senate itself.

[7] Law no. 81 of March 1993, concerning the election of mayors, presidents of provincial governments and of members of municipal and provincial councils. It contained a clause establishing that neither sex could account for more than two-thirds of the candidates for election to municipal and provincial councils. The adoption of this clause was strongly supported by an alliance between Christian Democratic and left-wing party activists, femocrats and WPAs (Guadagnini 1998).

[8] Alessandra Mussolini stated: 'Obligatory alternation is offensive to women, who do not need to be safeguarded in this way, but for what they are worth in the family, in their care of children, and in the work they carry out within society.' Cf. Bucci (1993).

Policy outcome

As stated, the law adopted in August 1993 provided that 75 per cent of seats would be assigned using the majority system and 25 per cent using a proportional system. A clause was included establishing that for the 155 (of 630) proportionally elected seats, lists should consist of candidates of both sexes in alternate order (zipping). A few years later a quota system was also introduced in the new law passed in February 1995 for the election of regional councils.[9]

However, in September 1995 the Constitutional Court outlawed electoral quotas.[10] According to the court, quotas were unconstitutional as they infringed the principle of equality incorporated in the constitution. In particular the quotas conflicted with article 3, which states that 'all citizens ... are equal before the law, without distinction of sex, race, etc.', and article 51, which states that 'All citizens of either sex can have access to public offices and elective posts under equal conditions.'

The court decision has to be considered the end point of the debate concerning the change in the voting system, since it abolished one clause included in the law passed by the National Assembly.

After the court decision, the percentage of women elected in the lower chamber, which had reached around 15 per cent in the 1994 election, dropped to 11.1 per cent in the 1996 and to 11.2 per cent in the 2001 election.[11]

Women's movement impact

Two specific reasons explain the initial success of quotas in the debate within the National Assembly. Advocates of quotas obtained policy satisfaction, first because the policy sub-system was weak and second because

---

[9] Law 43, 23 February 1995, concerning new regulations for election of councils in regions with an ordinary statute. The new electoral system provided for a double vote in a single round and on a single ballot sheet: one to assign 80 per cent of the seats, with a proportional system based on the territorial area of the provinces, the other to assign the remaining 20 per cent of seats using a majoritarian system covering a single regional area. The latter quota of seats was the reward destined for the regional list which obtained the greatest number of votes. The law contained a clause which prescribed that neither sex should account for more than two-thirds of the candidate lists for the seats to be assigned with the proportional system.

[10] Sentence 6–12 September 1995, no. 422, in the *Gazzetta ufficiale della Repubblica Italiana*, 1a serie speciale, 39, 20 September 1995.

[11] The number of women among the candidates for the election of the lower chamber dropped from 17.3 per cent in 1994 to 12.5 per cent in 1996 and was 13.9 per cent in the 2001 election.

it was generally held that the provision adopted was likely to be cancelled by the Constitutional Court,[12] which is exactly what happened. Thus, considering that the endpoint of the debate was the decision adopted by the court, the women's movement impact/state response can be classified as 'co-optation': in the first phase of the debate, held in the National Assembly, women were involved with the policy process and obtained policy satisfaction but afterwards the clause concerning quotas was abolished by the Constitutional Court.

Women's policy agency activities

During the period of the debate in parliament, the CNPPO was chaired by Tina Anselmi, an authoritative Christian Democrat who had many terms of office as an MP. Anselmi had been the first female minister in Italy. She strongly supported the adoption of quotas in the electoral laws as she was convinced that quotas were an unpleasant but necessary measure to overcome the situation of under-representation of women. In this debate, the role played by the CNPPO can be classified as marginal. The CNPPO advocated the goals of the integrated women's movement (see below) but was not successful in obtaining a gendered outcome: after the initial success achieved in the National Assembly, the quota clause was abolished by the Constitutional Court.

Women's movement characteristics

The women's movement characteristics in the first and second debates were basically similar. The movement was re-emerging, it was close to the left and it was still fragmented. The autonomous groups and cultural centres of difference feminism opposed the quotas, as they regarded them as a measure that accepted women's weakness. For them women's representation remained a low priority issue. By contrast, the integrated women's movement still prioritised increased women's representation. However, it was divided on the means to achieve this goal. While part of the integrated movement supported the introduction of quotas in the electoral laws, some opposed it, considering that other measures would be more suitable. These measures included: promoting political training for women; putting pressure on the parties to increase their nominations of women and on the media to give more coverage to

---

[12] The same reasons explain the success achieved in obtaining a quota system in the law adopted in March 1993, concerning local elections (cf. note 7).

women during electoral campaigns; creating 'talented women's data banks', that is lists of women suitable for candidacy to be submitted to the parties; and organising awareness-raising campaigns to promote votes for women.

Its divisions caused the integrated women's movement to miss the opportunity of using the debate on electoral laws to make public opinion aware of the problem of women's under-representation. In the 1990s, the question of women's limited presence in decision-making arenas was still considered by public opinion as a 'women's problem' and not as a question of democracy (Guadagnini 2000).[13]

Policy environment

Advocates of quotas achieved their initial success in the National Assembly in August 1993: there was fierce opposition to the inclusion of the quotas clause in the law, but it was approved because the policy environment was weak. Carlo Azeglio Ciampi was the president of the ruling government, supported by the Christian Democratic Party, the Socialist Party, the Social Democratic Party, the Liberals and left-wing Independents. The Ciampi government had to contend with the ongoing institutional transformation, a difficult economic climate (government deficit), and judicial investigations that involved every sector of the political, administrative, professional and economic elites. One-third of legislators who passed the law were under investigation by the magistrates of *Mani pulite*. In this period, the leading government parties – the Christian Democrats and the Socialists – broke up, and so did their traditional allies (Liberals, Social Democrats and Republicans).

Nevertheless, as stated, in 1995 the Constitutional Court outlawed the clause concerning quotas included in the law passed by the National Assembly, thus modifying the law itself. The Constitutional Court is a closed, male-dominated sub-system: the women's movement do not have access to it. At the time of the court decision, the policy environment was not as weak as before: the ruling government was led by Lamberto Dini and was supported by a centre-left majority.

---

[13] According to the data collected in two surveys carried out in 1998 and 1999, only just over half of all Italians (55 per cent) considered that a limited number of women in parliament was a problem and that women should be better represented. It should, however, also be said that there was a considerable difference between the sexes: the problem was more keenly felt by women (63.7 per cent) than by men (47.3 per cent) (Guadagnini 2000).

Debate 3: Amendment of article 51 of the constitution, 1997–2003

How the debate came to the public agenda

After the 1995 decision by the Constitutional Court, as the number of women elected at all levels continued to drop, a debate began on the need to modify the constitution in order to make it possible to adopt affirmative action without stirring up controversies about its constitutionality.

An initial attempt to introduce into the constitution the principle of equal opportunities of access to elective posts came about in the debate on the reform of decentralisation of power from the national to the local level. In 1997, the CNPPO submitted a number of constitutional amendments to the *Commissione bicamerale per le riforme costituzionali* (Bicameral Commission for Constitutional Reforms), presided over by Massimo D'Alema, secretary of the PDS. The commission was in charge of preparing a proposal on the constitutional reforms concerning federalism, the form of government and the judicial system. The amendments were incorporated in the committee's final document, but they could not be applied: the document was never approved by the National Assembly, because of disagreement between the political parties on the reforms proposed (Pasquino 1999). Nevertheless, in the constitutional reforms concerning decentralisation adopted in 2001 by a centre-left majority, an article was approved which stated that regional laws 'promote equal opportunities for access of women and men to electoral posts', thus making it possible to adopt affirmative action in regional electoral laws.[14] The ensuing success helped give new strength to the debate in favour of the reform of article 51 of the constitution, aimed at establishing the constitutional obligation to promote equal access to elective posts in all elections.

Furthermore, the debate gained impetus from the success achieved by the 'parity movement' in France, which obtained a constitutional amendment in 1999 that made it possible to adopt positive action in the electoral laws to guarantee sex equality in candidate lists (see chapter 5).

A number of constitution revision bills were put forward to introduce the principle according to which the law should promote equality of access for both women and men to public posts and elective offices. The first bill (2 March 1999) was proposed by Claudia Mancina, a DS MP, together with other centre-left members of both chambers. Other bills were subsequently introduced by MPs of the centre-left parties.

[14] Cf. note 2.

In 2001, when Berlusconi was the head of government, a bill was submitted, signed by various members of the government: by Prime Minister Berlusconi himself and by the Minister for Equal Opportunities, Stefania Prestigiacomo (*Forza Italia*), and the Minister for Constitutional Reform, Umberto Bossi (*Lega Nord*). To the existing paragraph stating 'All citizens of either sex can have access to public offices and elective posts under equal conditions', it added the following sentence: 'For this purpose the Republic promotes, by means of special measures, equal opportunities for women and men.' The passage of the amendment through the legislature was slow. As a constitutional law, it had to be passed twice by both the lower and the upper chamber. It was at last approved in February 2003.

Dominant frame of debate

Arguments in favour of the constitutional amendment referred to the decline in the number of elected women and to the need to take affirmative measures to neutralise the negative effects of the new electoral systems and parties' resistance to select women candidates. The reform was demanded in the name of equality, equal opportunities and the need to reverse the democratic shortfall caused by the under-representation of women. Comparison was frequently made with the experience in other European countries where women's representation rose steadily during the 1990s. Attention was also drawn to the regulations of international institutions such as the UN, the Council of Europe and the EU. Particular reference was made to France, where the constitutional amendment adopted in 1999 paved the way for the adoption of a number of regulations mandating parties to field 50 per cent female candidates in elections run with a proportional system, and establishing financial sanctions for those parties which do not observe the principle of an equal number of male and female candidates in elections run with a majority system (see chapter 5).

Gendering the debate

The debate was inherently gendered as it concerned a law designed to promote equal representation of women and men. Female experts in constitutional law and women from the centre-left parties, in particular from the DS, who first proposed the amendment, played a key role in the promotion of the debate. They were given support by their parties, which had already promoted the introduction of quotas in the new electoral laws in the 1990s.

The innovative element of this debate is the support given to the reform by women of centre-right parties including *Forza Italia* and the National Alliance Party (AN, heir of the MSI). Prominent members of these parties, such as Alessandra Mussolini of AN, who clearly opposed the electoral quotas in 1993, were now strong advocates of the constitutional amendment. Different reasons may account for this change of attitude. Women in right-wing parties became aware of how difficult it is to increase women's representation without affirmative action measures. In the second half of the 1990s, *Forza Italia* and AN had the lowest percentage of women elected to the lower chamber, 7.3 per cent and 4 per cent respectively. In addition an increasing number of women *voters* became aware of the problem of achieving equal opportunities. This is probably why the centre-right parties and the Berlusconi government supported the reform.

The constitutional amendment was inspired by the French experience. In France, the reform was the outcome of a lively and widespread debate held in newspapers, magazines and public assemblies. The debate helped revitalise the women's movement and put the question of equality of political representation onto not only the political but also the public agenda. In Italy the debate that preceded the adoption of the reform mainly involved the integrated women's movement: women elected at all levels, political party activists, WPAs at national and local levels, experts and some women's associations. It received limited media coverage (Beccalli 1999). It was the approval of the reform that actually encouraged the widest debate: several conferences and seminars were organised on how to implement the new law. These initiatives showed how there was considerable interest in this matter among women in general and widespread support among the various members of the women's movement on the need to promote equal opportunities in gender representation by means of affirmative action.

Policy outcome

The constitutional amendment was finally approved on 20 February 2003. The reform is permissive. It gives policy-makers the power to adopt adequate measures to promote equal opportunities in access to elective bodies.

The decision was followed by an implementation debate, a discussion about the real provisions to be adopted (Guadagnini 2003). A number of bills had been submitted which, in August 2004, had so far not been approved by the National Assembly. They included various proposals concerning today's diverse electoral systems. For the elections to municipal councils, a bill submitted by centre-left parties proposed quotas in the electoral lists for small municipalities (with fewer than 3,000 inhabitants) and the rule that on every list the gap between the number of candidates of each sex must not exceed one in larger municipalities. All measures should be temporary and should be applied for a limited number of years. For those elections run with a majority system, a number of bills proposed a reduction in the percentage of electoral expenses reimbursed to the parties presenting candidate lists that are unbalanced in terms of gender. A number of bills proposed the extension of party obligations to increase the percentage (from 5 to 10 per cent) of their public funding that is dedicated to initiatives designed to promote the participation of women in politics.

As far as European parliament elections are concerned (PR system with multiple preference votes), a law was approved in April 2004 (Law no. 90 of 8 April 2004) which provided that in the lists of candidates, 'neither of the two sexes may be represented by more than two-thirds of the candidates'. For the parties that did not respect this proportion, the amount of reimbursement of electoral expenses would be reduced to a maximum of half, in an amount directly proportional to the number of candidates over the number allowed. The regulation was to remain in force for ten years. The law was preceded by a lively debate between those (centre-left female activists, CNPPO) who demanded equal presence (50/50) of the two sexes in the lists of candidates, and those (centre-right women, Minister for Equal Opportunities, Prestigiacomo) who were in favour of the quota system that was finally approved. The law had positive effects. The number of female candidates in the 2004 elections rose 35 per cent and the number of women elected by 20 per cent (about double the percentage of women elected in 1999).

Women's movement impact

According to the RNGS model, the movement impact/state response can be classified as a 'dual response', as female MPs took part in the debate and in the decision-making process, and the policy outcome matched the objectives of those who promoted the reform.

Women's policy agency activities

In the second half of the 1990s, the overall structure of the WPAs was reinforced. In 1996, during the first centre-left government (presided over by Prodi), a Ministry for Equal Opportunities *(Ministero per le pari opportunità)* was created alongside the two existing commissions.

The ministry has the task of mainstreaming the principle of equal opportunities in all policies adopted by the government. It is a ministry without
portfolio that commands limited economic means and resources. At
municipal, provincial and regional level commissions for equal opportunities were finally set up and operated. In the late 1990s, new WPAs were
created in Piedmont where the Council of Elected Women (*Consulta delle
elette*) was established. It is composed of women elected from all parties in
regional, provincial and municipal elections, and its task is to promote
women's political participation and representation.

The WPA that intervened in the parliamentary debate was the Ministry
for Equal Opportunities, whose minister at the time of the debate was
Stefania Prestigiacomo, a young manager from Sicily and a member of
Forza Italia who was not involved in the feminist movement. Not only was
Prestigiacomo the signatory of a bill concerning the reform, but when the
law was adopted, she credited this success to the centre-right women.
The reform was also given a substantial boost by the CNPPO, chaired by
Marina Piazza, a feminist sociologist. In terms of the RNGS model,
WPAs played an insider role in gendering the debate.

Women's movement characteristics

The movement was still fragmented, but it was growing. In the late 1990s
the autonomous wing consisted of a greater number of groups and
associations than during the previous debates. The autonomous movement may be described as a vast archipelago of small groups working at
local level. They tended to have a structured organisation and to specialise
in individual issues. The groups work in issue areas typical of the feminist
movement such as women's health and culture (Della Porta 2003). Many
associations provide social services, particularly services related to the
fields of maternity, gynaecology, intercultural mediation and violence
against women. They organise cultural and vocational courses, guidance
courses for family problems, legal advice, helplines for female victims of
violence and so forth.

In contrast to the previous period, feminist groups adopted a more
pragmatic approach. They sought alliances to achieve practical objectives
and began to appreciate relationships with the institutions, especially at
local level. The fact that in most cases the groups require public funding has
increased awareness of the importance of having women in decision-making
posts at both the local and national levels. Even though the issue of
increased women's representation in institutional bodies was still a low
priority issue, there was a greater consensus on the need to adopt positive
measures for ensuring balanced representation. The autonomous women's

movement may be considered as close to the left. The integrated women's movement continued to prioritise the issue of women's representation and was moderately close to the left.

Policy environment

The debate ended with a decision adopted by the National Assembly. The sub-system can be considered as moderately closed in this debate: there was an agreement between political parties on the adoption of the amendment, since it only established a general principle and not specific, practical measures. The debate started and developed during the centre-left governments presided over by Romano Prodi (May 1996 to October 1998), Massimo D'Alema (October 1998 to April 2000) and Giuliano Amato (April 2000 to March 2001). The debate concluded during the second Berlusconi government (started in June 2001) composed of *Forza Italia*, *Allenza Nazionale*, *Lega Nord* and CCD-CDU (a party created out of the former Christian Democratic Party).

Conclusion

The impact of the women's movement and of WPAs in gendering the debate on political representation produced positive and negative results. In the first debate, success may be accounted for by the long struggle waged by women activists in the PCI. This resulted in an empowerment of women within the internal party organisation at the time of the debate, as a result of which a number of women were present in the party decision-making bodies. The fact that the majority of female leaders, officials and members adhered to the new party helped to create support from male leaders. The official PDS commitment to represent different social groups also facilitated the acceptance of women's demands.

In the second debate, the initial and short-lived success was mainly a result of the weakness of the policy environment. The reforms adopted in 1993 were approved at a time when parties and the political elite as a whole had been considerably delegitimised. The party system had crumbled and the new parties that had risen from its ruins were seeking a fresh look. The determination of a number of female MPs and the support given by the WPAs played a crucial role in ensuring the approval of quotas. Subsequent defeat was a consequence of the closure of the sub-system which adopted the final decision of the Constitutional Court, a male-dominated institution to which women did not have access. The fragmentation and the lack of cohesiveness of the women's movement on the issue of quotas prevented the debate from being used to raise public awareness of women's under-representation. The parties (with the exception of left-wing parties) continued to evade the issue and to select a limited number of female candidates.

In the third debate, the movement's success can be explained by a number of reasons. The law was permissive. Instead of requiring practical provisions that would have to be implemented to increase the representation of women, it stated a general principle. Such generality enabled a great number of actors to agree. It is likely that in the eyes of right-wing politicians the law was considered as a useful rhetorical strategy to show their positive attitude towards women's demands without committing themselves to any real action. In actual fact, the debate following the reform, the numerous legislative initiatives that had been presented, and the new regulations for the European elections adopted in 2004 showed that there is true determination by women not to let the reform be disregarded. Heightened awareness among public opinion, and among women voters in particular, of the gender gap in political representation probably helped reduce the hostility of the centre-right parties, which did not want to lose consensus among female voters.

The use by feminist activists of arguments relating to the legislation adopted by international organisations (UN, Council of Europe, EU) and to the backwardness of Italy as compared with other democratic countries proved to be an important element of pressure on reluctant male politicians.

Up to the end of the 1990s, the paradox in the Italian situation lay in the contrast between the activism of the integrated women's movement and the disappointing results achieved in terms of women's presence in elective posts. In the 1980s and in the early 1990s this might be explained by the lack of cohesion of the movement, which weakened feminist activists' attempts to achieve their goals. By the early 2000s there was a more widespread awareness of the problem of women's under-representation and of the need to adopt affirmative measures, the only ones able to oblige parties to include greater numbers of women in the candidate lists. Such awareness helps to explain the success achieved in gendering the debate on the constitutional amendment. The next step is to obtain effective measures to secure effective implementation of the amendment in all elections.

References

Baccetti, Carlo 1997, *IL Pds. Verso un nuovo modello di partito?* Bologna: IL Mulino

Bardi, Luciano 2002, 'Italian Parties: Change and Functionality', in Paul Webb, David Farrell and Ian Holliday (eds.) *Political Parties in Advanced Industrial Democracies*, Oxford: Oxford University Press, pp. 46–76

Beccalli, Bianca 1999, *Donne in quota*, Milan: Feltrinelli

Bertolino, Simone 2004, *Rifondazione comunista. Storia e organizzazione*, Bologna: IL Mulino

Bucci, Gianni 1993, 'Mezza listaè danna, la Polemica Cartimia.' *IL giornale*, 5 August

Ceccanti, Stefano and Salvatore Vassallo (eds.) 2004, *Come chiudere la transizione. Cambiamento, apprendimento e adattamento nel sistema politico italiano*, Bologna: IL Mulino

Corbetta, Piergiorgio and Arturo M. L. Parisi 1994, 'Ancora un 18 aprile. Il referendum sulla legge elettorale per il Senato', in Carol Mershon and Gianfranco Pasquino (eds.) *Politica in Italia. I fatti dell'anno e le interpretazioni*, Bologna: IL Mulino, pp. 141–60

Cotta, Maurizio and Pierangelo Isernia (eds.) 1996, *IL gigante dai piedi di argilla. Le ragioni della crisi della prima repubblica: partiti e politiche dagli anni '80 a Mani pulite*, Bologna: IL Mulino

D'Alimonte, Roberto and Alessandro Chiaramonte 1995, 'Il nuovo sistema elettorale italiano: le opportunità e le scelte', in Stefano Bartolini and Roberto D'Alimonte (eds.) *Maggioritario ma non troppo*, Bologna: IL Mulino, pp. 37–81

Della Porta, Donatella 2003, 'The Women's Movement, the Left, and the State: Continuities and Changes in the Italian Case' in Lee Ann Banaszak, Karen Beckwith and Dieter Rucht (eds.) *Women's Movements Facing the Reconfigured State*, Cambridge: Cambridge University Press, pp. 48–68

DONNE 2000 a cinque anni dalla Conferenza mondiale di Pechino. Le cose fatte, gli ostacoli incontrati, le cose da fare, Quaderni internazionali di vita italiana, Presidenza del Consiglio dei Ministri, Dipartimento per l'informazione e l'editoria, 1999. www.palazzochigi.it/pariopportunità

Dossier-provvedimento della Camera dei deputati 'L'elezione diretta del sindaco e la riforma del sistema elettorale locale. Lavori preparatori della legge 25 marzo 1993, n. 81', vols. I–XII, pp. 1–1920

Dossier n. 128/II, parte prima – quinta, XI legislatura, settembre 1995, Camera dei deputati, servizio studi, 'Nuove norme per l'elezione della Camera dei deputati. Lavori preparatori della legge 4 agosto 1993, n. 277', pp. 1–1898

Dossier n. 59/I, parte prima – terza, XII legislatura – marzo 1995, Camera dei deputati, servizio studi, 'Nuove norme per la elezione dei consigli regionali, lavori preparatori della L. 23 febbraio 1995, n. 43', pp. 1–942

Fusaro, Carlo 1995, *Le regole della transizione*, Bologna: IL Mulino
2000 'Elezione diretta del presidente e forme di governo regionale', in Alessandro Chiaramonte and Roberto D'Alimonte (eds.) *Il maggioritario regionale. Le elezioni del 16 aprile 2000*, Bologna: IL Mulino, pp. 35–58

Ginsborg, Paul 1996, 'Explaining Italy's Crisis', in Stephen Gundle and Simon Parker (eds.) *The New Italian Republic: From the Fall of the Berlin Wall to Berlusconi*, London and New York: Routledge, pp. 19–39

Guadagnini, Marila 1993, 'A Partitocrazia Without Women: the Case of the Italian Party System', in Joni Lovenduski and Pippa Norris (eds.) *Gender and Party Politics*, London: Sage Publications, pp. 168–204
1998, 'The Debate on Women's Quotas in Italian Electoral Legislation', *Swiss Review of Political Science*, 4, 3: 97–102

2000, *La stagione del disincanto? Cittadini, cittadine e politica alle soglie del duemila*, Turin: IL Segnalibro

(ed.) 2003, *Da elettrici a elette. Riforme istituzionali e rappresentanza delle donne in Italia, in Europa e negli Stati Uniti*, Turin: Celid

Ignazi, Piero 1992, *Dal Pci al Pds*, Bologna: IL Mulino

Morlino, Leonardo 1996, 'Crisis of Parties and Change of Party System in Italy', *Party Politics* 2, 1: 5–30

Parker, Simon 1996, 'Electoral reform and political change in Italy, 1991–1994', in Stephen Gundle and Simon Parker (eds.) *The New Italian Republic: From the Fall of the Berlin Wall to Berlusconi*, London and New York: Routledge, pp. 40–56

Pasquino, Gianfranco 1999, 'Autopsia della Bicamerale', in David Hine and Salvatore Vassallo (eds.) *Politica in Italia. I fatti dell'anno e le interpretazioni*, Bologna: IL Mulino, pp. 117–38

2002 *II sistema politico italiano. Autorità, istituzioni, società*, Bologna: Bonomia University Press

Verzichelli, Luca and Maurizio Cotta 2003, 'Italy: From "Constrained" Coalitions to Alternative Governments?', in Wolfang C. Müller and Kaare Strøm (eds.) *Coalition Governments in Western Europe*, Oxford: Oxford University Press, pp. 433–97

www.parlamento.it

www.senato.it

www.deputatids.it

www.dsonline.it/partito/aree/donne

Newspapers examined include: *L'Avvenire, IL Corriere della Sera, IL Giornale, La Repubblica, La Stampa, L'Unità*

Interviews include:

Tina Anselmi, president of the Commission for Equal Opportunities of the Prime Minister's Office in 1993

Laura Cima, member of parliament and member of the National Commission for Equal Opportunities

Francesca Izzo, co-ordinator of women in the Democratic Party of the Left (PDS)

Marina Piazza, president of the Commission for Equal Opportunities of the Prime Minister's Office

Chiara Valentini, journalist

High tides in a low country: gendering
political representation in the Netherlands

Jantine Oldersma

Introduction

The right to be represented was a central issue in the Dutch war of
independence (1568–1648) that resulted in the Republic of the Seven
United Provinces. The Netherlands, including Belgium, became a centralised kingdom in 1813 after the Napoleonic occupation; in 1830,
however, the Belgians revolted to become an independent kingdom.
The basic rules for representative government were formulated in 1848;
in 1917 universal suffrage, male and female, was won. The Dutch political system is based on proportional representation; the most important
legislative body is the second chamber, the first chamber having limited
powers. A multi-party system makes coalition governments a permanent
feature; political parties are key actors in the policy process.

Until the 1960s the political system was remarkably stable; Dutch
political parties followed the fault lines of society, forming Catholic,
Protestant and Social Democratic 'pillars'. An extensive system of corporatist 'advisory boards' played an important role in the 'consensus
democracy', providing institutionalised access to the policy-making process mainly for business and professional interests and labour unions
belonging to the three pillars (Andeweg and Irwin 1993).

From the 1960s onwards, when 'new' social movements demanded
more 'democracy', representation was regularly on the agenda in three
types of arenas: in the media, political parties and parliament. A new
political party, D66, demanding a more confrontational style of politics,
entered parliament with seven members in 1966. The women's movement was another important factor. Its core organisation, *Man-Vrouw-
Maatschappij* (MVM, Man-Woman-Society), founded in October 1968,
began campaigning for more women in politics during the 1972 election
and has subsequently put pressure on political parties to pay more attention to women's issues and women's representation. The demand for
more women in politics received media attention at every election thereafter. In the 1940s and 1950s the percentage of women in the second

chamber rose from 5 to almost 10 per cent. Towards the end of the 1970s the percentage hovered around 15, and towards the end of the century around 35 per cent. The first chamber, the city councils and the cabinets lag behind with approximately a quarter of female members. The percentage of women in the cabinet received a severe blow when a right-wing cabinet formed in 2002 came up with only one female minister out of a total of fourteen. This was remedied, however, a year later in a new right-wing cabinet after vigorous protests from women in the conservative parties.

Policy-making institutions

Parties and parliament are the most important players where political representation is concerned. Debates over representation, however, mainly affected parties on the left of the political spectrum. D66 made political representation their main concern, but the party has rarely succeeded in winning more than 5–10 per cent of the votes.

Selection of debates

The turmoil over democratic representation, brought to the political agenda by political parties, reached parliament in the 1980s. The *Commissie-Biesheuvel* reported in 1984 on reforms to strengthen the influence of voters. In 1989 a committee of parliamentary leaders of all parties (the *Commissie-Deetman*) made an inventory of frictions in the Dutch political and administrative system. Six sub-committees followed up on the initial analysis. The *Commissie-De Koning* examined the relationship between voters and elected officials, and the *Commissie-De Jong* studied the corporatist system. Both reported in 1993. Representation of women was an important issue in the 1970s and 1980s in two left-wing parties, the *Pacifistisch Socialistische Partij* (PSP, Pacifist Socialist Party) and the *Communistische Partij Nederland* (CPN), both of which would in the 1990s become part of *Groen Links* (Green Left). The struggle over political representation in the Social Democratic Party in the 1970s had profound consequences for national politics because the party took part in a governing coalition from 1973 to 1977. Women's representation became an issue in the right-wing parties in the second half of the 1980s.

In the 1970s the main debates about representation in the Netherlands were inside political parties. From these the debate about the 'action party' between 1967 and 1977 in the Social Democratic Party has been selected. Though this party did not take the lead in debates about representation, the fact that they commanded a larger proportion of the vote make them more interesting, from our point of view, than D66 or the left-wing splinter parties.

In the 1980s, debates about representation were mainly concerned with the political representation of women in elected positions. The debate about the second memorandum on equality policy has been chosen to highlight the discussions in the women's movement over the issue of representation.

In the 1990s, there were three important parliamentary debates about representation: on the electoral system, on the introduction of referenda in the constitution, and on corporatism. Proposals to change the proportional electoral system to a majoritarian system were watered down to a mixed system and then abandoned; the introduction of a corrective referendum was defeated by a narrow margin of one vote. However, the debate on corporatism has been chosen because this phenomenon has been considered one of the defining characteristics of Dutch political culture.

Debate 1: The Social Democratic Party (PvdA), 1966–1977

How the debate came to the public agenda

Between 1963 and 1966, the Social Democratic Party lost about a quarter of its voters. A group of party members, calling themselves the New Left (*Nieuw Links*), blamed the party's incumbent leaders; allegedly they were too inclined to accommodation and compromise. The party could only survive, they claimed, if it could win back the (presumably young) voters active in grass-roots organisations such as the student and the feminist movements. The New Left analysis of the party's problems became dominant in the party executive: in 1973 it pleaded for a reorganisation to turn the party into an 'action party' (Beck et al. 1978). In 1977 a new party platform incorporated these ideas.

Dominant frame of debate

The New Left wanted to make the socialist party more successful by 'polarisation' of the political spectrum. Organising the party in a more democratic way and linking it to social movements was seen as a crucial element in this strategy. In 1967 New Leftists published their views on party organisation in a pamphlet: 'Een partij om mee te werken' (A Party to Work With). The party should aim at polarisation in politics; expose oppositions and conflicts in society and represent them in the political arena. They argued for a more active membership, more democratic control and transparency, and for persuading incumbent functionaries to make room for new ones. In its organisational structure the 'action party' should reserve positions for active groups like young members and women. Referenda and decentralisation of candidate selection to local party branches should make the party more responsive to members. The party congress installed a committee to study these proposals and in 1968 it published a report (*Rapport van de Structuurcommisie*).

While the New Left was mainly interested in grass-roots participation and 'democratisation', an 'Amsterdam School' of political scientists within the party also pleaded for a more polarised style of politics. In their view, the introduction of a majoritarian electoral system combined with a directly elected prime minister would lead to more vitality and transparency in politics. The electoral losses of religious parties were interpreted as portending a full secularisation of voters. Dutch politics would become a bipolar system with a 'progressive' and a 'conservative' block. The 'pollution' of politics with such 'non-political concerns' as religion would soon be a thing of the past. The 1969 party congress accepted the principle of decentralised candidate selection and also gave the New Left a substantive bridgehead in the party executive. New Left members found their way into the party elite in the 1970s (Van Praag 1991).[1]

Gendering the debate

The Social Democratic Party's auxiliary organisation *Vrouwencontact* (Women's Contact) played a key role in gendering the debates within the party. The feeling in the 1960s was that separate women's organisations were outdated and that women should 'integrate' with the 'normal' party. *Vrouwencontact*, however, was revitalised under the influence of the feminist movement and could successfully claim to organise the grass-roots activists that the party wanted to woo (Van de Velde 1994, pp. 216–17).

Joke Smit and Hedy D'Ancona founded the first Dutch second-wave organisation, MVM. Both were members of the Social Democratic Party, but not of the party's auxiliary organisation. At their behest, in 1968, the executive distributed a questionnaire on the position of women to the members of *Vrouwencontact*. Concerns of the new women's movement, like better education and career opportunities, childcare and abortion

---

[1] To hasten this process, a substantial faction of party members argued that the party should declare that they would not enter into a coalition with the Catholic Party, but make a joint programme with other 'progressive' parties before every election (Van Praag 1991, pp. 66–7).

rights, turned out to be widely shared by the members. This resulted in a resolution adopted by the 1968 *Vrouwencontact* congress, demanding party support for these issues. In 1969 Ien van den Heuvel, a party activist with feminist leanings, was elected party chair, which facilitated the introduction of a feminist programme in the party itself. Following a joint effort by MVM members and *Vrouwencontact*, the election programme of 1971 was amended to include a chapter on equal opportunities for men and women, including a reference to legal abortions (Ribberink 1998, pp. 101–5).

The response of party women to Smit and D'Ancona's questionnaire showed that the concerns of feminism had a large following among Social Democratic women. The adoption of feminism worked the other way around as well: it attracted feminist women to *Vrouwencontact* and to the party. This enabled feminist party members to present themselves as a prime example of linking the party to 'new movements'. Local women's groups, in decline during the 1960s, flourished again in the 1970s (Beck et al. 1978). A campaign for preferential voting in 1972 doubled the amount of preferential votes for women on the Social Democratic list (Ribberink 1998, p. 229). Activists calling themselves *Rooie Vrouwen* (Red Women) took over *Vrouwencontact* and in 1975, the organisation formally changed its name to *Rooie Vrouwen*.

Vrouwencontact had been a pressure group for women in politics for most of its existence, and the feminist interest in the issue of representation naturally reflected with their concerns (Van de Velde 1994, p. 227). It served as a convenient stepping-stone for gendering the debate on 'democratisation' of the party, bringing women into the party and into the party elite. The feminist frame emphasising women's interests as well as the high level of grass-roots activity of their members fitted very well with the dominant frame of party activists. Although there was some resistance, based on the idea that female candidates might compromise the quality of politicians, this was not very strong.

Policy outcome

In 1973, women won a substantive representation (six of twenty-six members) on the committee to design a new party platform. At the party congress of 1977, the new platform, advocating more socialism as well as more feminism, was accepted. The *Rooie Vrouwen* pushed even more feminist issues through than had been in the draft. In 1975, the *Rooie Vrouwen* successfully lobbied the party executive for a quota for 25 per cent women on party lists. The party executive decided to ask the candidate selection committees in 1977 to strive for 25 per cent women; the 1977 congress also adopted 25 per cent as a target. In 1986 the party executive moved at congress to make the 25 per cent quota mandatory and to adopt a voluntary target of 50 per cent female candidates in party committees and on party lists (Van de Velde 1994, p. 230).

Women's movement impact

The party discourse was gendered: not only were feminist issues introduced into election programmes, the basic party document was also changed to incorporate feminism in 1977. The siege of feminists revitalised *Vrouwencontact* and more women took part in party committees and in the party executive, making this a clear case of dual response. The issue of women's representation was taken up by the party executive in 1971 and new measures were taken when efforts were not effective. The percentage of women on the party lists slowly increased during the 1970s and more so during the 1980s.

Women's policy agency activities

A women's agency at national level did not yet exist during the first part of this debate. The machinery for equality policy in the Netherlands was set in motion in 1974 by the Den Uyl administration (1973–77), a coalition cabinet of Social Democrats (PvdA), Democrats (D66) and the left wing of the Christian Democrats (ARP). In response to a postcard campaign and in view of the United Nation's International Women's Year, in 1975 a committee was formed, consisting of independent 'experts', to give advice on the needs of Dutch women. This *Emancipatie Kommissie* (EK, Emancipation Committee) mainly consisted of MVM members. It designed a five-year plan for equality policy, containing a programme and a blueprint for a national machinery (Emancipatie Kommissie 1976).

Vrouwencontact, however, could qualify in this case as a quasi-women's policy agency. It did have the capacity to impact on policy-making, and could prepare and elaborate policy proposals relative to party politics. *Vrouwencontact* was instrumental in persuading party members that feminist demands were widely shared by women in the party. The existing network and their access to party resources facilitated feminists in gaining access to policy-making circles within the party; proposals for quotas gained legitimacy because *Vrouwencontact* supported them. The organisation thus played an insider role.

When the party became the dominant factor in a left-wing coalition in 1973, members of MVM and *Vrouwencontact* entered the national arena to gain a foothold for feminism there.

Women's movement characteristics

The women's movement grew rapidly during the 1970s with a strong emphasis on grass-roots activity and direct action. They were very close to the left, and leaders of the movement were mostly members of left-wing parties, but – most clearly in the case of abortion – there were tensions between the autonomous part of the movement, who preferred independence from 'politics', and party members. The priority of the issue of women's representation for women inside the Social Democratic Party was high. They strongly believed that politics was very important if women's position in society were to be changed. The 'red women', first inside *Vrouwencontact* and later as *Rooie Vrouwen*, when the name of the organisation was changed, acted as a pressure group and mobilised women for political office. They were very cohesive on this issue and counter-movements did not develop. There were debates with other parts of the movement about the nature and desirability of party politics.

Policy environment

The policy environment during the 1970s, in the national arena and in the Social Democratic Party, was open. The Social Democratic Party elite was open to new ideas because they had suffered electoral defeat. They hoped to gain new voters by incorporating women and the young, making for difficulties when they became part of the governing coalition between 1973 and 1977. The unwillingness of activists of the 'new' movements to accept compromise in the course of coalition building eventually cost the party a second term in power. This traumatic event of winning the election but losing the coalition negotiations led to a recentralisation of candidate selection in the party, and diminished the sympathy for the new movements.

Debate 2: Equality policy plan, 1981–1985

How the debate came to the public agenda

Although the Netherlands had a junior minister and an agency in charge of equality policy from 1978 onwards, women's movement activists were dissatisfied with their accomplishments. The general feeling that the feminist cause was severely hampered by the lack of female representation in politics was voiced most impressively by Joke Smit at the beginning of the 1980s, when she pleaded for an independent women's party. In reaction to this, female members of parliament united in the *Kamerbreed*

Vrouwenoverleg (All Parties Women's Caucus) and agreed to work together on women's issues across party lines. Independent feminist intellectuals took the issue up by organising two conferences on feminism and political power (Bleich et al. 1982; Dorsman et al. 1983).

The issue of feminism and political power became a central issue in equality politics when the Social Democratic Party entered the cabinet in 1981. Hedy D'Ancona became junior minister for equality policy. She initiated a new policy plan, incorporating recent theorising about gender inequality. Unfortunately, the cabinet fell in May 1982 and a right-wing coalition took over in November 1982. Equality policy was taken over by Liberal Annelien Kappeyne van de Coppello, who proceeded with the programme left by her Social Democratic predecessor. The programme was translated into a policy paper in 1984, discussed with women's organisations and adopted by the cabinet in 1985.

Dominant frame of debate

The debate resulting in a new policy paper was mainly concerned with the conceptualisation of 'women'. In the first policy paper for equality policy, women were visualised as a backward group in society; to become 'normal' citizens they would have to be emancipated. This interpretation was in tune not only with male (expert) views of women, but also with dominant ideas in traditional women's organisations (Meijer 1996). Equality policy was needed to change mentalities and to 'educate' women. Traditional as well as some feminist organisations received subsidies from the *Directie Coördinatie Emancipatiebeleid* (DCE, the women's policy agency) to train women in political skills. In terms of representation, women were not thought to be ready to play a part in politics. Thus appropriate policies on representation meant teaching women the skills deemed necessary to function among male politicians. There was no place for policies to change selection procedures or introduce quota systems as they would compromise the 'quality' of candidates. Moreover, they were unnecessary – women would enter politics 'naturally', once they were better equipped (Oldersma 2002).

Gendering the debate

The new women's movement in the Netherlands in the 1980s did not see women as backward, but blamed their position on a society that was structurally biased against women. This is therefore a case in which an already gendered debate was 're-gendered' in a more feminist fashion by movement actors, party women and their allies in the women's policy agency. The standard conceptualisations of 'women', 'politics', 'the state' and 'representation' were all under attack during this period. The essentialism of early feminist notions of 'women' was denounced, but formerly antagonistic groups and organisations of women did join forces.

The nature of 'politics' and its potential to change society was an important theme of discussion. *Feminisme en politieke macht* (Feminism and Political Power, Bleich et al. 1982), a collection of papers written for a conference on women and politics in 1981, expressed many shades of distrust in 'politics'. 'Anarcafeminists' wanted to remain outside 'society'; 'radical feminists' saw 'politics' as irrelevant and wanted to develop 'the self'; 'revolutionary feminists' also saw politics or 'reformism' as irrelevant and wanted to fight the 'patriarchal class state'. Another theme was the corrupting influence 'politics' might have on 'women' (Outshoorn 1991). Activists saw compromise and deliberation as high treason against 'the movement'. Women in political parties and in labour unions as well as women from traditional women's organisations wanted to unite to gain more influence in politics. In 1982, the *Breed Platform Vrouwen voor Ekonomische Zelfstandigheid* (Federation of Women for Economic Independence) was launched and united the 'new' and the 'old' women's movements (De Jong and Sjerps 1987).

Feminist academics were also divided about the potential of politics to empower women. A structuralist wing advocated studying power relations in society as the best way forward. Another wing wanted to pay more attention to studying selection procedures and policy processes (Leijenaar and Saharso 1983; Stasse et al. 1982). The structuralist wing was influential in DCE policy in the 1980s and led to subsidies for organisations in civil society to hire a femocrat. The other wing did not influence policy before the 1990s, but was able to do important research commissioned by the Ministry of Home Affairs (Leijenaar and Jansen 1981). A symposium in 1983, where the commissioned report was presented, provided the opportunity to explain why a political system that excluded women could never be called truly 'democratic' (Outshoorn 1984). In 1989, when a female Social Democrat became Minister of Home Affairs, selection procedures became an object of policy.

Policy outcome

A committee of civil servants and experts formulated a Concept Beleidsplan Emancipatie (Concept Policy Plan on Equality) in 1984 that largely followed recent feminist theorising on gender inequality. Positions of influence in society and in politics are still male territory, the document states, and this is seen as one of the reasons why women are as yet unable to realise the changes they desire. The overall aim of the analysis was to shift the blame for women's under-representation from their putative backwardness to the gendered nature of unequal power relations. However, under-representation in politics received very little attention, and where it was mentioned it was presented as a problem of the backwardness of women. Women must be made aware of their position and helped to gain insight, the document states. They must organise socially and politically to realise the aim of structural change in society: 'This is why the proportion of women in public functions needs to grow' ... 'Support for the women's movement (taken broadly) is therefore an essential part of the government's policies for women.' The 'taken broadly' was to include traditional women's organisations, without which the necessary support of the Christian Democrats would not be forthcoming. The price for a policy on women in politics, thus, was a retreat into a more defensive policy frame.

This short clause formed the basis for granting subsidies to organisations that could hire, for a limited period, their own 'femocrat'. Nearly all political parties applied for one, to support their own auxiliary women's organisation, and to help define their view on women's issues. The selection of women candidates received a further boost from 1988 until 1992, when subsidies to political parties were granted under the condition that they would contribute to the selection of more women on the party list (Van de Velde 1994, pp. 299–311).

In 1985, the *Vereniging voor Vrouwenbelangen, Vrouwenarbeid en Gelijk Staatsburgerschap* (*Vrouwenbelangen*, Association for Women's Interests, Women's Work and Equal Citizenship) received a subsidy to support their organisation. *Vrouwenbelangen* was a direct descendant of the *Vereniging voor Vrouwenkiesrecht* (Association for Women's Suffrage), founded in 1894. It had a small membership of professional and politically active women from different parties. The 1985 International Women's Year provided the occasion for starting *Aktie m/v 50/50* (Action m/f 50/50), to stimulate attention to the issue of women in politics. *Vrouwenbelangen* formed a coalition with most political parties. The subsidy helped to professionalise the campaign and to give it staying power (Angerman 1994).

Women's movement impact

Women and women's organisations, feminist or traditional, were taken more seriously as participants in the policy process. Movement ideas were taken over with very little alteration, making this a case of dual response. Yet no specific policy on politics resulted. This was a result partly of divisions within the movement about the correct way forward, partly of lingering notions of the backwardness of women. A direct policy, confronting selection procedures and political culture, was unacceptable to the cabinet or, for that matter, to many women's organisations or political parties. Subsidies to women's organisations, however, did stimulate parties to pay attention to women's issues and to select women.

Women's policy agency activities

The leadership of the women's policy agency during this period changed from Christian Democrat to Social Democrat to Liberal. Hedy D'Ancona, feminist and Social Democrat, made an enormous impact by commissioning a new policy plan that gave the agency a cross-sectional scope and a mandate that clearly included political representation. The staff as well as the budget for research and subsidies increased considerably. Most of her ideas were taken over and developed further by Liberal Mrs Kappeyne van de Coppello, who turned out to be quietly feminist in her own way. D'Ancona moved the agency from the Ministry of Culture and Social Work to the Ministry of Social Affairs, where it remained. The agency played an insider role, trying to change prevailing political discourses by stimulating debate and research. The two conferences on women and political power mentioned above were subsidised; dissemination of the proceedings was financed, and a booklet on women in parliament was commissioned in conjunction with parliament itself. The agency's research policy prioritised research on power and politics and stimulated the publication of a number of studies into the gendered nature of Dutch politics. Lastly, the subsidy politics of the *Beleidsplan* were utilised to set femocrats to work on all political parties and on a front of feminists united around *Vrouwenbelangen* as well. The agency, albeit in a roundabout way, both gendered policy debates and advocated movement goals.

Women's movement characteristics

At the beginning of the 1980s the 'core movement' organisation, MVM, was still in existence; it would dissolve in 1988. The movement was a large conglomerate of service organisations, semi-commercial organisations and many women's networks inside political parties and unions. The women's movement was more or less consolidated in the course of the 1980s, but may more aptly be seen as growing as a consequence of the alliances with traditional women's organisations. This moved feminism away from its left-wing allies to a position somewhat removed from the left. Women in parliament united. During the 1980s nearly all political parties more or less adopted the goal of having more women on their lists. In that decade, politics as such was not a high priority issue for the women's movement, but it gained some strong advocates. This shift in alliances within the women's movement makes it difficult to state whether the movement was cohesive: this was not the case at the beginning of the 1980s, but cohesiveness was forged between different groups in the second half of the decade. There was no counter-movement, but a very small religious party, the *Staatkundig Gereformeerde Partij* (SGP, Calvinist), still refuses to put women on the list to this day.

Policy environment

A coalition of Christian Democrats and Liberals dominated Dutch politics from 1977 until 1989, with the exception of a brief spell between September 1981 and May 1982 when a CDA/PvdA/D66 coalition provided a window of opportunity for feminists. Overall, the power structure was closed, especially where women and politics were concerned: contemplating a policy of quotas or other direct ways to move more women in to political positions was unthinkable and there was no question of allowing women into policy networks. Hedy D'Ancona used her nine months in office as junior minister of equality policy to the full by drawing in feminists to write a policy plan that changed the conception of women and by designing a subsidy policy that created opportunities for feminist researchers and for femocrats. Though the political climate changed to conservative, the Liberal junior minister made sure that the women's policy agency remained a niche for feminism.

Debate 3: Corporatism, 1989–1997

How the debate came to the public agenda

In the 1970s, corporatism appeared on the policy agenda when 'Iron Rings' of interest organisations, civil servants and experts were blamed for frustrating 'progressive' politics.[2] In the 1980s, the corporatist channel was seen by right-wing governments as an obstruction to cuts in government funding. As a result of diligent weeding by a number of committees, the committee system slimmed down to about half its size during this decade (*Commissie-De Jong* 1993, p. 41). In 1989, D66

---

[2] Ex-prime minister Den Uyl attributed the failure of his own 'progressive' policies to obstruction by 'obscure' entanglements of civil servants and committee members (Van den Berg and Molleman 1980).

managed to put constitutional reform on the parliamentary agenda in the form of the *Commissie-Deetman*, formed by the leaders of all parties. The *Commissie-De Jong*, consisting of parliamentarians, was then asked to propose a renovation of the corporatist channel resulting in drastic restructuring.[3] The spirit of reform benefited from a parliamentary enquiry in 1992, inspired by the failure of attempts to restructure the welfare state (Commissie Buurmeijer 1993).

Dominant frame of debate

The debate about corporatism in the Netherlands was influenced by Anglo-Saxon political science rather than the more benign views expressed by Schmitter and Lehmbruch's 1979 volume. 'Overload' of the state by interest organisations was one major concern; the other was the threat that corporatism might pose to the 'primacy of politics'. In the report by the *Commissie-De Jong*, 'Raad op Maat' (Advice to Measure), published in 1993, a shift away from interest organisations towards expert advice was advocated. Good policy development required expert advice that served parliament as well as government. Interest representation might be useful, but only in policy implementation. In the liberal mood of the 1990s, the report of the *Commissie-De Jong* met with general acclaim. It was unanimously accepted in parliament and duly implemented. The report was criticised severely by Dutch academic experts who regretted the muffling of the voice of civil society and predicted that commercial consultancies would benefit, costing more and obscuring the process of consultation. These voices went unheeded (Oldersma and Woldendorp 1995).

Gendering the debate

In debates about gender and corporatism, the issue of descriptive representation fared much better than the issue of substantive representation. That women should be present was readily accepted, but the presence of expertise on gender issues or representatives of women's interests was a different matter. The main actors pleading for both types of representation were the *Emancipatie Kommissie* and its successor the *Emancipatieraad* (ER, Emancipation Council).

---

[3] It is worth noting that the *Commissie-De Jong* had two female members. The *Commissie-Deetman* itself had 33 per cent female members; the sub-committees together had only 6 per cent. These 6 per cent, two female members, were concentrated in the committee on corporatism, while the other five sub-committees were all male.

The first study of committee members in 1967 revealed that only 5 per cent were women. In a letter to all ministers, the *Nationale Vrouwen Raad* (NVR, National Women's Council), a federation of traditional women's organisations, drew attention to the statistics. The *Emancipatie Kommissie* called for more women in advisory bodies in the report it published in 1976. A survey of advisory bodies by its successor, the *Emancipatieraad*, in 1991 showed that the rules meant to stimulate the appointment of women were not only not implemented, but not even known to most officials (Emancipatieraad 1991). The council's advice was to set and implement targets. By 1993, the number of women in advisory bodies had risen to some 15 per cent. A survey of all committee members in that year showed that the goal, if not yet the practice, of descriptive representation had been taken on board by most political actors (Oldersma 1996). Commenting on the report of the *Commissie-De Jong* in 1994, the Emancipation Council stated that the introduction of twelve new 'strategic committees' gave the cabinet a unique opportunity to realise immediately its long-term aim, namely that advisory bodies should have 50 per cent female members. In the debate in parliament most parties agreed.

The history of substantive representation in the traditional corporatist channel is different. In 1981, the *Emancipatieraad* (1981–97) followed in the footsteps of the *Emancipatie Kommissie* (1975–81) to advise government on its policy on women. The selection of members posed problems. Representation of women's organisations would have to incorporate traditional women's organisations and thereby offend feminists. A committee of 'experts' from the women's movement would contain only feminists and was not acceptable to Christian Democrats. The compromise was a committee of 'independent' members, carefully mirroring party politics (Klink 2000). The ER was the main foothold of the women's movement in the corporatist system. Over the years it gained prestige in the eyes of movement actors as well as among politicians, as it could benefit from gender expertise developed at universities and in research institutions. It had a state-wide mandate and could largely follow its own agenda.

Though the ER, as an 'expert' committee, fitted the new policy, the *Commissie-De Jong* categorised it as (women's) interest group oriented and thus a candidate for abolition. The demarcations between new 'expert' committees would largely follow departmental boundaries and have no place for equality policy. The council, however, made a final attempt to fit equality policy in the new policy frame. If the advisory function were to be spread over the new committees, the *Raad* stated, then it would need to be formalised and members with expertise on equality policy would have to be included. In addition an expert centre was needed to monitor and stimulate the mainstreaming of gender advice for a limited period (Emancipatieraad 1994).

Policy outcome

In 1980, the Ministry of Culture, Recreation and Welfare issued rules to stimulate greater representation of women in advisory bodies, later endorsed by the cabinet. The *Beleidsplan Emancipatie* (1985) briefly argued for more women, as well as for more attention to gender by 'special' as well as 'normal' committees. In 1987, the cabinet issued guidelines aiming at a male/female ratio of 1:1 in advisory bodies. For every open place the possibility of appointing a woman should be actively considered.

The *Commissie-De Jong* developed a revolutionary plan for implementation of its proposals: the 'Desert Law' abolished all existing advisory bodies on 1 January 1997. In the new situation every department would have only one advisory body for strategic long-term planning, consisting of leading experts in the field. Descriptive representation remained on the agenda. The Home Office, concerned with implementing the reform of corporatism, installed a helpdesk to aid selectors to find women with expertise in their field. 'Top Link', an organisation sponsored by DCE, helped to find women if the resources of the ministries fell short. Installation of some committees had to be postponed until a satisfactory percentage of women had been found. The new committees averaged 37 per cent women, bringing the total to 20–25 per cent (Klink 2000).[4]

Proposals to guarantee substantive representation encountered problems when a new government took power. The *Emancipatieraad* lost a third of its members in 1993 and was dissolved in 1997. The new law that was to present the framework for further regulations did not mention the task of advising on equality policy; neither did laws to install the new committees. Members were not explicitly selected for their expertise on equality policy. The expert centre intended to stimulate and monitor the process of 'mainstreaming' advice on equality matters in the new committees was no longer on the agenda. Instead, the new leadership of the women's policy agency embarked on a mission to force all the institutions they subsidised to merge. This new 'expert centre' would both support movement activities and take the task of advising government in hand. This was the start of a long, drawn-out conflict between the 'women's movement' and the policy agency. Eventually, Equality was formed, an

---

[4] Some technical committees were not abolished after all, because the members' advice would be more expensive if given on a commercial basis.

expert centre on gender and diversity, subsidised by DCE and with an appointed executive board of independent feminists that has no formal status as an advisory body.

ER members lobbied for a successor in 1997, to guarantee that the new system of committees would take up equality issues. Pressure by women's organisations and women in parliament succeeded in 1998 when the government established the *Tijdelijke Expertise Commissie voor Emancipatie in het nieuwe Adviestelsel* (TECENA, Temporary Expert Committee for Emancipation in the New Advisory System), a small committee of experts in women's studies, to ensure the mainstreaming of the advisory structure. TECENA finished in 2001 and has no successor.

Women's movement impact

Though the women's movement did not receive complete policy satisfaction, this case has to be classified as dual response. Women were participants in the policy process, and the discourse on selecting members and on substantively representing women was gendered. In the end, female experts on equality policy succeeded in having a niche in the advisory committee system until 2001. The percentage of women on advisory bodies also rose considerably.

Women's policy agency activities

The women's policy agency was in the hands of several Social Democratic leaders from 1989 on. It was still cross-sectional, political representation was part of the mandate and it had substantial resources. Elske ter Veld, a feminist, used the ER to outline a policy on representation, including descriptive as well as substantive representation in the corporatist channel. DCE participated in a committee of civil servants about the advisory structure but could not save the ER, though Ter Veld managed to keep it floating in a cheaper version until 1997. The advice of the council to implement the 50 per cent rule for new committees and to form an expert centre to mainstream advice on equality issues was received well in cabinet, and two new politicians, Wallage at equality policy and Van Thijn at the Home Office, agreed to implement it.[5] The 1994 elections frustrated these plans. Equality policy went to Social Democrat Ad Melkert, whose main priority was labour market policies. The reform of

---

[5] Ter Veld stepped down because she disagreed with a new proposal to cut back on invalid pensions.

the corporatist system was in the hands of Kohnstamm, a D66 junior minister. Although it did change its policies in the middle of the debate, we have to call the agency an insider, as it both gendered debates and introduced women into the policy process.

Women's movement characteristics

The women's movement at the beginning of the 1990s was highly fragmented and highly professionalised. The ER, though not a women's policy agency, did have a large staff and did undertake the gendering of debates on policy networks, aided by academic experts. Feminists in the Social Democratic Party pushed through to the cabinet in 1989, but Christian Democrats and Liberals were also under pressure from feminist and female members. In the case of substantive representation, the Liberal chairperson of the ER lobbied the Social Democratic minister to act on plans, written by left-wing academic experts. There was no counter-movement. The issue had a high priority for a small group of dedicated women, mostly professionally interested in equality policy.

Policy environment

The return to power of the Social Democrats in 1989, in coalition with the Christian Democrats, provided the women's movement with new opportunities. The cabinet contained three women, including Hedy D'Ancona and a number of female junior ministers. The Home Office was in the hands of Social Democrat Ien Dales, who opened the policy network to women's representatives. In 1994, a coalition of Social Democrats, Democrats and Liberals came to power and effectively closed policy networks down again. Social Democrat Ad Melkert prioritised labour market policies and wanted the agency to form alliances with industry; at the Home Office Kohnstamm took over, a D66 politician who abhorred interest group politics.

Conclusion

State responses to the movement

In all three cases the conclusion is dual response, but there are some reservations. In the first case, feminists boldly set up camp in the Social Democratic Party, where they remain until the present day. In the second case, gendering did take place and women did come into the policy process, but they did not succeed in expanding the discourse to include the issue of representation. This did happen at the beginning of the third debate in terms of descriptive representation, but the demise of a feminist leadership and the coming to power of a non-feminist leadership, all Social Democrats, frustrated the discussions on substantive representation.

Women's policy agency activities and characteristics

In the first case the national women's policy agency did not exist, but we treated *Vrouwencontact* as a quasi-WPA. It was quickly taken over by feminists and was well placed to play an insider role within the party. The national WPA had a political leadership from its establishment in 1978, but feminist leadership was restricted to brief periods of nine months in 1981–2 and three years at the beginning of the 1990s. Including Liberal Mrs Kappeyne van de Copello, the sum total is a mere seven years in nearly three decades. In all three debates, however, feminist leaders were crucial in bringing representation to the policy agenda and in defining and redefining it in a non-essentialist way. Feminist attempts to argue that all women had common interests in politics soon faltered when political reality proved that opinions could and did differ. Women from different parties, however, became a unified force for the representation of women in politics when they eventually managed to agree on common policies. Women's unity, in the end, was not a given, but was forged in the policy process.

The women's policy agency provided linkages between different groups within the women's movement and between movement actors and the policy network around the issue of representation. This was done by commissioning and stimulating research, by subsidising conferences and, in the second half of the 1980s, by subsidising femocrats. Subsidies to women's groups and the advisory function of the EK helped to disseminate the results of research and discussion.

In retrospect, however, the move from welfare to socio-economic politics did not favour prioritisation of the issue of representation. The discourse of the PvdA/VVD/D66 coalition in the 1990s, characterised by its slogan 'work, work, work', led to definitions of women's equality as a socio-economic problem and obscured the political dimension even further. Nevertheless, the agency did manage to gender discourses on representation and introduced women into the policy process on both occasions that it had an opportunity to do so.

The feminist movement has always been ambivalent about representation: descriptive representation seemed desirable because it widened the constituency but it de-emphasised politics. Substantive representation has the opposite effect, which might partially account for its relative lack of support. In the second and third debates there was no strong and cohesive actor to advocate both substantive and descriptive representation: in the first debate there was such an actor and in that case feminists were very successful.

As all three debates met with a dual response, it seems fair to conclude that the Dutch state has been open to feminist concerns. There are some caveats, however, as the measure of openness for the issue of representation has clearly shifted over time. In the first debate, the Social Democratic Party was very open to feminists and provided them with a wide-open window of opportunity when they led the governing coalition. But their periods in power were interruptions to right-wing rule. Even when they were in power, policies directly influencing the political system were anathema to left- and right-wing politicians. Nevertheless, the second debate shows that in the 1980s, equality of representation policies were designed and were successful, but they maintained a discourse of women's backwardness. Despite a promising start to the 1990s when the Social Democratic/Liberal/D66 coalition came to power, the minister in charge of the women's policy agency during the later part of the third debate de-prioritised the issue of women's substantive political representation.

Women's representation has progressed immensely in the Netherlands over the past thirty years, despite disagreement among feminists and right-wing coalitions. Movement actors, however, succeeded in framing the issue in a way that resonated with the prevailing political winds. The contribution of femocrats, able to transform any type of policy frame into a suitable policy, is considerable.

References

Andeweg, Rudy B. and Galen A. Irwin 1993, *Dutch Government and Politics*, London: Macmillan

Angerman, Arina 1994, 'Women in Politics: the Case of M/V 50/50, the Action Men/Women 50/50', paper presented at the seminar '*Effective Strategies and National Machinery*', New York

Beck, W., W. Van de Bunte, P. Nieuwenhuijsen, R. de Rooi, W. J. van Velzen, P. Viehol, R. Vos and W. van de Zandschulp (Werkgroep Partij in Actie) 1978, *Partij, parlement, activisme*, Deventer: Kluwer (WBS-cahiers)

Berg, Joop T. J. van den and Henk A. A. Molleman 1980, *Crisis in de Nederlandse politiek*, Alphen aan den Rijn: Samsom

Bleich, Anet, Freda Droes, Elsbeth Etty, Saskia Grotenhuis and Marijke Linthorst (eds.) 1982, *Feminisme en politieke macht, Vol. I: Posities, problemen en strategieën*, Amsterdam: De Populier

Commissie-Biesheuvel 1984, *Rapport van de Staatscommissie van Advies inzake de Relatie Kieser-Beleidsvorming*, The Hague: Staatsuitgeverij

Commissie-Buurmeijer 1993, *Rapport enquêtecommissie uitvoeringsorganen sociale verzekeringen*, The Hague: SDU

Commissie-Deetman 1990–1, *Rapport bijzondere commissie Vraagpunten*, Proceedings Second Chamber, 21 427, nr 3

Commissie-De Jong 1992–3, *Raad op maat. Rapport van de bijzondere commissie Vraagpunten Adviesorganen*, Proceedings Second Chamber, 21 427, nr. 29

Commissie-De Koning 1992–3, *Het bestel bijgesteld*, Proceedings Second Chamber, 21 427, nrs. 36–7

Dorsman, Willy, Elsbeth Etty, Monique Leijenaar, Marijke Linthorst and Tineke de Nijs (eds.) 1983, *Feminisme en politieke macht, Deel II: Herverdeling van de betaalde en onbetaalde arbeid*, Amsterdam: De Populier

Emancipatie Kommissie 1976, *Aanzet voor een vijfjarenplan, revisie positie van de vrouw, rolverdeling vrouw-man*, The Hague: Emancipatie Kommissie

Emancipatieraad 1991, *Vrouwen in politiek en openbaar bestuur*, The Hague: Emancipatieraad

1994, *Met het oog op mei 1997. Toekomstige advisering met betrekking tot het emancipatiebeleid*, The Hague: Emancipatieraad.

Jong, Brenda de and Ina Sjerps 1987, 'Zweven in de breedte. Vier jaar Breed Platform Vrouwen voor Ekonomische zelfstandigheid', *Socialisties-Feministiese Teksten* 10: 145–64

Klink, Elsbeth 2000, 'Pleitbezorgers en policy windows. De institutionalisering van de integratie van emancipatie-aspecten in het nieuwe adviesstelsel', Master's thesis, Unversity of Leiden

Leijenaar, Monique H. 1989, *De geschade heerlijkheid*, The Hague: SDU

Leijenaar, Monique H. and L. Janssen 1981, *Vrouwen in de lokale politiek: eenonderzoek naar het funktioneren van vrouwelijke raadsleden in Nederland*, Mededelingen no. 8, Unversity of Amsterdam, Department of Politics, Amsterdam

Leijenaar, Monique H. and B. Niemöller 1983, *Barrières voor Carrières. Vrouwen in het Openbaar Bestuur*, Amsterdam: FSW-A/M en T/UvA

Leijenaar, Monique H. and Sawitri Saharso 1983, *Vrouwen en politieke macht. Trendreport*, The Hague: VBEO

Meijer, Irene Costera 1996, *Het persoonlijke wordt politiek. Feministische bewustwording in Nederland 1965–1980*, Amsterdam: Het Spinhuis

Ministerie van Sociale Zaken en Werkgelegenheid 1985, *Beleidsplan Emancipatie*, The Hague: Ministerie van Sociale Zaken en Werkgelegenheid

Oldersma, Jantine 1996, *De vrouw die vanzelf spreekt, gender en representatie in het Nederlandse adviesradenstelsel*, Leiden: DSWO-Press

2002, 'More Women or More Feminists in Politics? Advocacy Coalitions and the Representation of Women in the Netherlands 1967–1992', *Acta Politica: International Journal of Political Science* 37: 263–83

Oldersma, Jantine and Jacob J. Woldendorp 1995, 'Belangenvertegenwoordiging en beleidsadvisering: geniet, maar drink met mate', in Kees van Kersbergen and I. M. A. M. Pröpper (eds.) *Publiek debat en democratie*, The Hague: SDU, pp. 81–98

Outshoorn, Joyce V. 1984, 'Meer vrouwen in de politiek? Argumentaties van voorstand(st)ers toen en nu', in Ministerie van Binnenlandse Zaken, *Vrouwen in politieke functies*, The Hague: Verslag van een studiedag

1991, 'A Distaste of Dirty Hands: Gender and Politics in Second-Wave Feminism', in Tayo Andreasen, Anette Borchorst, Drude Dahlerup, Eva Lous and Hanne Rimmen Nielsen (eds.) *Moving on: New Perspectives on the Women's Movement*, Aarhus: Aarhus University Press, pp. 175–87

Praag, Phillip van, Jr. 1991, *Strategie en illusie. Elf jaar intern debat in de PvdA (1966–1977)*, Amsterdam: Het Spinhuis

Ribberink, Anneke 1998, *Leidsvrouwen en zaakwaarneemsters, een geschiedenis van de aktiegroep Man Vrouw Maatschappij (MVM) 1968–1973*, Hilversum: Verloren

Schmitter, Phillipe and Gerhard Lehmbruch 1979, *Trends toward Corporatist Intermediation*, Beverly Hills/London: Sage

Stasse, Hanneke, Trees Mom and Marijke Eijkmans 1982, *Staat en seksestrijd, Naar een feministische staatstheorie*, Amsterdam: SUA

Velde, Hella van de 1994, *Vrouwen van de partij. De integratie van vrouwen in politieke partijen in Nederland, 1919–1990*, Leiden: DSWO-Press

Wetenschappelijke Raad voor het Regeringsbeleid 1977, *Adviseren aan de overheid*, The Hague: Staatsuitgeverij

9 The women's movement, gender equality agencies and central-state debates on political representation in Spain

Celia Valiente

Introduction

This chapter examines the role of the Women's Institute (*Instituto de la Mujer*, WI) and the women's secretariat of the Spanish Socialist Workers' Party (*Partido Socialista Obrero Español*, PSOE) – hereafter 'PSOE women's secretariat' – in three central-state debates on political representation in Spain since 1983. The WI is the main central-state level women's policy office in Spain.[1] As the analysis in this chapter demonstrates, the WI and the PSOE women's secretariat were able to represent women's movement goals and gender the frame of two debates on political representation: the discussion that in 1988 led to the adoption by the PSOE of a 25 per cent women's quota, and in 1997 resulted in the increase of this quota to 40 per cent. In the third discussion (on a mandatory 40 per cent women's quota for all parties submitted by the PSOE in 2001), an energetic PSOE women's secretariat was unable to counteract the WI, whose activities were not feminist. Women were allowed to participate in the policy process but the policy outcome (the rejection of the bill in 2003) was contrary to the demand advanced by the women's movement.

The women-friendly outcomes of the first two debates occurred under governments formed by the PSOE. The women's movement was at a stage of consolidation and the active WI and PSOE women's secretariat were attentive to the development of measures to increase women's political representation. This success of the women's movement was facilitated by the presence of a left-wing party in office. Change of government to the Conservative People's Party (*Partido Popular*, PP) was the reason for the unfavourable outcome of the third debate.

In other countries, the issue of political representation of specific groups of society is discussed in terms not only of gender but also of ethnicity. Not so in post-authoritarian Spain, where the topic has been

---

[1] For research on the WI, see Threlfall (1996, 1998) and Valiente (1995, 1997, 2001a, 2001b, 2004).

debated mainly in terms of women's presence in representative institutions. Therefore, in general, debates on gender and political representation are the Spanish discussions on political representation.

Generally speaking, since the 1980s Spanish public debates on women's political representation have four characteristics. First, deliberations are chiefly on women's quotas in political parties. Parties are the main actors in the Spanish political system, and the second wave of the feminist movement includes significant proportions of women who belonged to both women's groups and left-wing parties. The main left-wing parties and coalitions have women's quotas. An example is the electoral coalition United Left (*Izquierda Unida*, IU), which was created in 1986 by the association of the Communist Party and other parties to the left of the PSOE. The debate on women's political representation developed principally (although not exclusively) on the left of the political spectrum. By contrast the conservative PP remained strongly against quotas. The PP participated actively in the discussion on quotas only after the late 1990s when it responded to mobilisation by women on the political left in favour of mandatory quotas for all parties.

Second, generally constitutional issues and women's political representation were discussed jointly only from the late 1990s. At that time opponents to mandatory quotas declared them to be unconstitutional. Previously constitutional matters were not a central topic in public discussions of political representation. Comparatively speaking, Spain was a young democracy formed after the death of Franco in 1975. Most policy actors were reluctant to reform the 1978 constitution because it was a product of negotiation and compromise reached with difficulty by the main parties during the transition to democracy. The existence of *Euskadi Ta Askatasuna* (ETA) terrorism make changes in the constitution unlikely until the Basque conflict is settled, because the independence of the Basque country (the terrorists' goal) implies a constitutional reform. Thus there was a reluctance to 'constitutionalise' issues of political representation.

Third, the discussions on political representation are conducted mainly (but not exclusively) at the central-state level. The main left-wing parties and coalitions that have women's quotas (the PSOE and the IU) are central-state-based political organisations. The bill to impose a 40 per cent women's quota on all parties was submitted in November 2001 by the PSOE to the central-state legislature. However, in the twenty-first century deliberations on women's representation gained importance at the regional level. In 2003, two regions governed by the PSOE (alone or in coalition), the Balearic Islands and Castile-La Mancha, were in the process of establishing mandatory quotas of 50 per cent of women and men in alternative positions (the so-called zipper lists) for all parties for their regional elections.

Finally, debates on political representation often contained references to international events. Examples include initiatives to increase the presence of women in institutions taken successfully in other countries such as the Nordic states, measures that failed because these were declared unconstitutional, such as in France in the early 1980s and Italy in 1993, and strategies promoted by supra-national organisations and institutions, such as the United Nations or the European Union.

Selection of debates

Institutions that make representation policy

The political representation of citizens at the central-state level is regulated in general terms by the constitution and in detail by the 1985 General Electoral Act of 19 June (*Ley Orgánica 5/1985, de 19 de junio, del Régimen Electoral General,* hereafter '1985 General Electoral Act'). Acts are made and amended in the legislature.[2] Political parties, through formal and informal rules, recruit candidates to represent citizens in political institutions. In short, the legislature and the political parties make representation policy in Spain.

Universe of policy debates

The WI was created in 1983. Hence there was no possibility of women's policy agency intervention in debates before that date. The PSOE was in power between 1982 and 1996 and after spring 2004. It was the main opposition party between 1996 and spring 2004. Three party discussions on women's representation resulted in action to increase women's political representation. These were the approval of a 25 per cent women's quota for internal party positions and on party electoral lists in January 1988, the endorsement of a new 40 per cent quota in June 1997, and the submission to the legislature of a bill to reform the 1985 General Electoral Act, making a women's quota of 40 per cent mandatory for all parties in November 2001.

The IU has usually been the third largest nationwide political party in national elections. In the late 1980s, an internal party debate on women's

---

[2] The legislature is composed of two chambers: a lower chamber called the Congress of Deputies, and an upper chamber called the Senate. Members of the Congress of Deputies are elected by proportional representation under the D'Hondt system with closed and blocked lists. The vast majority of senators are elected by a majority system.

political presence finished with the 1989 commitment to a women's quota of 30 per cent for internal party positions and on party electoral lists. Two other IU discussions culminated in the adoption of new women's quotas of 35 per cent and 40 per cent in 1990 and 1997 respectively (Ramiro 2000: 225–6).

At regional level, a debate on women's political representation preceded the June 2002 Act requiring the alternation of men and women on the lists of all political parties competing in regional elections in the Balearic Islands (*El País*, 18 June 2002: 21). A similar measure was adopted in the region of Castile-La Mancha (Act 11/2002 of 27 June on the reform of Electoral Act of Castile-La Mancha 5/1986 of 23 December). The government then lodged an appeal to the Constitutional Court on the grounds that the two acts were unconstitutional.[3] On 15 October 2002, the court decided to deal with the appeal (*El País*, 18 October 2002: 23). Implementation of the policy was suspended until the court pronounced its sentence.

Selection of debates

The three debates chosen for close investigation in this chapter resulted in the approval of a 25 per cent women's quota by the PSOE in 1988 (the first debate), the establishment of a 40 per cent women's quota by the PSOE in June 1997 (the second debate), and the rejection in 2003 of the PSOE bill to endorse a 40 per cent women's quota mandatory to all parties submitted to the legislature in November 2001 (the third debate). The three debates fulfil the RNGS model criteria of decisional system importance, life cycle and issue area salience. Regarding *decisional system importance*, the three discussions developed within a political party (the PSOE) but the final part of the third debate took place in the legislature. The three debates took place at the central-state level. The above-mentioned regional debates could not be analysed in this chapter because they were still taking place when the research was completed. All of the debates had extensive *life cycles* – the topic of citizens' representation has been more or less continuously discussed since 1983. Between them the debates covered the whole life cycle so far of political discussion of this issue: the first took place in the 1980s, the second in the 1990s, and the third from the 1990s on. In terms of *issue area salience*, the three

---

[3] The Constitutional Court is the supreme interpreter of constitutionality, and can rule that laws are unconstitutional and invalid. It reviews laws made by the Spanish legislature, the national executive and regional governments, and its decisions apply to the whole territory of Spain and cannot be appealed (Heywood 1995: 105–6).

debates refer to all the arguments on political representation advanced by major policy actors in Spain.[4]

Debate 1: Endorsement of a 25 per cent women's quota in the socialist party, 1987–1988

How the debate came to the public agenda

In the 1970s, and especially in the 1980s, feminists within the PSOE continuously denounced the low presence of women in top political decision-making positions. In the 1977, 1979, 1982 and 1986 general elections, the percentage of women members of the Congress of Deputies was 6 per cent. Women's political representation in the PSOE did not increase; its proportions of women deputies were 9, 5, 9 and 7 per cent in successive elections (Instituto de la Mujer 1994: 79–80). But as a result of feminist pressure, the thirty-first PSOE federal congress in January 1988 discussed a proposal to institute a 25 per cent women's quota for internal party positions and on electoral lists (Partido Socialista Obrero Español-Secretaría de Participación de la Mujer 1988: 1).

Dominant frame of debate

The debate focused on questions about the low presence of women in Spanish politics. Was it a serious problem that in the first decade of Spanish democracy the presence of women in political decision-making positions was very low? If so, what were the causes of this problem? Could this problem be solved? If so, what would be the potential solutions? Is it fair to reserve a proportion of political positions to any particular sector of the population (women)?

Gendering the debate

The debate was gendered at the outset, because both supporters and (to a lesser extent) opponents of the quota made explicit references to women and men. Some opponents attacked quotas by using the classic anti-feminist argument of the left: that feminist demands were particularistic and bourgeois deviations from the main objective of a socialist party (the improvement of the status of the working classes) (Bustelo 1979: 13;

---

[4] The sources for this chapter mainly consist of published documents from the WI, the women's movement and the PSOE; secondary analysis; and press articles from *El País* (the main newspaper of general information with nationwide coverage).

Partido Socialista Obrero Español 1988a: 114). Other opponents were more conciliatory. They agreed that the low presence of women in top positions in the party and the state was a problem, but argued that its cause was a matter of supply, that there was a shortage of women with enough qualifications and ambition to hold decision-making positions. A quota would not solve this scarcity of potential female candidates (Threlfall 2001: 4). Actually, women were in short supply in the party as a whole; they were about 15 per cent of members (Gallego 1994: 670).

PSOE feminists used several arguments to defend the quota. They countered that women were absent from the hierarchy of the party and the state because they were discriminated against in subtle and not so subtle ways, and not because there was an insufficient supply of potential female candidates (Threlfall 2001: 4). Advocates argued that in the absence of quotas men would never voluntarily release power, since many party men seek power for its own sake, while numerous women want power to improve society and help others. PSOE feminists time and again pointed out that, historically, left-wing parties have not supported (and have often even opposed) feminist causes. However, PSOE feminists believed and hoped that left-wing parties would have the potential to be women-friendly because of their general commitment to equality (Bustelo 1979: 14; 1980: 8–9; Partido Socialista Obrero Español 1988b: 26–9). They reminded their opponents that the Socialist International recommendation on the measures to increase women's presence in political decision-making positions should be adopted by member parties (Threlfall 2001: 5). Finally, pragmatic arguments were made. Quotas are gender-equality measures that would help the PSOE win a higher share of the women's vote in subsequent elections by presenting a more feminised image and attracting more women's votes (Bustelo 1979: 14).

Policy outcome

At the thirty-first PSOE federal congress (22–24 January 1988), delegates passed the 25 per cent women's quota for party positions and electoral lists (Partido Socialista Obrero Español 1988c: 84). Thereafter, the proportion of female PSOE MPs rose steadily, to reach the level of 28 per cent of PSOE deputies and 23 per cent of PSOE senators in the 1996 election (Instituto de la Mujer 1994: 80–2; 1997a: 98–9).

Women's movement impact

The Spanish women's movement is composed of two branches: the feminist branch and the non-feminist branch. Individuals and organisations that consider themselves feminist comprised the feminist branch of the women's movement (hereafter 'the feminist movement'). It has been amply researched, so this chapter refers mainly to this branch. The non-feminist branch of the women's movement consists of house-wives' associations, cultural and religious groups, widows' organisations, mothers' groups and the like. Hardly any research has been conducted on these organisations.

During the transition to democracy, the problem of the relationship between feminism and mainstream politics was raised in most feminist gatherings. Some feminists thought that an important level of formal and real equality could be attained through state action. It was thus important that women were present in political decision-making arenas. Other feminists rejected mainstream politics altogether, because they saw the state as a site that actively contributed to the perpetuation of unequal gender relations. At the end of the 1970s, the feminist movement was bitterly split between supporters of both positions. However, this division eroded slightly during the 1980s and more in the 1990s, mainly for three reasons. First, the 1982 PSOE electoral victory meant that for the first time since the 1930s a socialist party governed Spain. Some feminists thought that this would be a unique opportunity to improve women's rights and status. Second, the WI policy of subsidising the women's movement meant that groups that did not want to relate to the state would have considerably fewer resources than groups that dealt with the state and received money from it. Third, the increasing energy put by many feminist groups into the delivery of services to the female population focused the attention of feminists on the details of the man-agement of services and away from general and theoretical discussions on the state (Durán and Gallego 1986: 208–12; Gallego 1994: 671; Scanlon 1990: 95–8).

Party developments

In the PSOE, the main advocates of measures to improve women's political representation (including quotas) were feminist activists and leaders, many of whom belonged (or had belonged) both to the party and to feminist associations in civil society. The PSOE accepted women (PSOE feminists) representing gender interests in the process. By adopt-ing the 1988 quota of 25 per cent, the PSOE answered one of the demands of the sector of the feminist movement pursuing higher levels of women's political representation. Thus, the PSOE's reaction to (a sector of) the feminist movement was a *dual response*.

Women's policy agency activities and characteristics

The WI was officially created in 1983 (Act 16 of 24 October). The scope of the WI is very broad. It has five comprehensive goals: to promote policy initiatives for women through formal enactment of policy statements; to study all aspects of women's situation in Spain; to oversee the implementation of women's policy; to receive and handle women's discrimination complaints; and to increase women's knowledge of their rights. The WI is a permanent bureaucratic agency. Until 1988 the WI was a part of the Ministry of Culture, one of the least important in the Spanish state. Located within a ministry rather than having a cabinet position, the WI was distant from major power centres. In the mid-1980s, the WI did not yet have an extensive staff and budget, but was in the process of gaining them. Between 1983 and 1988 the director was Carlota Bustelo, a well-known feminist activist who had been a member of the Women's Liberation Front (*Frente de Liberación de la Mujer*, FLM). The FLM foundational document demanded amongst other things 'the incorporation of women into all social, productive, *political* and creative tasks' (emphasis added; translation by Celia Valiente – Seminario de Estudios Sociológicos sobre la Mujer 1986: 36–7). Carlota Bustelo was also a PSOE deputy during the first legislative term (1977–9). In protest at what she considered to be an insignificant and unacceptable proportion of female PSOE MPs, she refused to continue as an MP into the second legislative term (1979–82) (Threlfall 1996: 120). Women's political representation was one of the high priorities of the WI in the mid- and late 1980s.[5]

Some members of the WI were able to push demands for women's political representation into the PSOE debate on quotas in the 1980s because they belonged (or had belonged) to the party, the WI, and/or the feminist movement. The case of Carlota Bustelo was not unique. For instance, Matilde Fernández, elected as a member of the PSOE executive committee in charge of the Women's Secretariat in 1984 (Threlfall 1998: 85) and latterly Minister of Social Affairs (1988–93), belonged to the WI's advisory council.[6] In this way, members of the WI played the role of an *insider* in the 1988 PSOE debate on quotas.

---

[5] This high priority is reflected, for instance, in the special attention paid to the topic by the WI's journal titled *Women* (*Mujeres*). Pages on the matter can be consulted in: 1984, No. 2: 42; No. 4: 6–13, 18–25, 28–30, 49–56, 84–5, 95–7; 1986, No. 12: 3, 6–23, 28–34.

[6] Since 1985, the WI director has been aided by the advisory council (*Consejo rector*), which is primarily composed of representatives from the major ministries and (up to the 1990s) six people who had demonstrated a long commitment to gender equality (Matilde Fernández among them).

The PSOE women's secretariat was also an *insider* in the 1988 debate on women's quotas, since it incorporated the goal of the part of the movement interested in mainstream politics into its own positions (a higher women's presence in politics achieved through quotas) and inserted these gendered policy demands into the dominant frame of the debate on the PSOE quota. That the demands of PSOE feminists could be heard was partly because they previously gained organisational status within the party. In 1976, a women's caucus, Woman and Socialism (*Mujer y Socialismo*), was formed in the PSOE and in 1981, a member of the caucus was elected to the PSOE's executive committee, with others following her in successive years. Carlota Bustelo (first WI director, 1983–8) was the main advocate of the foundation of Woman and Socialism. In December 1984, party leaders decided to institutionalise the women's caucus at the federal executive level, whereupon it became the women's secretariat. The feminists in the secretariat successfully added clauses involving women's issues to PSOE congress resolutions, electoral programmes, and other documents. The PSOE women's secretariat has a broad and cross-sectoral mandate, since it is in charge of gender equality within the party. It is a permanent bureaucratic agency of the party. It is part of the Federal Executive Committee; therefore it is close to the major power centres. It has a medium institutional capacity (staff and budget), and has generally been headed by feminists. Women's political representation was one of the highest priorities of the PSOE women's secretariat from the 1980s (Durán and Gallego 1986: 213; Folguera 1988: 124–5; Threlfall 1985: 48–9; 1998: 82–3).

Women's movement characteristics

After emerging in the 1960s and early 1970s, and growing from 1975 to the early 1980s, the feminist movement was in a stage of consolidation by the mid- to late 1980s. The Spanish feminist movement, while not negligible, has been historically weak, its activities involving only a minority of women. The movement occasionally showed some signs of strength, however. For example, it organised national feminist conferences regularly attended by between 3,000 and 5,000 women. In comparison with other western countries, the feminist movement in Spain does not have high visibility in the mass media. In the 1980s, most of the feminist groups were very close to the left. Political representation was a priority for one of the sectors of the feminist movement that believed that state policy could improve the status of women, but it was not a unifying issue for the movement as a whole. The part of the movement interested in political representation was cohesive. Movement organisations active on the issue agreed on the frame and proposals, although each group tended to pressurise the political party to which it was closest. Left-wing political parties were thus a privileged location for feminist advocates of political representation. Conservative politicians openly opposed women's quotas. They provided arguments against quotas in the general discussion on the issue, but could not directly intervene in the debate within the PSOE. Thus the strength of the counter-movement to women's quotas may be characterised as moderate.

Policy environment

Since the 25 per cent quota was an internal PSOE rule, the policy environment of this measure was not only the state but also the PSOE. The structure of this policy sub-system was moderately closed to feminist demands. PSOE feminists could take part in the decision-making process at federal congresses because some of them already belonged to the party hierarchy, and they and others successfully pressurised highly ranked PSOE officials. In contrast, members of the feminist movement inter-ested in political representation but not belonging to the PSOE could not participate in PSOE federal congresses. The policy frame that initially shaped the debate at the thirty-first federal congress was compatible with the frame in which movement goals were expressed by activists because both frames referred to the same issues (although in different ways). In the late 1980s, the PSOE controlled the executive and had an absolute majority in both chambers in the legislature.

Debate 2: Endorsement of a 40 per cent women's quota in the socialist party, 1992–1997

How the debate came to the public agenda

The concept of 'parity democracy' was introduced at the European Summit of Women in Power held in Athens in 1992. PSOE feminists took up the parity democracy issue, generated a continuous debate in the party and pressurised the party hierarchy to increase the 25 per cent quota to 40 per cent.

Dominant frame of debate

The discussion of parity democracy in the PSOE in the 1990s addressed and extended the questions already raised in the first debate. There was discussion about whether it was the right moment to increase the women's quota, and whether the party might better concentrate on the resolution of more pressing problems.

Gendering the debate

As in the case of the previous debate, participants in this debate raised explicitly gendered questions, although defenders of the 40 per cent women's quota did so more often than opponents. Supporters of the new quota argued that left-wing parties need quotas because of their differences from right-wing parties. The parties of the right, it was argued, maintain a 'social Darwinist' ideology that resists special measures to ensure women's representation. These parties believe that only the most qualified and capable individuals within parties reach power positions. Nothing prevents women from competing in that race. When party women are good enough, they will reach top positions. If fewer women than men are present in the upper ranks of parties and state, then this difference is a result simply of women's inadequate performance in the competition. Left-wing parties are ill disposed to such theses, because these parties are (or should be) more sensitive and critical to pre-existing inequalities that impede some groups (Partido Socialista Obrero Español 1988b: 26–9; 1997: 207).

Policy outcome

As a result of sustained PSOE feminist pressure, delegates at the thirty-fourth PSOE federal congress (20–22 June 1997) discussed and approved the increase of the internal and electoral women's party quota to 40 per cent (Partido Socialista Obrero Español 1997: 207). Subsequently, the proportion of women who became PSOE deputies increased from 28 per cent in 1996 to 37 per cent in 2000 and to 46 per cent in 2004. The percentage of women among PSOE senators decreased from 23 per cent to 17 per cent between 1996 and 2000 and increased to 27 per cent in 2004 (Instituto de la Mujer 1997a: 98–9; 2002; 2004).

Women's movement impact

The sector of the Spanish feminist movement pursuing parity democracy in the 1990s and the twenty-first century (hereafter 'the Spanish parity movement') consists of feminist leaders and activists in political parties and in women's organisations, primarily from the left. It includes feminists from the PSOE and the IU. In terms of feminist associations, the parity movement grew out of well-known women's groups mainly linked to political parties, including (among others) the Federation of Progressive Women (*Federación de Mujeres Progresistas*), close to the PSOE, and the Dolores Ibárruri Foundation (*Fundación Dolores Ibárruri*), close to the IU. Other less well-known feminist organisations, such as the Forum of Feminist Politics (*Forum de Política Feminista*), are also mobilised in favour of parity democracy.[7]

Spanish parity feminists pressurised the hierarchy of left-wing parties to increase the already existing women's quotas. The 1997 PSOE move to increase its quota to 40 per cent coincided with the goals of the sector of the feminist movement active on the issue of political representation. Within the PSOE, feminists were consistently among the main participants in the internal deliberation on the new quota. Thus, the PSOE's reaction to the women's movement was a *dual response*.

Women's policy agency activities and characteristics

This second debate ran across two very different political periods: between 1992 and spring 1996 (socialist rule); and between spring 1996 and June 1997 (conservative rule). During both periods the WI was a cross-sectional permanent bureaucratic part of the state with a broad policy mandate, and was distant from major power centres (between 1988 and 1996 the WI depended on the Ministry of Social Affairs, and after 1996 on the Ministry of Labour and Social Affairs). In the 1990s, the WI's administrative capacity was high as it boasted an extensive staff and budget. Between 1991 and 1993, the WI director was a feminist lawyer, Purificación Gutiérrez, and between 1993 and 1996, a feminist sociology professor, Marina Subirats (Threlfall 1998: 86). In the 1990s (until 1996), political representation was one of the top priorities of the WI.[8]

Until the 1996 PSOE electoral defeat, the WI incorporated the women's movement goal of parity democracy into its own positions, leading many activities on the matter domestically and abroad. WI officials advanced the aim of the 40 per cent quota within the socialist party because some of them also belonged to the PSOE and even to the party hierarchy. Others were very close to the PSOE: WI directors Carmen Martínez-Ten (1988–91) and Purificación Gutiérrez, and Ministers of

---

[7] For more on the Spanish parity movement in comparison with that of France, see Jenson and Valiente (2003).

[8] Many sources document this priority status in the 1990s. Most issues of the WI periodical journal *Women* (*Mujeres*) contain pages on the topic: 1990, No. 2: 27, 33; 1992, No. 9: 14, 26–30; 1993, No. 10: 28–9; 1993, No. 12: 24–5; 1994, No. 13: 22–6; 1995, No. 18: 16; 1996, No. 21: 6–8.

Social Affairs Matilde Fernández (1988–93) and Cristina Alberdi (1993–6), among others. Thus, the activities of some WI members (until spring 1996) could be characterised as those of an *insider*.

In spring 1996, the conservative PP came to power. While the institutional characteristics of the WI remained the same as during the period between 1992 and 1996, the leadership and the priority given to political representation both changed. In 1996, the PP appointed Concepción Dancausa as WI director. She was a civil servant with no ties with the feminist movement and apparently with no previous significant experience in the policy area of women's rights (*Mujeres* 1996, No. 22: 5). Political representation was a topic of very low priority for the WI during the years of conservative rule. The main WI policy document of the late 1990s was the Third Gender Equality Plan (Instituto de la Mujer 1997b), which ran from 1997 to 2000. It is divided into ten sections. The shortest sections are on 'power and decision-making' and 'environment' (three pages each). The devices contained in the Third Gender Equality Plan to foster participation of women in decision-making were 'soft measures', such as the promotion of research, the improvement of statistics, and support for training programmes for potential female decision-makers. The Third Gender Equality Plan did not establish numerical targets of political representation. After the 1996 PP electoral victory, the WI did not participate in the internal PSOE debate on political representation. It was neither an advocate for movement goals (quotas) in the PSOE decision-making process, nor did it gender PSOE policy definitions on the issue. Between spring 1996 and the 1997 PSOE federal congress, the WI activities regarding the PSOE debate were therefore *symbolic*.

As was the case in the first debate, during the whole debate on the PSOE 40 per cent women's quota, the PSOE women's secretariat continued to be a cross-sectional bureaucratic agency of the party with a broad mandate. It was close to the major power centres, it had a medium institutional capacity, and it was headed by feminist leaders very interested in parity democracy and very active in the PSOE debate on the 40 per cent women's quota (Threlfall 1998, 2001). Then, the PSOE women's secretariat played the role of an *insider* in this debate.

Women's movement characteristics

Most feminist movement characteristics were unchanged from the first debate. The feminist movement was in a stage of consolidation, and was very close to the left. Political representation was an issue of high priority for an important sector of the feminist movement, which was cohesive on the matter, and faced a moderate counter-movement contrary to quotas from the PP and women's groups close to the conservative party, such as Women for Democracy (*Mujeres para la democracia*). As shown above, in the second debate, feminist activism in support of quotas was located not only in left-wing political parties (as in the first debate), but also (although to a lesser extent than in parties) in women's groups to some degree autonomous from political parties.

Policy environment

The structure of the policy environment where the PSOE 40 per cent women's quota was approved in June 1997 was moderately closed for the sector of the feminist movement interested in political representation. Members of this sector who did not belong to the socialist party could not participate directly in the internal party debate, but PSOE feminists could take part in the discussion and played a major role in it. Joaquín Almunia, the PSOE leader who prepared the political document on the model of the party to be discussed and voted on at the thirty-fourth congress (and who became PSOE general secretary in that very congress), was in general moderately favourable to feminist causes. The frame that shaped the debate on the proposal of the 40 per cent women's quota was expressed in terms that were compatible with movement goals as expressed by activists. The 1993–6 PSOE government was a minority government supported in the legislature by the regionalist Catalan coalition, Convergence and Union (*Convergència i Unió*, CiU). Between the elections of spring 1996 and spring 2000, the PP formed a minority government supported by three regional parties or coalitions of parties, CiU, the Canary Coalition (*Coalición Canaria*, CC) and the Basque Nationalist Party (*Partido Nacionalista Vasco*, PNV). However, the PNV withdrew its support for the government around the middle of the legislative term.

Debate 3: The 2001 socialist bill on mandatory quotas for all parties, 1998–2003

How the debate came to the public agenda

In August 1998, the PSOE announced that it would submit a bill to reform the 1985 General Electoral Act in order to require all electoral lists to limit their candidates of the same sex to no more than 60 per cent. In other words, the bill would, if approved, mandate 40 per cent minima of each sex for all political parties. The IU supported the idea, but the governing PP strongly opposed it (*El País*, 31 August 1998: 18).

Dominant frame of debate

The same issues discussed in the first two debates were prominent in the third debate. However, in addition, constitutional matters were present in this discussion, because opponents to mandatory quotas agreed that mandatory quotas were unconstitutional. The right of a party to impose any rule of candidate selection on other parties was also debated.

Gendering the debate

Supporters of mandatory quotas were situated on the left of the political spectrum and tended to use gendered arguments. They argued that a democracy of high quality is one in which half of the population (women) is politically represented by significant proportions of women. Some documents in favour of mandatory quotas presented gender parity as an end in itself, as a matter of justice (see for instance Alberdi 1998; Chicano 1999; Ruiz-Tagle 1999). While they were fighting for the right of women to be elected, PSOE parity activists represented themselves as followers of the first suffragists who fought for the right of women to vote. In the same documents gender parity was also claimed on the basis that female activists maintained a broader social and feminist agenda. Advocates claimed that if women and men were equally represented in the political arena, policy outcomes would be different and more positive. Policy outcomes would better meet the particular needs of women. Policies would be elaborated in a more consensual way. Public measures would include the interests not only of women but also of other, less privileged groups. Moreover, the distinction between the private and the public was averred to be fictitious since the personal is political. Responsibilities should then be shared: political decision-making should not be the monopoly of men, as family and caring responsibilities should not be the monopoly of women. Care services in the welfare state had to be developed, to help women and men combine their professional and family responsibilities.

The most vocal opponents of quotas were conservatives. They were less likely to use gender notions than were supporters of mandatory quotas. In common with conservative policy actors in other countries, the PP and women's associations close to it thought it was wrong to intervene in the recruitment process in order to elect more women. The process had to be 'fair' and 'neutral', so that the 'best people' (including women) could be elected. Some conservative leaders and activists accepted 'soft' measures (such as encouraging women to stand for office) but opposed 'hard' ones (quotas). PP politicians termed quotas a form of discrimination (*ABC*, 27 January 2002: 28). Others claimed that only the

PP gave women real opportunities to gain the centres of power, in contrast to the artificial quotas of the PSOE. They used as evidence the increase in the numbers of PP women in elected office after the party won the general elections of 1996 and 2000 (*ABC*, 27 January 2002: 28; *El País*, 30 January 2000: 29; Nasarre 2002).

Policy outcome

In November 2001, the PSOE submitted a bill to the legislature on the reform of the 1985 General Electoral Act to make parity mandatory. The bill was debated and rejected in the legislature on 8 April 2003.[9]

Women's movement impact/State response

Continuous mobilisation in favour of higher levels of women's political representation and mandatory quotas has been a feature of Spanish politics since the late 1990s. Parity activists actively sought the advice of constitutional experts, some of whom declared that the bill was constitutional. They based their judgment on article 9.2 of the constitution which states that public power will promote the conditions under which citizens' freedom and equality are real and will facilitate citizens' participation in political, economic, cultural and social life (see, for instance, Peces-Barba 1999).

The PSOE bill on mandatory quotas was submitted in November 2001 to the legislature by two PSOE female deputies: Micaela Navarro, PSOE Women's Secretary, and María Teresa Fernández de la Vega, PSOE parliamentary spokesperson, who is known for her support of feminist causes. Female MPs played a central role in the parliamentary debate on the bill, a common phenomenon when the legislature is considering a women's issue. Thus, the state's response to women's movement parity advocates was one of *co-optation*, because the state accepted parity advocates in the policy-making process but did not give policy satisfaction to the parity mobilisation.

Women's policy agency activities and characteristics

The characteristics of the WI in this third debate were similar to the second phase of the second debate. The WI was a cross-sectional permanent bureaucratic agency distant from major centres of power. Its mandate is

---

[9] The debate in the legislature can be consulted in the Congress of Deputies' web page (www.congreso.es).

broad and its extensive staff and budget gave it a high administrative capacity. In 2000, the PP appointed Pilar Dávila del Cerro as WI director. She was a former civil servant. To my knowledge, she had no ties with the feminist movement. She had significant experience in the policy area of women's rights because she was the WI sub-director between 1996 and 2000. Between September 2002 and March 2003, the WI director was Carmen de Miguel y García (a civil servant with expertise in trade issues). She was then replaced by Miriam Tey de Salvador (a professional with a previous career in the private publishing sector). Political representation was not a WI priority during conservative rule.

After the 1996 PP electoral victory, the WI did not support mandatory quotas. In the late 1990s, in reaction to the concept of 'parity democracy', the PP coined the expression of 'balanced representation' (*representación equilibrada*) (Jenson and Valiente 2003: 92). The WI produced a Fourth Gender Equality Plan in March 2003, extending the Third Equality Plan, which theoretically expired in 2000, until March 2003. According to the Third Equality Plan, the goal to be achieved regarding women and politics was 'balanced participation' (*participación equilibrada*) (Instituto de la Mujer 1997b: 55). This wording is also present in the Fourth Equality Plan to be implemented between 2003 and 2006 (Instituto de la Mujer 2003: 23–5). As in the Third Plan, the section on gender equality in decision-making is the shortest section. It offers 'soft measures' such as the improvement of statistics and research on the matter but not numerical targets (quotas). Thus, women's policy agency activities are *non-feminist* because the WI did not advocate the goals of the parity advocates. Instead it defended the weaker goal of balanced participation and the weaker method of soft measures.

The characteristics of the PSOE women's secretariat during the third debate were the same as during previous debates. With a medium administrative capacity and headed by a feminist socialist (Micaela Navarro) between 1997 and 2004, the PSOE women's secretariat continued to include women's political representation as one of its top priorities. The PSOE women's secretariat advocated the goal of the parity movement in the debate. It intervened in and gendered the debate. An example is the intervention by Micaela Navarro (not only PSOE women's secretary but also an MP) who defended the PSOE 2001 bill in the 8 April 2003 parliamentary debate.

Women's movement characteristics

As in previous debates, the feminist movement was in a stage of consolidation, was very close to the left and faced a moderately strong counter-movement opposing quotas. The priority given to political representation by the sector of the feminist movement interested in the topic was high. This sector of the movement was cohesive, but cohesion did not mean frequent joint actions by different women's organisations. The location of activities of parity activists included not only autonomous women's groups and political parties (as in the second debate) but also the legislature. Parity activism was feminist.

Policy environment

The final part of the debate on the 2001 PSOE bill on the 40 per cent women's quota for all parties took place on 8 April 2003 in the legislature. It has some characteristics of closed policy environments: parliamentary proceedings are codified through regular meetings and rules, and participation is limited to leaders of political parties with parliamentary representation. The PP used its absolute majority in the legislature to reject the bill altogether. The frame of the parliamentary discussion prior to the rejection was compatible with that used in the women's movement to discuss political representation, since both frames deal with the same topics (although in a different manner).

Conclusion

This chapter has shown that the women's movement, the WI and the PSOE women's secretariat inserted their policy preferences in two of the three debates that preceded the most important public decisions on political representation (more specifically, on women's quotas) since the 1980s. The presence of the women's movement, WI and PSOE women's secretariat in these two debates occurred while political representation was an issue of high priority for both the movement and the women's policy agencies. The fact that the socialist party was in office was a key element for the policy success of the movement, the WI and the PSOE women's secretariat. In contrast, in the third debate the women's movement and the PSOE women's secretariat were still very attentive to the issue of political representation but did not secure approval of the bill, even though women participated extensively in the whole discussion. The closed policy environment and the low priority given to political representation by the WI were two major factors in the rejection of the PSOE bill on a 40 per cent mandatory quota for all parties.

Quotas have been implemented in the PSOE and constitute the main variable explaining the increase of women's presence in political decision-making positions (Threlfall 2001: 29). Although women's quotas have been adopted exclusively by left-wing parties, the improvement in women's political representation is not a phenomenon restricted to left-wing politics. In part as a reaction to left-wing quotas, since the 1990s, the presence of conservative female politicians has also increased, to 28 per cent of PP deputies and 25 per cent of PP senators in 2004 (Instituto de la Mujer 2004). Ironically the indirect influence on political representation of the movement and policy machineries under socialist governments has been more extensive than their effect in the left side of the political spectrum.

References

ABC, 27 January 2002

Alberdi, Cristina 1998, 'Democracia y ciudadanía', *El País*, 2 November: 26

Bustelo, Carlota 1979, *La alternativa feminista*, Madrid: Partido Socialista Obrero Español

1980, *Mujer y socialismo: para cambiar la vida*, Madrid: Partido Socialista Obrero Español

Chicano, Enriqueta 1999, 'Democracia paritaria', *El País*, 25 January: 30

Congress of Deputies' web page: www.congreso.es

Durán, María Á. and María T. Gallego 1986, 'The Women's Movement in Spain and the New Spanish Democracy', in Drude Dahlerup (ed.) *The New Women's Movement: Feminist and Political Power in Europe and the USA*, London: Sage, pp. 200–16

El País, 1987–2003

Folguera, Pilar (ed.) 1988, *El feminismo en España: Dos siglos de historia*, Madrid: Fundación Pablo Iglesias

Gallego, María T. 1994, 'Women's Political Engagement in Spain', in Barbara Nelson and Najma Chowdhury (eds.) *Women and Politics Worldwide*, New Haven and London: Yale University Press, pp. 661–73

Heywood, Paul 1995, *The Government and Politics of Spain*, London: Macmillan

Instituto de la Mujer 1994, *Las mujeres en cifras: Una década, 1982–1992*, Madrid: Instituto de la Mujer

1997a, *Las mujeres en cifras 1997*, Madrid: Instituto de la Mujer

1997b, *Third Gender Equality Plan*, Madrid: Instituto de la Mujer

2002, *Las mujeres en cifras*, Madrid: Instituto de la Mujer; retrieved 26 September 2002 from www.mtas.es

2003, *Fourth Gender Equality Plan*, Madrid: Instituto de la Mujer; retrieved 15 April 2003 from www.mtas.es

2004, *Las mujeres en cifras*, Madrid: Instituto de la Mujer; retrieved 18 August 2004 from www.mtas.es

Jenson, Jane and Celia Valiente 2003, 'Comparing Two Movements for Gender Parity: France and Spain', in Lee Ann Banaszak, Karen Beckwith and Dieter Rucht (eds.) *Women's Movements Facing the Reconfigured State*, New York: Cambridge University Press, pp. 69–93

Mujeres, 1983–6, 1990–6

Nasarre, Eugenio 2002, 'Las "listas cremallera"', *El País*, 28 June: 28

Partido Socialista Obrero Español 1988a, *Aspectos y problemas de la vida política española: Programa 2000*, Madrid: Pablo Iglesias

1988b, *Estrategias para la igualdad de sexo: Programa 2000, cuadernos de debate*, Madrid: Siglo XXI

1988c, *Resoluciones aprobadas por el 31 Congreso Federal, Madrid, 22–24 de enero de 1988*, Madrid: Partido Socialista Obrero Español

1997, *Resoluciones aprobadas por el 34 Congreso Federal, Madrid, 20–22 de junio de 1997*, Madrid: Partido Socialista Obrero Español

Partido Socialista Obrero Español-Secretaría de Participación de la Mujer 1988, *Mujer-hombre: 125 medidas para la igualdad*, Madrid: Partido Socialista Obrero Español

Peces-Barba, Gregorio 1999, 'La cuota femenina en las candidaturas electorales', *El País*, 1 July: 15–16

Ramiro, Luis 2000, 'Incentivos electorales y límites organizativos: Cambio y elección de estrategias en el PCE e IU, 1986–1999', Ph.D. dissertation, Florence: European University Institute, Department of Political and Social Sciences

Ruiz-Tagle, María Á. 1999, 'La paridad, UN derecho de ciudadanía', *El País*, 6 April: 36

Scanlon, Geraldine 1990, 'El movimiento feminista en España, 1900–1985: Logros y dificultades', in Judith Astelarra (ed.) *Participación Política de las Mujeres*, Madrid: Centro de Investigaciones Sociológicas and Siglo XXI, pp. 83–100

Seminario de Estudios Sociológicos sobre la Mujer 1986, 'El movimiento feminista de España: De 1960 a 1980', in Concha Elena Borreguero, Catena, Consuelo de la Gándara and Maria Salas (eds.) *La mujer española: De la tradición a la modernidad, 1960–1980*, Madrid: Tecnos, pp. 29–40

Threlfall, Monica 1985, 'The Women's Movement in Spain', *New Left Review* 151: 44–73

1996, 'Feminist Politics and Social Change in Spain', in Monica Threlfall (ed.) *Feminist Politics and Social Transformation in the North*, London and New York: Verso, pp. 115–51.

1998, 'State Feminism or Party Feminism?: Feminist Politics and the Spanish Institute of Women', *The European Journal of Women's Studies* 5, 1: 69–93

2001, 'Towards Gender Parity? Women in Party Politics', unpublished manuscript

Valiente, Celia 1995, 'The Power of Persuasion: the *Instituto de la Mujer* in Spain', in Dorothy McBride Stetson and Amy G. Mazur (eds.) *Comparative State Feminism*, Thousand Oaks, CA: Sage, pp. 221–36

1997, 'State Feminism and Gender Equality Policies: the Case of Spain (1983–95)', in Frances Gardiner (ed.) *Sex Equality Policy in Western Europe*, London: Routledge, pp. 127–41

2001a, 'A Closed Sub-system and Distant Feminist Demands Block Women-Friendly Outcomes in Spain', in Amy G. Mazur (ed.) *Making Democracies Work for Women: State Feminism, Women's Movements, and Job Training Policy*, New York: Routledge, pp. 111–30

2001b, 'Gendering Abortion Debates: State Feminism in Spain', in Dorothy McBride Stetson (ed.) *Abortion Politics, Women's Movements, and the Democratic State*, New York: Oxford University Press, pp. 229–45

2004, 'State Feminism and Central State Debates on Prostitution in Post-Authoritarian Spain', in Joyce Outshoorn (ed.) *The Politics of Prostitution: Women's Movements, Democratic States and the Globalization of Sex Commerce*, Cambridge: Cambridge University Press, pp. 205–24

10 Party feminism, state feminism and women's representation in Sweden

Diane Sainsbury

Introduction

Issues of political representation in Sweden during the past four decades have been influenced by two processes: the modernisation of the world's second oldest written constitution adopted in 1809 and a struggle over extending democracy. Constitutional reform and enlarging democracy provided a contradictory setting – both hospitable and unfavourable – to women's demands for better political representation. Until recently feminist actors and perspectives were generally marginalised in discussions on constitutional reforms, with women at the last minute expressing apprehension that a specific reform would adversely affect their representation. By contrast, the discussion on extending democracy and promoting equality offered a discursive opportunity of crucial importance to the impressive growth of women's representation.

Besides issues of the day, aspects of the Swedish understanding of political representation have formed an auspicious environment. Historically social representation has had a strong tradition, dating from the establishment of the four estates parliament in 1435. This parliament originally rested on a broader basis than similar bodies elsewhere and survived much longer (until 1866). Social representation, combined with a constitutional provision that interested parties should be consulted in the decision-making process, and the idea of a representative bureaucracy paved the way for corporatist arrangements in policy-making and subsequently in administration. The political parties, in particular the Social Democrats, the Centre Party and the Conservatives (the Moderates since 1969), which have represented the interests of workers, farmers and business respectively, also carried on the tradition of social representation. The principle of proportional representation, which furthers representation of a broad spectrum of interests and ideas, has also been central to Swedish politics. It has been reflected not only in the electoral system since 1911 but also in the distribution of the chairpersons of parliamentary committees, the county governors, and in some cases local and regional government executives. Lastly, the Swedish notion of citizenship is inclusive, pertaining to all members of society. Its inclusiveness is demonstrated in the voting rights of groups that do not have the franchise in many other western democracies, such as non-citizens who are legal residents and citizens in prison. In summary, the environment was characterised by a political culture of egalitarianism, a strong tradition of social representation, and the principles of proportional representation, consultation and inclusiveness.

It is in this context that women's representation in parliament rose from slightly less than 15 per cent in 1970 to 45 per cent in 2002, and representation in the cabinet climbed from roughly 10 to 50 per cent. Gains in elected office have also been accompanied by a dramatic increase of women in appointed positions from the late 1980s onwards. Currently the proportion of women in some appointed offices approximates their share of elected positions. This chapter examines the impact of the women's movement and women's policy agencies – and more specifically feminist ideas and actors – on increasing the political representation of women in elected and appointed offices.

Selection of debates

The policy sub-systems that make the most important decisions about political representation vary according to type of office involved – elected or appointed positions. For *elected* office the key institutions or arenas are the political parties. It is the prerogative of the parties to select the candidates and draw up party lists. Moreover, there is little legislation regulating Swedish parties. For *appointed* positions in the state bureaucracy, the policy sub-system is much more complex, involving actors in government, the major interest organisations and the parties. Sweden has an unusual administrative system. The ministries are primarily involved in policy formulation with a staff numbering a few hundred civil servants in each ministry, while implementation of policy is assigned to separate national administrative agencies. This arrangement also gives ad hoc inquiry commissions a unique role in policy-making, and in some instances, the commissions draft legislation. Formally it is the government that appoints the members of inquiry commissions and administrative boards. Prior to the 1990s the corporatist composition of the boards of the national administrative agencies, regional bodies and several inquiry commissions gave responsibility to the major interest organisations to nominate persons for these positions. The political parties also make nominations, and in the 1990s party nominations became increasingly important with the supposed abandonment of the corporatist form of representation.[1]

The universe of debates on political representation since 1960 consists of a dozen or so major debates. They centred on modernising parliament (elimination of the indirectly elected upper chamber) and the electoral system (reducing disproportionality in representation and increasing voters' influence in the election of candidates), improving the representation of poorly represented groups (women, immigrants, young people and the elderly), and the citizenship rights of both immigrants and emigrants.

I have selected the following three debates: first, the debate on greater democracy and more women in politics (1967–72); second, the debate on quotas for administrative bodies (1985–7); and third, the debate on establishing a women's party in the wake of the decline of women's parliamentary representation (1991–4). This selection meets several of the RNGS project criteria. The debates span four decades and thus meet the life-cycle criterion. They also occurred in different arenas and had high saliency. The initial debate, however, occurred before women's policy agencies as defined by the RNGS project existed. The most difficult decision has concerned the debate occurring in the 1990s – choosing either the debate on the women's party or that on greater influence of voters in the election of party candidates. The choice of the debate on the women's party is based on its much higher saliency. It should be noted, however, that the outcomes of these two simultaneous debates have very different implications for women's representation. The debate on the women's party improved the position of female candidates on most party lists in the 1994 and 1998 elections, and strengthened the principle of alternating female and male candidates on party lists. By contrast, the 1998 change in the electoral system reduces the importance of party lists by giving the voters the option to indicate a preference for a specific candidate, which can alter the order of candidates elected to office.

For a variety of reasons, it was feared that the new electoral system would have a negative impact on women's representation. These fears were not transformed into reality during the first parliamentary elections after the reform. In the 1998 and 2002 elections women's representation continued to inch upwards (42.7 per cent in 1998 and 45.3 per cent in 2002), and the number of women elected to parliament was slightly higher than it would have been otherwise. However, the full impact of the new electoral system has still to be felt. Only between one-quarter and one-third of the electorate utilised its option to vote for a candidate in

---

[1] For a more detailed discussion of the Swedish political system, see Arter (1999); Einhorn and Logue (2003).

addition to a party; as a result, ten or twelve candidates in each election entered parliament, and they comprised a mere 3–4 per cent of the members of parliament.

Debate 1: Greater democracy and more women in politics, 1967–1972

How the debate came to the public agenda

The issue of women's representation grew out of a larger project to place gender equality on the public agenda. The push to put gender equality on the agenda came from two sources: first, a network of academics who launched a debate on sex roles in the early 1960s, and second, the women's organisations of the political parties. Of the women's organisations, the efforts of the Social Democratic Women's Federation (SSKF) were the most important. In the mid-1960s it published Woman's Equality (*Kvinnans jämlikhet*), an ambitious programme of reform. Its proposals dealt with taxation, labour market policy, family law, education, social security and public services; and they were eventually incorporated in the Towards Equality programme, adopted by the 1969 party congress. Ironically, the demand for women's representation was not included in the 1964 women's programme, and the problem of under-representation of women in public office was only briefly mentioned in the Towards Equality programme (*Jämlikhet* 1969: 24, 94). Emphasis on other reforms to achieve equality of women and men initially eclipsed the issue of women's representation.

Among the first to voice the demand for increased political representation for women were the reform communists. The 1967 programme of the Left Party-Communists (VPK), 'Socialist Alternative', contained a strong plank advocating equality of the sexes. It proclaimed, 'Women are also under-represented in the leadership of the Labour Movement organisations. It is a blatant injustice and a threat to democracy that half of the population of Sweden is poorly represented on boards and executive committees' (Socialist Alternative 1967: 13). The Centre Party women, who had the poorest representation in parliament in the 1960s, were also very early in pointing to women's under-representation as a contradiction in democratic principles (Larsson 1973). By 1968 the demand began to gain momentum, and it was raised in many quarters and across the political spectrum. The women's organisations of the political parties, the Fredrika Bremer Association (a women's rights organisation founded in 1884) and the reform communist party called for more women in politics.

Dominant frame of debate

All proponents framed the demand for women's representation in similar terms. From the outset, the dominant frame or the master frame was the implications for democracy. The problem was the deficient functioning of Swedish democracy, manifested in gross under-representation. Women were half the citizenry, but only a small portion held political office.

Gendering the debate

Women gendered the wider debate on extending democracy and promoting equality. The equal right of participation and influence – or equality in power and influence – was central to the Towards Equality programme but the thrust of the demand was to extend participatory rights to the economy and the immediate environment – on the job, at school and in the neighbourhood. Furthermore, the programme trumpeted that the demand for equality concerned everybody but without relating it to the sexes: '[T]he demand for equality encompasses broader spheres [than economic differences] and concerns all members of society ... Equality requires a society where ... individuals have greater opportunities to participate in the decision-making processes that influence his [sic] everyday situation' (Jämlikhet 1969: 13). This general demand for equal participation and influence was gendered by underlining women's representation and the inequalities in the political representation of women and men.

At the same time women framed their claims in *ungendered* terms. They made their claims as voters and citizens – not as women. As citizens they demanded that the principle of equal rights to political office be translated into reality. Framing the issue of women's representation as citizens' rights had several strategic advantages. First, it enhanced unity among women. Politically organised women constituted a minority within each of the parties, and they were divided along partisan lines. As citizens they had equal rights and were joined together in redressing the denial of their rights. Second, as half the citizenry, women were entitled to a corresponding share of the seats. Third, framed as a contradiction of democratic principles, the demand for increased representation for women was hard to argue against. In fact, everyone concurred in principle, and all the party leaders expressed their support of more women in office.

Policy outcome

This debate produced two distinct outcomes. The first was the initial adoption by the political parties of guidelines for women's representation in party and elected office. In 1972 the Liberals were the first party to adopt such guidelines. The party conference decided that women were entitled to at least 40 per cent of the posts in all party bodies (Sandberg 1975: 80). Eventually the Social Democrats also adopted guidelines. At its 1978 congress the party laid down the following guidelines: the share of women in elected public office ought to reflect their proportion of the population; while in the case of party office, women's share ought to be in proportion to female party membership, which then totalled roughly one-third of party members. The Social Democratic Women's Federation had proposed that neither sex should have more than 60 per cent of the positions, and that quotas should be introduced if a fair distribution of positions could not be reached through agreement between the sexes (Karlsson 1996: 160).

The second outcome was the establishment of the Advisory Council on Equality between Men and Women in late 1972. It was attached to the Office of the Prime Minister; the first chairperson was Thage G. Peterson, the key administrative officer (the permanent under-secretary) of the prime minister, and Anna-Greta Leijon headed the council's secretariat (Karlsson 1996). After the 1973 election Leijon entered the cabinet as Assistant Minister of Labour with 'special responsibility for women's issues', and she later became the chairperson of the council (Leijon 1991: 119).

Women's movement impact

Both outcomes corresponded with feminist goals, and women were pivotal in the process. However, at the time the initial guidelines were a disappointment to women, but in a long-term perspective they were the beginning of a process in which the parties set forth guidelines and recommendations that women could use in their fight to gain elected office.

Of special interest is the creation of the Advisory Council. Many accounts of its formation fail to note the role of women. Instead Prime Minister Olof Palme's speech at the 1972 party congress has been hailed as a turning point, and he is assigned credit for its establishment (e.g. Elman 1995: 241; Karlsson 1996). On the basis of these accounts, the outcome would be classified as pre-emption. This interpretation, however, overlooks the actions of the SSKF.

Embittered by the results of the 1968 and 1970 elections, which actually decreased their share of the parliamentary delegation, Social Democratic women mounted their own campaign for more women in politics. As part of the campaign, the SSKF congress in 1972 drafted a six-point resolution on gender equality. One point was to appoint a special task force at cabinet level to monitor and promote issues related to women's equality (Fagerström 1974: 45). Subsequently the party congress adopted a decision supporting the establishment of a working group on gender equality at cabinet level, which led to the Advisory Council's formation. In other words, the creation of the council corresponded to the demands of the SSKF, and therefore should be categorised as a dual response. Party women proposed the council, and it was eventually staffed almost entirely by women.

Women's policy agency activities

This debate pre-dated the existence of women's policy agencies. However, the women's organisations of the parties were inside agitators, and they can to some extent be regarded as quasi-women's policy agencies seeking to advance women's representation in descriptive and substantive terms through direct access to party decision-makers. Compared with their counterparts in other countries, the women's sections of the parties, especially those of the Liberals and the Social Democrats, have strong traditions as independent associations. The independent position of the Social Democratic women's organisation has afforded both advantages and limitations. The SSKF has often developed its own policy positions and lobbied for them inside the party, but independence has also entailed a more peripheral position in the party. For example, the SSKF is much less integrated in the party organisational hierarchy than the women's sections of the non-socialist parties. Party by-laws do not guarantee full representation at the party congress or in the national committee and the executive committee. Importantly, however, the SSKF does have the right to attend and express its views at meetings of these bodies, although its representatives lack the right to vote unless they are elected as a delegate to the congress or as a member of the committees. Nor did the SSKF have direct access to the cabinet at this time, which may have prompted its proposal for a body at cabinet level.

Women's movement characteristics

The initial demands for more women in politics preceded the emergence of the new women's movement. The major feminist actors were the members of organisations established during the first wave of the women's movement – the Fredrika Bremer Association and the women's organisations of four of the political parties: the Conservatives, the Liberals, the Centre Party (formerly the Agrarians) and the Social

Democrats. The demand for political representation was originally over-shadowed by other reforms, but by 1972 it had top priority and was a pan-partisan concern. Its increasing priority paralleled the early growth of the movement and the political mobilisation of women. The new women's movement initially strengthened leftist forces but simultaneously posed a challenge to the Social Democrats. The main organisation associated with the new movement was Group 8 and its affiliates. Group 8 was formally established as an independent socialist feminist organisation in 1970.

Policy environment

The policy sub-system was the political parties, and as such the system was only open to party members – or around one-third of the electorate at the time. The party congress/conference, where the party leadership often predominates, makes decisions on nomination rules and guidelines. In terms of access it was a moderately closed system, but importantly the system was not closed to women. In terms of decision-makers few women were delegates to the party congress/conference or in positions of party leadership during the period of the debate.

Because this type of decision is an internal party matter, the composition of the government is less significant than when the issue requires a parliamentary decision. More important is the nature of party competition, and whether measures to improve women's representation are perceived to strengthen or weaken the parties' competitive positions. In the 1968 election the Social Democrats experienced a sweeping victory, receiving 50 per cent of the vote, and they formed the only majority non-coalition government in their history. However, the Social Democrats' hold on majority power was short-lived, and the elections of the 1970s were highly competitive contests where a fraction of the vote determined control of the executive. The 1970 election – the first under the party leadership of Olof Palme – resulted in a drop in electoral support but not a loss of government. Unhappy with the election results, the Social Democrats were bent on reversing the downward trend, and the votes of all groups became critical.

In short, strategic and ideological imperatives conjoined, offering a window of opportunity. Strategically the Social Democrats were under pressure as both the right and the left outflanked them on the issue of women's representation. The pressure was keenly felt because the party wanted to lay claim to the issue of gender equality. On the right, the Fredrika Bremer Association brought up the issue of quotas and mounted a campaign, 'More Women in Politics', in 1972–3. The Liberals were first to adopt guidelines for party office – setting 40 per cent as a goal for women's representation. The transformation of the Communist Party into a leftist alternative emphasising women's issues and the emergence of Group 8 as an independent socialist women's organisation also gave Social Democratic women extra leverage (Karlsson 1996). Moreover, all parties were vying for the support of women, especially those whose interest in politics had been fired by a growing and enthusiastic women's movement. Ideologically the radicalisation of the Social Democratic Party emphasising greater democracy and equality offered a discursive opportunity. How could the party present itself as a proponent of greater democracy and at the same time not improve its own record on women's representation? The party's emphasis on equality also made it especially difficult to deny the legitimacy of women's demands for equal representation.

Debate 2: Quotas for appointed positions, 1985–1987

How the debate came to the public agenda

During the first year of its existence (1973), the Advisory Council to the Prime Minister on Equality between Men and Women wrote to the government, pointing out that few women were members of inquiry commissions or on the boards of national administrative agencies. In 1975 the council went on to criticise the low representation of women in regional administrative bodies (Sandberg 1975: 81).

Reports to the UN offered opportunities for agenda setting and advancing positions for negotiations. *Step by Step*, a national plan for gender equality that also served as the report to the 1980 United Nations Women's Conference, stressed the necessity to improve women's representation in the corporatist and bureaucratic channels (*Step by Step* 1979: 103–21). The Swedish government's report to the 1985 UN Women's Conference in Nairobi, *Side by Side*, also brought up the issue, contrasting the poor representation of women on national administrative boards, regional bodies and inquiry commissions with their advances in elected office. The stated goal of the government was to increase women's representation so that both sexes were included in *all* administrative bodies by 1991 (*Side by Side* 1985: 90). It identified the problem as the freedom of organisations and their failure to nominate women despite the government's request that a man and a woman be nominated for each position. The same year, the Minister of Gender Equality, Anita Gradin, appointed an inquiry commission to propose measures to increase women's representation in the state bureaucracy.

Dominant frame of debate

As in the first debate, women's under-representation was the problem. It contradicted democratic principles and women's under-representation in appointed office was more pronounced than in elected office. The commission's final report argued that government bodies should represent the will of the people and be a mirror of the population. Representative democracy required that women and men participate in decisions in the same proportions and on equal terms (SOU 1987: 51). Increased women's representation was a matter of increasing democracy and widening the basis of decision-making. For democratic reasons, increased women's representation was a goal in itself, but it was also a means – a means to promote new issues and points of views and make them politically relevant. In this instance the goal was policies jointly formulated by women and men that accommodated the interests of all.

Gendering the debate

The commission gendered decision-making in the state bureaucracy, stressing that administrative bodies make decisions that distribute resources but women and men have different concerns. Without women representatives in these bodies, decisions would fail to take into account the interests of women and their priorities. Examples of conflicts of interest between the sexes, mentioned by the commission, were different priorities concerning investments in road construction vis-à-vis public transport, social services and work time. The commission also pointed out that certain women's issues only reached the policy agenda through women's efforts, such as women's representation, gender equality, women's health issues, shelters for battered women, pornography and prostitution (Sou 1985: 4–6).

Finally, the commission argued: '[w]e live in a male society where men's experiences and values are the norm', insisting that changes in attitudes were insufficient to eliminate women's subordination. Attitudes were usually embedded in power structures; what was needed was changes in power. 'Today men dominate politics and consequently have a profound influence on women's lives. If women are to gain real influence over their own lives, they must gain entry to the councils where decisions are made. The goal is that women and men share power, influence and responsibility in all spheres of society' (Sou 1985: 4–5). It also declared that if women were to acquire their fair share of decision-making power, men had to relinquish power and influence.

Policy outcome

The most controversial proposal of the commission was the introduction of quotas. It recommended quotas and drafted a bill to this effect. At the same time the commission mixed strong words and recommendations with a conciliatory stance. The commission stated its firm conviction that only quotas would achieve quick results. However, as a concession, it had chosen a 'softer' approach as a sign of its confidence in the nominating organisations' assurances that they only needed more time. Accordingly, the commission recommended that the government give the organisations a chance to show their good intentions by nominating more women. Strategically, the commission's concession put the onus on the nominating organisations. Quotas could be avoided if they nominated women. The commission also laid down specific targets for women's representation on administrative bodies and inquiry commissions: 30 per cent by 1992, 40 per cent by 1995 and 50 per cent by 1998. If the goal of 30 per cent was not reached by 1992, the commission proposed the introduction of legislated quotas.

The commission and its proposals set in motion a remarkable growth in women's representation in appointed positions. At the time of the commission's investigation in the mid-1980s, women held roughly 15 per cent of the positions, but in the late 1990s over 40 per cent of the members of inquiry commissions and the boards of national administrative agencies were women. In the case of the prestigious position of general director of an administrative agency or head of an inquiry commission, women increased their share to approximately 30 per cent compared with around 5 per cent in the mid-1980s (Ds A 1986, 4: 32; Bergqvist 1997: 235; *Kommittéberättelse* 1999: 395). Still these gains fell short of the target of 50 per cent set for 1998, and growth in women's representation on regional bodies was lower and more uneven.

Women's movement impact and women's policy agency activities

This debate represents a dual response *par excellence* – women were central in the debate as well as the policy process and the outcome corresponded to the goals of the women's movement. The activities of women's policy agencies were critical to the response and are clearly classified as insider. From the start, the drive to increase women's representation in appointed positions in the state administration has been a project of femocrats involved in women's policy machinery. The Advisory Council to the Prime Minister first brought it up as an issue. The council, together with its successors – an all-party commission that drafted a national gender equality plan and the Minister of Gender Equality – worked to get the issue on to the policy agenda and to keep it there, using the reports to the UN women's conferences as a vehicle. Femocrats were not only involved in agenda setting, they also framed the debate, gendering the decisions of the state bureaucracy by emphasising their relevance for women. Feminists were also in charge of the inquiry commission leading to legislation, the government bill, and the eventual evaluation to see whether the targets for women's representation were fulfilled (Bergqvist 1994: 104–5). Furthermore, when the Social Democrats returned to power in 1982, they consolidated the position of the Minister of Gender Equality, increasing her resources (Pincus 1998). Most decisive, however, the women's policy agencies had a mandate, which they had carved out for themselves.

Women's movement characteristics

In the 1980s some observers and even activists believed that the women's movement was in decline; and there were signs of waning. The most visible organisation of the new women's movement – Group 8 – was losing members. Nevertheless it seems more appropriate to view the 1980s as a period of consolidation. The decline of Group 8 was partially offset by its members joining the Left Party-Communists, and the membership of the women's sections rose, reaching a peak during the time of the debate. Women also continued to consolidate their positions at all levels of elected office. New feminist organisations, such as the women's shelter movement, were growing (Gustafsson et al. 1997), and women in trade union organisations made steady gains. Networks of feminist academics were created through funding provided by the research unit under the Minister of Gender Equality. Finally, women's activism, measured as various forms of individual political participation, increased compared with the previous decade (Sainsbury 1993; cf. Stark 1997: 230–1).

The key actors were very close to the parties of the left. The issue of women's representation was of high priority to the movement as a whole but there were divisions over quotas as a means to increase representation. The conciliatory move by the commission prevented an open rift among women over the issue of quotas. The compromise also largely defused a counter-movement that the proposal for quotas produced.

Policy environment

In the 1982 election the Social Democrats won 46 per cent of the vote and formed a minority government based on a left majority in parliament, and the party remained in power for the rest of the decade. The policy sub-system was moderately closed. The main actors in formulating policy – the expert commission and the Ministers of Gender Equality – formed a tight circle, but several other actors had a potential veto. As part of the policy-making process, commission reports are sent out to interested parties for comment in what is known as the remiss system. Negative comments during the remiss procedure can kill a proposal, while favourable opinions strengthen it. In this instance, the labour market organisations also held a trump card by virtue of their power of nomination. Furthermore, the media often scrutinise commission reports, and the commission's first report generated much controversy in the media. These features, together with a preference for inclusive decisions, worked in favour of the compromise solution.

Debate 3: The establishment of a women's party, 1991–1994

How the debate came to the public agenda

Women's representation in parliament fell from 38 per cent to 34 per cent in the 1991 election; it was the first time since 1928 that there was a major setback. Women were both angered by their weakened position in parliament and fearful of the consequences. Immediately after the election, women formed a network, the 'Support Stockings' (*Stödstrumporna*), whose rallying cry was 'Half the power, full pay'. Their goals included improving women's representation in parliament and preventing the new coalition government headed by the moderates from dismantling the public sector and women-friendly policies (Stark 1997).

Dominant frame of debate

In a more pronounced fashion than previously the issue of women's representation was framed in terms of power, as evident in the demand for 50 per cent of the power. One network leader explained the emphasis on power in the following way: 'women, with far less access to economic resources, at least have votes. Power in the democratic process is more accessible than economic power' (Stark 1997: 241). The problem was the failure of parties to nominate women. The solution, proposed by the Support Stockings, was to start a women's party that would put up its own list of candidates in the 1994 election. The establishment of the party depended upon whether the major parties selected sufficient female candidates to reinstate and even improve women's parliamentary representation so that they held half the power.

Gendering the debate

The parties' failure to nominate women was blamed on men's power and a male political culture in the parties. Feminists now more emphatically gendered power and the parties, and network spokeswomen adopted an adversarial stance. In the Social Democratic women's magazine in early 1992, Maria-Pia Boëthuis – a leading Support Stocking – maintained that men in overalls were still the party norm. She further complained, 'Your guys have not listened [to women] and in the process they have committed political suicide' (*Morgonbris* 1992: 3). In short, the Support Stockings gendered both the problem and the solution of the debate. The problem was male power and the solution was a women's party.

Social Democratic women also pointed to the male political culture of the party, but this sort of argument was wedded to the master frame of women's representation – its implications for democracy. A report on women's representation in the party noted that the Social Democrats had a tradition of representing working-class men that had shaped the party's organisation and functioning. It concluded that if women were not represented, male interests and knowledge would govern decisions, and that under-representation meant that democracy was incomplete (SD 1993: 3, 16). Similarly in the 1993 party congress debate, an active trade union woman argued, 'The problem is not women but a political culture that has failed to take women's views seriously; it has failed to realise that women's exclusion from political bodies is a problem for democracy' (SD 1993 kongressprotokoll, B: 32–3). Finally, the programme adopted by the congress declared: 'The foundation of democracy is the equal worth of all human beings. Gender equality entails the same rights, obligations and opportunities for men and women. To achieve gender equality is to broaden democracy' (SD-programme 1993: 15).

Policy outcome

On the eve of the election the Support Stockings confidently predicted that no matter which parties made gains in the election, the proportion of women MPs would increase (Boëthuis et al. 1994). Indeed women's parliamentary representation rebounded, reaching a new high of 40 per cent in the 1994 election. A further outcome was that at the 1993 party congress the Social Democrats changed their by-laws to stipulate that the party lists provide an equal distribution of sexes. Party women's share of parliamentary seats rose from 41 per cent to 48 per cent in the 1994 election, and the Social Democratic government that came into office had the first cabinet in which women and men were equally represented.

Women's movement impact

The outcome – dual response – was the product of the combined pressures of women inside the parties and the external women's movement. In this debate the external movement, and especially the network, figured much more prominently than previously. Obviously, the threat to start a women's party was critical, and party women utilised this threat during the candidate selection process. The Support Stockings also backed up the threat by mounting several campaigns as shows of movement strength. Among them was a sticker and button campaign to emphasise that the movement was everywhere, even in the men's lavatories in the parliament building. The Support Stockings also held a women's tribunal in Stockholm to scrutinise the non-socialist government's roll back of the public sector, and they urged that similar tribunals be organised across the country.

Within the Social Democratic Party, the SSKF joined forces with women in top party positions: Mona Sahlin, then the first woman general secretary of the party and later deputy prime minister; Ingela Thalin, a member of the party executive committee; and Margot Wallström, former Minister of Gender Equality. Sahlin and Wallström were also members of the working group to analyse party losses in the 1991 election. In addition to pointing to the threat of a women's party during nominations, Social Democratic women used the threat in a different way. In the words of Margareta Winberg, president of the SSKF: 'Let us demonstrate that the Social Democrats are the women's party in Sweden' (SD 1993 kongressprotokoll B: 35). A working group chaired by Wallström charted women's representation in a report entitled *Are the Social Democrats a Women's Party?* (*Är socialdemokraterna ett kvinnoparti?*). It found that women's representation was highest (approximately 40 per cent) in parliament, the executive committee and the national committee (*partistyrelse*), but in key positions in local politics (chairpersons of municipal executive boards, the parliamentary constituency organisations, municipal constituency organisations (*arbetarekommuner*) and the local chapters), women's representation was much poorer – ranging from 12 per cent to 22 per cent. To become a women's party, the report concluded, women must have the same opportunities to influence society as men. This demand encompassed all elected positions, chairpersons and party functionaries (SD 1993). Simultaneously, as an alternative to this demand, SSKF women proposed special women's lists (Eduards 1992; SD-motioner 1993). In effect, SSKF women pursued the same tactics as the Support Stockings but inside the party. If the party did not act to improve women's representation, women would introduce their own lists.

Women's policy agency activities

In this debate the WPAs were symbolic. They did not enter the debate, and they were not involved in the process of restoring women's representation in parliament. Nor would they have supported the quota solution adopted by the Social Democrats. The WPAs had other tasks and were fully occupied with improving women's representation in appointed positions as part of the five-year gender equality plan adopted by parliament in 1988. The non-socialist government pledged to continue to work along the lines of the plan. The post of Minister of Gender Equality went to the Liberals who have been part of the alliance advocating radical policies to secure equality between women and men. Instead it was a quasi-WPA that played the insider role. The SSKF gendered the debate, complaining about the male political culture of the party and welcoming a dialogue with the Support Stockings. Now, however, top party women aided the SSKF by throwing their political weight behind the demand for equal representation of women and men in all public and party offices.

Women's movement characteristics

The 1990s witnessed a resurgence of the women's movement. The impressive mobilisation across classes and generations was heralded as a 'new women's movement' (e.g. *Morgonbris* 1992: 3). Its newness was reflected in a new generation of activists, new tactics, more emphasis on networking than previously, and a much stronger presence of trade union women. The key organisers of the Support Stockings were women academics and publicists mostly on the left, but they were not party members. Several had been active in Group 8 and radical feminist campaigns of the 1970s and 1980s. The network and the movement represented a wide range of political views, but both were united in giving top priority to the goal of increasing women's political representation. The idea of a women's party provoked hostile criticism across the political spectrum and sometimes ridicule; network leaders also paid a high personal price, having to endure harassment at work and hate mail (Stark 1997). Nonetheless, this counter-movement was politically ineffectual mainly because the leading members of the network preferred not to start a women's party. The failure to form a women's party, however, drove a wedge into the leftist part of the movement; young radical feminists who viewed women organising as women as the ultimate challenge to the patriarchal order regarded the failure as a betrayal (Ulmanen 1998).

Policy environment

The government was a minority centre-right coalition composed of the Moderates, Liberals, Centre Party and Christian Democrats. The Moderates held the post of prime minister, and the government's parliamentary base included the right-wing populist New Democrats. Together with the New Democrats, the Moderates had made sizeable gains and interpreted their victory and the rightward shift in the electorate as a mandate for change.

As in the first debate, the political parties were the arena of decisions. In three respects the policy sub-system was now more fluid and open. The Support Stockings practised the tactics of disruption by creating uncertainty. They kept threatening to form a party but always at the last minute postponed the decision. If they had acted upon their threat, it is likely that the new party would have thrown the party system into a state of disarray. Opinion polls indicated that a women's party formed by the Support Stockings could attract 25 per cent of the vote – some reports claimed as much as 40 per cent (Stark 1997). Furthermore, the media were a major player in the debate, showering attention on the Support Stockings and booming up the prospects of a women's party. The constellation of party strength also added an element of uncertainty. The 1991 election not only removed the Social Democrats from office; it was their worst election since 1928. The disaster at the polls caused much soul searching within the party, opening up space for new ideas and the acceptance of previously controversial proposals. Moreover, opinion polls showed that supporters of left parties were most prone to vote for a new women's party. Finally, the votes of women were perceived as especially important to the left parties. In recent elections, a larger proportion of women than men had voted for the Social Democrats and the Left Party.

Conclusion

In the major debates on the political representation of women, feminists have been successful in achieving dual responses from the state and the political parties. The debates produced a change in policy content corresponding to movement goals, and they fundamentally altered the understanding of democratic representation. Women participated in the policy process, and women's political representation reached impressive levels in a cross-national context.

The gains in representation resulted from party feminists and state feminists working in tandem. Party feminists concentrated on improving women's representation in party and elected offices. They also spearheaded the move to create WPAs and have filled the key ministerial positions. Femocrats turned their energies to bettering women's representation in appointed positions in the state bureaucracy.

The advances involved the activities of both women's policy agencies and quasi-women's policy agencies. In the first debate quasi-women's policy agencies within the parties achieved initial successes, while the activities of women's policy agencies were both effective and necessary to the outcome in the second debate. The insider position afforded unique opportunities to influence the formulation and implementation of policy. The crucial determining factor in this debate was the existence of a mandate. Since nominations to elected office are the prerogative of the political parties and state intervention in party activities has been minimal, this area was largely outside their jurisdiction but posts within the state were not. In the third debate it was again the women's party organisation, but now in alliance with individual high-ranking women party members, that influenced the outcome.

Specific characteristics of the women's movement help to explain these successes. Consistently high priority was assigned to the goal of increasing women's political representation, and the movement was united behind this goal. The initial framing of the issue as the equal rights of the citizenry reinforced movement unity. In the second debate, the proposal to introduce quotas was divisive but the commission's compromise restored unity. The pan-partisan nature of the goal of women's representation was also essential to the outcome of more women's nominations across most of the political spectrum in the third debate. The stage of the movement varied (emergence and growth, consolidation and resurgence respectively) but this conceals an important common denominator – the women's movement was not in decline but gaining strength. Most significantly, movement access to major decisional arenas strengthened over time through the institutionalised presence of women. The location of feminist activists, working both inside and outside the political parties and the state, has also been of key importance to movement success. The stance of the movement has often been proactive rather than reactive. This stance was possible because of the lack of an organised counter-movement. At an early date, the political parties went on record in support of women's representation, and the positive positions of the parties limited the space for an overt counter-movement to emerge.

Of the policy environment variables, the importance of frame fit stands out. The master frame of women's representation has been its implications for democracy, and the emphasis on women's under-representation as a glaring contradiction to democratic principles has had enormous resonance. It appears to have been especially great when the policy sub-system is the parties, possibly because they see themselves as the main vehicles for a functioning representative democracy. In contradiction to the assumption that openness provides the most favourable policy environment, feminist successes have occurred in closed or moderately closed sub-systems. Because of their institutionalised presence, women have had access and opportunities to influence policy outcomes even in closed sub-systems.

With regard to the parties in power, the Swedish case offers evidence both for and against the hypothesis that women's movements are more effective when parties of the left are in government. On the one hand, the ascendancy of the left from the mid-1960s to the mid-1970s promoted a public discourse on equality and greater democracy that feminists used, triggering the growth of women's representation in elected and appointed positions. The movement has been more effective in increasing women's representation compared with most other countries in this book, and the Social Democrats have been the dominant party in power. Moreover, it was a Social Democratic government that established the first WPA. On the other hand, the non-socialist government created additional WPAs and formalised the post of the Minister of Gender Equality. Furthermore, during the last debate the parties in power were a centre-right coalition. Despite this, the outcome was a dual response. In other words, the party in power is not a necessary condition for a dual response, especially when the policy sub-system is the political parties. In addition, women experienced little success in improving their representation during the first two decades of the post-war period when the Social Democrats were also the party of the government. Then a critical factor was missing – the widespread political mobilisation of women.

Finally it needs to be stressed that the women's movement has not influenced the outcomes of all debates on political representation. The basic explanation lies in the low priority many feminists have given to debates not specifically dealing with women's representation. Furthermore, several of these debates have caused heated partisan controversy between the left and the right, such as voting rights for immigrants in parliamentary elections, undermining the prospects for an alliance of women across parties. Such divisions can neutralise party women who have been a political force essential to the successes of bringing women into elected office. In short, two of the major prerequisites of feminist success in increasing the political representation of women – movement unity and high priority – have not existed in several other debates.

214   *Diane Sainsbury*

References

Arter, David 1999, *Scandinavian Politics Today*, Manchester: Manchester University Press

Bergqvist, Christina 1994, *Mäns makt och kvinnors intressen*, Skrifter utgivna av Statsvetenskaplig föreningen i Uppsala 121, Uppsala: Acta Universitatis Upsaliensis

1997, 'Korporatismens nedgång – kvinnornas framgång?', in Anita Nyberg and Elisabeth Sundin (eds.) *Ledare, makt och kön* (SOU 1997: 135), Stockholm: Ministry of Labour, pp. 212–44

Boëthius, Maria-Pia, Ebba Witt-Brattström and Agneta Stark (eds.) 1994, *Kvinnors lilla lista*, Stockholm: Norstedt

Ds A 1986, 4. *Ska även morgondagens samhälle formas enbart av män? Kartläggning av könfördelningen i central och regional statsförvaltning*, Stockholm: Ministry of Labour

Eduards, Maud L. 1992, 'Against the Rules of the Game: On the Importance of Women's Collective Actions', *Rethinking Change: Current Swedish Feminist Research*, Stockholm: The Swedish Council for Research in the Humanities and Social Sciences, pp. 83–104

Einhorn, Eric S. and John Logue 2003, *Modern Welfare States: Scandinavian Politics and Policy in a Global Age*, Westport, CT: Praeger

Elman, Amy 1995, 'The State's Equality for Women: The Equality Ombudsman', in Dorothy McBride Stetson and Amy G. Mazur (eds.) *Comparative State Feminism*, Thousand Oaks, CA: Sage, pp. 237–53

Fagerström, Eva 1974, 'Fler kvinnor i politiken – en studie av det socialdemokratiska partiets and kvinnoförbundets åtgärder för att nå detta mål mellan valen 1970 och 1973', unpublished paper, Department of Political Science, University of Stockholm

Gustafsson, Gunnel, Maud Eduards and Malin Rönnblom 1997, *Towards a New Democratic Order? Women's Organizing in Sweden in the 1990s*, Stockholm: Publica Nordstedts juridik

Jämlikhet 1969, *Första rapport från SAP-LO:s arbetsgrupp för jämlikhetsfrågor*, Stockholm: Prisma

Karlsson, Gunnel 1996, *Från broderskap till systerskap. Det socialdemokratiska kvinnoförbundets kamp för inflytande och makt i SAP*, Lund: Arkiv

Kommittéberättelse 1999, Regeringens skrivelse 1998/99: 103

Kvinnans jämlikhet 1964, Stockholm: Tiden

Larsson, Maj 1973, *Kvinnor i tidsspegel. En bok om Centerns kvinnorförbund*, Stockholm: LTs förlag

Leijon, Anna-Greta 1991, *Alla rosor ska inte tuktas!* Stockholm: Tiden

Morgonbris, 1992–4

Pincus, Ingrid 1998, *Från kvinnofrågor till könsmaktstruktur*, Kvinnovetenskapligt forums arbetsrapport nr. 1, Örebro: University of Örebro

Sainsbury, Diane 1993, 'The Politics of Increased Women's Representation: the Swedish Case', in Joni Lovenduski and Pippa Norris (eds.) *Gender and Party Politics*, London: Sage, pp. 263–90

Sandberg, Elisabet 1975, *Equality is the Goal*, Stockholm: Advisory Council to the Prime Minister on Equality between Men and Women

SD 1993, *Är socialdemokraterna ett kvinnoparti?* Stockholm: Socialdemokraterna

SD 1993 kongressprotokoll B, *Protokoll. Socialdemokraternas 32:a kongress 15–21 september 1993*, Stockholm: Socialdemokraterna

SD-motioner 1993, *Motioner. Socialdemokraternas 32:a kongress 15–21 september 1993*, Stockholm: Socialdemokraterna

SD-programme 1993, *De nya uppdragen – for arbete, omtanke och framtidstro. Antaget vid socialdemokraternas partikongress den 15–21 september 1993*, Stockholm: SSKF

Side by Side 1985, *A Report on Equality between Women and Men in Sweden 1985*, Stockholm: Ministry of Labour

Socialist Alternative 1967, official English translation of the party programme adopted by the 1967 congress of the Left Party-Communists

SOU 1987: 19, *Varannan damernas*, Stockholm: Ministry of Labour

Stark, Agneta 1997, 'Combating the Backlash: How Swedish Women Won the War', in Ann Oakley and Juliet Mitchell (eds.) *Who's Afraid of Feminism: Seeing through the Backlash*, London: Hamish Hamilton, pp. 224–44

Step by Step 1979, *National Plan of Action for Equality 1979*, Stockholm: Ministry of Labour

Ulmanen, Petra 1998, *(S)veket mot kvinnorna och hur högern stal feminismen*, Stockholm: Atlas

11 Party government and women's representation debates: the UK

Joni Lovenduski

Introduction

Although parliament is formally sovereign, UK decision-making is determined by party government. Supported by a single member simple plurality electoral system that normally produces working majorities for the winning party in the House of Commons, governments are dominated by a cabinet composed of majority-party politicians that is in turn dominated by the prime minister and a few other senior ministers. Party government secures the centralisation and closedness of the political system. Party discipline secures passage of government bills. Formally accountable to the House of Commons, the power of the cabinet is such that the system is frequently referred to as an 'elected dictatorship'. Major decisions are taken by a combination of a minister, their policy advisers and civil servants. Details of decisions are worked out in the civil service where legislation and other policy documents are drafted. The formal arrangements conceal the extent to which decisions are significantly influenced by the 'Number 10 policy machine'.

Political representation takes place in both elected and appointed bodies. The rules and procedures that determine who becomes a representative differ by sector. For elected bodies the political parties make the most important decisions about who are the elected representatives because nomination of candidates is a party matter, subject to very few external constraints. In contrast, the nature of the electoral system is a constitutional matter, subject to considerable regulation. Until recently trade unions, business and employers' associations, interest and advocacy organisations and civil service officials made nominations for vacant positions in government-appointed bodies whose membership is formally agreed by ministers. Activity in support of equality of women's representation brings at least three international actors into the decision-making frame: the United Nations, the European Union and the Council of Europe. As with other members of the European Union, EU legislation takes precedence in its areas of competence, which, since the 1997

Amsterdam Treaty, have included equality provision for the composition of decision-making bodies. The key institutions in which British political representation takes place pre-dated representative democracy. David Judge argues that British political institutions did not accommodate to popular sovereignty. This sequence suggests that institutions adapted inadequately to take account of democratic responsibilities. As a result, discussion of political representation in Britain is replete with paradoxes in which common assumptions about the democratic nature of the system are not expressed in institutional arrangements (Judge 1999: 19–20). The growth of 'governance' with its array of appointed bodies exacerbates this disjunction. Whereas models of representative government suggest simple flows of power between the represented and their MPs, modern systems of 'governance' differentiate the represented and their relations with government (Judge 1999: 121). Between 1970 and 2001 the rules of the game changed for both elected and appointed offices. The most important changes in the rules about elected office included the introduction of new elected bodies at regional level with accompanying new electoral systems, reform of the structure of local councils and changes in the system of elections to the European parliament. Political parties repeatedly adjusted their rules about the selection of candidates, but their control over nomination was neither challenged nor altered. Rule changes for appointed office included the introduction of a system of self-nomination and public advertisement of vacancies.[1]

Universe of debates

In the post-war period British debates about political representation preoccupied only a few groups of political reformers interested in altering the constitution. Led by the Charter 88 group a movement for constitutional reform gained support in the 1980s. Political representation issues were a central part of its agenda. This group of intellectuals and activists was able to mobilise informed opinion and secure support in the political class. Demands included the establishment of Scottish and Welsh parliaments with powers to tax, directly elected by some form of proportional representation; devolution of power to the English regions; proportional representation for parliamentary (Westminster), local and European elections; the reform of the House of Lords to an elected second chamber with the abolition of its hereditary principles.

---

[1] The Standing Committee on Standards in Public Life first reported in 1996. It has changed the rules on public appointments to make them more transparent.

Much of the Charter 88 programme was incorporated into the election manifesto of the Labour Party, elected in 1997. After 1997 reforms included devolution of some parliamentary powers to new assemblies under proportional electoral systems in Scotland, Wales and Northern Ireland, partial reform of the House of Lords, some modernisation of the procedures of the House of Commons, reform of local government, the establishment of the Greater London Assembly headed by a London mayor and the beginnings of a programme of regionalisation in England. The European Convention on Human Rights was incorporated into British law in the 1998 Human Rights Bill. In addition, changes in the regulation of UK political parties from the 1990s were described by influential commentators as amounting to constitutional change (Beetham et al. 2002). These events generated debates that created unprecedented opportunities to raise issues of women's representation.

The movement for equality of women's representation pre-dated the reform and modernisation movements by many years. Comparatively and historically, women's representation in the House of Commons was low, rising slowly in the 1980s and more rapidly in the 1990s to a peak in 1997 of around 18 per cent at Westminster (Appendix 1). At the 1997 general election a record number of women MPs were elected to the House of Commons. Subsequently activists were able to ensure a substantial presence of women in the newly formed Scottish parliament and Welsh Assembly, and were immediately engaged in improving women's share of seats in the European parliament, in local government and in publicly appointed bodies.

Notable was the use made by women's advocates of the opportunities afforded by the Scotland and Wales devolution debates. Feminists, many of them political party members, intervened in this process to become part of the movement for change. In Scotland their goal was a legislature in which women held 50 per cent of the seats and were well represented in its cabinet and executive. Under the umbrella of the Scottish Women's Co-ordinating Group they lobbied the Constitutional Convention and the political parties to gender the debate. They drew attention to the kind of electoral system that would most benefit women and secured agreement from party leaders to this effect. As the prospects for devolution became more promising equality advocates were involved in discussions about institutional design. The achievement of feminist advocates in Scotland was considerable. When the first Scottish parliament opened for business 37 per cent of its members were women. In its first executive women were 30 per cent of ministers, and women took 41 per cent of the committee places including six of seventeen convenorships (Mackay 2003). Its blueprint included arrangements for inclusive consensual and co-operative ways of doing business. In Wales where a similar process occurred, women won 40 per cent of the seats in the new assembly. In both countries the absence of incumbents was an important opportunity for feminists. After elections in 2003 women were 40 per cent of members of the Scottish parliament and 50 per cent of members of the Welsh National Assembly. This example illustrates well the principles of successful intervention in British politics. It was a process that involved classic political strategies. Engagement in debate, an understanding of the rules of the game, the mobilisation of support, the formation of alliances, the remaking of political discourse, and the accumulation and dissemination of expertise all operated to affect the rules of the game.

Prior to 1997 much of the activity over women's representation took place within the political parties, especially the Labour Party, in the trade unions and in women's advocacy organisations, many of them ad hoc and short lived. After 1997 activity expanded into the legislature and government as women and some male supporters in parliament and in government set about mobilising support for and sensitising opinion to the need for special measures to achieve equality of representation. When the general election of 2001 returned fewer women to the House of Commons than in 1997, government acceded to demands for changes in the law so that there would be no legal obstacles to parties wishing to introduce quotas of women candidates. Accordingly the Sex Discrimination Electoral Candidates Bill was introduced by the government in the autumn of 2001 and received Royal Assent in 2002.

Debates about political representation in Britain are of three main types. First, constitutional debates deal with the architecture of the system. Second, debates about the rules of the game are mainly but not exclusively carried on within political parties during periods of opposition. Such debates are highly salient because the political parties are the foundations of the architecture of British government. Third, presence debates treat both the composition and the existence of decision-making bodies and may have important implications for the organisation of the machinery of government. Not least because of the fluid nature of the uncodified UK constitution, the three kinds of debate do not operate within clearly defined boundaries. They may and do spill over into each other as the discussion below suggests.

Women's policy machinery

At government level the Women's National Commission (WNC), with responsibility for ensuring consultation between government and women's organisations, was established in 1969. The Equal

Opportunities Commission (EOC) was established by the Sex Discrimination Act of 1975 as a cross-sectional agency with responsibility to oversee the sex equality legislation. From 1986 a ministerial group on women's issues operated under the aegis of the Home Office; in 1992 it became a cabinet committee, its brief to consider women's issues on a cross-sectional basis. A succession of cabinet members were given, in addition to their other responsibilities, the 'women's portfolio', which they sometimes accepted only reluctantly (Lovenduski and Randall 1993). In 1997 the Labour government inaugurated a Ministry for Women. The ministry took over responsibility for much of the equality machinery and the minister worked with a cabinet committee on women, which later was renamed the Women and Equality Committee to signify concern with other equalities, such as homosexual rights. Since 1997 there have normally been two 'Ministers for Women', one at cabinet level and a junior minister who takes day-to-day responsibility for women's equality issues. As we go to press the UK government is in the process of establishing a single equality unit with responsibility for all equality legislation, a change expected to take place in 2006. Most British political parties also have quasi-WPAs, which consist of women's offices, committees and shadow ministries.

Selection of debates

The selected debates took place in the Westminster decisional system. To represent the decisional system it is necessary to cover the political parties, the executive and the legislature. To represent the time span of the existence of women's policy machinery, it is necessary to begin in the 1970s. Accordingly, one debate is selected from each part of the system, one from each decade of the life of the policy machinery and one from each sector of government. The three debates are on the reform of public bodies, 1979–81; the role of trade unions in Labour Party candidate selection, 1993; and the modernisation of parliamentary sitting hours, 2002.

All the debates addressed issues of central importance to presence in decision-making throughout Britain and resulted in an end-point decision in a major institution during the lifetime of a women's policy agency. Each received widespread media coverage, was the subject of parliamentary questions or other prominent discussion, and led to extensive further debates. The devolution debates described briefly above have not been selected because, although of some constitutional significance, they directly affected only a small proportion of the population (less than 15 per cent). In addition they are widely written about elsewhere (Mackay et al. 2002, 2003; Russell 2003).

Debate 1: Reform of public bodies, 1979–1981

How the debate came to the public agenda

In common with other liberal democracies, modern UK government is characterised by the delegation of a number of responsibilities to appointed committees, commissions, tribunals and regulatory agencies, known as quasi-autonomous non-government organisations (Quangos). They receive government funding to dispose of a significant amount of power and resources. Although appointed by government they are by convention at least partly autonomous. Debates about their accountability frequently occur, generating considerable parliamentary and media discussion. The debate between 1979 and 1981 was about the need to reform the Quango system, which was judged to be out of control, unaccountable and costly. Prime Minister Thatcher took an interest in their reduction after her election in 1979. The debate centred on the need to cut the costs of running Quangos and eliminate duplication of tasks and other inefficiencies. Attention focused on the growth of Quangos over a ten-year period. The end point was in two parts: the publication of the Pliatzky Report (*Report on Non-Departmental Public Bodies*) in 1980, followed by the publication of *Non-Departmental Public Bodies: a Guide for Departments* in 1981. The 1980 report recommended changes that were partly implemented and reported in the following year (Pliatzky 1980, 1981).

This was the first of a series of debates on the nature and composition of UK public bodies. Prime Minister Thatcher promised to eliminate the inefficiencies and expense of Quangos.[2] Cuts in the social services and education began in 1979. In the same year Leo Pliatzky, a senior treasury civil servant, was appointed to review the functions of Quangos, identify which were non-essential and recommend guidelines for reviewing Quangos in the future.

Policy outcome

The first of the two Pliatzky Reports recommended a moderate cull and included a list of Quangos that should be targeted for drastic budget and staff cuts or elimination altogether. The 1981 report identified executive bodies, with expenditure on capital and current account approaching £5,800 million, and employing approximately 217,000 staff. In addition,

---

[2] A clear-out of the previous regime's appointments is a normal activity for incoming UK governments.

Pliatzky identified 1,561 advisory bodies, and found that it was impossible to count the number of tribunals.

The policy outcome was a review of the functions of Quangos, the abolition of more than 400 of them, reduction in the budgets given to remaining Quangos, reduction in staff and public appointments to them (3,700 ministerial appointments and 250 permanent posts), guidelines to ensure their accountability to parliament, guidelines to ensure any new Quangos were evaluated before being established, and establishment of thirty-one new bodies to take over the functions of the eliminated Quangos! Guidelines were established for reviewing Quangos at least once during each parliament. Subsequently regular reports on public bodies were published including annual press notices listing separately bodies that had been created and abolished since the previous report.

Dominant frame of debate

In keeping with Thatcherite rhetoric the problem was identified as the inefficiency and expense of Quangos. The dominant discussion frame was of efficiency and the reduction of government spending. Blame was put on successive governments and government departments and the practice of 'hiving off' government functions to non-departmental bodies. The frame did not fit with women's movement goals.

Gendering the debate

Parliament did not discuss the effects of the elimination and reduction of Quangos in gendered terms. No specific parliamentary consideration was given to how the reduction/elimination of Quangos, particularly in education and health sectors, might affect women. However, there was discussion of women's representation in the debate about appointments to the new public bodies that were established to replace the Quangos (*The Times*, 5 March 1980). Jo Richardson MP, later Shadow Minister for Women, argued in the House of Commons that women should be better represented in public appointments. She argued for equality provision to be written into the statutes on public appointments. The government responded by pointing out that women were listed among the candidates for Quango positions.

In the press both substantive and descriptive representation were discussed. Substantive issues were also trailed in a related debate about the effects of government cuts in public expenditure, which elided with the Quango debate. Concerns originated with reports by trade unions and the EOC. An article in *The Times* (11 July 1980) discussed the loss of women's administrative jobs as part of the cuts affecting the education system and questioned the government's attacks on bureaucracy, stating that very few administrative jobs existed prior to these cuts. The press drew attention to cuts to Quangos in areas predominantly used by women. Press reports presented women as a distinct group, mainly in relation to men. Women and men had different social roles. Most of the articles described women as a group who moved between the public and private sphere. For example, it was stated that education cuts 'force women back into the home'. Differences among women were explicitly discussed. The public/private divide was discussed prominently in terms that depicted women making gains in the public sphere through education and increased job opportunities, and then being the first to lose status either through job loss or because of responsibilities such as childcare, not assigned to men. No solution to the problem was offered. By contrast, descriptive representation, discussed in the appointments debate, led to a clear proposal made by the Shadow Minister for Women to mandate the inclusion of women.

The debate was gendered in three ways. First, the effects of Quango cuts were analysed in terms of women's issues, particularly the effects of health, education, social services and manpower cuts, and their disproportionate importance to women was made explicit. Second, the debate considered issues that affected women more than men, such as the role of carer, and what this means when cuts take place; an example was the elimination of day nursery places in the education system. Third, the public/private divide was invoked in gendered terms.

Women's policy agency characteristics and activities

The Equal Opportunities Commission was itself under some threat as it was a Quango. It intervened in the debate mainly via the press and also made a case for its own continuation as a necessary implementation agency. With responsibility for sex equality issues the EOC and trade union equality officials argued that cuts in Quangos would have a negative impact on women's employment and training. The Manpower Services Commission (another Quango) made the same arguments. The Shadow Minister for Women argued for the greater representation of women among public appointees. At the time of the Pliatzky Reports the EOC and the WNC could be described as marginal. They attempted unsuccessfully to raise women's issues in the debate but had only rudimentary and arguably pre-feminist conceptions of women's interests. Neither agency was well respected, and both were remote from centres of power and thought to be weakly led by a succession of party political appointees who had no loyalty to the women's movement.[3] The EOC, with a budget of about £1.2 million in 1981, was better resourced than was the WNC, which consisted of a small office led by a junior civil servant.

Women's movement characteristics

British feminism was revitalised in the 1970s when the Women's Liberation Movement emerged and established feminist organisations gained strength in the trade unions and some political parties. By the end of the decade the movement was divided into a radical, autonomous wing and liberal and socialist wings that were increasingly associated with the political parties. The movement can therefore be thought of as comprising autonomous and integrated feminists analogous to the other movements described in this volume. At the beginning of the 1980s the women's movement was divided over issues of difference and over strategic and tactical concerns. Organisationally it was fragmented, characterised by numerous autonomous and affiliated (to parties, trade unions, professional associations, etc.) feminist groups. The autonomous movement was not interested in women's political representation. The affiliated movement was close to the left. Scattered individuals engaged the issue, but there was little coherent movement organisation. Most contemporary accounts of the women's movement suggested that it was in decline. However, a substantial women's movement within the trade unions and the Labour Party was (re-)emerging and would soon have an appreciable impact. In retrospect, however, the early 1980s might be seen as a period of consolidation as feminists learned to operate in mainstream politics in order to resist new right policies that were thought to be harmful to women. There was no counter-movement on the matter of women's public appointments.

Policy environment

This was the first Thatcher government. The policy system was closed. The political initiative largely belonged to the prime minister and senior members of the cabinet. The dominant image of women in the debate was

---

[3] Commissioners were appointed on conventions of modified bipartism whereby the head was a nominee of the governing party and the deputy head was nominated by the opposition party, with others nominated by trade unions, business associations and the voluntary sector.

the participation of the anti-feminist, anti-Quango, anti-spending Prime Minister Margaret Thatcher.

Women's movement impact

This issue was definitely a concern for unions and Quangos, which were prominent in the debate. The women's movements did not figure prominently in the debate. They were seldom mentioned in the press in relation to the cuts to Quangos. At this stage issue priority was low. The autonomous women's movement did not take up issues of political representation and was not much concerned with mainstream politics, while the integrated movement had not yet found a coherent voice. Women's movement impact was negligible; there was no state response. No legislation resulted from the gender perspectives of the debate. The Pliatzky Reports made no recommendations on women's representation. However, there was an aftermath. The EOC began an active campaign for and monitoring of women's representation on public bodies. In 1986 the Women into Public Life campaign was launched by a coalition of women's organisations. The head of the EOC, Baroness Platt, spoke in support of the campaign from the platform of the launch meeting. In 1988 civil servants advising ministers on public appointments were given guidelines by the Cabinet Office (which has responsibility for public appointments) and the EOC on how to find women suitable for such posts. Annual reports on public appointments since 1986 include reference to women's share of new appointments. The issue remains on the agenda and is a prominent concern of the Women and Equality Unit, which devotes a section of its website to public appointments.

Debate 2: The role of the trade unions in the selection of parliamentary candidates for the Labour Party, 1993

How the debate came to the public agenda

During Labour's four successive periods of opposition after 1979 repeated debates over party organisation took place in a process of modernisation that afforded many opportunities for feminist advocates to intervene. Issues of descriptive political representation were addressed in terms of candidate selection and de-selection, leadership selection, the composition of the party's ruling National Executive Committee (NEC), the rules governing election to the shadow cabinet, the enfranchisement of party members in internal decision-making, the scope and role permitted to internal factions and tendencies, and control over the promises of the election manifesto.

After their 1992 general election defeat, Labour modernisers initiated another wave of party organisational reforms. Believing that the influence of trade unions, which were affiliated via the party's federal structure, was electorally damaging, modernisers sought to reduce this influence on party decision-making. Unions had special voting rights that gave them 'block votes' on important decisions at all levels of the party including leadership selection, candidate selection and policy matters. The debate on the selection of parliamentary candidates was brought to the 1993 party conference by leader John Smith as part of a package of measures designed to reduce trade union influence and especially to remove the block vote.

To understand the debate one needs to be familiar both with candidate selection and with wider debates in the Labour Party between 1979 and 2001. British electoral candidate selection is almost entirely a party matter. The main decisions take place at constituency level. In the early 1990s trade unions had considerable influence over constituency selections because they were affiliated to the party at constituency as well as at national level. Affiliation gave them guaranteed places on constituency selection committees and entitled them to a fixed percentage of votes in constituency candidate selection decisions. Their vote was normally cast by local union officials in support of trade union candidates who were usually men. There was no obligation for the local officials to ballot their members before casting their vote.

Several months before the autumn annual conference, which is the party's supreme decision-making body, Smith proposed that trade unions give up their fixed share of the votes so that each party member would have one equally weighted vote. Smith needed to persuade unions to cast their votes in favour of one member, one vote (OMOV), thereby reducing their own power in the party. The controversial move was fiercely resisted.

Policy outcome

The proposal for OMOV was narrowly approved by party conference by a vote of 47.5 per cent to 44.4 per cent, marking the end point of the debate. The resolution included a clause establishing a system of all-women shortlists (AWS) in half of the party's winnable and safe seats in the next general election. Constituency parties chose their parliamentary candidates from a shortlist of nominees of the various affiliated branches. The AWS proposal therefore meant that local selectors in some constituencies could consider only women when they chose their parliamentary candidate. The AWS clause was crucial to John Smith's victory. The modernisers won because one trade union, the Manufacturing, Science and Finance Union (MSF), which opposed OMOV, decided to abstain because it favoured AWS (Lovenduski and Norris 1994). The clause was inserted at the behest of the Women's Committee, a subcommittee of the party's NEC. The NEC Women's Committee debated the options at a meeting attended by John Smith who committed himself to implementing the proposal. OMOV was subjected to a clause-by-clause vote at the 1993 conference. The clause establishing all-women shortlists was overwhelmingly passed (Short 1996). The party quickly implemented the policy.

Dominant frame of debate

The debate on candidate selection was polarised between modernisers who favoured OMOV and traditionalists who favoured the retention of some form of electoral college that privileged the trade unions. Founded by the trade unions in order to facilitate the representation of their members and interests, the Labour Party was attuned to the requirements of descriptive representation. The debate was conducted in terms of who should decide who the representatives would be. The issue of union power within the party informed a discourse in which descriptive and substantive representation were inseparable. The dominant (public) discourse of the debate was based on arguments about fairness, equity, representation and policy improvement, and hence fit well with the demands of the women's movement.

Gendering the debate

The gendering of the OMOV debate was made explicit in the clause of the resolution that established all-women shortlists. The crucial actors who gendered the debate were Clare Short, who was chair of the NEC Women's Committee, Deborah Lincoln, who was party women's officer, the members of the NEC Women's Committee, trade union equality officials and women's sections, and a number of supportive party leaders and officials including the party director of organisation, Peter Coleman. The debate took place when the movement for women's representation in the party was ascendant. Through the activities of women's advocates organised in the party and unions a series of quotas had been established at every level of the party except candidacy for legislative office, where a *target* of 40 per cent was set in 1989. When it first emerged, the demand for AWS was a radical claim made by Labour Women's Action Committee, a leftist feminist fraction that campaigned for AWS in *every* seat. Gradually the tactic gained wider support. The influential Labour Women's Network became an advocate of the strategy. However, although the women's conference of the party voted regularly throughout the 1980s to introduce the system in selection, it was repeatedly voted down at the party's annual conference and less effective methods were adopted instead. During the 1980s changes were made to the nomination and application stages of candidate selection. For example, constituencies were required to shortlist a woman if one applied. These stratagems had little effect, however, and the number of female MPs grew only very slowly. The problem was how to gain support in the party for more effective measures to elect female MPs. The breakthrough came when advocates switched their claim to a system of all-women shortlists in only *half* of Labour's vacant and winnable seats. Their position was strengthened when advocates suggested a means of implementing the proposal by holding regional consensus meetings in which constituency Labour parties would be invited to volunteer to select from a women-only list (Labour Women's Network 1994; Short 1996). Because the demand was for only half of the available seats and because its implementation was to be achieved by consensus, it could be argued that the proposal was fair.

In the course of the debate the rights of female voters to be represented by women and the rights of female party members to be nominated were explicitly asserted. Within the party discussion of the proposal ranged across substantive policy issues, the necessity for the party to present a women-friendly image and the necessity for women to be represented by women. Claims were made that increasing women's representation would increase the party's appeal to female voters and its ability to produce policies that incorporated women's perspectives (Short 1996; MacDougal 1997).

WPA and QWPA characteristics and activities

Party QWPAs, including the NEC Women's Committee, the Shadow Minister for Women and the party Women's Office, were extremely active. Insider strategies were used to gain the support of party leader and union leaders. The Smith leadership was sympathetic to its goals. Senior party and trade union women were active and influential. By 1993 most unions had active women's officers and internal equality movements. For most of the 1990s the women's officer of the party was an influential senior figure. QWPA activities were supported by many party women's sections at branch, constituency, regional and national level. The cross-sectional scope of the QWPA was backed by the women's officer and included membership support, training, candidate matters, representation and policy and communications; hence it was relatively extensive in terms of sex equality and women's issues. The Women's Office, headed by Deborah Lincoln, provided support for a hierarchy of women's committees throughout the party and acted to promote women's movement goals. Activists included many MPs and women who entered the House of Commons in the subsequent 1997 election, including Angela Eagle, Fiona MacTaggart and Barbara Follett. They had important support from sympathetic men. In 1993 the QWPA leadership was particularly close to both the sympathetic party leadership and the party women's movement. It advocated women's movement goals and gendered the debate both in the sense that it ensured that issues of women's presence were included and by relating women's representation to issues of difference and exclusion. In contrast to the QWPAs, WPAs were not active in the debate, which was not at that time part of their mandate. Neither the EOC nor the WNC, whose characteristics had not changed since the first debate, were empowered to intervene in party debates.

Women's movement characteristics

In this debate the relevant sections of the women's movement were those mobilised within the Labour Party. By 1993 there was a substantial women's movement within the party. Activists organised both to secure women's political presence and to make sure their interests were represented (Lovenduski and Randall 1993; Perrigo 1996). Other actors included trade union feminists, often women's officers or equality officials who were also members of the Labour Party. Key figures included Anne Gibson (senior official of the MSF, the union whose abstention secured the OMOV decision). The MSF was explicit that its decision was determined by its support for all-women shortlists. As explained above, the clause-by-clause voting on the OMOV approved it, hence OMOV victory secured the all-women shortlist proposal.

The Labour Party itself occupied the centre and left of the political spectrum in 1993. Within this configuration the most influential fractions were on the centre-left of the party. Increasing women's presence was a high priority for the integrated movement, which had already succeeded in increasing women's representation within the party hierarchy. Advocates were able to draw on well-placed supporters who were crucial to the implementation stage of the policy when it was necessary for constituencies to agree to select candidates from women-only shortlists.

A strong counter-movement existed, mainly based in constituencies where the policy was likely to frustrate the ambitions of 'favourite sons'. Their voices were not decisive in the conference debate, but later they became very important in the implementation process and were able to overturn the policy in the courts three years later. The EOC, then led by a Conservative appointee, intervened after the debate when two male party opponents to the decision decided that their right to be a representative was infringed by the all-women shortlist procedure. Supported by the EOC they took their case to an industrial tribunal, which ruled the procedure to be illegal under the Sex Discrimination Act (*Jepson and Dyas Elliot v. Labour Party* 1996). However, on the debate in question there was no counter-movement.

Policy environment

The moderately closed policy environment was a complex internal party configuration of procedures, officials and factions. It is classified as moderately closed rather than closed because the recently installed internal quotas of women on party decision-making bodies afforded access for feminist activists. However, the traditionally masculinist culture of the Labour Party continued to be a barrier to women. This culture, despite considerable recent improvement, was underpinned by pervasive traditional trade union values. Historically union organisational practices were imported wholesale into the party and still dominated in 1993. Indeed this is what the debate was about. This was a policy environment accessible only to well-established, politically skilful labour movement activists.

Women's movement impact

There was no state response to this debate, which was an internal party matter. Although there was resistance, increasing women's representation found at least some resonance with the culture of the party. The notion that a representative must be a member of the group she represents, for example, is a principle borrowed from trade union principles of descriptive representation. Inside the party the decision is an example of a dual response. Within the Labour Party, women's advocates were accepted into the policy-making process and feminist goals were agreed. The debate outcome confirms recent research by Caul (2000) who argues that pressure from senior party women is a major factor explaining party adoption of gender quotas. Opponents of all-women shortlists were not much heard in the conference where the focus was on OMOV principles.

Debate 3: Modernisation of the House of Commons: parliamentary sitting hours, 2001–2002

How the debate came to the public agenda

During the 1990s parliamentary reform was discussed in the press in articles, editorials and letters to the editor from private citizens. Public opinion polls included items on reform which was also supported by civic organisations and the business community. The reform of House of Commons procedures is the responsibility of the Leader of the House, who is also a member of the cabinet. The Leader chairs the parliamentary modernisation committee set up in 1997 in the House of Commons and the modernisation sub-committee of the cabinet (Rogers and Walters 2004). The issue of sitting hours was raised at the first meeting of the Parliamentary Labour Party after the 1997 election. Prior to the reforms commons debate frequently continued beyond the 10 p.m. finishing hour and, until the 1997 parliament, often went on into the small hours of the morning. All-night sittings were regular events.

The problem was that parliament was thought to be inefficient (it took a long time to pass bills), old-fashioned (it worked according to practices devised for the nineteenth century including a fair amount of ritual and fancy dress) and not particularly successful at scrutinising government. A powerful system of party 'whipping' controlled MPs, operating a system that included control over career progress, timetable and information. Sitting, or working, hours were therefore only one of several perceived problems, but one which had considerable support from new MPs. But the Leaders of the House, Anne Taylor and then Margaret Beckett, believed that such reform would be unpopular and resisted the idea until a letter calling for hours reform, originated by Anne Campbell and circulated by Fiona MacTaggart (both feminist MPs), obtained 200 signatures from members. When Robin Cook, a keen moderniser, became Leader of the House in 2001, he let it be known that he favoured sitting hours reform and acted to ensure that it was included in the Modernisation Committee proposals (Cook 2004). The proposals debated in October 2002 included various measures to streamline procedures and make the commons more efficient, including changing the hours of work, reforms to debate procedures, timetabling, the carry-over of bills from one session to the next and time limits on MPs' speeches. Proposed changes to parliamentary working hours proved very controversial.

Dominant frame of the debate

The dominant frame was the nature and future of democratic institutions. Differences between women and men were discussed within that frame. The themes were modernisation and democratisation. Those who favoured change argued that the public was entitled to the best attention their MPs could give. *The Times*, for example, argued that the current sitting hours led to the routine scheduling of important decisions at late hours when 'everyone involved is mentally unfit to make them and no one else is up to hear that they have been made' (times.online.co.uk, 30 October, accessed 4 November 2002). Those who favoured reform argued that normal hours would be more democratic and efficient, more family friendly, better suited to the media, better for the health of MPs and better suited to the modern era. Robin Cook expressed concern about low voter turnout in the 2001 general election, which he associated with the need to make the work of the Commons more accessible to the electorate. In a speech to the Hansard Society he stated that 'We must enhance the status of the House of Commons as a representative chamber, so that it is seen as a robust and effective part of the process of government decision making' (Hazell et al. 2003). Opponents, including some Labour backbenchers, believed the reforms would further increase executive power at the expense of the legislature. They argued that the changes would further marginalise Westminster, make MPs look lazy, diminish the effectiveness and importance of committee work, and create a metropolitan elite of those MPs whose constituencies were near Westminster. Older MPs (few in number – more than half of the Commons has experience only of Blair as prime minister and only 7 per cent were MPs during Mrs Thatcher's premiership), including Gwyneth Dunwoody, drew attention to the powers that had been lost by parliament. In short the debate was framed in a complex set of arguments in which concerns about democracy and accountability were cross-cut by considerations of institutional continuity, professionalisation and representation. Divisions between and among female and male MPs of the various political parties from northern and southern regions made it difficult to characterise the issue in conventional political terms. The frame of modernisation, efficiency and democratisation was compatible with women's movement goals.

Gendering the debate

For feminists the debate and discussion around women's under-representation rapidly elided into discussion about the barriers to women that current parliamentary practice presented (Lovenduski 2005). The issue of the parliamentary culture and its brutal and family-hostile working hours and practices was highlighted by many female Labour MPs. Press attention increased when Labour MP Tess Kingham announced that she would stand down at the 2001 general election because it was impossible to combine being a mother to her children with the demands made on an MP. Her view, shared by many, was that evening hours of business and especially frequent late-night sittings were unnecessary. Many commentaries about Commons reform made reference to its likely impact on women. Both Joan Ruddock, former Minister for Women, and Barbara Follett, the founder of the British EMILY's List,[4] were at the forefront of demands for a more family-friendly parliamentary regime. However, although sympathetic, those responsible for organising the vote on hours believed that explicit reference to gender dimensions of the reforms might cost them the support necessary to get the new arrangements through. They therefore advised advocates to play down the family-friendly arguments of some supporters, even though such arguments were made by both women and men.[5] Even so the issue of family friendliness was aired by MPs during the debate. Caroline Flint said that the late Commons hours affected family life and that she did not wish to return to her family at weekends too exhausted to be a good mother to her children. Oona King drew attention to the need for MPs to fulfil their family responsibilities. The views of the family-friendly proponents were widely reported in the media. The gendering of the debate was rudimentary. The few references to difference, to sexuality and other issues of the body were made in reports from feminist organisations such as Fawcett, not in parliament. Public debate and media reports tended to depict women as a unitary group. For example, they used the terms gender and sex interchangeably and implied that women and ethnic minorities were necessarily separate rather than cross-cutting categories. The parliamentary debate did not address issues of differences among women or the possibility that women might bring different perspectives to the parliamentary agenda. Gender was invoked in the dichotomous terms of equal opportunities, of removing obstacles and barriers to women most often seen as constrained by a traditional division of labour.

---

[4] EMILY's List is a Labour Party group formed to raise and allocate funds to aid women seeking to become candidates. It is modelled on the US organisation of the same name (see chapter 12).

[5] Discussions between author and Meg Russell (see note 7).

Policy outcome

In September 2002, Robin Cook announced plans to rationalise the hours by shortening the twelve-week summer break and abolishing late-night sittings. On a free vote (that is, free of official party whipping) with an exceptionally large turnout of MPs and with considerable behind the scenes activity by supporters and opponents of reform, the proposal to pilot a changed schedule of sittings was accepted. According to *The Times* 'whoops of joy' by female MPs greeted the announcement of the result, an indication that for some MPs the issue of women's representation was part of the frame. Thus the policy outcome coincided with the goals of the movement, a dual response.[6]

Women's policy agency characteristics and activities

WPA activities included reports and seminars on the issue, press releases and public announcements. Their mandate extended by the Amsterdam Treaty, they favoured increased women's representation and should be regarded as advocates of women's movement goals. The Women and Equality Unit put the transcript of the parliamentary debate on its website; the EOC, perhaps emboldened by the provisions of the Amsterdam Treaty, officially supported modernisation in its statements and press releases. The WNC used its extensive email circulation list to draw attention to the debate. An email was circulated asking those on the circulation list to write to their MPs to stress the importance of family-friendly sitting hours for parliament. WPA activities were thus insider.

Women's movement characteristics

The affiliated women's movement developed significant professional capacities by the end of the twentieth century. First, women's advocacy organisations became more skilled at lobbying on issues of political representation, at placing their views in the press and at networking with influential politicians, journalists, think tanks and experts. An important example is the Fawcett Society. Once a suffrage organisation, it was revitalised in the 1990s. By the end of the decade Fawcett was central to campaigns for women's political presence.

Second, feminist advocates expanded their affiliations, increasing and extended their memberships of and activity in influential lobbying

[6] The decision was partly overturned in a parliamentary vote on 26 January 2005 when the pilot scheme was due to expire. This issue is likely to be revisited by subsequent parliaments.

organisations, review bodies, trade unions and pressure groups.[7] Feminists were also active and prominent in the electoral reform movement, in Charter 88 and as part of various think tanks such as the Institute for Public Policy Research, the Bow Group and so forth. Such infiltration may be seen as evidence of a very advanced stage of movement consolidation. Similar developments took place in the wider women's movement, which now was more supportive of women's political representation. For example, the Women's Budget Group adopted a proposal to increase the proportion of women in decision-making bodies to at least 40 per cent. Some feminists were unwilling to engage political institutions but their views were rarely if ever heard in the debates on constitutional reform. Although formally cross-party, the movement organisations engaged in the debate have best access to the political left and should thus be characterised as close to the left. There was no feminist counter-movement. Counter-movement was the work of the traditionalists in parliament and to a lesser extent of the political right.

Policy environment

The policy environment was moderately closed. A feminist presence in the cabinet after 1997 increased access for feminist advocates but in a closed system. The first Blair government (1997–2001) only grudgingly honoured its pledge to put women's issues at the heart of government (Lovenduski 2005). After 2001 first Sally Morgan and later Patricia Hewitt became Minister for Women. Both were feminists under whom the WPA became more powerful and competent.

Women's movement impact

Movement impact may be classified as dual response because feminist advocates participated in the debate and women's movement goals were realised.

---

[7] For example, Sheila Diplock became executive director of the Hansard Society after leaving Fawcett. Becky Gill, political officer of Fawcett, moved to the TUC. Laura Shepherd Robinson went from Fawcett to the General and Municipal Workers. Alice Brown was appointed to the Neil Committee and later became public policy ombudsman for Scotland. Deborah Lincoln, a Labour Party women's officer in the early 1990s, was made special adviser to the Minister for Women. Meg Russell, former Labour Party women's officer, went first to the Constitution Unit and then to become political adviser to Robin Cook on House of Lords reform.

Conclusion

All the selected debates addressed long-standing issues that surfaced and resurfaced between 1970 and the present. Arguably the proportion of the fragmented women's movement interested in issues of women's representation expanded over the years of the debates. None of the decisional systems may be regarded as open in RNGS terms, a finding that is congruent with most assessments of UK party democracy. Parliament and the parties with their elaborate procedures, rules and conventions are moderately closed, whilst the executive with its limited participation and closely managed procedures and access is closed. However, the policy environment did vary between issues and over time. The executive was more open during the modernisation debates than it was during the Quango debates. This development appears to be the result of the favourable location of feminist advocates in the party in power. In the third debate the women's policy agencies and the women's movement co-operated, parts of the debate were gendered and considerable political skill was assembled to press women's movement demands.

All three debates touched on women's descriptive and substantive representation. However, the discourse was one in which differences among women were rarely considered and the notion that men have gender largely unexplored. Yet there is evidence that the gender implications of Commons modernisation were well understood by opponents. The day after the vote to change working hours, the traditional, conservative and anti-feminist tabloid the *Daily Mail* raised the alarm about the reforms, declaring that what was under threat was masculinity and respect for the traditional skills and abilities of men. Such sophistication is rarely found in the coverage of more sympathetic press commentators.

The research suggests that the women's movement began the period at a stage of decline but that the integrated movement consolidated after 1979. It was close to the left, operating in the Labour movement and in the Liberal Democratic Party. By 2001 it had some support on the right of the political spectrum, as prominent Conservative women became more vocal advocates of women's representation. The counter-movement waxed and waned. For example, it re-emerged in the Liberal Democrats after 2001 when that party rolled back its commitment to equality of representation, reducing the number of guaranteed places for women on its European parliament electoral lists.

Prior to 1997 WPAs had no mandate to influence women's elected representation. Their efforts during the Quango debate were rooted in concerns about women's economic position, which was within their mandate. In the Labour Party debate on OMOV, the party QWPA was both present and connected to party feminists. The QWPA in the Labour Party was remarkably effective, possibly because of a widely held consensus that political parties are the appropriate forums in which to make decisions about political representation. In addition the Labour Party QWPA worked closely with advocates of women's political equality in the women's movement.

It is notable that all three debates have a considerable, and continuing, aftermath. The Quango debate turns out to have been the first of many, and debates on candidate selection led to legal change permitting parties to adopt quotas of women in 2001. Some mobilisation of MPs discontented with the changed working hours was apparent at the end of 2003, and their votes proved decisive in 2005. This research highlights the necessity for advocates of women's representation to mobilise in political parties. It is likely that the successful establishment of party machinery and infrastructure may be a precondition for effective state machinery. Assuming that government will change hands at some time in the future, then in the UK continuation of effective WPA will require at least some integration of machinery and movement in all of the political parties.

Acknowledgements

Alison Warner of Nuffield College Oxford conducted some of the research for this chapter. Meg Russell, Deborah Lincoln and Mary Ann Stephenson all supplied important information and gave their time. Meg Russell, Deborah Lincoln, Dionyssis Dimitrakopoulos, Diane Sainsbury and Alan Ware offered helpful comments on earlier drafts of this chapter.

References

Beetham, D., Iain Byrne and Pauline Ngan 2002, *Democracy under Blair: a Democratic Audit of the United Kingdom*, London: Politicos Publishing
Caul, M. 2000, 'Political Parties and the Adoption of Candidate Gender Quotas: a Cross-National Analysis', *The Journal of Politics* 63, 4
Cook, Robin 2004, *The Point of Departure*, London: Simon and Schuster
Democratic Audit 1999, *Making a Modern State: a New and Democratic Second Chamber for Britain*, Democratic Audit Paper No. 17, Colchester: Democratic Audit
EOC 1988, *Women and Public Appointments: Guidelines for Government Departments*, Norwich: KMSO
Hazell, R., O. Gay, A. Trench, S. King, M. Sandford, R. Masterman and L. Maer 2003, 'The Constitution, Consolidation and Cautious Advance', *Parliamentary Affairs* 56: 156–9
Judge, David 1999, *Political Representation*, London: Routledge

Labour Women's Network 1994, *Uphill All the Way: Labour Women into Westminster*, London: Labour Women's Network

Lovenduski, J. 1997, 'Gender Politics: a Breakthrough for Women', in Pippa Norris and Neil Gavin (eds.) *Britain Votes 1997*, Oxford: Oxford University Press, pp. 708–19

  2001, 'Gender and Politics: Critical Mass or Minority Representation', *Parliamentary Affairs* 54, 4: 743–58

  2005, *Feminizing Politics*, Cambridge: Polity Press

Lovenduski, Joni and Pippa Norris 1994, 'Political Recruitment: Gender, Class and Ethnicity', in Lynton Robins, Hilary Blackmore and Robert Pyper (eds.) *Britain's Changing Party System*, Leicester: Leicester University Press

Lovenduski, J. and V. Randall 1993, *Contemporary Feminist Politics*, Oxford: Oxford University Press

MacDougal, Linda 1997, *Westminster Women*, London: Vintage

Mackay, Fiona 2003, 'Women and the 2003 Elections: Keeping up the Momentum', *Scottish Affairs* 44: 74–90

Mackay, Fiona, E. Meehan, T. Donaghy and A. Brown 2002, 'Women and Constitutional Change in Scotland, Wales and Northern Ireland', *Australasian Parliamentary Review* 17: 35–40

Perrigo, Sarah 1996, 'Women and Change in the Labour Party', *Parliamentary Affairs* 49, 1: 17–25

Pliatzky, Leo 1980, *Report on Non-Departmental Public Bodies*, Cmnd 7797, London: HMSO

  1981, *Non-Departmental Public Bodies: a Guide for Departments*, London: HMSO

Rogers, Robert and Rhodri Walters 2004, *How Parliament Works*, fifth edition, London: Pearson Longman

Russell, Meg 2003, 'Women in Elected Office in the UK 1992–2002: Struggles, Achievements and Possible Sea Change', in A. Dobrowolsky and V. Hart (eds.) *Women Making Constitutions: New Politics and Comparative Perspectives*, London and New York: Palgrave

Short, Clare 1996, 'Women and the Labour Party', *Parliamentary Affairs* 49, 1: 17–25

12 Women's policy agencies, the women's movement and representation in the USA

Janine A. Parry

Introduction

Debates over political representation are pervasive in the USA.[1] Pluralist by design, many of the country's core political values and institutional arrangements are premised on the belief that the number of voices in the process is at least as important as the outcome produced. Definitions of representation thus tend to focus on opportunities for participation in public decisions. A host of the key constitutional and statutory developments of the twentieth century are telling in this regard, including direct democracy, secret ballots, primaries, expanded voting rights, campaign finance reform, eased voter registration, and more. American affinity for the rhetoric of representation has hardly resulted in participatory parity, however. The US Congress remained less than 14 per cent female in 2003; the state legislatures averaged just 23 per cent women members (ranging from 37 per cent in Washington to 9 per cent in South Carolina); and only six women – a record – currently serve as governors.

Another aspect of representation in a democratic system, especially one so heavily draped in formal constitutionalism, is the manner in which citizens are identified under its governing document. The Equal Rights Amendment (ERA) of the 1970s and early 1980s addressed this matter with respect to sex. Its ratification would have produced both practical and symbolic effects. In the former case, most analyses conclude that it would have elevated the consideration of sex discrimination cases to the level of strict scrutiny, the judiciary's highest threshold for examining publicly sponsored differential treatment. Labour regulations and educational opportunities would have been greatly altered as a result. With respect to its symbolic importance, scholars have made the case that formal, especially constitutional, language matters greatly.

[1] The author would like to thank Dorothy McBride Stetson for her expert guidance on this project, and the National Science Foundation (Grant #SES-0084580) for its financial support of the research reported in this chapter.

239

According to DuBois, for example, 'concepts of rights, individualism, and equality have had a distinct impact on the way that women have understood themselves and have expressed their sense of their proper position in society' (quoted in Zimmerman 1991: 188). Political representation, then, is a matter of identity and citizenship as much as it is a chance to participate in the day-to-day hum of politics.

Selection of debates

In addition to selecting debates reflective of both definitions above, it was important to consider that the US political environment places conflicts about political representation in several places simultaneously. Though party organisations are notoriously weak and not among the key decision venues, multiple arenas are found in the many layers of American government. The most important of these are the US Congress and the fifty state legislatures. The former, after all, has been the only source of constitutional change in the nation's more than 200-year history (though only with the consent of at least three-quarters of the states), and the constitution establishes the very definition of citizenship from which the rights of voting and office holding are derived. Filling in the gaps in such provisions have been decisions of the US Supreme Court and federal statute (passed by both chambers of Congress and signed by the president). The national constitution, however, leaves not only the ratification of national amendments to the states but also the details of elections, making them the key venues for political representation debates. Decisions about voter eligibility, campaign finance and (sub-national) candidate qualifications remain the sole domain of the states.

With these considerations in mind, three cases were selected from a rich universe of national and state-level debates: ERA ratification in Arkansas; term limits for Michigan state officials; and eased nationwide voter registration through the National Voter Registration Act (NVRA). The first was a battle to alter the US constitution. Stretching from the 1970s into the early 1980s and providing an example of political representation in its more abstract form, the ERA debate – especially the state-by-state ratification battle – demanded that Americans address the matter of citizenship in a manner akin to the epic civil rights struggles of the 1950s and 60s. The Michigan term limits case is representative of a policy issue that raged nationwide in the early 1990s, and resulted in capped terms for elected officials in nearly half the states. Finally, the NVRA presents a policy debate over a 'plain Jane' federal statute, one that, though formally initiated in 1988 and closed by 1993, has been pervasive in American politics. Taken together, these three cases, spread among the key decision systems in American politics, capture the most salient political representation conflicts in the decades spanning from 1970 to 2000.

Debate 1: ERA ratification in Arkansas, 1972–1977

How the debate came to the public agenda

The addition of an explicit recognition of sex equality to the US constitution was proposed in 1923 by a 'radical' wing of the victorious suffragists. Though congressional passage was not achieved until 1972, nearly half the states voted to accept the proposed amendment the same year, and in early 1973 it seemed 'virtually assured' that Arkansas would join the rapidly growing list of ratifying states. ERA-backers, including the state chapters of the Women's Political Caucus, the Federation of Business and Professional Women, and the League of Women Voters (LWV) as well as the Governor's Commission on the Status of Women (GCSW), had been contacting policy-makers since the spring of 1972, and had received public declarations of support by Democratic Governor Dale Bumpers and several legislators (Woodruff 1972; Talbot 1972). But on 15 January a busload of South Arkansas women calling themselves the 'Committee for the Protection of Women' disembarked at the state capitol building to express objections to the radical changes they claimed the ERA would invoke. The ratification debate in Arkansas was officially underway.

Dominant frame of debate

Law-makers and journalists considered ratification by the Arkansas General Assembly a foregone conclusion – at least at the outset. After all, nearly one-half the states and almost two-thirds the number needed for ratification had consented to the amendment already; it was widely expected that Arkansas would follow suit. Proponents had been actively courting legislators for nearly eight months, reassuring them that a constitutional guarantee of sex equality would affect 'legal rights only, not social customs'. Indeed, by 11 January 1973 the ratification resolution's chief sponsor in the Senate proclaimed twenty-two affirmative vote commitments from his colleagues, four more than needed, and the House of Representatives' version had been co-sponsored by more than half the chamber, 'assuring its passage' (*Arkansas Gazette* 1973). In short, the dominant frame of the early debate in Arkansas as elsewhere was that ratification of the Equal Rights Amendment was a non-contentious – even symbolic – gesture that women wanted and deserved.

Gendering the debate

The debate was quickly reframed, and regendered, however, once the opposition arrived. Central among the themes soon engaged by the 'pro' and 'anti' camps was whether the Equal Rights Amendment was necessary. Opponents of the measure insisted that women already had gained the legal rights they needed with the passage of the Equal Pay Act in 1963, the Civil Rights Act in 1964 and the Equal Employment Opportunity Act in 1972. The Fourteenth Amendment to the US constitution also was presented as evidence that Congress already had the power to ameliorate any remaining inequities between men and women. National anti-ERA champion Phyllis Schlafly articulated this position during visits to Arkansas, cautioning that the measure only stood to deny women the 'extra' rights and privileges they had been granted, particularly in matters related to the workplace and the military. Advocates of ratification acknowledged the text of the Fourteenth Amendment and other measures but pointed to the Supreme Court's failure to interpret such provisions as strictly in sex discrimination cases as it had in cases related to race or ethnicity.

Another issue of ample dispute was whether adoption of the ERA would reduce the rights and privileges granted to women, or instead expand them to men. Opponents argued the former position, charging that the amendment would nullify laws that afforded 'special protection' to women. Among these were the rights of women to be supported by husbands and women's rights to their husbands' property. Equally threatening was the amendment's impact on the military draft. No one, warned one state senator, would 'want to see these sweet, tender little bodies with their heads torn off by shrapnel' (Steinmetz 1973). Proponents countered that most of the legal changes required by the amendment's passage were likely to take the form of female-specific laws being extended to males. In the case of military service, expert testimony concluded 'the ERA will not require that all women serve in the military any more than all men are now required to serve'. Women who were physically unable or unqualified, who were conscientious objectors, or who were exempt due to particular responsibilities (e.g. those with dependants) would not have to serve (US Congress 1972: 13).

A third theme was the degree to which the ERA's passage would alter traditional relations between women and men. Opponents suggested that the naming of children would become muddled, placing obstacles in the way of tracing lineage later in life. Proponents insisted that the amendment required equality in legal matters only, not in cultural customs. Similarly, concerns about biblical interpretations of male–female relationships surfaced. Carrying placards reading 'From the breadmakers to the breadwinners', the anti-ERA contingent based their message on the customary, and reputedly Bible-based, vision of femininity. A debate that was gendered at the start as a simple matter of justice was successfully regendered as a threat to the social order, particularly woman's accepted place in it.

Policy outcome

Shortly after the arrival of the El Dorado contingent, surprised legislators moved to address their concerns by proposing the addition of a 'draft protection' amendment to the proposal, debating a resolution to amend the state constitution 'to preserve the right of the General Assembly to enact legislation giving special rights and privileges to women', and – ultimately – refusing to vote on the issue in the 1973 session. Pro-ERA momentum never recovered. After a February 1975 poll revealed, for example, that nearly two-thirds of the House membership had decided against the measure, it was consequently left to languish in committee. Proponents who pressed the assembly to again take up the issue in the following session saw similar results. By the spring of 1977, the Arkansas ERA ratification effort was effectively dead.

Women's movement impact

Regardless of a near-perfect match between the goals of the women's policy agency – the GCSW – and the goals of the other feminist activists (not to mention the support of both political parties and numerous churches), the substantive policy change sought was not achieved. Thus, this debate presents an example of co-optation. The state received individual female activists and constituencies into government, but failed to concede to feminists' goal. Instead, conservative powerbrokers relied upon the objections of a vocal counter-movement, insisted that they were merely arbitrating a 'women's war', and refused to grant the women's movement an important form of political representation.

Women's policy agency activities

Demonstrating vastly more life than its predecessors, the Arkansas GCSW of the 1970s became deeply entangled with the women's movement and the ERA-ratification effort (Parry 2000). While it also conducted research in the areas of employment, education, government, health and childcare, it placed the ratification of the Equal Rights

Amendment high on its agenda. Though the unit's administrative capacity during the decade was minimal, it did have a broad mandate that covered – or at least did not prohibit – its active endorsement of the ERA. It also had an independent (if small) budget, maintained moderately close ties with the state's progressive governors during the period of the ERA debate, and was guided by some of the state's most respected and accomplished feminist leaders.

The GCSW thus worked collaboratively with – even indistinguishably from – other actors in the feminist movement in the ERA struggle. Commissioners moved freely between the GCSW, the League of Women Voters, the Arkansas Women's Political Caucus and other pro-ratification organisations. Such interchangeability of personnel might suggest that the Arkansas GCSW operated as an insider, wholly incorporating – and prioritising – women's movement goals and rhetoric in gendering a policy debate of great significance to both. The problem, however, is that neither the GCSW nor the women's movement won the 'gendering' war in this case. No longer a simple matter of symbolic equality nor an overdue tool for the advancement of women, the debate saw the ERA regendered by its opponents into a threat to the 'right' of women to be financially supported, to have access to sex-segregated restrooms, to be non-combatants in military conflicts, etc. In this case, then, the women's policy agency activities are best characterised as marginal.

Women's movement characteristics

With respect to the characteristics of the feminist movement, the ERA's early chances for ratification in Arkansas looked encouraging. Cohesion among the state's pro-amendment groups was strong, and by early 1973 the measure's passage had become the priority item on the movement's agenda. The state chapters of Business and Professional Women, the League of Women Voters, and the American Association of University Women, long vibrant on other issues in the state, were actively lobbying on behalf of the measure, and were working in tandem with the GCSW. What little state labour presence there was at the time also had come to support the ratification position by 1977. Endorsements also were acquired from the state Democrat and state Republican parties, the *Gazette*, and many mainline churches. The caveat to this happy condition lay in the strength of the counter-movement in this debate. It was numerically smaller, but formidable in volume and rhetoric. As in venues around the country, Arkansas anti-feminists (and imported ones such as Schlafly) successfully cast the ERA as anti-motherhood, anti-man and – most importantly – anti-woman. This fact, together with a political environment inconducive to change, killed ERA ratification in Arkansas.

Policy environment

Arkansas's failure to ratify the ERA was largely a result of a policy environment in which the central powerbrokers possessed a negligible commitment to equal rights, and to the policy process. On the first score, it was a host of conservative state legislators, not the relatively liberal governors of the 1970s, who maintained responsibility for deliberating over the merits of ratification. The former's record on progressive change was not promising. The fact that Representative Paul Van Dalsem was an early champion of the amendment in the House is telling in this regard. Van Dalsem was widely perceived to be pushing ratification in 1973 to atone for an infamous declaration ten years earlier that women who meddled in politics should remain 'barefoot and pregnant' (Thompson 1998). Van Dalsem's meagre efforts to advance the measure broke down when he angered his colleagues by delaying a vote on an unrelated matter. They retaliated by blocking his pro-ERA resolution. Such contempt for the 'normal' legislative process was a consequence of the low electoral competition – and thus closed policy environment – endemic to the twentieth-century American South. Arkansas's legislative turnover had long been among the lowest in the country, leading to the rise of powerful, forty-year veterans who often were stalwart protectors of the status quo (Blair 1988). The result was a secretive, 'old school' modus operandi, an environment in which backroom deals were frequently struck and votes were conducted by voice if at all. New ideas – feminist or otherwise – were destined to fail.

Debate 2: Term limits in Michigan, 1991–1992

How the debate came to the public agenda

The late 1980s and early 1990s were ripe for the re-emergence of term limits in American politics. A banking scandal in the US House, a floundering economy and dismally low electoral competitiveness at the national level produced a sour mood. The solution – or at least, in many eyes, a just punishment to be exacted on the 'ruling class' – was to cap the number of terms elected officials could serve. Receiving little support for the idea from national office holders (despite polls which consistently registered overwhelming public support), term limits advocates turned to the individual states, especially those in which citizens could take policy matters into their own hands through the mechanisms of direct democracy. California, Colorado and Oklahoma led the way in 1990 by limiting the service of their state legislators. Activists in other states soon followed suit, adding to their proposals caps on the terms of executive officers as well as members of Congress.

Michigan – which recently had seen lower-than-average state legislative turnover and other signs of increased legislative professionalisation and at the time was represented by some of the longest-serving national elected officials in the country – was among these other states. Though at least two earlier Michigan petition drives failed to produce the necessary number of signatures to present voters with a term limits proposal, in December 1991 proponents submitted nearly 150,000 more signatures than required. The measure was among the most comprehensive of any proposed: state representatives were limited to three two-year terms, state senators to two four-year terms, state executive officers to two four-year terms, US Representatives to three two-year terms, and US Senators to two six-year terms. In addition, a lifetime cap was to be placed on service at each level.

Dominant frame of debate

Proponents painted a picture of a term-limited Michigan as one enjoying the leadership of 'citizen legislators' – preferably from business backgrounds – rather than 'career politicians'. By implication, anyone could make a bid for public office, serve a few terms, and return home before becoming too cosy with crooked lobbyists and too comfortable with the trappings of public life. (This was a claim that the anti-term-limits alliance of 36-year congressional veteran John Dingell, the Upjohn Corporation, the Big Three automakers and the unions buoyed considerably.) Term limits opponents relied upon equally familiar arguments: inexperienced law-makers would be at the mercy of complex issues, career civil servants and professional lobbyists; citizens, faced with lame-duck incumbents, would lack leverage over representatives in their final terms; and a term-limited Michigan would find its national power diminished in comparison with the congressional delegations of non-term-limited states. Good government groups further scolded that term limits were a shortsighted solution to the long-term problem of weakened government accountability. Common Cause activists, for example, championed campaign finance reform as an alternative that would 'give challengers a better shot', while the League of Women Voters favoured greater citizen responsibility in carefully examining the actions of their representatives. As League President Fran Parker repeatedly insisted in printed news accounts, Michigan already had term limitations: they were called elections (Daubenmier 1992; GONGWER 1991).

Gendering the debate

Participants in the Michigan term limits debate made few public arguments about the issue's gender implications. Though the activist who spearheaded the campaign once noted that term limits would 'destroy the good ol' boy system' by opening 'things up for more women, more minorities to serve', little more was said on that point by him or anyone else (Boyle 1992). Instead, in Michigan and nationwide, concern over the preponderance of white males serving in elective posts remained secondary to punishing current office holders regardless of their demographic characteristics. Further, while there was some scholarly discussion in the 1980s and 1990s of the role of incumbency as an obstacle to women's political progress (see, for example, Burrell 1994), most groups advancing women in politics either remained silent or expressed ambivalence about the idea. A spokeswoman for the Women's Campaign Fund, for example, noted at the time that mandatory election turnover 'opens the system'. Yet, she added, 'the slate is wiped clean and there's not a lot of places for those (currently elected) women to go' (Decker 1991). Gloria Woods, then president of Michigan NOW (National Organization of Women), recalled similar feelings among her membership: 'We did not take a stand in part because our closest allies in the legislature were Democrats,' she noted, 'mostly women, all of whom would be termed out if the legislation passed.' Further, 'it was not at all clear that the possible gains women *might* make with term limits would mean an overall gain in allies ...' (Woods 2002). Gender, then, was not central to the framing of this debate.

Policy outcome

Intermittent polls conducted through the summer and autumn of 1992 revealed strong majorities in favour of the adoption of term limits in Michigan, and the measure ultimately won the approval of nearly 60 per cent of the voters. Two post-election legal challenges were mounted, but the state forged ahead with state-level implementation in 1998, making it one of nineteen states to adopt term limits of some variety, and one of several to see little change in its proportion of women legislators (NCSL 1998; Schneider and Schaffer 1999). It is ironic in light of the movement's largely congressional origins that the sections of the numerous state provisions targeting national-level officials were later struck by the US Supreme Court (*US Term Limits, Inc. v. Thornton*, 1995). Thus, by the late 1990s members of numerous state legislatures and many of their executive branch peers found themselves subject to mandatory electoral turnover; this despite the fact that the majority of state officials – including those in Michigan – had voluntarily, and regularly, exited their posts for decades.

Women's movement impact

Evaluating the impact of the women's movement is especially difficult in this case. While the female elites who were involved in the debate (e.g. the heads of the League of Women Voters and Common Cause) largely opposed the idea, women voters facilitated its super-majority approval at rates equivalent to men. In neither case, however, was the advancement of women much articulated in the deliberations. After the dust had settled, however, several women's movement actors publicly expressed doubt that term limits would advantage women. Thus, if we consider both the opposition of the female LWV and Common Cause activists during the main debate period (though it was not based in gendered thinking), the ambivalence of NOW, and the post-election scepticism of many women's movement activists, the relationship between the women's movement and official response in the Michigan case can best be described as co-optation. Term limits were adopted over the – albeit barely articulated and/or belated – objections of the Michigan women's movement actors.

Women's policy agency activities

The current Michigan Women's Commission was established by statute in 1968. With a staff of three, a budget of about $300,000 and a broad mission, the unit was among the best resourced in the country at the time of the term limits debate. Yet, many activists criticised Governor Engler's 1991 decision to revoke the commission's independent status and move it under the umbrella of the state Department of Civil Rights (Boyle 1994). As a consequence of this reorganisation or, perhaps, in reaction to the changed partisan balance in the governor's appointees (from Democrat to Republican) from commissions past, many in Michigan's independent women's movement were critical of the unit's 1990s record. NOW president Gloria Woods praised the commissioners in 1994 for their 'concern and caring', for example, but suggested they had failed to be voices of leadership for women. 'They need to be out there speaking for us. Unfortunately, they've been quiet,' she said (Boyle 1994). A review of the commission's publications – especially its newsletter *Michigan Women* – over its forty-year history suggests that it was engaged in a narrower range of policy advocacy activities in the 1990s than in the 1970s and 1980s. In terms of the role of the commission in Michigan's adoption of term limits, there is a silent symmetry between the women's policy agency activities and the women's movement. While a few members of the latter group showed late awareness of the gender implications of such a policy, neither much engaged the matter. Thus, the value of the intervening variable is symbolic.

Women's movement characteristics

Michigan long has had a relatively rich relationship with the second wave women's movement. In 1962 it became the first state to establish (under gubernatorial prerogative) its own women's commission (Harrison 1988). The adopted home of a pivotal figure in the women's movement nationally (Democratic US Representative Martha Griffiths who in 1972 steered the Equal Rights Amendment out of the House Judiciary Committee), it also included a state-level sex equity provision in its 1963 constitution and ratified the national ERA. Signs of continued vibrancy – including consolidation and cohesion – abound. The state was home in the 1980s to a coalition of twenty-six women's groups – the Michigan Women's Assembly – devoted to 'women's economic self-sufficiency, choice, and the success of the Equal Rights Amendment' (Moen 1991). Another coalition – supplemented by an alliance with the state's formidable union presence – emerged in the mid-1990s to combat, successfully, attacks on affirmative action. The Michigan women's movement, like that in other states in recent decades, is close to the Democratic Party, or at least allied with Democratic legislators with whom they share common policy goals (Woods 2003). A counter-movement exists in Michigan to be sure, but does not appear to have been particularly strong during the debate period, perhaps because the ascendance of conservative Republican John Engler to the governorship reduced the perception of a feminist threat. Regardless, the fact that women's movement actors were divided on the term limits issue (as noted above) make its absence from the feminist agenda no surprise.

Policy environment

Michigan's moralistic culture joined contemporary political conditions to provide a nurturing environment for a policy of mandatory electoral turnover (Browne and VerBurg 1995). A weakened economy, a series of national political scandals, the perception of a 'governing class' and, most importantly, the availability of the initiative – an enormous exception to an otherwise closed policy sub-system – as a means to circumvent the state's elected representatives facilitated the measure's adoption. In addition, after two decades of slim majorities or split control in the state legislature, Michigan Democrats – a party less enamoured of the idea – were in the minority during the debate period. Republicans held the majority in the state Senate, and the state House was closely divided. And, though several former Democratic governors were active in the 'anti' campaign, Governor Engler offered considerable support to the term limits cause.

Debate 3: National Voter Registration Act, 1988–1993

How the debate came to the public agenda

Voter turnout in the USA suffered a noticeable decline in the second half of the twentieth century (Rosenstone and Hansen 1993; Cooper 2000). While the reasons for this development are complex, state and national policy-makers of the 1980s and 1990s zeroed in on relaxing the country's voter registration requirements as the cure for voter malaise. Because the vast majority of adult Americans have a driver's licence, linking voter registration to visits to the Department of Motor Vehicles (DMV) provided a logical means to reduce some of the 'costs' traditional to the process, including tight controls on the place and time of registration. The states first experimented with this type of reform in 1975 when Michigan began training DMV employees to assist in voter registration; Alaska, Arizona and Colorado followed suit in the early 1980s. By 1993, two-thirds of the states had established some kind of 'motor-voter' programme (*Congressional Digest* 1993).

Spurred by the earlier state actions and by 'good government' groups like the League of Women Voters, federal motor-voter legislation was introduced in Congress in 1988. It required all states to supply registration forms at motor vehicle agencies as well as state offices serving welfare recipients, the unemployed and the disabled. Though the House passed the measure in 1990 and 1991, Republican members blocked floor consideration in the Senate. Republican President George Bush eventually received a compromise measure in July 1992, but promptly vetoed it. When an override effort failed in the Senate two months later, Democrat Bill Clinton made the matter a campaign issue in his bid for the presidency that autumn. Indeed, when Clinton assumed office in January

1993, congressional Democrats elevated national motor-voter legislation to the top of the agenda.

Dominant frame of debate

This conflict emerged as a highly partisan one in which nearly all of the arguments advanced were seen as thinly veiled references to the potential political advantage for Democrats in reaching out to unregistered voters. The measure's sponsors insisted this was not their aim. Al Swift (D-WA) said he sought to reach the 92 per cent of the population that had regular contact with the state DMV and the remaining 8 per cent (largely the disabled and low-income and/or inner-city residents) through other agencies only because it was a convenient way to interest voters in elections. In answering the suggestion of angling for 'political advantage' for his party, Swift pointed to early twentieth-century voting reforms that had indisputably targeted immigrants and minorities as 'undesirables' in the political process. Erasing this stain by making registration easier, he maintained, was the measure's 'only aim' (Sammon 1993a, 1993b).

Opponents were careful to applaud the bill's objective of increased voter turnout, and confined their objections to its presumed secondary effects. The risk of election manipulation and burdensome administrative costs were primary among these. By restricting states' authority regularly to purge voter rolls of inactive registrants, increasing the burden on state election officers to verify and track the current addresses of mail-in registrants, and presenting registration opportunities to potentially ineligible persons, they argued, the country would see 'duplications, triplications and quadruplications' of voter registration forms and soaring state election budgets. The opposition also raised the possibility that public assistance recipients would feel 'coerced' into registering and voting in a particular way (Senate Report 1989). Finally, some Republicans openly challenged the nature of the non-DMV registration venues Democrats proposed. 'All of us are interested in extending the right to vote to all,' asserted one exasperated Representative. 'But at unemployment and welfare offices only? . . . if you want to pick a party affiliation of these people, take a guess. You won't pick ours' (Sammon 1993a).

Gendering the debate

Participants in the debate took little note of its potential gender implications, at least explicitly. But implicit references – to the impoverished, the working poor and clients of social service agencies – were abundant.

When the Senate temporarily stripped the measure of the registration requirements at agencies other than the DMV, for example, the president of the LWV said the move suggested 'that voting is a constitutionally guaranteed right only for some Americans; low-income and jobless citizens, as well as citizens with disabilities, need not apply' (Sammon 1993c). The job of making it explicit that these low-income, jobless citizens were most likely to be women fell to political scientist and reform activist Frances Fox Piven. In a 1996 write-up chastising some states' efforts to thwart NVRA implementation, Piven, and co-author Richard Cloward, wrote:

The most contentious part of the [measure] is the requirement that public assistance recipients be offered registration. The reason is obvious. Public assistance recipients are the most Democratic constituency in the electorate. They are (1) not well educated, poor, young, unmarried black and Hispanic women, many of whom could be registered in [social assistance] agencies, as well as working women and men who receive Food Stamps or Medicaid to supplement their low wages or lack of health benefits; and (2) not-well-off elderly, especially women, many of whom could be registered in Food Stamp and Medicaid agencies. (Piven and Cloward 1996: 40)

Similarly, in *CQ Researcher*'s later examination of low voter turnout, Piven uses a gendered illustration to support her contention that workday election dates are the primary reason voting rates have remained low despite national motor-voter reform. 'Work time has increased so much among American adults,' she notes. 'Think about a working mother who has to take the kids to day care before she can go to work, and then pick them up in the evening, and they may not even be in the same location. If she doesn't have a car, going out and voting is not going to be high on her list of priorities' (Piven quoted in Cooper 2000). The issue frame in this debate thus might be characterised as gender-subtle.

Policy outcome

Encouraged by the election of Democrat Bill Clinton, motor-voter backers moved quickly to push the measure forward in 1993. It passed easily through the House Administration Committee in late January, then through the House itself – largely along partisan lines (259–160) – in a matter of days (Sammon 1993a). After suffering somewhat more trouble in Senate committee, the measure ultimately cleared the upper chamber, 62–36, with six Republicans joining the Democrats to make it filibuster proof (Sammon 1993b). The final measure, Public Law 103–31, required states to allow people to register to vote when applying for a driver's licence and interacting with certain public agencies (though not unemployment compensation sites); states also had to provide for mail registration. Signed by the president on 20 May 1993, the National Voter Registration Act (NVRA) took effect on 1 January 1995.

Women's movement impact

Of the actors involved in the conflict, only one – Piven – articulated an expressly gendered frame of reference. Though numerous members of the LWV played an active role (it was a League-backed ballot initiative in fact that brought about Colorado's 1984 motor-voter programme), their participation was offered in a non-gendered way (Savage 1990). Yet, the frequent references by League spokeswomen and others to the poor and to public agency clientele indisputably suggest to any moderately savvy political actor that women would be disproportionately advantaged by this measure. Likewise, a 1996 resolution at the annual meeting of the National Organization for Women reveals that the organisation later realised NVRA's potential in combating the Republican gains of 1994 (NOW 1996). Together, such observations move this case toward dual response. Women who were friends of the feminist movement were involved in the policy process, and the state offered substantive policy change in congruence with their wishes.

Women's policy agency activities

There has not been a full-fledged women's policy agency at the national level in the United States since the demise of a series of short-lived presidential commissions in the 1970s, though various advisory councils and commissions of a specialised nature do exist. Most important among them is the US Women's Bureau. Established within the Department of Labor in 1920 to advance the interests of female labourers, its mandate gradually has been broadened to encompass all manner of workplace equality and anti-discrimination efforts. It does not include, however, issues of elections or political representation and thus did not partake in this debate; hence its role was symbolic.

A quasi-WPA, the Congressional Caucus for Women's Issues (CCWI), would have been the most likely candidate for involvement on an issue of this sort. It also was absent, however, also making its role symbolic. Established in 1977, the CCWI was a legislative service organisation of Congress bringing together a group of office holders with common interests. Guided over the years by a host of the most widely recognised feminist members of Congress (e.g. co-chairs Patricia Schroeder, D-CO and Olympia Snowe, R-ME), it served as a 'nexus' between congresswomen and women's groups, enjoying the support – and advancing the policy demands – of feminist organisations including NOW (making it a quasi-WPA). Membership dues ($1,800 for congresswomen and $900 for congressmen in the early 1990s) had long allowed the caucus to hire staff, produce publications, and host media and advocacy events, but a surge in affiliations after the 1992 elections (in which a record number of women were elected) led to an unprecedented degree of institutionalisation during the 103rd Congress. According to Gertzog (1995), this surge in size and capacity enabled the caucus to play an instrumental role in several key policy debates of the 1990s, especially on health equity, family and medical leave, and domestic violence and sexual assault. A close connection to the White House after Clinton's election facilitated its success. Yet, while members also took up the banners of, among other issues, financial aid for college students with children, childcare for participants in national job training programmes, tax code reform and reproductive choice (marking a fundamental shift in the caucus's past voice on the issue), there is no evidence that the CCWI weighed in on expanded voter rights.

Women's movement characteristics

With respect to the women's movement, some have suggested that various developments of the 1980s resulted in a diminished women's movement in the 1990s (Costain 1992). Yet, the adoption of the 1993 motor-voter act in some ways coincided with a rejuvenation of feminist policy activism in the USA. Not only did both popular and scholarly interest in 'the gender gap' and women's candidacies burgeon, but female activists demonstrated increased levels of political sophistication that enabled them to counter the decline in mass membership among movement organisations. From the massive expansion of women's political action committees, or PACs, dedicated to making campaign contributors to female candidates (e.g. EMILY's List[2]), to the establishment and growth of women-oriented think tanks (e.g. the Institute for Women's Policy Research), to the lobbying alliances crafted by direct service providers (e.g. the national Coalition against Domestic Violence), by the early 1990s the national network of women's policy organisations had mastered 'insider tactics' (McGlen and O'Connor 1998; Spalter-Roth and Schreiber 1995). Thanks to a continued alliance with the Democratic

---

[2] EMILY is an acronym for Early Money is Like Yeast. Founded in 1985 EMILY'S list is the largest and best known of the women's PACs in the USA. Its contributors seek to elect pro-choice Democratic women to national, state and local office.

Party and the election of its first president in twelve years, too, the movement also experienced several key policy victories. Among these were the
rescission of the 'gag rule' in family planning policy, the adoption of the
Family and Medical Leave Act, and executive and judicial rejection of a
'partial birth abortion' ban. Policy setbacks – including attacks on abortion rights and a controversial welfare reform package – certainly
occurred as well, a fact that speaks to the strong and cohesive counter-
movement which yet retained much of its 1980s influence in Congress
and the courts. Nowhere in this flurry of activity, however, was mention
made of loosened voter registration rules.

Policy environment

The fact that both chambers of Congress were Democratically controlled during precisely the same years as the voter registration debate,
and that Democrats had regained control of the White House by the
time of its resolution, was extremely significant to NVRA's passage. It
also impacted the dominant discourse of the early 1990s. The loss of the
White House after twelve years, and the loss of the one congressional
chamber they had managed to dominate only briefly since the Second
World War, set Republicans on edge. And with good reason. NVRA was
one of a trio of political reform bills that Democrats pressed for in the
early months of the Clinton administration. Many Republicans fought
all three (the others involved campaign finance reform and loosened
rules on political activism by federal employees), fearing a formula for
'permanent Democratic control' should they be adopted (Alston 1993).
Finally, in terms of the penetrability of the debate arena, decision sub-
systems in the USA are rarely more open than congressional debates,
especially those as widely publicised and easily graspable as the 'motor-
voter' proposal. The conflict – which occurred in committee, on the
chamber floors and in the media – consequently attracted a plethora of
policy experts, party activists, lower-level elected officials, government
reformers and others.

Conclusion

These debates on political representation in the USA suggest a limited state
response to the women's movement. Only in the case of eased voter registration did feminists see dual response. In the other two debates – ERA
ratification in Arkansas and term limitations in Michigan – the policies
adopted ran counter to movement goals. This may not come as any great
surprise in light of the absence of state feminism in these cases. Only the

Arkansas women's commission made an effort – if an unsuccessful one – to gender the debate in a manner congruent with women's movement goals. In the case of Michigan term limits and the national move to ease voter registration, the WPAs were conspicuously absent.

Such a spotty record for the women's movement is primarily attributable to the policy environment, especially the party in power. In each case, though it is less clear in the largely voter-driven situation in Michigan, the majority party (or faction) achieved policy victory. Even the strength of the counter-movement in the battle over the Arkansas ERA would not have triumphed without the assistance of conservative Democrats in the legislature. That women's movement characteristics were not essential to shaping these debates is not to suggest, however, that feminists were in decline, lacked cohesion or failed to align themselves with friendly power players. It is more likely the case that many of the major late-twentieth-century debates over political representation were not priority issues for second wave feminists in the USA. In fact, if the Michigan Women's Commission and the Congressional Women's Caucus failed to inject gendered language into political representation debates (making them merely 'symbolic'), we see here that it was largely because the women's movement did too. Why?

There are two possibilities. The first is that in their fervour to effect substantive policy change in 'women's issues' (e.g. reproductive health, childcare, sex equity in education and the workplace, etc.), activists overlooked the potential for the kind of procedural policy change that debates over political representation necessarily engender (see Rochon and Mazmanian 1993). Why bother with voter registration when abortion rights are under attack? Whether over-committed or simply negligent, women's movement activists may have admonished those in the seats of power to 'remember women', but underestimated the potential of mandatory electoral turnover and eased voter registration actually to place women in those seats of power.

The second possibility is that many advocates for women's rights considered the thorough gendering – and regendering – of the Equal Rights Amendment to have been the very cause of its demise, and therefore a tactic to be avoided in future struggles. Recall that the ratification debate occurred at the beginning of the period under study, leaving the remaining conflicts to occur after this crushing disappointment. One lesson to extract from such a defeat is that if you want to win, make the issue about anything *except* women, particularly substantive changes in their status (see Mansbridge 1986). Several of the Arkansas actors in fact raised this point about their later activities on behalf of women's rights, suggesting that it led many of them to engage in a kind of 'stealth feminism' (Blair 1998). But, if the absence of gendered elements in the debates explored here does indeed represent an intentional post-ERA strategy, activists of the new century may want to proceed with caution. They may have been defeated in the most significant gendered debate of our time, but this chapter reveals that the sex-neutral language of 'good governance' offers no guarantee.

References

Alston, Chuck 1993 'Democrats Flex New Muscle with Trio of Election Bills', *Congressional Quarterly Weekly Report* 51, 12: 643–5

Arkansas Gazette 1973, 'Legislative Ratification Appears Certain for Equal Rights Proposal', 11 January: 4A

Blair, Diane D. 1988, *Arkansas Politics and Government: Do the People Rule?*, Lincoln: University of Nebraska Press

1998, Personal interview, Fayetteville, AR, 10 May 1998

Boyle, Jacquelynn 1992, 'Term Limits, B: Yes', *Detroit Free Press*, 4 November 1992: 3A

1994, 'New Director Defends Panel', *Detroit Free Press*, 26 September 2002: 1B

Browne, William P. and Kenneth VerBurg 1995, *Michigan Politics and Government: Facing Change in a Complex State*, Lincoln: University of Nebraska Press

Burrell, Barbara 1994, *A Woman's Place is in the House: Campaigning for Congress in the Feminist Era*, Ann Arbor, MI: University of Michigan Press

Congressional Digest 1993, 'Voter Registration Reform', 72: 67–96

Cooper, Mary H. 2000, 'Low Voter Turnout', *CQ Researcher* 10: 835–55

Costain, Anne B. 1992, *Inviting Women's Rebellion: a Political Process Interpretation of the Women's Movement*, Baltimore: The Johns Hopkins University Press

Daubenmier, Judy 1992, 'Limiting Terms isn't the Answer, Group Says', *Detroit Free Press*, 8 June 1992: 8B

Decker, Cathleen 1991, 'Money May Play a Bigger Role in Elections', *Los Angeles Times*, 11 October 1991: A1

Gertzog, Irwin N. 1995, *Congressional Women: their Recruitment, Integration, and Behavior*, second edition, Westport, CT: Praeger

GONGWER News Service, Inc. 1991, 'Legislators Net $6.6 Million from PACs; Group Seeks Reform', *Michigan Report*, 21 October 1991: 1–2

Harrison, Cynthia 1988, *On Account of Sex: the Politics of Women's Issues, 1945–1968*, Berkeley: University of California Press

Mansbridge, Jane J. 1986, *Why We Lost the ERA*, Chicago: University of Chicago Press

McGlen, Nancy E. and Karen O'Connor 1998, *Women, Politics, and American Society*, Upper Saddle River, NJ: Prentice Hall

Moen, Gerri 1991, 'LWVMI Works in Coalition with Michigan Women's Assembly', *Michigan Voter* 38: 2

NCSL (National Conference of State Legislatures) 1998, '1998 Pre-Election Turnover', accessed on 13 September 2002 at http://www.ncsl.org/ programmes/legman/elect/pretrn.htm

NOW 1996, 'Women's Vote: Use it or Lose it', resolution adopted at the Annual Conference of the National Organisation for Women, 28–30 June, Las Vegas, NV, accessed on 10 January 2003 at http://www.now.org/organiza/ conferen/1996/resoluti.html#act

Parry, Janine A. 2000, 'What Women Wanted: the Arkansas Governor's Commissions on the Status of Women and the ERA', *Arkansas Historical Quarterly* 59: 265–98

Piven, Frances Fox and Richard A. Cloward 1996, 'Northern Bourbons: a Preliminary Report on the National Voter Registration Act', *PS: Political Science & Politics* 29: 39–42

Rochon, Thomas R. and Daniel A. Mazmanian 1993, 'Social Movements and the Policy Process', *Annals of the American Academy of Political and Social Science* 528: 75–87

Rosenstone, Steven J. and John Mark Hansen 1993, *Mobilization, Participation, and Democracy in America*, New York: Macmillan

Sammon, Richard 1993a, '"Motor Voter" Rides a Fast Track through the House', *Congressional Quarterly Weekly Report* 51, 6: 264

    1993b, 'Senate Kills Filibuster Threat, Clears "Motor Voter" Bill', *Congressional Quarterly Weekly Report* 51, 5: 1221

    1993c, 'Negotiations Begin on "Motor Voter"', *Congressional Quarterly Weekly Report* 51, 14: 837

Savage, Harlin 1990, 'States Discover Innovative Way to Register Elusive Voters', *The National Voter* 89: 12–15

Schneider, M. Bryan and Jody Sturtz Schaffer 1999, 'Annual Survey of Michigan Law', *The Wayne State Law Review* 45: 557

Senate Report 1989, S. Rpt. 101–140 on S. 874, 'National Voter Registration Act of 1989', 26 September 1989, CIS NO:89–S683–12

Spalter-Roth, Roberta and Ronnee Schreiber 1995, 'Outsider Issues and Insider Tactics: Strategic Tensions in the Women's Policy Network during the 1980s', in Myra Marx Ferree and Patricia Yancey Martin (eds.) *Feminist Organisations: Harvest of the New Women's Movement*, Philadelphia: Temple University Press, pp. 105–27

Steinmetz, Tucker 1973, 'Jones' Amendment Seals Doom of ERA in Senate', *Arkansas Gazette*, 2 February: 1A

Talbot, Tish 1972, 'State Women's Groups Plan Drive to Support Rights Amendment in '73', *Arkansas Gazette*, 12 November: 10A

Thompson, Robert 1998, 'Barefoot and Pregnant: the Education of Paul Van Dalsem', *The Arkansas Historical Quarterly* 57, 4: 377–407

US Congress 1972, Senate, Judiciary Committee, *Equal Rights for Men and Women*, 92nd Congress, 2d sess.

US Term Limits, Inc. v. Thornton (93–1456), 514 US 779 (1995)

Woodruff, John 1972, 'Women's Political Caucus Endorses Rights Amendment', *Arkansas Gazette*, 14 May: 1A

Woods, Gloria 2002, electronic (e-mail) interview, 3 October

2003, electronic (e-mail) interview, 6 January

Zimmerman, Joan G. 1991, 'The Jurisprudence of Equality: the Women's Minimum Wage, the First Equal Rights Amendment, and *Adkins v. Children's Hospital*, 1905–1923', *The Journal of American History* 78, 1: 188–225

13   Conclusions: state feminism and political representation

Joni Lovenduski, Claudie Baudino, Marila Guadagnini, Petra Meier and Diane Sainsbury

Women's movements and state feminism

The main purposes of this study of the politics of political representation decisions are, first, to determine and explain variations in the success of women's movements in opening democratic processes to women's participation and concerns, and, second, to explore whether the state, as a result of effective WPA activities, has intervened to achieve such success.[1] Let us now return to our original questions, the questions that framed this comparative study. Do women's policy agencies matter? And if so, why? Have WPAs made democracies more representative and democratic? Have WPAs advanced the demands of the women's movements in a way that has indeed improved representation in both descriptive and substantive terms?

In this chapter we combine the evidence from the eleven countries to answer our core research questions. We make a comparative analysis of the results of the country studies that have been presented in a more detailed and discursive manner in the individual chapters by applying the model presented in chapter 1. There are costs and benefits to this approach. Inevitably and regrettably our comparative analysis loses much of the wealth of detail and insight provided by the authors of the country chapters. But with comparison we gain the ability to detect trends in the capacity of women's policy agencies to help women's movements and women in general to participate in and influence decisions about policy on political representation.

Debates about political representation may differ from those on other policy areas for a number of reasons. First, debates about who may be

---

[1] This chapter was written by Joni Lovenduski using summary and analytical materials supplied by the other editors. The final version benefited from extensive comments by Diane Sainsbury. We are also grateful to Amy Mazur and Dorothy Stetson for offering an exemplary map of the terrain of debate analysis in their earlier books for the project and to Joyce Outshoorn for letting us see advance chapters from her book on prostitution debates.

260

representatives are often constitutional debates, subject to special procedures in addition to or instead of normal legislative processes. Thus we find that such institutions as constitutional courts may be involved, or referenda may be held or enhanced legislative majorities may be necessary to make decisions. Second, many of the debates about political representation of the past thirty years have been debates specifically about the presence of women in decision-making institutions. They are gendered at the outset at least insofar as they draw attention to the presence of men and the absence of women from political decision-making. Therefore the central research question shifts to one of how the debate frames of women's movement and WPAs affect an already gendered discourse. In many cases, especially in the 1990s and later, we are looking at the extent to which gendering alters in debates that were explicitly gendered at the outset. Third, major divisions in movements between integrated and autonomous feminists may take on a different significance as, for the most part, integrated feminists mobilise their political skills to engage political institutions while autonomous feminists, although often supportive of claims for presence, in practice remain preoccupied with other concerns. Fourth, the role of the political parties comes to the fore and may be more important than the state in decision-making. As stated in the introduction to this volume, in European systems of party democracy it is political parties that make the crucial decisions about who our representatives should be. There is considerable institutional variation here. One such variation is the extent to which political parties are constitutionalised, otherwise regulated and therefore subject to legal intervention in their decision-making. However, although decisions about political representation may eventually play out in state institutions, their formulation and development tends to be a party matter. Political parties decide whether to take action on the issue and also determine such procedural matters as whether political representation should be part of the mandate of state women's policy agencies. Thus in many debates not only are the internal party institutions established to promote women in the party more important actors than WPAs, but they also have similar characteristics and mandates to state WPAs. In this research such institutions are called quasi-women's policy agencies (QWPAs) and are considered separately from WPAs.

Women's movements and political representation: variations and trends

In our comparative analysis we use country-based definitions of feminism as our benchmark. In the preceding eleven chapters each author employs the definitions of feminism that are current in the country under consideration at the time of the debate. Thus we are able to keep in view the diversity of women's movements and feminisms that characterise each country, while at the same time having the benefit of a definition that is comparative. On the whole the women's movements described in this collection did well. Most were in a period of growth or consolidation. Although our coverage is not comprehensive, the debates cover a considerable time span; hence our sketch of the movement is more than a collection of scattered images. Only in Germany did women's movements decline over the long term. The movements have not resisted the impact of time. In many countries they were in a period of re-emergence or growth during one or more debates, suggesting a cyclical evolution. The movements were generally close to the left, with the exception of parts of the movement in the Finnish and Swedish debates, where in some cases they were both close to the left and pan-partisan.

Women's political representation was often not an immediate demand of the 'new' women's movements. Other issues, such as economic rights and reproductive rights, had higher priority. There were also differences in the timing of raising women's representation issues. In the Netherlands, Sweden and Finland equality of women's representation was raised in the 1960s. In the 1970s it arrived on the agenda in Austria, Germany, the UK and the USA. In the 1980s quotas of female representatives became a topic in many countries. By the end of the decade women's political representation was an issue in all of the countries discussed in this volume, an effect not only of women's movement activity but also of opportunities afforded by extensions of mandate brought to women's policy offices by the Amsterdam Treaty in EU countries. The late 1980s and 1990s also witnessed debates on women's access to administrative positions and posts on appointed bodies. Electoral and constitutional reforms were increasingly the subject of debate in the 1980s and 1990s.

The scope of the debates

The debates deal with several facets of political representation. A central concern was the presence of women in decision-making positions, that is the equal access of women and men to various sites of decision-making in the policy process, with some considerable emphasis on equal representation in elected assemblies and cabinet positions. Women's movements also attempted to secure women's presence in public administration and in the public bodies charged with preparing legislation. Internal party positions were a target for mobilisations. Debates dealt with both the mechanisms of and preconditions for political representation and the nature of representation itself. Among the mechanisms discussed, most attention was paid to electoral systems and their impact on which people are represented and to formal quotas and their effects. Debates on the preconditions of political representation focused on citizenship and constitutional amendments to guarantee the equal rights of men and women or to promote equal access to political office.

The debates occurred in diverse policy arenas and reflected an impressive array of strategies to achieve equal representation between the sexes. Strategies ranged between the two extremes of recommended guidelines (voluntary) and constitutional reform (compulsory). They included the introduction of formal party quotas and legislated quotas, the launching of the zipper system (alternating candidates of each sex on the party ballot) and a system of all-women shortlists, attempts to tie public party funding to the nomination of female candidates, special subsidies to encourage women to enter politics, threats to create a women's party or to present all-women lists of candidates as alternatives to the regular party lists, affirmative action and the establishment of gender equality or women's policy machinery in parties and in government.

The policy settings of debates on political representation have varied. Political party guidelines and regulations are normally the prerogatives of the parties, with decisions confined to party organisations and members. The first step to winning elected office is nomination and the political parties are the nominators. In nearly a quarter of the debates the parties were the major decisional arena (Table 13.1). In this respect the issue of political representation differs from previous issues explored by the RNGS network – job training (Mazur 2001), abortion (Stetson 2001) and prostitution (Outshoorn 2004). In those debates on representation where the outcome was a law or a constitutional reform, the executive and the legislature were the key arenas of decision-making. The special arrangements typically required for constitutional amendments, however, often increases the number of veto sites. For example, constitutional courts may affirm or reverse the policy decision as they did in France in the 1980s and Italy in the 1990s.

The issue of women's representation came to the public agenda via a number of routes. A common route was the general discourse on democracy. A closely related pathway was discussion on renewal or modernisation of a party or another major institution. A further catalyst was disappointments regarding the lack of progress in the numbers of women in office or the way previous reforms to improve women's representation were implemented. In most debates on women's representation it was women who brought the issue to the public arena, but several debates also reveal the importance of male allies and cross-gender alliances.

Table 13.1 *Content and outcome of policy debates*

	Outcome
Austria	
AU1 Access to the cabinet, 1975–1979	25% women in cabinet, accept integration of women in policy process.
AU2 Civil service reform, 1981–1993	Equal treatment law with most of women's movement objectives incorporated.
AU3 Public party subsidies, 1994–1999	Women's quota not linked to party finance.
Belgium	
BE1 Quotas for electoral lists, 1980–1994	Government adopts law mandating at least 25% women on lists to 1999, at least 33% after 1999.
BE2 Quotas for advisory committees, 1990–1997	Women to make up at least one-third of advisory bodies.
BE3 Quotas for federal government, 1991–1999	Articles allowing insertion of minimum quota of women/men not opened for revision.
Finland	
FI1 Independent electoral associations to nominate candidates, 1972–1975	Government accepts independent electoral commissions.
FI2 Quotas for party executive in the Finnish People's Democratic League (SKDL), 1986–1987 *Party debate*	Party adopts internal quotas of 40% women/ men in all executive structures.
FI3 Quotas in the Equality Act of 1995, 1991–1995	Quota of 40% women/men for all indirectly elected public bodies.
France	
FR1 Change in voting system for local elections, 1982	National Assembly agrees to 25% women/ men quota. Constitutional Court over throws, thus constitutionalising issue.
FR2 Change in voting system for parliamentary elections, 1985	Voting system changes, women's presence does not.
FR3 The parity reform, 1999–2000	Law establishes various obligations and provisions mandating parties to make 50% nominations of women at various levels of election. Most effective provisions for sub-national or EU elections.
Germany	
GR1 Quota rules in the Social Democratic Party (SPD), 1977–1988 *Party debate*	Party agrees to quotas of women candidates and internal positions.
GR2 Second Federal Equal Rights Law, 1989–1994	Basic Law amended to acknowledge the state's commitment to realising gender equal- ity. Equal rights law mandates nominations of 1 man/1 woman for each position on decision- making bodies until parity is reached.
GR3 Reform of Nationality Law, 1998–1999	Nationality law allows dual citizenship until age 23 for those born to non-German parents in FRG.

Table 13.1 (*cont.*)

	Outcome
Italy	
IT1 Creation of the Democratic Party of the Left (PDS), 1989–1991 *Party debate*	New party forms committed to sex equality with quotas of 40% women/men in all internal bodies, congress delegations and candidate lists. Establishes women's committee and sections.
IT2 Reform of electoral law for the lower chamber of parliament, 1991–1995	Mixed electoral system 25/75 adopted. Zipping for list candidates, outlawed by Constitutional Court in 1995.
IT3 Constitutional amendment to promote equal opportunities for access to political office, 1997–2003	Amendment permits equal opportunities policies for access to political office.
Netherlands	
NL1 Reform of the Social Democratic Party (PvdA), 1966–1977 *Party debate*	Party adopts new programme that includes women/men quotas on lists.
NL2 Equality Policy Plan, 1981–1985	Subsidies for parties to hire femocrats.
NL3 Corporatism, 1989–1997	Various measures to increase women's presence on advisory bodies. (But equality advisory bodies weakened.)
Spain	
SP1 Women's quota of 25% in the Socialist Party (PSOE), 1987–1988 *Party debate*	Agrees women/men quota of 25% for internal party positions and electoral lists.
SP2 Women's quota of 40% in the PSOE, 1992–1997 *Party debate*	Agrees to increase above quotas to 40%.
SP3 Mandatory quotas for all parties, 1998–2003	Mandatory quotas for all parties rejected.
Sweden	
SW1 Greater democracy and more women in politics, 1967–1972	Parties adopt guidelines for women's presence in elected and party office. Advisory Council on Equality between Women and Men established.
SW2 Quotas for appointed positions, 1985–1987	Commission establishes targets for women in elected office, threatens mandatory quotas if not achieved.
SW3 The establishment of a women's party, 1991–1994	Parties increased numbers of women deputies, SD changed rules to provide for equal distribution of women on party lists. Women 48% of legislators and 50% of government.
United Kingdom	
UK1 Reform of public bodies, 1979–1981	Public bodies audited and culled.
UK2 Candidate selection in the Labour Party, 1993 *Party debate*	One member one vote agreed with clause mandating all-women shortlists. Record number of women elected 1997.

Table 13.1 (*cont.*)

	Outcome
UK3 Parliamentary working hours, 2001–2002	Working hours reformed to more family-friendly times.
United States	
US1 Equal rights amendment ratification in Arkansas, 1972–1977	Legislature did not vote on ERA, killing issue in the state.
US2 Term limits in Michigan, 1991–1992	Term limits adopted.
US3 National Voter Registration Act, 1988–1993	Voter registration made easier.

Gendering the debates: political representation and the research question

Presence is not the only dimension of political representation that we consider. Answering the central question of whether or not WPAs make democracies more democratic involves determining whether WPAs play a crucial role in increasing the influence of the women's movement on policy outcome (substantive representation) and/or in increasing the physical presence of women or representatives of the women's movement in policy debates (descriptive representation). The question of whether women's movements 'gender' debates about increasing women's presence in political office suggests an absolute answer. But in representation policy, because so many debates are gendered from the outset, the answer may be a matter of degree. In this volume twenty-one of the thirty-three selected debates were debates specifically about women's representation and twelve debates in seven countries were about other aspects of representation. Hence we are in a position to compare initially gendered and non-gendered debates. In addition, nine of the debates take place inside a political party, allowing an inspection of the effects of party arrangements for making representation decisions and for accommodating women's demands.

As in the cases of job training, abortion and prostitution (Mazur 2001; Stetson 2001; Outshoorn 2004), the frames, or problem definitions, of political representation debates as they develop are crucial to understanding the influence of women's advocates, both inside and outside government. Strategically, women's movements try to insert their definition of political representation into the dominant discourse about the issue. As for other issues the women's movement frame is likely to be that the policy is central to women's rights, which must also have the highest priority. However, on this issue, as we have already noted, the strategic options may differ.

We have so far identified two particular problems in assessing political representation debates. First, we risk circularity because we are here using debates about women's political representation to test propositions about women's political representation. Second, as we have seen, because so many contemporary debates about political representation are explicitly about women's representation, many of the debates we are examining are gendered at the outset, a phenomenon also encountered in other RNGS debates. The sensible way of treating the first problem is to pay careful attention to process and sequence of events to avoid circularity in our arguments. To address the second problem we can assess whether the gendering changes in accordance with feminist interventions in the course of a debate. To make such arguments we can imagine a parameter based on careful definitions of sex and gender. Sex, defined as a biological division, is situated at one end of the parameter while gender, defined as the social constructions of biological sex, is at the other. Whilst sex is a dichotomous variable, gender is a continuum of feminine/masculine differences. The sex variable is a basis for claims from justice for equal descriptive representation in democratic states. The gender variable also illuminates claims for substantive representation; hence a range of policies that affect women's concerns or affect women and men differently may be discussed as the debate unfolds (Lovenduski 2005).

Accordingly we can assess changes in the gendering of debates in terms of whether claims are made for procedural (descriptive) or substantive representation or both. Claims for women's descriptive representation are cast in terms of numbers (or proportions) and invoke arguments from justice. Claims for substantive representation are cast in terms of policy effects and invoke arguments about the consideration of gender differences in policy-making. This distinction is helpful when we think about the dominant frame of the debates. Strategically, women's movements seek to gender policy debates about political representation, that is, they seek to establish that the debate is about women. They may also wish to establish that women are a diverse category. However, the rationale is that, once it is established that the debate is about women, then women will be included in the policy process. This assumption informs the framework of our study. Hence for each debate we ask the following question: Did women's movement actors succeed in gendering the dominant frame of the debate and did they gain access to the policy process during the debate?

There are two categories of debate to consider here: first, debates that were mainly and explicitly about women, that is, debates initially framed in terms of women's representation; and second, debates that were not explicitly about women. The logic of our comparative model suggests we start with debates that were not explicitly about women. Of the thirty-three

Table 13.2 *Gendering of debates*

Not explicitly about women	Quotas debates	Presence debates	Substantive women's concerns
FI1, FR2, GR3, IT1, IT2, NL1, NL3, UK1, UK2, UK3, USA2, USA3	AU3, BE1, BE2, BE3, FI2, FI3, FR1, FR3, GR1, IT3, SP1, SP2, SP3, SW2	AU1, NL3, SW1, SW3	AU2, GR2, USA1
12 debates	14 debates	4 debates	3 debates

debates, twelve were not explicitly and mainly about women's representation (Table 13.2). However, in three of these debates, IT1, IT2 and UK2, women's representation was a consideration from the outset. Of the remaining nine debates, seven (FR2, IT2, NL1, NL3, UK1, UK3 and in a very minimal way USA3) became gendered in that issues of women's representation were inserted by women's movement actors and were considered at least partly in terms of women's interests. In IT2, NL1 and NL3 interventions by women's movement actors led to the adoption of quotas to ensure women's presence. In the cases of USA2 and GR3 no claims for women's representation were made even though the terms of the debate were compatible with feminist goals to increase women's representation. In the case of USA1 it seems that the gendering of the debate reversed as a strong counter-movement was able to (re)establish traditional gender roles as central to the dominant discourse. In the case of FI1, the debate about independent electoral associations to nominate candidates, the women's movement did not attempt to gender the debate because electoral laws were perceived to be part of 'high' politics and a gender-neutral issue. We return to these debates below.

The remaining twenty-one debates focused explicitly on women, and hence were framed in gendered terms from the outset. Fourteen of these debates were about quotas, defined as measures to permit or require minimum presences of women (or maximum presences of men) in decision-making arenas. Thus, including the second Italian and the first and third Dutch debates, we have considered a total of seventeen debates about quotas of women. Quotas to ensure the presence of women are very much on the political agenda. (For a full rundown of measures to adopt quotas of women worldwide see www.quotaproject.org.) They are a procedural or numerical strategy, which is believed by many women's movement actors to lead to substantive effects. In the debates analysed here, proposals to have quotas of women in representative and other decision-making arenas offered women's movement actors opportunities to frame debates in both descriptive and substantive terms. The favoured argument was that it takes a certain minimum presence of women to ensure that women's concerns are considered.

In general, in the debates that from the outset were about women, women's movement actors sought both descriptive and substantive representation. For example, in the Austrian debate about women's access to the cabinet and the German debate about quota rules in the Social Democratic Party, an initial discussion around women's rights to have the same presence as men developed to include considerations of the nature of gender differences.

Table 13.2 also shows that in eight countries all three debates were or became gendered and in the other three, two of the debates were gendered. On the whole this suggests that once gendered, political representation debates thereafter tend to include women's concerns. However, the difficult cases of USA1, USA2 and GR3 are indicators that this cannot be taken for granted. Women's movement intervention continues to be necessary to the maintenance of a gendered frame in discussions of political representation.

Comparing debates: the model applied

Chapter 1 describes the RNGS model of state feminism and explains the relationships that are hypothesised to exist between WPAs and women's movements. In this chapter we consider whether or not the WPAs were, in the thirty-three debates, the most important factor behind the success or failure of the women's movement to influence the debates on political representation. According to the RNGS model, the impact of the women's movement and the response of the state are considered as dependent variables potentially influenced by two independent variables: the characteristics of the women's movement and the various dynamics of the policy environment. The impact of WPA activities and characteristics are conceptualised as intervening variables. The model therefore suggests that the extent to which the women's movements are able to influence the state in terms of political representation is linked to the activities and characteristics of the WPAs. Accordingly if these independent variables influence the women's movement's impact on the state, their influence partly depends on the activities of WPAs (see figure 1.2).

We now turn to the sorting and classification of the qualitative data presented in the country chapters to enable a cross-national comparison. We therefore return to the hypotheses set out in chapter 1.

H.1 Women's movement activists in democratic states have tended to be successful in increasing both substantive representation as demonstrated by policy content and procedural/descriptive representation as demonstrated by women's participation.

The first proposition examines variations in the success of women's movements in thirty-three political representation debates. The movement impact typology that is used here sorts impact according to the effect on the descriptive representation or presence of women in the debate and the substantive representation, that is the incorporation of women's movement concerns in the debate outcome. The coding of outcomes is as follows: dual responses occur when women have achieved both descriptive and substantive representation. Co-optation is descriptive representation only, pre-emption is substantive representation only and no response indicates neither substantive nor descriptive representation were achieved.

Broadly speaking the data in Table 13.3 confirm the first hypothesis. Overall women's movements were successful in gaining access to the policy process or at both gaining access to the policy process and securing outcomes that corresponded with women's movement goals (see Table 13.3). In particular women's participation in the policy process stands out: they participated in twenty-seven debates. Moreover, in seventeen debates the movement made both a procedural and a substantive impact and therefore achieved a dual response. This means that feminists participated in the debate and all, or more usually some, of their demands were met. In a further ten debates women's movements were participants but did not achieve a substantive effect. In one debate

Table 13.3 *Women's movement impact in thirty-three political representation debates*

Country	Dual response	Co-optation	Pre-emption	No response
Austria	AU1, AU2	AU3		
Belgium		BE1, BE2, BE3		
Finland	FI2, FI3			FI1
France		FR3	FR1	FR2
Germany	GR1	GR2		GR3
Italy	IT1, IT3	IT2		
Netherlands	NL1, NL2, NL3			
Spain	SP1, SP2	SP3		
Sweden	SW1, SW2, SW3			
United Kingdom	UK3			UK1, UK2
USA	USA3	USA1, USA2		
Total	17	10	1	5

feminist demands were pre-empted. Researchers have classified only five of the debates as 'no response', that is totally unsuccessful for the movement as they neither participated in nor influenced the debate. However, in two of these debates the movement viewed the debate as not especially relevant to the goal of increasing women's representation, and therefore kept a very low profile. In only two countries, Belgium and France, did the movement fail to achieve a dual response on any debate.

H.2 Women's movement activists in democratic states have tended to be more successful where women's policy agencies have acted as insiders in the policy-making process, that is, have gendered policy debates in ways that coincide with women's movement goals.

To measure their role in achieving movement success we classify WPAs in terms of whether or not their position on the debate coincided with women's movement goals and their ability to insert gendered perspectives into the dominant frame of the debate. Gendering the debate in terms that are congruent with movement definitions is an important step in gaining representation in policy content. So, agencies that both agree with movement goals and are successful in gendering or re-gendering the debate in accordance with movement definitions are classified as insider. Agencies that take a women's movement position but do not affect the debate are marginal, agencies that gender the debate in ways that do not coincide with movement goals are non-feminist, while agencies that do neither are symbolic.

Table 13.4 classifies the thirty debates for which a WPA was present from the start of the debate. Three debates, AU1, NL1 and SW1, are therefore excluded. They will be picked up again towards the end of this chapter. In this part of the analysis debates that took place in political parties but in the presence of a state WPA are analysed in terms of the activities of the WPA. Thus the findings presented in Tables 13.4 to 13.12 result from a strict interpretation of the model. We address the part played by party QWPAs towards the end of the chapter when we consider what another possible interpretation of the debates may indicate. According to Table 13.4 WPAs supported women's movement positions in fifteen debates and successfully inserted women's movement definitions in twelve. In thirteen cases WPAs did not attempt to intervene in the debate on behalf of the women's movement, and in two cases agencies intervened in ways that did not coincide with women's movement goals.

Women's policy agencies were most likely to be either insider or symbolic actors in political representation debates. Whilst insider activities tended to be associated with a dual response, symbolic activities were evenly distributed across the categories of response. Table 13.5 shows that insider WPA activities enhanced women's movement impact. WPA

Table 13.4 *WPA activity by country and debate*

Country	Insider	Marginal	Symbolic	Non-feminist
Austria	AU2		AU3	
Belgium	BE1		BE3	BE2
Finland	FI3		FI1, FI2	
France	FR3		FR1, FR2	
Germany	GR2		GR1, GR3	
Italy	IT3	IT2	IT1	
Netherlands	NL2, NL3			
Spain	SP1, SP2			SP3
Sweden	SW2		SW3	
United Kingdom	UK3	UK1	UK2	
USA		USA1	USA2, USA3	
Total	12	3	13	2

Note: AU1, NL1 and SW1 are not included because WPAs were not in existence at the time the debates began.

Table 13.5 *Women's policy agency activity and movement impact (N cases)*

	Insider	Marginal	Symbolic	Non-feminist	Total
Dual response	9	–	5	–	14
Co-optation	3	2	4	2	11
Pre-emption	–	–	1	–	1
No response	–	1	3	–	4
Total	12	3	13	2	30

activities were insider in twelve debates, of which nine resulted in a dual response. However, not all insider WPA activities are associated with movement success and not all movement success is associated with insider status.

Of the fifteen cases of policy failure (eleven co-optations and four no response), eight were linked to symbolic WPA activities, while the remainder were distributed across the categories. Overall the findings indicate that insider WPA activities tend to be linked to successful outcomes and that symbolic WPA activities may be linked to unsuccessful outcomes. These findings raise the question of what kinds of agencies are able successfully to act on women's movements' behalf.

H.3 Women's policy agencies with institutional capacity as defined by type, proximity, administrative capacity and mandate have been more effective than agencies with fewer resources and less capacity in providing linkages between women's movements and policy-makers.

We predicted that agencies with greater resources and administrative capacity will be more successful. The capacity of a WPA classifies its scope and type of organisation (political, administrative or bureaucratic), its proximity to political power, its administrative capacity in terms of resources, the inclusion of political representation in its mandate, and its leadership (feminist or not).

The thirty debates yield up to thirty-six observations of WPAs because there are, as mentioned above, a number of debates in which more than one WPA was present. The scope of all of the WPAs is characterised by the authors as cross-sectional; hence we can eliminate this factor as an explanation of variations. In twenty-seven observations they are political, mainly in the sense that they are headed by political appointees chosen by the government. In twenty-seven observations the WPAs were near to the centre of power, usually the prime-minister or the cabinet. Most agencies had limited or moderate administrative capacity or resources. In twenty-six observations leaderships are classified as feminists for all or part of the debate. Only in twelve WPAs are leaderships described as non-feminist for all or part of a debate. A similar variation is evident in WPA mandates; in twenty-four cases the issue was close to the mandate, in eleven it was not. How do these characteristics map onto WPA activities?

Table 13.6 shows that insider agencies are likely to be political, to be located in close proximity to power, to have feminist leadership and to include political representation policies in their mandate. A comparison of the characteristics of insider and symbolic agencies reveals considerable similarity: both types are likely to be political, have feminist leaders and to be located close to centres of power. However, symbolic agencies are less likely to include political representation in their mandate. Thus, a major difference between symbolic and insider agencies is the inclusion of political representation in their mandate. Marginal agencies contrast with insider agencies in terms of type. In summary, the WPA characteristics that stand out are type, proximity, leadership and mandate. However, only mandate distinguishes between insider and symbolic WPA activities. To support or reject hypothesis 3 it is necessary to examine the role of the agencies both in relation to the characteristics of the women's movements and in relation to the policy environments, the subject of hypothesis 4.

H.4 Variations in women's movement characteristics and/or policy environments explain variations in both women's policy agency effectiveness and movement activists' success in increasing women's representation.

To examine linkages between women's movement characteristics, policy environments, agency effectiveness and movement success, we first relate

Table 13.6 *Characteristics of WPA and WPA activities*

	Type			Proximity		Administrative capacity			Leadership		Mandate	
	Administrative	Political	Judicial	Close	Distant	High	Medium	Low	Feminist	Non-feminist	Close	Not close
Insider	3	14	1	12	5	2	6	6	14−2*	5+2*	15	2
Marginal	2	1	–	2	1	–	–	3	2	2	2	1
Symbolic	2	11	–	12	1	2	3	5	11	2	5	8
Non-feminist	1	1	–	1	1	2	–	1	1	1	2	–
Total	8	27	1	27	8	6	9	15	26−2	10+2	24	11

Note: No WPA in AU1, NL1, SW1.

*Change of leadership type during debate.

Two observations FI3, IT1, IT3, UK3. Four observations FR3.

NL3: leadership change from feminist to non-feminist in 1994.

SP2: leadership change from feminist to non-feminist in 1996.

Missing observations: proximity BE1,2; administrative capacity FR1,2,3.

movement characteristics and policy environment to agency effectiveness, then to movement success. The Belgian and Italian authors distinguish between integrated and autonomous feminists, and other authors make analogous distinctions in some debates. Integrated feminists are those who had or sought purchase in the political system, mainly via parties of the left, whilst autonomous feminists may have been interested in the issue but were not organised in political institutions. We report the observations of integrated women's movements because integrated movements sought to engage the political system in debates.

The research design proposes that the stage of the women's movement at the time of the debate (whether emerging, growing, in consolidation or decline), its closeness to the left, the priority of the issue and cohesion on the issue, and the strength of the counter-movement explain differences in WPA effectiveness. Specifically we expected agencies to be most effective in assisting movements at stages of growth or consolidation, close to the left, unified on the issue to which they gave a high priority and acting against a weak counter-movement. It seems that on this issue all of the women's movements were close to the left. Only in one case (FI3) was part of the movement not classified as close to the left, and in this case the part close to the left was so substantial that we have entered it as close to the left. We can therefore discard 'proximity to the left' from the analysis of political representation debates and it does not appear in Table 13.7. Stage of growth, issue priority and movement cohesion are the characteristics most associated with insider agency activities. As expected, symbolic and non-feminist WPA activities were less associated with high issue priority and more with low movement cohesion on the issue. However, their pattern of movement stage was similar for both insider and symbolic agencies, leaving us with issue priority and cohesion as the major variables that differed between insider and symbolic agency activities. Perversely a strong or moderately strong counter-movement appears to be associated both with insider and symbolic WPAs, a point to which we return below. Overall the case studies do not permit us to draw strong conclusions about the impact of other women's movement characteristics on women's policy agency activities.

Similarly the fourteen cases of movement success are associated with movement cohesion and the priority given to the issue (Table 13.8). Co-optation is associated with low movement cohesion, but not with low issue priority, a finding that requires some more unpacking. Most authors underline the priority attached by the movement to the issue as a potential explanation of movement success (or its absence as an explanation of lack of success). The Austrian, Finnish, German and Swedish cases all suggest that high or moderate issue priority is associated with

Table 13.7 Women's movement characteristics and women's policy agency activity

	Stage			Priority		Cohesion		Counter-movement		
	Emerging/growth	Consolidation	Abeyance/decline	High/moderate	Low	Cohesive	Not cohesive	Strong	Moderate	Weak/none
Insider	3 cases FR3, NL2, IT3	8 cases AU2, BE1, FI3, NL3, SP1, SP2, SW2, UK3	1 case GR2	12 cases AU2, BE1, FI3, FR3, GR2, IT3, NL2, NL3, SP1, SP2, SW2, UK3		11 cases AU2, BE1, FI3, FR3, GR2, IT3, NL3, SP1, SP2, SW2, UK3	1 case NL2	1 case FI3	5 cases FR3, GR2, SP1, SP2, SW2	6 cases AU2, BE1, IT3, NL2, NL3, UK3
Marginal	2 cases IT2, USA1	–	1 case UK1	1 case USA1	2 cases IT2, UK1	1 case USA1	2 cases IT2, UK1	1 case USA1	–	2 cases IT2, UK1
Symbolic	3 cases GR1, SW3, UK2	7 cases AU3, BE3, FI1, FI2, IT1, USA2, USA3	3 cases FR1, FR2, GR3	6 cases BE3, FI2, GR1, IT1, SW3, UK2	7 cases AU3, FI1, FR1, FR2, GR3, USA2, USA3	6 cases BE3, FI2, IT1, UK2, USA3, SW3	7 cases AU3, FI1, FR1, FR2, GR1, GR3, USA2	1 case USA3	4 cases FI2, GR1, SW3, UK2	8 cases AU3, BE3, FR1, FR2, FI1, GR3, IT1, USA2
Non-feminist	–	2 cases BE2, SP3	–	2 cases BE2, SP3	–	2 cases BE2, SP3	–	–	1 case SP3	1 case BE2
Total	8	17	5	21	9	20	10	3	10	17

Table 13.8 *Women's movement characteristics and impact*

	Stage			Priority		Cohesion		Counter-movement		
	Emerging/growth	Consolidation	Decline	High	Not high	Cohesive	Not cohesive	Strong	Moderate	Weak/none
Dual response	6	8	–	13	1	11	3	3	5	6
Co-optation	3	7	1	9	2	5	6	2	3	6
Pre-emption	–	–	1	–	1	–	1	–	–	1
No response	1	1	2	–	4	1	3	–	1	3
Total	10	16	4	22	8	17	13	5	9	16

Note: Includes observations for integrated movements in Belgium and Italy 1, 2, 3.

success. In thirteen of the fourteen successful results for the movement, the issue was of high priority. Feminists were at least moderately cohesive on the issue in eleven of the fourteen cases. However, high issue priority and movement cohesion do not guarantee policy success. In the two cases where high issue priority and movement cohesion led to co-optation the movement faced a strong counter-movement on the issue, although the movements were in stages of consolidation in one case (SP3) and growth in the other (USA3). Otherwise the perverse counter-movement effect described above continues in Table 13.8 which shows that in eight of the cases of dual response a strong or moderately strong counter-movement was active in the debate. In summary, the most striking associations with success are high movement issue priority and cohesiveness.

The type of WPA activities may also be affected by the policy environment. The distinction between moderately closed and closed policy environments appears to have explanatory value. The relationship between WPA activities and policy environment is presented in Table 13.9. Insider WPAs faced moderately closed policy environments in nine debates and closed environments in three.

Symbolic WPA activities took place in moderately closed policy environments in four debates, in closed environments in six and in open policy environments in three cases.

The presence of the left in power may enhance WPA capacity to represent women's movements. The left was in or shared power during nineteen debates. The absence of the left from government was more likely to be associated with symbolic agency activities. Compatible issue frame fit, on the other hand, did not distinguish between insider and symbolic WPA activities, while incompatible issue frame fit was associated with marginal WPA.

How does the policy environment affect movement impact?

Mapped onto the policy environment, movement impact is most affected by the presence of the left in power and by the issue frame fit of the debate (Table 13.10). In nine of the fourteen observations of dual response the left was in power. The dual responses gained under centre or right-wing control are not a refutation of the hypothesis. In the Swedish case, the third debate was the creation of a women's party and, although this debate took place under a right-wing government, its effects were most felt in the Social Democratic Party. A similar argument may be made about the debates over the transformation of the Italian Communist Party, in the German Social Democratic and British Labour parties. However, the left was in or sharing power in ten of sixteen instances in

Table 13.9 *Policy environment and women's policy agency activities*

	Open?		Left in power?			Frame fit		
	Open/moderately open	Moderately closed	Closed	Left in/shares power	Left not in power	Matching	Compatible	Incompatible
Insider		9 cases FI3, FR3, GR2, IT3, NL3, SP1, SP2, SW2, UK3	3 cases AU2, BE1, NL2	9 cases AU2, BE1, FR3, NL2, NL3, SP1, SP2, SW3, UK3	3 cases FI3, GR2, IT3	3 cases AU2, IT3, SW2	8 cases BE1, FR3, GR2, NL3, SP1, SP2, FI3, UK3	1 case NL2
Marginal			3 cases IT2, UK1, USA1	2 cases IT2, USA1	1 case UK1			3 cases IT2, UK1, USA1
Symbolic	3 cases IT1, USA2, USA3	4 cases FI1, GR1, GR3, SW3	6 cases FI2, AU3, BE3, FR1, FR2, UK2	7 cases AU2, BE3, FI1, FR1, FR2, GR3, USA3	6 cases GR1, IT1, SW3, UK2, USA2, FI2	4 cases AU3, FI1, FR2, USA3	8 cases BE3, FI2, GR1, GR3, IT1, UK2, USA2, SW3	1 case FR1
Non-feminist			2 cases BE2, SP3	1 case BE2	1 case SP3		1 case SP3	
Total	3	13	14	19	11	7	17	5

Note: NL2: described as right with left window; AU1, NL1, SW1 NA: no WPA.

Table 13.10 *Policy environments and movement impact*

	Open/moderately open	Moderately closed	Closed	Left in power	Left shares power	Left not in power	Frame fit matching	Frame fit compatible	Frame fit incompatible
Dual response	2	9	3	9	–	5	4	9	1
Co-optation	1	3	7	2	4	5	1	8	2
Pre-emption	–	–	1	1	–	–	–	–	1
No response	–	1	3	2	1	1	2	1	1
Total	3	13	14	14	5	11	7	18	5

Note: NL2: Left window.

which a dual response was not achieved. That is, six of eleven instances of co-optation, the only instance of pre-emption and three of the four instances of 'no response'. In two of the instances of 'no response' (FR1 and GR3) the women's movements were not interested in the issue. It may be that the theory that women's movement impact is enhanced by the presence of the left in government should be revisited. The discourse frame fit was matching or compatible in thirteen of the fourteen cases of dual response, as it was in nine of the eleven cases of co-optation and three of the four no responses, suggesting that appropriate wider discourse on an issue may be necessary but is not a sufficient condition of feminist policy success.

To summarise so far, in fifteen debates WPA activities were classified as insider or marginal and in fifteen as symbolic or non-feminist. In nine of the debates in which WPA activities were insider or marginal a dual response was achieved from the state. Our final research question is to assess whether the agencies are necessary and effective links between the movements and the state. This question is expressed as three related hypotheses.

H.5 Women's policy offices have tended to provide necessary and effective linkages between women's movement activism and substantive and procedural responses by democratic states.

H.5A If women's policy offices are necessary and effective linkages between movement activism and state substantive and procedural responses, then variations in movement resources and policy environments will have no independent relation to state responses.

H.5B If women's policy offices are not necessary and effective linkages between movement activism and state substantive and procedural responses, then variations in women's movement resources and policy environments will be directly related to variations in state responses, regardless of women's policy office activities.

The relationships set out in H.5 are described in Tables 13.11 and 13.12. Table 13.11 classifies the characteristics of women's movements and policy environments that suggest a relationship with the dependent variable, movement impact. Table 13.12 shows the same variables controlling for the potential intervening variable of WPA activities. If agency activities are unnecessary to or impede women's movement success, then the direction of the relationships between independent and dependent variables displayed in Table 13.11 will diminish. If agency activities assist or enhance women's movement activities, then the direction will increase. The sorting and classification process left six variables in play: movement issue priority and cohesion, the openness of the policy sub-system (environment), the presence of the left in power,

Table 13.11 *Women's movement characteristics and policy environments by women's movement success – dual response*

	Yes (%)	No (%)	N
		Dual response	
Priority high	59	41	22
not high	13	87	8
Cohesive yes	65	35	17
no	23	77	13
Policy system open	67	33	3
moderately closed	69	31	13
closed	21	79	14
Left in/sharing power yes	47	53	19
no	45	55	11
Frame fit matching	57	43	7
compatible	50	50	18
incompatible	20	80	5
Counter-movement strong/moderate	57	43	14
weak/none	38	62	16

Table 13.12 *Effects of women's movement characteristics and policy environments on women's movement success by policy agency activities*

	Insider/marginal dual response			Symbolic/non-feminist dual response		
	Yes(%)	No(%)	N	Yes(%)	No(%)	N
Priority high	64	36	14	50	50	8
not high	–	100	1	14	86	7
Cohesion yes	73	27	11	67	33	6
no	25	75	4	11	89	9
Policy sub-system open	–	–	–	67	33	3
moderately closed	78	22	9	40	60	5
closed	33	67	6	14	86	7
Left in /sharing power yes	70	30	10	22	78	9
no	40	60	5	50	50	6
Frame fit matching	100	–	3	33	67	3
compatible	56	44	9	40	60	10
incompatible	33	67	3	50	50	2
Counter-movement strong/moderate	42	58	7	67	33	6
weak/none	63	37	8	11	89	9

the extent of the discourse frame fit, and strength or presence of the counter-movement. When compared with Table 13.11 results show that insider and marginal WPA activities assist women's movements in reaching goals, as most of the relationships become stronger when controlled for WPA activities. Table 13.11 suggests a strong link between the relative openness of the policy environment and movement policy success. Where the policy environment was open or moderately closed the movement was more likely to achieve a dual response. For debates during which the policy sub-system was classified as closed, the movement was seldom successful.

Do the results support the proposition that activist WPAs assist movement success in achieving their demands on political representation? We have shown in Table 13.11 an association between movement success and cohesion, issue priority and an open or moderately closed policy subsystem and a strong or moderately strong counter-movement, but little or no association with matching or compatible frame fit, left in power or sharing power. Let us consider these associations in more detail.

Issue priority and cohesion

In terms of issue priority Table 13.11 shows that when the movement attached a high priority to political representation issues a dual response was more likely. The, also stronger, association between policy failure and low movement priority for the issue mirrors this finding. Both the associations between high issue priority and policy success and between low issue priority and policy failure increase in Table 13.12 for insider/marginal agencies. Hence insider/marginal WPA activities may boost movement success where issue priority is high. However, they are not able to overcome the disadvantages of ascribing low priority to the issue. Where movements gave the issue being debated low priority they were unlikely to be successful, whatever the type of agency activity. In half of the cases in which WPAs did not support women's movement goals and issue priority was high, the outcome was a dual response. Hence WPA activities on women's behalf may not be necessary to successful policy outcomes if issue priority and movement cohesion are high.

The strong association between movement cohesion and success apparent in Table 13.11 is mirrored by a strong link between policy failure and low movement cohesion. The impact of movement cohesion increases for insider/marginal agencies as shown in Table 13.12, suggesting that activist WPAs may boost the success rates of cohesive movements. The findings for symbolic and non-feminist agencies just about support this proposition. The table shows that cohesive movements may be less likely to be successful in the absence of activist WPAs. Finally, movement cohesion is strongly associated with high issue priority. When the issue priority is high, the movement tends to be cohesive. Overall analysis of the two women's movement characteristics of issue priority and cohesion offer a modest amount of support for the proposition that WPAs assist the achievement of policy success by women's movements.

Policy environment

How did variation in WPA activities associate with variation in the policy environment? Table 13.12 shows that where the policy sub-system was moderately closed or closed, activist WPAs boosted success rates while symbolic and non-feminist agency activities were less likely to be associated with movement success and more likely to be associated with policy failure.

The left in power

All of the movements were classified as close to the left, hence we expected to find an association between movement success and the left in power or sharing power. This association is absent in Table 13.11, but appears in Table 13.12 for insider and marginal agency activities, mirrored by an association between policy failure and the left not being in power for symbolic and non-feminist agency activities. When the left is in power activist agencies are more likely to be successful than when the left is not in power. In contrast non-activist agencies are likely to be unsuccessful when the left is in power and equally successful or unsuccessful when the left is not in power.

Finally the data in Table 13.12 show that when the left was not in power movements were successful in fewer than half of the debates where WPAs were insider. Hence there is some support for the prediction that insider or marginal agency activities may boost any positive effects that result from the presence of the left in government. In one debate, USA1, variable indicators require a classification of the very right-wing Southern Democrats in Arkansas in the 1970s as part of the left; hence the boost is stronger than it appears to be. When the left is in government, activist WPAs are more persuasive while non-activist agencies may impede movement effectiveness. To summarise, WPA activities could not overcome the disadvantages of the absence of the left from power but boosted the success of movement actors when the left was in or sharing power.

Discourse frame fit

Matching or compatible debate discourse was associated with dual responses in eight of fifteen cases where WPAs were insider or marginal. Where WPAs were symbolic or non-feminist only five of fifteen debates led to dual responses. However, insider WPAs were associated with movement success in only one of the three cases in which frame fit was incompatible, while WPAs classified as symbolic or non-feminist were associated with failure in one of the two cases in which frame fit was incompatible. Therefore a matching or compatible discourse frame was more likely to be associated with policy success when insider WPAs were present than when they were not. Overall the frame fit findings indicate that insider or marginal WPAs are able to capitalise on favourable discourse frames but not to overcome unfavourable frames, whilst symbolic and non-feminist WPAs can do neither.

Counter-movement strength

Table 13.11 suggests that the presence of a strong or moderately strong counter-movement is associated with movement policy success and that a weak counter-movement is associated with policy failure. Table 13.12 reverses that relationship for activist agencies but retains it for non-activist WPAs. Insider/marginal agency activities and strong counter-movements are less likely to be associated with movement policy success, while weak counter-movements are more likely to be so associated. For symbolic/ non-feminist agency activities the association between strong and weak counter-movements and movement policy success is shown to be stronger in Table 13.12 than in Table 13.11. This perverse association invites discussion. Table 13.7 showed that strong and moderate counter-movements are associated with movement cohesion. In twelve of the twenty instances of a strong or moderate counter-movement, the women's movement actors are classified as cohesive. Conversely weak counter-movements are associated with low movement cohesion. In eight of the seventeen debates where counter-movements were weak, movement actors were classified as not cohesive. These associations (small) suggest that a strong or moderately strong counter-movement may enhance movement cohesion, a possibility that merits further research.

The patterns described so far confirm that activist WPAs provided effective linkages between movement and state, particularly where the left was in or sharing power, the policy environment was not closed, discourse frame fit was matching or compatible with women's movement actor goals, and women's movement actors were cohesive on and gave high priority to the issue. Under these conditions WPAs provided a boost to movement chances of policy success in debates about political representation. Activist WPAs were apparently unable to compensate when women's movement actors did not give the issue high priority and/or were not cohesive, and issue frame fit was incompatible.

Exceptions

Having explored the majority of cases, we can now turn to the exceptions in order to describe fully the patterns of state feminism presented in this study and to fill out our analysis. There are two patterns that run against the overall direction of the findings: five dual response/symbolic cases and three co-optation/insider cases. The first cluster of exceptions suggests that WPA activity makes no difference. However, in three of these cases – GR1, FI2 and IT1 – the WPA had no mandate to intervene in the debates. These cases are discussed in more detail in the next section. The remaining two debates in the category are the Swedish women's party debate and the USA National Voter Registration Act debate. In the Swedish debate the movement threatened to establish a women's party if steps were not taken to improve the number of female deputies at the next election. It was addressed to the parties and was especially felt in the Social Democratic Party, hence was in many respects a party debate. In the USA3 case the dual response classification is a very close call as the gendering of the debate was minimal, amounting to only two interventions. Thus the first cluster of exceptions may be explained in terms of the model.

Insider activities were not associated with a dual response in only three cases: BE1, GR2 and FR3. In both the Belgian and the German debates, although the frame fit was compatible, neither movement was cohesive and the left was not in power. Moreover in the case of GR2 the debate was not a top priority for the movement, and hence the obstacles to success were almost insurmountable. However, in the French case the movement was cohesive, the frame fit was compatible, issue priority was high and there was a strong counter-movement, but the right was in power. The impact was classified as co-optation because women's movement actors, though initially influential, lost control over the implementation provisions for the policy. Inevitably party priorities were reasserted and women were not nominated for winnable seats in the following election to the national legislature. This exception underlines the importance of political parties to debates about political representation.

Overall the exceptions point to the importance of political parties where insider agencies are more likely to have purchase. Political parties must want or be required to promote sex equality if women are to take up their rightful share of places in elected assemblies.

So far we have discussed debates in terms of their major characteristics as political representation debates and their impact on the state. The debates presented here offer the opportunity to explore two further dimensions of political representation policy debates. As mentioned above we have a set of debates in which decisions were reached inside political parties and a set of debates that were not explicitly about women's representation. Both warrant additional exploration.

Party debates

The close relationship between women's movements and political parties of the left affects the outcome of policy debates on women's political representation. Our debates enable us to explore this relationship further. Seven of the thirty debates analysed in Tables 13.4 to 13.12 took place inside political parties: FI2, GR1, IT1, SP1, SP2, SW3 and UK 2. In addition AU1 and NL1 also took place inside political parties, a total of nine party debates. For such debates we should consider the role of quasi-women's policy agencies, that is, agencies that perform WPA functions but are not formally mandated by the state. QWPAs are most likely to be found in political parties and major interest and professional associations, but we also present in other institutions such as trade unions or legislatives (see USA3). Party QWPAs were in existence in eight of the party debates (all but FI2).[2] In six cases the QWPA activities were insider and the result was a dual response. Were we to classify results of internal party debates on the basis of QWPA activities rather than state WPA activities, we would have more cases of dual response/insider and fewer cases of dual response/symbolic. It should be noted, however, that in the two Spanish debates the overlap between party control of the WPA and the PSOE QWPA obscures the effectiveness of the QWPA, although there is no doubt that its role was insider. In the Italian case the party was in transition from the PCI to the PDS. The previous QWPA activities in the PCI ensured the gendering of the debate about creating a new political party. In the UK, Germany and the Netherlands, party QWPAs gendered the debates and assisted feminists to achieve a dual response within the party. All the party debates took place in parties of the left and are further

---

[2] Finnish political parties have women's sections that perform similar tasks to QWPAs in other parties. They are relatively independent, receive directly a special portion of the party subsidy and are a form of institutionalised feminism within the political parties. They are therefore classified as women's movement actors.

evidence of the close relationship between women's movements active on the issue of political representation and the left.

The interactive process appears to be one in which feminists active in the parties operate both to empower the QWPAs and to bring the issue to the agenda, thus providing opportunities for QWPAs to act. Moreover party QWPAs appear to be important to the establishment of WPAs as illustrated in the cases of AU1, NL1, UK2 (for the Ministry for Women and Equality) and SW1.

This does not mean that there are no right or centre parties that take up issues of women's representation. We have shown that, increasingly, such parties do seek to increase women's political representation (see chapters on Belgium, Germany, Italy and Spain). It is striking that QWPAs facilitated policy success on this issue in all cases where they acted. The findings support the proposition that the location of women's movements inside political parties is strongly associated with movement success.

Debates not initially about women's political representation

Twelve of the debates in seven countries were not specifically about women's political representation: FI1, FR2, GR3, IT1, IT2, NL1, NL3, UK1, UK2, UK3, USA2 and USA3. They therefore offer the opportunity for an especially robust test of the impact of women's movements on the state. In this discussion, where debates took place inside an institution in which a QWPA was present, we use the observations of QWPA activities in the tables (IT1, UK2 and USA3).

The debates cover a range of issues about political representation, including candidate selection, the acquisition of citizenship, the nature of the electoral system, voter registration procedures, the arrangements for appointments to corporate bodies, parliamentary working arrangements and term limits. These debates support the majority findings. The majority of the cases resulted in policy success; four of the five cases of dual response were associated with insider or marginal WPA or QWPA activities, moderate to high issue priority, cohesion on the issue for the movement and either the left was in power or the debate took place inside a party of the left. The direction of the associations generally increased between Tables 13.13 and 13.14, indicating that agencies enhanced women's movement policy success under favourable conditions. By contrast co-optation and no response results were generally associated with symbolic WPA activities. Similarly the results for symbolic/non-feminist WPA activities highlight that high issue priority, movement cohesion and left in power were necessary for movement success. Symbolic agencies were associated with movement failure even when the other predictors of

Table 13.13 *Debates not explicitly about women's political representation by priority, movement cohesion, left in power, policy environment and issue frame fit*

	Dual response		
	Yes(%)	No(%)	N
Priority high moderate	71	29	7
not high	0	100	5
Cohesive yes	75	25	8
no	0	100	4
Left in/sharing power, or inside left party yes	60	40	10
no	0	100	2
Policy environment open	75	25	4
moderately closed	75	25	4
closed	0	100	4
Frame fit matching	67	33	3
Compatible	57	43	7
Incompatible	0	100	2

Note: Party debates classified by QWPA.

Table 13.14 *Debates not explicitly about women's political representation by priority, cohesion, left in power and QWPA/WPA activities*

	Insider/marginal Dual response			Symbolic/non-feminist Dual response		
	Yes(%)	No(%)	N	Yes(%)	No(%)	N
Priority high	100	–	4	100	–	1
not high	50	50	2	–	100	5
Cohesion yes	100	–	5	100	–	1
no	–	100	1	0	100	5
Left in /sharing power or inside left party yes	100	–	3	17	83	6
no	–	100	1	50	50	2
Policy environment open	100	–	2	50	50	2
moderately closed	100	–	2	–	100	2
closed	50	50	2	–	100	2
Frame fit matching	100	–	2	–	100	1
compatible	100	–	3	33	67	3
incompatible	–	100	1	–	100	2

success were present. These findings support the proposition that activist WPAs and QWPAs assisted but may not have been essential to movement success on this type of issue. In common with the majority findings they suggest that activist agencies boosted positive effects of association with the left, while non-active agencies appeared to be associated with negative effects. Overall the ambiguous results of this association suggest that women's movement friendships with the left are not necessarily beneficial. This is an area in which more research is needed.

Nation-state patterns

The methodological decision to take policy debates on political representation as our unit of analysis means that researchers were able to examine patterns of movement activism and state response on the issue over time, within countries and cross-nationally. Thus nation-state trends are findings of the study. If strong nation-state patterns emerge then the benefits of studying policy debates instead of nation-states are limited. Accordingly, having discussed patterns of women's movement success and WPA activities, we turn finally to a consideration of national patterns. Some evidence that the national context has an effect is to be found in the content of the debates. For example, debates about quotas in electoral laws took place in Belgium, France and Italy where there were particularly low levels of elected women's representation in the 1980s and early 1990s (see Appendix 1).

But when we look at national patterns in terms of movement impact we find substantial variation. In only three countries is the impact of women's movements consistent over the three debates: Belgium, the Netherlands and Sweden (Table 13.3). In Sweden and the Netherlands policy-makers met women's movement demands for substantive and procedural representation in all three debates. In two of these debates (SW1 and NL1) there were no WPAs in existence at the time the debates began. By contrast the Belgian state consistently incorporated women as participants in the debates but did not meet substantive demands. Whilst the Belgian debates took place over a relatively short period of time, both the Swedish and the Dutch debates were spaced over the whole thirty-year period. Overall, however, consideration of the national context does not appear to be decisive. There is variation in the ability of WPAs to increase the access of women to the state in eight of the eleven countries discussed in this volume. In four countries the response was the same in two debates. In two countries, Austria and Spain, the debates followed the same sequence of success in the first two debates and failure in the third. In Finland the movement failed in the first debate, in which it was not interested, but succeeded in the second and third. In the UK the movement achieved neither descriptive nor substantive political representation in the first debate, it was present in the second debate and achieved political representation in the third debate. In Austria and Spain the movement achieved a dual response in the first two debates but a co-optation in the third. The explanations, however, differ. In Austria the first two debates saw a cohesive women's movement that gave the issue a high priority. While the third debate undoubtedly affected women's interests, the women's movement was not cohesive and issue priority was low. In Spain the first two debates were party debates that took place while the left was in power for all or part of the time, but the third debate occurred under a right-wing government.

The data offer some evidence that EU policy is important in debates about women's political representation. During the 1990s the experience of EU policy gradually accustomed policy actors to the significance of gender gaps. Policies to correct such gaps in representation gradually became more legitimate, a process that accelerated after 1997 when the Amsterdam Treaty included provision for positive action to bring about equality between women and men in decision-making. Claims for balanced representation that were initiated by the left in the 1980s were taken up by the right in the 1990s when corrective policies were passed and implemented under some right-wing governments.

Overall the case is not so much of nation-state patterns but of party patterns, and, as we have shown, analysis of party debates enhances the findings drawn from analysis of state debates.

The relative unimportance of the national context is surprising. When we examine the data on actual levels of women's political representation across the countries and the time period we find massive variations (Appendix 1). At the beginning of the twenty-first century women's share of elected national positions was four times as high in Sweden as it was in Italy. In most countries women's descriptive representation rose over the period under study, but between 1970 and 2000 WPA effectiveness did not appear to increase. In the 1970s WPAs were successful in two of five cases, in the 1980s they were successful in three of seven cases, in the 1990s they were successful in six of fourteen cases. Although in the early 2000s they were successful in three of four cases, overall, increases in women's presence in elected assemblies are not, on the face of it, associated with increases in WPA success. However, we have seen that women's movement characteristics have an effect on WPA success especially when the political circumstances are favourable, that is when the left is in power.

We might expect that, as women's movements are institutionalised, measured in terms of the presence of women in decision-making positions, WPA roles are both mediated and enhanced. The movement has access to institutions through the women who have been elected. Cohesion among elected women is increased not least because there is a higher percentage of women elected in most of the parties. Over time party differences on issues of women's presence decrease as their numbers become more equal across parties. Many of the chapters in this volume emphasise the importance of a consistent presence of feminist policy-makers and many of the successes occurred when the parties associated with feminists were in power and the capacities and/or mandates of WPAs expanded.

State feminism

Are women's policy agencies state feminist in the context of political representation debates? More broadly, does the establishment of state feminism create feminist elites who substitute for women's movements? For western Europe the answer to the first question appears to be yes. Experts classified the activities of twelve state agencies as insider and three as marginal. In every country except the United States examples of insider WPAs supporting women's movement goals on the issue of increasing women's political representation were identified. Our findings suggest a state feminist presence in ten of the countries under consideration. Overall the findings support a theory of state feminism. However, the results also show that state feminism alone is not enough. Women's movement characteristics provide much of the explanation for policy success. Thus state feminism must be supported by cohesive movements united around an issue to which they give high or at least moderate priority. The long-standing and widespread feminist concern that state feminism functions properly only when associated with effective women's movements is borne out by the results of this study and illustrates the importance of the second question. The preoccupation of feminists with establishing state agencies to promote women's equality and to bring movement concerns into the state is justified as a strategy that brings benefit to women by enhancing their success in policy debates about political representation.

Finally the results also support the decision to select the policy debate as a unit of analysis to allow longitudinal and cross-national patterns to emerge. The assumptions of the research design are supported by the data. The sorting and classification of observations to test core hypotheses of the RNGS model has produced meaningful results. These results show that, by establishing WPAs, states offer institutional resources that act to support goals defined by women's movements. The definition of feminism in local terms during each debate has prevented concept stretching but enabled generalisation about movements across countries.

References

Lovenduski, Joni 2005, *Feminizing Politics*, Cambridge: Polity Press

Mazur, Amy (ed.) 2001, *State Feminism, Women's Movements and Job Training: Making Democracies Work in a Global Economy*, New York and London: Routledge

Outshoorn, Joyce (ed.) 2004, *The Politics of Prostitution: Women's Movements, Democratic States and the Globalisation of Sex Commerce*, Cambridge: Cambridge University Press

Stetson, Dorothy McBride (ed.) 2001, *Abortion Politics, Women's Movements and the Democratic State: a Comparative Study of State Feminism*, Oxford: Oxford University Press

Appendix 1   Tables of women's representation in eleven countries

Table 1 *Women in the Austrian parliament since 1949*

Year	Number of women		Percentage of women	
	minimum	maximum	minimum	maximum
1949–53	10		6.3	
1953–6	11		6.7	
1956–9	10		6.3	
1959–62	11		6.7	
1962–6	11		6.7	
1966–70	11		6.7	
1970–1	8		4.8	
1971–5	11		6.0	
1975–9	14		7.7	
1979–83	18		9.8	
1983–6	17	18	9.3	10.9
1986–90	21	28	11.5	15.3
1990–4	36	46	19.7	25.1
1994–6	39	46	21.3	25.1
1996–9	47	52	25.7	28.4
1999–2002	47	53	25.7	29.0
2002–	61	63	33.3	34.4

Note: Due to the fluctuations in the number of female MPs during legislative periods since 1983, the minimum and maximum number of female MPs for each subsequent period is provided. For example, there were eighteen changes to the number of women in parliament for the period 1990–6. The reason for these frequent changes is that, since the 1980s, there has been a clandestine rule that MPs resign their seats upon appointment to the government. The resulting fluctuations in the composition of parliament have generally worked to women's advantage.

Table 2 *Women in the Belgian federal parliament since 1945*

Year of election	Women in the House of Representatives %	Women in the Senate %	Women in the (federal) parliament %
1946	1.4	5.9	2.1
1949	2.8	4.0	3.3
1950	3.3	4.0	3.6
1954	4.2	3.4	3.8
1958	4.2	3.4	3.8
1961	5.1	1.7	3.6
1965	3.3	1.1	2.3
1968	3.7	0.0	2.0
1971	2.8	2.8	2.8
1974	6.6	6.6	6.6
1977	7.0	8.8	7.8
1978	7.5	10.4	8.9
1981	5.6	11.6	8.3
1985	7.5	11.4	9.3
1987	8.4	8.1	8.3
1991	9.4	10.8	10.1
1995	12.0	23.9	15.8
1999	23.3	28.2	24.9
2003	35.3	31.0	33.9

Note: All data represent the percentage of women in the respective assembly at the beginning of the legislature.
Source: Leen Van Molle and Ehaie Gubin 1998, *Vrouw en politiek in België,* Tielt: Lannoo; Valeric Verzele and Carine Joly 1999, La représentation des femmes en politique après les élections du 13 Juin 1999, Brussels: CRISP; www.senate.be; www.dekamer.be

Table 3 *Women in the Finnish parliament since 1945*

Year of election	Number of women	Percentage of women
1945	17	8.5
1948	24	12.0
1951	29	14.5
1954	30	15.0
1958	28	14.0
1962	27	13.5
1966	33	16.5
1970	43	21.5
1972	43	21.5
1975	46	23.0
1979	52	26.0
1983	62	31.0
1987	63	31.5
1991	77	38.5
1995	67	33.5
1999	74	36.5
2003	75	37.0

Table 4 *Women in the French parliament since 1945*

Date of election	Total number of seats	Number of women elected	Percentage of women elected
National Assembly			
October 1945	586	32	5.5
June 1946	586	30	5.1
November 1946	619	42	6.8
June 1951	627	22	3.5
January 1956	627	19	3.0
November 1958	579	8	1.4
November 1962	482	8	1.7
March 1967	487	11	2.3
June 1968	487	8	1.6
March 1973	490	8	1.6
March 1978	491	20	4.1
June 1981	491	26	5.3
March 1986	577	34	5.9
June 1988	577	33	5.7
March 1993	577	35	6.1
June 1997	577	63	10.9
June 2002	577	71	12.3
Senate			
June 1947	314	22	7.0
May 1949	317	12	3.8
July 1952	317	9	2.8
July 1954	317	9	2.8
November 1956	317	9	2.8
July 1958	314	6	1.9
October 1960	307	5	1.6
December 1962	271	5	1.8
October 1964	273	5	1.8
October 1966	274	5	1.8
September 1968	283	5	1.8
September 1971	282	4	1.4
September 1974	283	7	2.5
September 1977	295	5	1.7
September 1980	304	7	2.3
September 1983	317	9	2.8
September 1986	319	9	2.8
September 1989	321	10	3.1
September 1992	321	16	5.0
September 1995	321	18	5.6
September 2001	321	35	10.9

Table 5 *Women in the German parliament (Bundestag) since 1949*

Year	Number of seats	Number of women elected	Percentage of women elected
1949	410	28	6.8
1953	509	45	8.8
1957	519	48	9.2
1961	521	43	8.3
1965	518	36	6.9
1969	518	34	6.6
1972	518	30	5.8
1976	518	38	7.3
1980	519	44	8.5
1983	520	51	9.8
1987	519	80	15.4
1990	662	135	20.4
1994	672	177	26.3
1998	669	207	30.9
2002	603	198	32.8

Source: Kolinsky, Eva 1988 'Women and Politics in Western Germany', in Marilyn Rueschemeyer (ed.) *Women in the Politics of Postcommunist Eastern Europe*, New York: M.E. Sharpe; Election Resources on the Internet, www.ElectionResources.org.de; Federal Statistical Office of Germany, www.destatis.ed/e_home.htm; *Bundestag* web page, www.bundestag.de.

Table 6 *Women in the Italian parliament since 1945*

Year of election	Number of women	Percentage of women
1948	41	6.9
1953	34	5.6
1958	22	3.6
1963	29	4.6
1968	18	2.8
1972	25	3.9
1976	53	8.4
1979	52	8.2
1983	50	7.9
1987	81	12.8
1992	51	8.1
1994	95	15.1
1996	70	11.1
2001	71	11.2

Table 7 *Women in the Dutch parliament since 1945*

Year of election	First chamber	Second chamber	Community councils	Cabinet
1948	2	5	2	0
1950	2	5	2	0
1955	4	8	3	0
1960	5	9	4	8
1965	7	10	4	0
1970	5	8	7	7
1975	5	9	10	7
1980	9	14	13	7
1985	21	17	16	15
1990	27	20	19	21
1995	23	33	22	27
2000	24	36	23	27
2003	24	37	23	31

Table 8 *Women in the Spanish parliament since 1977*

Year of election	Total number of seats	Number of women elected	Percentage of women elected
Chamber of Deputies			
1977	350	22	6.3
1979	350	21	6.0
1982	350	22	6.3
1986	350	23	6.6
1989	350	51	14.6
1993	350	55	15.7
1996	350	77	22.0
2000	350	99	28.3
2004	350	126	36.0
Senate			
1977	248	6	2.4
1979	208	6	2.9
1982	253	11	4.3
1986	251	14	5.6
1989	255	33	12.9
1993	256	32	12.9
1996	208	31	14.9
2000	259	63	24.3
2004	259	65	25.0

Source: Instituto de la Mujer 1994, *La mujer en cifras, una década, 1982–1992* [Women in Numbers, a Decade, 1982–1992], Madrid: Instituto de la Mujer, pp. 79–82 (1977–1989 data); Instituto de la Mujer 1997, *Las mujeres en cifras 1997* [Women in Numbers, 1997], Madrid: Instituto de la Mujer, pp. 98–9 (1993–1996 data); Instituto de la Mujer 2003, *Mujeres en cifras* [Women in Numbers], Madrid: Instituto de la Mujer (2000 data); retrieved 29 October 2003 from www.mtas.es.

Table 9 *Women in the Swedish parliament since 1945*

Year of election	Number of women	Percentage of women
1945	18	7.8
1949	22	9.6
1953	28	12.2
1957	29	12.6
1959	31	13.4
1961	32	13.7
1965	31	13.3
1969	36	15.4
1971	49	14.0
1974	74	21.1
1977	75	22.6
1980	92	27.8
1983	96	29.5
1986	108	30.9
1989	131	37.5
1992	115	32.9
1994	141	40.4
1998	149	42.7
2002	158	45.3

Note: In 1971 the bicameral parliament was transformed into a unicameral body. The data before 1971 refer to the lower chamber of the *Riksdag*.

Table 10 *Women in the UK parliament since 1945*

Year of election	Number of women	Percentage of women
1945	23	3.8
1950	21	3.4
1951	17	2.7
1955	24	3.8
1959	25	4.0
1964	29	4.6
1966	26	4.1
1970	26	4.1
1974 (February)	23	3.6
1974 (October)	27	4.3
1979	19	3.0
1983	23	3.5
1987	41	6.3
1992	60	9.2
1997	120	18.2
2001	118	17.9

Note: Figures are for the lower chamber (the House of Commons).

Table 11 *Women in the US Congress and state legislatures since 1945*

| Year of election | US Congress %[1] | | | State legislatures %[2] |
	Senate	House	Total	Total (both chambers)
1945	0	3	2	
1947	1	2	1	
1949	1	2	2	
1951	1	2	2	
1953	2	3	2	
1955	1	4	3	
1957	1	3	3	
1959	2	4	4	
1961	2	4	4	
1963	2	3	3	
1965	2	3	2	
1967	1	3	2	
1969	1	2	2	
1971	2	3	3	5
1973	0	4	3	6
1975	0	4	4	8
1977	2	4	4	9
1979	1	4	3	10
1981	2	5	4	12
1983	2	5	4	13
1985	2	5	5	15
1987	2	5	5	16
1989	2	7	6	17
1991	4	6	6	18
1993	7	11	10	21
1995	9	11	11	21
1997	9	12	12	22
1999	9	13	12	22
2001	13	14	14	22
2003	14	14	14	22.4

Notes: [1] All figures exclude women delegates to US territories. [2] Data are not available for the period pre-1971.

Source: Center for American Women in Politics, Rutgers University.

Appendix 2 The RNGS model: summary of variable descriptors

Cluster One: Characteristics of women's movement actors

Stage
1 Emerging/re-emerging: formation of new organisations; rehabilitation of older organisations toward new goals.
2 Growth: expansion in numbers of organisations, activities.
3 Consolidation: organisations have structure, endurance and regular support; institutionalised in community and government arenas.
4 Decline/abeyance: decrease in organisations, members and activities over the period; latent organisational activity primarily by individuals.

Closeness to left
1 Very close: groups formally ally with or work with political parties and/or trade unions of the left. Ideas from the movement are taken up by left-wing parties in party platforms. Activists have internal power positions in the left-wing parties.
2 Close: groups formally ally with or work with political parties and/or trade unions of the left. They do not have internal power positions in the parties or unions and if the left takes up the ideas of movements they do so without stating so and bring these ideas to fit the party line.
3 Not close: movement and the left are remote or hostile to each other.

Priority of issue
1 High: issue is one of the top priorities of the women's movement activists and serves to forge alliances among the various wings and tendencies.
2 Moderate: not a uniting issue, but is a priority for some activists and organisations.
3 Low: not a priority for any organisation, but mentioned by some. Not on the agenda. Not present at all on agendas of individuals and organisations in the movement.

Cohesion

1 Cohesive: movement organisations active on the issue agree on the frame and/or policy proposals.
2 Divided: movement organisations active on the issue disagree on the frame and/or policy proposals.

Counter-movement

1 Strong: prevalent and proactive movement aimed at issue or issues taken up by different parts of the women's movement.
2 Moderate: counter-movement less active against women's movement issues.
3 Weak: nearly moribund or non-existent.

Cluster Two: Policy environment

Policy sub-system level

Structure
1 Open: organisation is amorphous, no common rules or conventions; participation is wide and changing with a variety of interest group representatives and free agents. Power balance shows no clear chain of command.
2 Moderately closed: organisation is more clearly defined but changing over time. Participation shows some regular actors but some free agents around. Power balance shows several actors trying to dominate the group but no single line of command.
3 Closed: codification of system through regular meetings and rules. Participation is limited with few free agents. Power balance shows one major actor controls policy space and parameters of the arena. A single policy community mobilises around the issue.

Issue frame fit

1 Matching: issue frame that initially shapes the debate is expressed in terms that are similar to movement goals as expressed by activists.
2 Compatible: issue frame that initially shapes the debate is not expressed in terms that are similar to movement goals as expressed by activists.
3 Incompatible: issue frame that initially shapes the debate is expressed in terms that are in conflict with (oppose) movement goals as expressed by activists.

Party or coalition in power

1 Strong left-wing control: left-wing parties may have majority in popularly elected legislative chambers and the presidency/executive.

2 Moderate left-wing control: left-wing parties may have the popularly elected chambers only and not the president. In the USA the left may have majority in only one elected chamber of the legislature.

Index

Made in United States
Troutdale, OR
09/06/2023